Transportation and the Culture of Climate Change

Energy and Society
Brian Black, Series Editor

OTHER TITLES IN THE SERIES

Energy Culture: Art and Theory on Oil and Beyond
Edited by Imre Szeman and Jeff Diamanti

On Petrocultures: Globalization, Culture, and Energy
Imre Szeman

Oil and Urbanization on the Pacific Coast:
Ralph Bramel Lloyd and the Shaping of the Urban West
Michael R. Adamson

Oil and Nation: A History of Bolivia's Petroleum Sector
Stephen C. Cote

Transportation and the Culture of Climate Change

Accelerating Ride to Global Crisis

Edited by Tatiana Prorokova-Konrad

WEST VIRGINIA UNIVERSITY PRESS / MORGANTOWN

ISBN
Cloth 978-1-949199-63-5
Paper 978-1-949199-64-2
Ebook 978-1-949199-65-9

Library of Congress Cataloging-in-Publication Data
Names: Prorokova, Tatiana, editor.
Title: Transportation and the culture of climate change : accelerating ride to
        global crisis / edited by Tatiana Prorokova-Konrad.
Other titles: Energy and society.
Description: First edition. | Morgantown : West Virginia University Press,
        2020. | Series: Energy and society | Includes bibliographical references
        and index.
Identifiers: LCCN 2020015449 | ISBN 9781949199635 (cloth) | ISBN
        9781949199642 (paperback) | ISBN 9781949199659 (ebook)
Subjects: LCSH: Transportation—Environmental aspects. | Transportation—
        Social aspects. | Transportation, Automotive—Environmental
        aspects. | Transportation, Automotive—Social aspects. | Petroleum as
        fuel—Social aspects.
Classification: LCC HE147.65 .T75 2020 | DDC 303.48/32—dc23
LC record available at https://lccn.loc.gov/2020015449

Book and cover design by Than Saffel
Cover image by shutterzomb / Shutterstock

Contents

Introduction. Carbonization as a Choice: Environmental
Ethics, Mobility, and Energy Options
Tatiana Prorokova-Konrad and Brian C. Black
    1

PART I

Mobility and the Environment

1. Using Heritage and Ecological Systems Thinking to Inform
   Resilient Automobility Design
   Barry L. Stiefel
       21

2. Bikes for Children, Cars for Adults: Postwar American
   Transportation Culture and the Legacy of Moving Images
   James Longhurst
       41

3. E-Scooters and the Urban Micromobility Revolution
   Matthew C. Swanson
       63

PART II

Car Cultures

4. "Carbolization": Cars, Carbon Emissions, and the
   Global Discipline of Automobility
   Gordon M. Sayre
       83

5. Hydrocarbon Enslavement and Fantasies of Freedom
   Patrick D. Murphy
       103

6. Suicide Machines: Bruce Springsteen, Ballard,
   and Broken Heroes on a Last Chance Power Drive
   David LaRocca
       123

7. Remainders of the Fossil Regime: Automobility Regression   151
    in Three Post-Apocalyptic Novels
    Brent Ryan Bellamy

PART III
Film, Energy, and Climate Change

8. Intermodal Aesthetics and the Otherwise of Cargo   173
    Megan Hayes and Jeff Diamanti

9. Nature Guarding "Her Treasures" in Oil Comedies: The   191
    Case of *Local Hero* and *Fubar: Balls to the Wall*
    Robin L. Murray and Joseph K. Heumann

10. Boom/Bust: Tragic Logistics and Accelerationist Comedy   211
    in Petroleum Transport
    C. Parker Krieg

11. Trafficking in Petronormativities: At the Intersections   227
    of Petrofeminism, Petrocolonialism, and Petrocapitalism
    Sheena Wilson

    Contributors   259
    Index   263

Carbonization as a Choice: Environmental Ethics, Mobility, and Energy Options

Tatiana Prorokova-Konrad and Brian C. Black

From the "romance of the open road" to a passion for "muscle cars" and even to the everyday necessity of personal travel to work, school, or the fulfillment of other basic needs, the movement of the modern human relies on devices to carry us. As scholars apply more scrutiny to developed humans' reliance on energy from fossil fuels, it quickly becomes evident that one of the most significant sectors of usage is personal transportation.

In general, energy use is one of the basic fashions in which humans interact with nature. The heat made of fire from wood or the protein derived from hunted game marked some of our most primitive energy exchanges. Organizing and distinguishing between these exchanges allows historians to accentuate transitions between energy sources which then lays bare how certain sources of energy differ from one another. Clarity on the differences between energy sources reveals most profoundly, for instance, how expansive but unsustainable is the reliance on fossil fuels for energy that began in the mid-nineteenth century.

No energy transition is a simple flip of a new "switch" following the discovery or adoption of new sources of power. For instance, from 1890 and into the 1910s, America's roadways were a wild laboratory of various transportation devices as inventors sought to fill the role that human and animal power had played for centuries: basic human movement through the surrounding landscape. From the horse buggy to the bicycle, from the Stanley Steamer to the Model T, devices serving the same purpose—including the first electric cars—derived their energy from a variety of sources. Competition and influence determined that the internal-combustion engine would power autos of the future. However, this choice was reinforced and supported by public will, political decisions, and laws such as zoning. Humans determined that the twentieth century would be powered by fossil fuels such as petroleum, and the marketplace provided them the flexibility to create a landscape of drive-thrus and filling stations.[1]

Abundant supplies and existing or emerging technology were part of the rationale for applying fossil fueled energy to transportation; however, this output demanded increased supplies. Growth in the transportation sector in the twentieth century resulted in a nonrenewable economic expansion of massive proportions. The significance of this shift forced historian John McNeill to dub the century as "peculiar" in the human past. He continues in *Something New Under the Sun*: "Although there are a few kinds of environmental change that are genuinely new in the twentieth century . . . for the most part the ecological peculiarity of the twentieth century is a matter of scale and intensity. . . . We have probably deployed more energy since 1900 than in all of human history before 1900."[2] To reconfigure our understanding of the human past in order to respect the gravity of this transition, McNeill worked with leading scientists to argue that our current geological epoch be redefined as the "Anthropocene," an era in which Earth's future came to be determined by the activity of one species—the human. In factoring in the additional knowledge of the pollution created by the burning of fossil fuels, historian Andreas Malm, in *Fossil Capital*, deems the burning of coal, petroleum, and other fossil fuels throughout history as "so many invisible missiles aimed at the future."[3] These scholars refer to the high-energy era of the twentieth century as the "Great Acceleration."

During this high-energy existence of the Anthropocene, data reveals that today 26 percent of global energy use fuels transportation. As part of the reinterpretation of the implications of carbon burning, we must look again at the choices we have made and continue to make related to personal movement. Part of our reassessment must be a fuller consideration of the ethical choices that drive our selection of "rides," our method for moving through the landscape.

In the following pages, *Transportation and the Culture of Climate Change* opens a critical discussion of the specific role played by fossil-fuel-powered transport in our planet's ongoing environmental crisis and uncovers the challenges created by fantasies of speed, mobility, and consumption, all of which cause irrevocable social and environmental transformations. Because we have barely begun to really pose questions about the numerous ways we are interpolated with fossil-fuel transport, this collection seeks to fill this lacuna, drawing attention to transportation as a powerful force triggering climate change during a time when our culture swiftly became a "petroculture."[4]

Tracing the enigmatic and tacit relationship between global warming and transport through the examination of various cultural artifacts (including oil comedies, environmental documentaries, post-apocalyptic novels, and pop music), this collection aims to understand how such artifacts have created a cultural understanding about humanity's addiction to and obsession with transport on the one hand, and its myopic attitude to the inevitable, drastic ramifications of environmental changes and/or a pathological fear of global warming on the other.

Recognizing and altering the pervasiveness of this particular technological form of transportation—whose myriad forms range from petroleum-powered vehicles to asphalt road surfaces created exclusively for the purpose of facilitating mobility among individuals and through territories—are crucial tasks for humanity today. It is particularly significant in the sort of long-term eco-thinking that demands that profound cultural, social, and political changes must occur immediately. Understanding the true nature of fossil-fuel transport as an essential contributor to ecological decline will help reenvision not only oil and our dependency on it but also what the society of the future should look like— to imagine a world in which capitalist comforts created in the twentieth and twenty-first centuries will finally be recognized as *ecologically archaic*, leading to sweeping transformations in lifestyle and in the sociocultural order.

Transportation as an Ethical Choice

The implications of this reconsideration are sweeping and foundational: transportation as we know it today enables mobility and speed for individuals and societies. Often, it is a decisive force driving capitalism and national economic, cultural, and political development. From this essential beginning, our current mobile, petrocultural identity was formed. Particular from other forms of transport, the automobile has become one of the most desired and, it seems, necessary commodities of modern life. Cars now fill the streets of cities and towns worldwide, helping to connect people and places while also causing fundamental conceptions of time and distance to be reimagined.

The expectations invested in the automobile have also reshaped geographies and changed our bodily experience. In this process, these vehicles have emerged as, collectively, one of the greatest threats to the environment. In particular, CO_2 emissions from transport using fossil fuels are one of the crucial causes for global climate change. Scholars argue that "all forms of transportation (including planes, trains, automobiles, boats, and so on)" are responsible for around "15% of global greenhouse emissions."[5]

The implications of the automobile have also become a scary and paradoxical touchstone of our culture in literature, film, and the visual arts. Cultural media have celebrated the might of technology, the necessity of mechanization, and humanity's inability to exist and progress without transport by air and over water and land. From John Steinbeck's *The Grapes of Wrath* (1939) to George Miller's *Mad Max* (1979) and its sequels to Gary Paulsen's *The Car* (1994) to Chris Wedge's *Monster Trucks* (2016) and beyond, numerous texts portray human existence as being improved and in certain cases even *enabled* through transportation. At the same time, these vigorously powerful narratives draw the attention of audiences worldwide to the problem of climate change as has been caused by industrialization and immensely intensified by transportation.

Today, the ubiquitous human nomadism made possible by transportation is taken to be normal. At the same time, air pollution and climate change resulting in large part due to emissions from fossil-fuel transport remain unnoticed—perhaps willfully by some, while others criminally silence the voicing of environmental concerns at a time when ever greater comforts and levels of prosperity and development are pursued by the capitalist world. Transportation is a crucial component of this dialogue. Cars have possessed "high visibility in the social landscape and cultural imagery over the last century" and continue to bear remarkable social significance.[6]

Given its variety of implications, the car must be seen as an *eco*-social phenomenon, influencing ecology and damaging, destroying, and transforming the biosphere. While scholars have recognized fossil-fuel transport as a capitalist phenomenon, they have yet to enjoin this significance to its ecological impact, particularly climate change.

Although many people understand that climate change is the most urgent environmental problem currently facing humanity, there has nevertheless been no sufficient action taken that can be said to have prevented or minimized the deadly effects of climate change. Possible explanations for this inaction include the nature of the crisis, particularly its invisibility or, rather, the deficient visibility of the crisis. Commenting on the "expansive" nature of global warming, Adam Trexler points out that "tail-pipe and smokestack emissions can lead ultimately to storm surges or rising sea levels on the other side of the globe. Similarly the effects of species loss can be difficult to see, even when they participate in ecosystems worth billions of dollars."[7] The disasters caused by climate change can remain unnoticeable to many of us because we simply cannot see them in our everyday lives, or because we choose not to notice them, adopting a colonialist, racist, and/or simply unintelligent way of thinking, considering certain geographical territories to be less important than others, as well as believing that Western, largely white populations are more important than people in developing nations, indigenous peoples, and other groups.

Our habit of complacency is likely another possible reason for our inaction. As Eric Cazdyn and Imre Szeman write:

> At present, we continue to act within . . . [the] limits, accepting them as the way things are and the way they have to be. We cede to governments the rationale and logics by which our societies are planned and organized. For all manner of impending crises—the end of fossil fuel, the proliferation of disease, the rise in the earth's temperature—we await the abstract entity called "science" (or the market, or God, or compassion) to save us in the nick of time.[8]

We often become indifferent to what, in principle, are our own lives and the continuing existence of life itself. Climate change is a grave problem in which "billions of people, including you and me, are implicated: buying food grown with petrochemicals; working in offices or shops or factories powered by coal plants; driving in cars or riding in buses or flying in planes that burn fossil fuels; or using the furnace or air conditioner that come with our home."[9] If each and every one of us is guilty, then only through a collective effort can we influence the situation and lift the planet out of the crisis. Changing the transport systems and our attitude towards transportation in general is one of the ways to deal with the problem.

When considering transportation, it must be seen as a direct expression of a larger relationship with energy. Fossil fuels—and oil in particular—are therefore viewed both in this introduction and in most of the essays in this collection as an integral part of the phenomenon of transportation. The burning of fossil fuels—the process that is used on a vast scale to enable transportation via ground, air, and water—affects the planet in decisive ways and changes its climate. The intensive use of fossil fuels began during the Industrial Revolution. By the end of the nineteenth century, scientists were already aware that the CO_2 released when fossil fuels are burned warms the planet, but at that time this was not considered to be all that significant a problem. Only in the 1950s and 1960s did scientists begin making renewed warnings about the deadly effects of CO_2 emissions, and by the 1970s and 1980s these concerns began to be regarded as *the* fundamental issue affecting the planet. The problem was raised again in 1988, by the NASA scientist Dr. James Hansen.

Finally, the UN's Intergovernmental Panel on Climate Change made its first assessment report in 1992, and in 1997 the Kyoto Protocol put forth a call for action to minimize global warming.[10]

Coal, oil, and natural gas have provided us with multiple comforts, but at a high cost—environmental degradation and the prospect of the planet's destruction. "Oil and its outcomes—speed, plastics, and the luxuries of capitalism, to name a few—have lubricated our relationship to one another and the environment for the duration of the twentieth century";[11] oil has become the mediator between humans and the environment as well as a dangerous weapon that we have used to systematically and continuously deteriorate specific ecosystems and the earth's environment as a whole. Brian Black and Marcy Ladson succinctly pinpoint the crux of the matter: "Although remarkable innovations converted inanimate energy into products of all types, at the most basic level industrialization was constructed on a foundation of shifting priorities and ethics."[12] When discussing climate change and humanity's role in causing and sustaining it, a consideration of ethics is crucial. Dominating and destroying nature, our actions have proved unethical and abusive. We *chose* to destroy the planet; we *chose* to carbonize.

Seen through this lens, transport becomes a seminal component of the high-energy existence and a particularly compelling example of humanity's continued selfishness and indifference to the problem of global warming. Why were there no satisfactory reforms that would reflect our acknowledgement of transport's deadly effect on the environment and help us transition out of our role as destroyers so as to become peaceful coinhabitants with the earth's other organisms and stewards of the planet's ecology? The simple explanation is that modern transport is too convenient for our species to compromise.

The role of oil as a mediator between humanity and the environment is intensified by the economic value of fossil fuels. Energy is viewed to be "at the nexus of people, environment, and economic development."[13] Talking about carbon as a "commodity"[14] is thus particularly helpful when outlining the relationship between transport and the environment. We buy carbon to burn it and pollute the environment. The world of haste that we have created, with consumerism and globalization in its forefront, dictates a pervasive anti-environmental way of being: live *now*, think myopically, and take the future for granted.

To understand fully *how* and *whether* transport can be limited and/or become more environmentally friendly, one needs to define the role of transport and mobility in our lives. Both transport and mobility are valuable cultural goods. The thought of eliminating or even just limiting access to transport and mobility might only cause hysteria and urge one to appreciate transport even more. This sort of response proves the deadly dependence that we have artificially cultivated, thinking of transport as a life necessity equal to the air we breathe.

If, hypothetically, there were no transport, the everyday life that we are now accustomed to would turn into chaos, and our first reaction would most probably be panic: we would wonder how to get to school or to work, pick up a child from kindergarten, buy groceries, and so on. Transport has, indeed, become a necessity; but the way it is used has also become an absurdity. Think about how often you (or somebody you know) have driven a car when you really did not need to; or consider various facilities, like the "drive-thrus" at banks, fast-food restaurants, and Starbucks, that promote mobility and the idea of being inside a car as a lifestyle.

As the cultural value of transport was glorified, it shifted from being a means of survival, development, and a sign of civilization, and has been long regarded a part of one's very self. Stephanie LeMenager calls the car the "symbol of middle-class self-definition."[15] David Louter claims: "The automobile, the very symbol of technology destroying an older way of life, offered mobility and freedom."[16] John Whitelegg observes: "The car can liberate the self-imprisoned soul from its perceived boredom in a limited geographical area. It can confer strong feelings of power, external signs of material wealth, sexual mastery and status."[17] Yet it is noteworthy that while such understandings of transport can be applied to literally every human being, they are particularly promoted and extolled in Western countries, especially the United States, where in many parts of the country owning a car has become the only way to connect to other people and to travel to other territories.

During the Cold War, for example, "demonstrating the superiority of U.S.-style capitalism was an important weapon in the fight to maintain popular support for the Western alliance in the struggle with communism." Therefore, technological products like "new washing machines, televisions, and automobiles"[18] were the means to contrast the highly developed American society with certain other nations. That development also manifested itself in the promotion of car ownership, which had been articulated by the federal government as early as the 1950s: "When Congress funded construction of the interstate highway system, nearly all of the basic patterns underpinning the creation of car-centered landscapes—as well as nearly all of the most significant environmental problems related to heavy car use—were firmly in place. With these changes, the United States became Car Country."[19] It was also in the 1950s that the car and the environment became entangled: "By the 1950s, the fact that automobiles could reach speeds up to 100 miles per hour and that over 40,000 miles of freeways were in the making shifted the ecological significance of cars."[20]

Of course, ultimately the effective mobility offered by cars and other forms of automotive transport and their heavy use have had serious environmental ramifications. It is, however, interesting that the relationship between transport and the environment has also been shaped culturally, making the perception and experience of the ecologically negative effects of transportation a culturally mediated phenomenon. Whitelegg points out the paradoxical coexistence of the car's positive and negative effects:

> The car and the lorry are frequently described as bringers of freedom, progress, independence and economic growth. The advertising world supplies numerous images in support of this vision of freedom and mastery over nature. It is no accident that these images are based on speed, power, open roads, attractive scenery and sexuality. The attractiveness and seductiveness of the car is deeply embodied in our culture and in our psychology. . . . In spite of the growth in our knowledge about the negative environmental, social and economic effects of private car use, the car still commands powerful support.[21]

It is both shocking and fascinating to witness how transport defines our relationship to nature. Christopher W. Wells explores the humanity/nature relationship via a discussion centering on and limited to the United States, claiming that "in Car Country, driving and sprawl have become essential, interlocking components of American lives, landscapes, and relationships with the natural world."[22] We suggest a careful application of this theory to the global world, for the use of transport has resulted in interventions *everywhere* in the natural world, although, of course, to varying degrees.

Thinking that "roadlessness remains the defining characteristic of modern wilderness"[23] is particularly helpful here. "For Americans, the car and the road enable the sense of radical materiality—feeling embodied—that has been theorized as ecological affect."[24] And although the road is not exclusively associated with transport (consider for example, beaten paths), the road is the primary symbol of mobility. Mobility is, in turn, an intervention in the wilderness that results in a destruction of natural wilderness (a place can no longer be wild once a human-made road is there). Transport, thus, not only prompts the building of more roads, it can itself make roads. So-called off-road vehicles, although they function *off* the road, can themselves create roads, turning impassable regions into landscapes of mobility. The use of transport can thus be described as a mechanical intervention in the natural world. Our wish to stay mobile results in two serious environmental issues: pollution and the re-structuralization/destruction of the natural landscape.

Finding Our Way Forward

The way to reduce the effects of transport on the environment, hence, requires a twofold solution. First, emissions must be reduced, and, second, the intervention of transportation in the natural world must be minimized.

Reducing emissions is a crucial step in solving the problem of global warming. But it entails the finding of alternative energy sources. Imre Szeman has been extensively discussing the problem of energy, seeing our dependence on fossil fuels as the major obstacle to a cleaner environment. He claims: "It's impossible to address global warming without significant changes in our use of fossil fuels. This is widely known. Making these changes means becoming different subjects who embrace a different collectivity and sociality—subjects who decide to no longer be creatures of petroculture. This is less well known. We don't just need to find new sources of energy and cut down on our use of fossil fuels. *We need to invent new ways of being, belonging, and behaving—and to do so quickly.*"[25]

The connection that Szeman skillfully draws among energy, humanity, and the environment, interpreting the environmental crisis also as a cultural crisis, is crucial to our understanding of the problem's scale. At the same time, regarding this information numerically and realizing that "over 90 percent of the products and services in the consumer economy depend upon oil inputs for manufacture, transport, or both. Without oil, the entire economy would grind to a standstill within weeks,"[26] we realize that the implementation of the necessary changes represents perhaps a more difficult task than any that humanity has ever had to carry out. And Szeman realistically concludes: "We have no models of such intensive and extensive social transformation."[27]

The promotion of "the large-scale use of oil" by "the British and American political elites"[28] has brought temporary comforts—but it has also caused the global ecological crisis. Transitioning from oil to alternative sources is, however, necessary not only for the environment but also for us in terms of our lifestyle: peak oil will inevitably force us either to find alternatives so as to maintain our everyday life on the same level or to go back to life before the discovery and mass consumption of oil: "Oil is limited, and its use pulls closer that larger limit of the Earth's environment, of which it is simultaneously a part (limit) and an other (catastrophe) that the future would be better off without."[29] Continuing to nourish the idea that Szeman wittily dubs the "fiction of surplus,"[30] as well as believing in the impossibility of energy crisis, is preposterous, considering the known facts about the limited reserves of fossil fuels that remain on Earth. To do so will, in the end, multiply the dread of global warming when we have no choice but to reckon with it.

The approach that would allow "a more sustainable mobility"—that is, "less car use, more public transport, more walking and cycling"[31]—seems particularly useful when addressing questions involving transport and the environment. Another way to reduce emissions is to use "refined transportation and heating fuels."[32] And while the rebuilding of engines and the refining of fuels are tasks that, requiring special skills, can be fulfilled only by scientists and engineers, the choice of *what kind of* transport to use, and *when* and *if* to use it, can be made by every one of us. What we can now observe are territorial approaches to environmental problems. For example, several European countries, including the Netherlands, Denmark, Germany, and Switzerland, have earned the reputation of being bicycle countries, because much of their population consciously chooses to travel by bicycle when it is possible not to use cars, buses, and other means of fossil-fuel-powered transport. This example is excellent but has limitations; for instance, in the United States "bicycling only accounts for 1% of all trips."[33] At the same time, some of the larger cities in the United States have found ways to actively contribute to reducing the effects of global warming. Jennifer L. Rice discusses the example of Seattle: "Through the *territorialization* of carbon—the active creation and quantification of bounded and ordered spaces of carbon-producing activities and simultaneous reproduction of local government jurisdictional capacities—Seattle is able to regulate, administer, and monitor policies on climate change."[34]

One can thus notice that despite the *global* cultural and economic addiction to transport, action is taken *locally*. This is, of course, a useful way to deal with the problem; yet it is truly useful only when *all* communities act. Nevertheless, it is apparent that the problem is of great complexity and includes multiple factors that must be considered, as John Cohen writes: "Greenhouse gas emissions per person depend on income, technology, demographic factors like household size, city size, and population density in built-up areas, institutional and economic factors like the availability of public transport at reasonable cost and convenience, and a host of behavioral factors like people's propensity to walk, bike, carpool, or drive solo to work."[35] While the restructuring of the system is a profoundly complicated task, entailing the changing of transport *culture* itself, the effectiveness of such a transformation is beyond doubt.

Indeed, "by far the greatest environmental benefit of bicycling and walking . . . is that they bypass the fossil fuel system to which the American economy has been addicted."[36]

The other problem that transport causes is the restructuring of the landscape. Highways are part of our cultural being; yet, if we realize that roads and bridges are created intentionally to facilitate human mobility, we can envision the scale to which wild nature has suffered directly from our roads and means of transport. When discussing "the impact of roads on the environment," we should consider "the effects of roads on wildlife populations . . . or population fragmentation . . . , impacts on plant populations or changes in the abiotic components of ecosystems . . . , the deterioration in the quality of the atmosphere and hydrosphere . . . , and irreversible changes in landscape."[37]

The impact that transport and mobility have and continue to exert on the environment is monumental. When discussing climate change and the ways to minimize its effects, we tend to think in terms of "prevention and mitigation."[38] How do we apply this strategy to reduce the consequences of transportation? In her book *Living Oil: Petroleum Culture in the American Century*, LeMenager draws on an interesting example from the 1970s: "At a Survival Faire in San Jose, California, in 1970, organizers bought a new car and buried it as a symbol of the task they saw confronting ecology action groups—essentially the task of creating an entirely new energy and transportation infrastructure, getting the country off of oil and cars."[39] It is exactly this idea of "getting [*the world*] off of oil and cars" that is useful today. It is, indeed, the only way to "prevent and mitigate" the consequences of global warming. Yet the fascination with transport and the possibility of being mobile (paradoxically, even if one does not want to travel or does so very rarely) are so strong that they condition our choice to use transport, no matter the ramifications. LeMenager writes: "Cars made the human body more valuable, pleasurable, and fun. They also caused, and still cause, more human deaths per day than any single agent, forcing questions about human consumption, the price of the mediated self made possible by cheap energy."[40]

Transport is fascinating for its dual extremity: it murders (e.g., the sinking of *Titanic* in 1912, the plane crashes on 9/11, the slow killing of the planet via emissions, etc.) but also provides an array of opportunities (e.g., studying and working at a place of one's choice, gaining financial stability and independence, staying mobile and thus remaining open to everything that today's world has to offer). Transport is a sub-space in our world, and stopping to use it, to be able to be onboard and transported elsewhere, might sound to some like stopping to live in one's house. Transport is a considerable part of our culture that is as hard to transform as it is for us to stop using fossil fuels—but we do not have an alternative. Writing about "today's monopsony of automotive and oil industries" as a historically avoidable phenomenon, for gasoline was just one of the options for fueling a car among "steam, electric batteries, alcohol, diesel, and biodiesel fuels," Gordon Sayre points out that "the barriers to its [the monopsony's] decline may be as much behavioral as technological."[41]

The tight connection between our already invented vehicles and our habituation to the way they function, therefore, becomes the major complexity of transport culture. Moreover, as in the case of "energy transitions"—"once a society adopts a new energy source, older ones are abandoned. This has rarely happened"[42]—it is as probable that once we have found other ways to stay mobile, we will continue to rely on polluting transport (consider the illustrative, although of course not ideal, case with bicycles). It is thus important to change not just the vehicles we use but "the infrastructure and behavior that constitute automobility"[43] and transport culture in general. Perhaps the most dangerous aspect of the climate change problem has been formulated by Szeman: "The desire to be saved remains an enduring part of our political landscape, whether we put our faith in science, religious figures or in politics."[44] Yet neither science, nor religion, nor politics will ever be able to save us from the deadly ramifications of climate change; we ourselves must abandon the habit of carbonizing and instead choose an ethical approach to the environment and to ourselves—which, it seems, will be possible only if we change our culture.

Organizing This Book

Focusing on the issue of "(auto)mobility" as a dangerous cultural reality, this book demonstrates the rupture between humans and nature that became visible with the emergence of transportation but has particularly intensified in recent times due to overt petrodependence. Engaging with such issues as (psychological and physical) addiction and consumerism, this collection of essays examines transportation as a complex industry not only to illustrate the "slow violence" (as outlined by Rob Nixon)[45] that characterizes ecological decline but also to uncover the bald human savagery towards the environment and fellow humans as a result of a carelessness rooted in a lack of education as well as the intentional adoption of short-sighted pragmatism and greed.

Thematically, the book is organized around a number of key issues related to the problem of cultural production and a critique of the role played by transportation in relation to nature, climate, and the environment. The collection provides a cultural understanding of the automobile and automobility as a procapitalist, antienvironmentalist phenomenon and of its position vis-à-vis other means of transport. Zeroing in on the intertwined malaise of capitalism and consumerism, the collection broadly comments on the problem of addiction and auto/petro-dependency as a social and ecological phenomenon, as well as on the means of commercial colonization, so that climate change is readily understood as a problem caused by the "West" but sustained by both the "West" and the "East." Juxtaposing the issues of oil, transportation, and climate change, as these are reflected in numerous cultural artifacts, the book brings to light the array of notions connected to the problem of global warming as well as outlines an impressive display of the ways through which transportation not only aggravates ecological decline but also makes it particularly difficult to deal with. *Transportation and the Culture of Climate Change* is thus not only a book that studies cultural portrayals of transportation and global warming but is also, in a way, a humanities scholars' guide that facilitates our understanding of the complexity of anthropogenic climate change and the profound role of transport and the phenomenon of mobility in causing and speeding the warming of our planet.

Transportation and the Culture of Climate Change is divided into three sections—"Mobility and the Environment," "Car Cultures," and "Film, Energy, and Climate Change"—to discuss transport (and the phenomenon of transportation) along with its influence on the environment, as reflected culturally from various perspectives.

Section one, "Mobility and the Environment," focuses on various means of transport that designate humanity's obsession with mobility. Barry L. Stiefel's "Using Heritage and Ecological Systems Thinking to Inform Resilient Automobility Design" zeroes in on the automobile as a cultural artifact to examine the historical component of the automotive heritage. Stiefel uses environmental and historical context to theoretically describe the necessary evolution that would allow a car to be holistically resilient in design and function and responsive to the dynamically changing world that we are living in. James Longhurst's chapter "Bikes for Children, Cars for Adults: Postwar American Transportation Culture and the Legacy of Moving Images" discusses people's overt unwillingness to use bicycles instead of cars. Specifically, Longhurst examines the messages of educational shorts and select Hollywood films from the 1950s to the 1980s to understand the cultural challenges of promoting adult bicycle transportation as a means of reducing greenhouse gas emissions in the twenty-first century. Finally, Matthew C. Swanson's "E-Scooters and the Urban Micromobility Revolution" focuses on e-scooters as an alternative means of transportation in cities, including Los Angeles, and argues that the meteoric rise of e-scooters has invigorated an urban micromobility revolution, a shift toward smaller, less energy-intensive modes of transportation for traveling shorter distances. Swanson claims that despite potential difficulties with e-scooter acceptance and success in cities, such as safety, urban scale, and perception among minority and lower-income populations, e-scooters can contribute to decarbonization efforts by replacing short automobile trips, including rideshares.

Section two, "Car Cultures," focuses exclusively on cars. It discusses humanity's addiction to this means of transport, as well as how car technology has had a toxic effect on nature and the environment. In " 'Carbolization': Cars, Carbon Emissions, and the Global Discipline of Automobility," Gordon M. Sayre examines the process of "carbolization"—the term that he has coined to describe the combined impact of rising carbon emissions, climate change, and the growing global fleet of cars—as a form of imperialist discipline, whereby global subjects become motorists who interact in traffic, and who now nearly all share the externalities of cars: congestion, pollution, resource depletion, and collision fatalities. In the chapter that follows, "Hydrocarbon Enslavement and Fantasies of Freedom," Patrick Murphy discusses the complexities of "car culture" and its effects on the environment. The author claims that transportation plays an ongoing role in facilitating and encouraging instant gratification and consumption from the fast food drive-thru window, to the online order and pickup of groceries, to the Amazon delivery network. The environmental costs of the car culture lifestyle with these components are largely hidden from or invisible to the public, who are discouraged by consumerism from thinking about long term effects and costs. David LaRocca's "Suicide Machines: Bruce Springsteen, Ballard, and Broken Heroes on a Last Chance Power Drive" directs attention to the imaginative landscape of driving and argues that in these realms we encounter raw emotion, mythic power, and dynamic interrelationships of cultural forms and norms. LaRocca's special focus is on the music of Bruce Springsteen, especially song lyrics from the 1970s, J. G. Ballard's novel *Crash* (1973), and the eponymous film made by David Cronenberg in 1996. LaRocca dwells on some ways in which the invention of conceptual and emotional relationships to automobility may have inadvertently "driven us" to destruction, and invites the reader to reflect further on our own, individual and collective, relationship to the means and machines of automobility. The section concludes with Brent Ryan Bellamy's "Remainders of the Fossil Regime: Automobility Regression in Three Post-Apocalyptic Novels." This chapter takes up three post-apocalyptic novels that engage directly with questions of transportation and automobility regression: John Varley's *Slow Apocalypse* (2012), Peter Heller's *The Dog Stars* (2012), and Emily St. John Mandel's *Station Eleven*

(2014). The selected post-apocalyptic novels figure conveyance and vehicles after the networks, supplies, and infrastructures making them both possible and functional have been destroyed. Bellamy argues that such explorations of the remainders of the fossil regime prove instructive for understanding the scale and importance of energy transition today.

Section three, "Film, Energy, and Climate Change," pays close attention to the relationship between the environment, petroleum, and consumerism, and the way it is represented in film. It opens with Megan Hayes and Jeff Diamanti's "Intermodal Aesthetics and the Otherwise of Cargo." In this chapter, Hayes and Diamanti read Noël Burch and Allan Sekula's *The Forgotten Space* (2010), Lucien Castaing-Taylor and Véréna Paravel's *Leviathan* (2012), and Shezad Dawood's *Leviathan Cycle* (2017–) as aesthetic and conceptual interventions into the antinomy of political economy and political ecology: enabling capital's abstraction of maritime space by way of the cargo ship and its largely unregulated labor and environmental envelope to start rubbing up against the simultaneous enlivening of the ocean's marine biology amidst the toxic trails of the shipping industry's greenhouse gas emissions. By capsizing their axis of orientation to the ship, Hayes and Diamanti bring environmental/energy humanities into dialogue with new/historical materialism. Their contention is that a critical vocabulary able to see the ship from the sea up, instead of the sky down, is indispensable to any critique of energy and climate in turn, and that a reorientation to the vantage point of this vocabulary begins in the in-between of *The Forgotten Space* and *Leviathan*. In "Nature Guarding 'Her Treasures' in Oil Comedies: The Case of *Local Hero* and *Fubar: Balls to the Wall*," Robin L. Murray and Joseph K. Heumann examine comedy's complicated relationship with oil, arguing that comedy sees oil as a source of spectacular effects, a comedic prop for gags and pratfalls, as well as a more serious plot source. Despite how, as Stephanie LeMenager suggests, oil's "biophysical properties have caused it to be associated with the comic 'lower bodily stratum,' in Mikhail Bakhtin's phrase," Murray and Heumann suggest that comic films might better address oil as the "shit and sex" of entertainment and reveal the stink behind the flare.[46] By drawing on comic tropes, individual and communal stories, and a productive nostalgia, Murray and Heumann assert that the oil comedies *Local Hero* (1983) and *Fubar: Balls to the Wall* (2010) begin to expose the smell. Instead of suggesting oil and the environment around it can live interdependently, *Local Hero* and *Fubar: Balls to the Wall* reveal the real costs of oil extraction to both human and nonhuman nature. C. Parker Krieg's "Boom/Bust: Tragic Logistics and Accelerationist Comedy in Petroleum Transport" argues that by turning to the peripheral industries that support oil extraction, we can recognize the broader material networks and economies which organize contemporary petroculture, transportation, and climate. The chapter explores the Smithsonian Channel's series *Boomtowners* (2015) and the Canadian mockumentary *FUBAR II* (2010). These unexpected genres, according to Krieg, point to unexpected links in the material networks of North American petroculture. This section, and the book itself, concludes with Sheena Wilson's "Trafficking in Petronormativities: At the Intersections of Petrofeminism, Petrocolonialism, and Petrocapitalism," where the author discusses how the culture of climate change in North America is shaped by patriarchal and colonial capitalist fantasies of mobility, which de-limit what is deemed possible when it comes to imagining the future of energy. Drawing on Michelle St. John's documentary film *Colonization Road* (2016) and an Ethical Oil advertisement campaign, the author argues that these fantasies of mobility are deeply embedded in extractivist dreams based on the circula-tion of petrocapital, thus demanding the dispossession of Indigenous lands, and the exploitation of women and other marginalized groups. Consequently, this chapter concludes with the assertion that any energy transition must reach beyond techno-scientific solutions for a post-carbon world; it must in-volve a literal and figurative *power shift* around which to mobilize feminist and decolonial politics in the interest of just futures.

Putting this collection together, we envisaged that *Transportation and the Culture of Climate Change* would appeal to an academic audience whose fields of studies include environmental history, eco-criticism, and energy humanities, and who are interested in the cultural responses to global warming, striving to understand the disastrous nature of climate change. *Transportation and the Culture of Climate Change* invites its readers to (re)consider such issues as environmental ethics, transport, and mobility from the perspective of the environmental humanities, and to think how the culture that we so swiftly created over the course of the twentieth century has excluded nature as well as the prospects of a safe and clean environment from the horizons of our future.

NOTES

1. For further discussion of this trend, see Brian C. Black, *Crude Reality: Petroleum in World History* (Lanham: Rowman & Littlefield, 2012).
2. J. R. McNeill, *Something New under the Sun: An Environmental History of the Twentieth-Century World* (New York: W. W. Norton, 2000), 39.
3. Andreas Malm, *Fossil Capital: The Rise of Steam Power and the Roots of Global Warming* (London: Verso, 2016), 7–9.
4. Imre Szeman, "Energy, Climate and the Classroom: A Letter," in *Teaching Climate Change*

in the Humanities, ed. Stephen Siperstein, Shane Hall, and Stephanie LeMenager (London: Routledge, 2017), 46.

5. Karen Pinkus, "Air," in *Energy Humanities: An Anthology*, ed. Imre Szeman and Dominic Boyer (Baltimore: Johns Hopkins University Press, 2017), 421.

6. Mike Featherstone, "Automobilities: An Introduction," in *Automobilities*, ed. Mike Featherstone, Nigel Thrift, and John Urry (London: SAGE, 2005), 1.

7. Adam Trexler, "Mediating Climate Change: Ecocriticism, Science Studies, and *The Hungry Tide*," in *The Oxford Handbook of Ecocriticism*, ed. Greg Garrard (Oxford: Oxford University Press, 2014), 205.

8. Eric Cazdyn and Imre Szeman, *After Globalization* (Hoboken: Wiley-Blackwell, 2013), 5–6.

9. Trexler, "Mediating Climate Change," 205.

10. John A. Duvall, *The Environmental Documentary: Cinema Activism in the 21st Century* (New York: Bloomsbury, 2017), 85.

11. Sheena Wilson, Imre Szeman, and Adam Carlson, "On Petrocultures: Or, Why We Need to Understand Oil to Understand Everything Else," in *Petrocultures: Oil, Politics, Culture*, ed. Sheena Wilson, Adam Carlson, and Imre Szeman (Montreal: McGill-Queen's University Press, 2017), 15.

12. Brian Black and Marcy Ladson, "The Legacy of Extraction: Reading Patterns and Ethics in Pennsylvania's Landscape of Energy," *Pennsylvania History: A Journal of Mid-Atlantic Studies* 79, no. 4 (2012): 378, accessed May 15, 2018, https://muse.jhu.edu/article/488541.

13. Richard A. Simmons, Eugene D. Coyle, and Bert Chapman, "Global Energy Policy Perspectives," in *Understanding the Global Energy Crisis*, ed. Eugene D. Coyle and Richard A. Simmons (West Lafayette: Purdue University Press, 2014), 29.

14. Samuel Randalls, "Broadening Debates on Climate Change Ethics: Beyond Carbon Calculation," *The Geographical Journal* 177, no. 2 (2011): 129, accessed May 15, 2018, http://www.jstor.org/stable/41238021.

15. Stephanie LeMenager, *Living Oil: Petroleum Culture in the American Century* (Oxford: Oxford University Press, 2014), 26.

16. David Louter, *Windshield Wilderness: Cars, Roads, and Nature in Washington's National Parks* (Seattle: University of Washington Press, 2006), 20.

17. John Whitelegg, *Critical Mass: Transport, Environment and Society in the Twenty-First Century* (London: Pluto Press, 1997), 17.

18. Colin Divall, "Mobilizing the History of Technology," *Technology and Culture* 51, no. 4 (2010): 938, accessed May 15, 2018, https://muse.jhu.edu/article/403273.

19. Christopher W. Wells, *Car Country: An Environmental History* (Seattle: University of Washington Press, 2012), xxxii.

20. Stephanie LeMenager, "The Aesthetics of Petroleum, after *Oil!*," *American Literary History* 24, no. 1 (2012): 71, accessed May 15, 2018, https://muse.jhu.edu/article/465478.

21. Whitelegg, *Critical Mass*, 17.

22. Wells, *Car Country*, xxxiv.

23. Paul S. Sutter, *Driven Wild: How the Fight against Automobiles Launched the Modern Wilderness Movement* (Seattle: University of Washington Press, 2002), 18.

24. LeMenager, "The Aesthetics of Petroleum," 73.

25. Szeman, "Energy, Climate and the Classroom," 46. Italics added.

26. Duvall, *The Environmental Documentary*, 128.

27. Szeman, "Energy, Climate and the Classroom," 47.

28. Amitav Ghosh, *The Great Derangement: Climate Change and the Unthinkable* (Chicago: University of Chicago Press, 2016), 74.

29. Imre Szeman, "Crude Aesthetics: The Politics of Oil Documentaries," *Journal of American*

Studies 46, no. 2, *Oil Cultures* (2012): 438, accessed May 15, 2018, http://www.jstor.org/stable/23259144.

30. Szeman qtd. in Lindsey Green-Simms, "Automobility," in *Fueling Culture: 101 Words for Energy and Environment*, ed. Imre Szeman, Jennifer Wenzel, and Patricia Yaeger (New York: Fordham University Press, 2017), 59.

31. Veronique Van Acker, Ben Derudder, and Frank Witlox, "Why People Use Their Cars While the Built Environment Imposes Cycling," *Journal of Transport and Land Use* 6, no. 1 (2013): 61, accessed May 15, 2018, http://www.jstor.org/stable/26202647.

32. Joseph E. Aldy et al., "Designing Climate Mitigation Policy," *Journal of Economic Literature* 48, no. 4 (2010): 919, accessed May 15, 2018, http://www.jstor.org/stable/29779703.

33. Peng Chen, Jiangping Zhou, and Feiyang Sun, "Built Environment Determinants of Bicycle Volume: A Longitudinal Analysis," *Journal of Transport and Land Use* 10, no. 1 (2017): 656, accessed May 15, 2018, http://www.jstor.org/stable/26211749.

34. Jennifer L. Rice, "Climate Carbon, and Territory: Greenhouse Gas Mitigation in Seattle, Washington," *Annals of the Association of American Geographers* 100, no. 4, *Climate Change* (2010): 930, accessed May 15, 2018, http://www.jstor.org/stable/40863612. Italics in original.

35. Joel E. Cohen, "Population and Climate Change," *Proceedings of the American Philosophical Society* 154, no. 2 (2010): 165, accessed May 15, 2018, http://www.jstor.org/stable/41000096.

36. Komanoff, Roelofs, Orcutt, and Ketcham qtd. in Simon Kingham and Paul Tranter, "Cycling and Sustainable Transport," in *Cycling Futures*, ed. Jennifer Bonham and Marilyn Johnson (Adelaide: University of Adelaide Press, 2015), 131.

37. Jędrzej Gadziński, "The Impact of Local Transport Systems on Green Infrastructure—Policy Versus Reality: The Case of Poznan, Poland," *Urbani Izziv* 26, *Green Infrastructure in Central, Eastern and South Eastern Europe* (2015): 66, accessed May 15, 2018, http://www.jstor.org/stable/24920948.

38. Ursula Kluwick, "Talking about Climate Change: The Ecological Crisis and Narrative Form," in *The Oxford Handbook of Ecocriticism*, ed. Greg Garrard (Oxford: Oxford University Press, 2014), 502.

39. LeMenager, *Living Oil*, 26.

40. LeMenager, "The Aesthetics of Petroleum," 72–73.

41. Gordon Sayre, "Automobile," in *Fueling Culture: 101 Words for Energy and Environment*, ed. Imre Szeman, Jennifer Wenzel, and Patricia Yaeger (New York: Fordham University Press, 2017), 54.

42. Christopher Jones, "The Carbon-Consuming Home: Residential Markets and Energy Transitions," *Enterprise & Society* 12, no. 4 (2011): 792, accessed May 15, 2018, https://muse.jhu.edu/article/458164.

43. Sayre, "Automobile," 56.

44. Imre Szeman, "New Habitat," *Resilience: A Journal of the Environmental Humanities* 1, no. 1 (2013): 3, accessed May 15, 2018, https://muse.jhu.edu/article/565572.

45. Rob Nixon, *Slow Violence and the Environmentalism of the Poor* (Cambridge: Harvard University Press, 2011).

46. LeMenager, *Living Oil*, 92.

Part I
Mobility and the Environment

CHAPTER 1

Using Heritage and Ecological Systems Thinking to Inform Resilient Automobility Design

Barry L. Stiefel

Since the late nineteenth century, the proliferation of commercially made motor vehicles (i.e., trucks, motorcycles, etc., here forward automobiles) has profoundly impacted the development of nearly every aspect of modern society. Their effect includes the contemporary landscape and how billions of people move from one place to another, which is why automotive heritage is relevant and should be used to inform future design for sustainable resiliency.[1] Designers and engineers who do not learn from the automotive past could repeat its failures. An example was when car companies experimented with "lifetime" fluids and filters, which made it impossible to clean filters and address other necessary general maintenance issues.[2] These mistakes then become consumer problems, in addition to the secondary effects pertaining to safety and environmental quality. For instance, will replacing all contemporary internal combustion engine automobiles on the road, which since 2010 have numbered over a billion worldwide, with electric and hybrid vehicles necessarily be the best course of action?[3] While tailpipe emissions would be significantly reduced, disposing of the billion or more problematic automobiles and making new ones to replace them could (even if melted down for recycling) "break" the planet when resources and energy expended for manufacturing this great change are taken into consideration. For the built environment, heritage preservation best practices have found that the "greenest" building is the one already built, because the environmental "debt" for construction, materials extraction, and embodied energy have already been expended. What if renewable materials, heritage preservation practices, and sustainable design were used to inform an alternative means of automobility?

Understanding the past orients consumers and grounds designers for addressing contemporary issues pertaining to transportation, which will need to be planned in such a manner that it does not adversely affect the environment.

Beginning in the 1920s, General Motors conceived of making the automobile a fourth need, in addition to food, clothing, and shelter.[4] By the mid-twentieth century, the automobile industry in North America and Europe, along with the assistance of many government policies for which companies like General Motors lobbied, achieved their goal of automobiles becoming a necessity through the development of automotive-dependent landscapes. Many could no longer travel to and from home, work, school, places of commerce, or recreation without an automobile, whether within municipalities or between one city and another. Mass transit systems by rail in many urban areas, as well as those that connected communities across rural expanses, were purposely defunded and neglected in order to promote the automobile.[5] In place of mass transit infrastructure was built great expanses of road systems to enable automobile use, which also deterred walkability. It is precisely the twentieth-century landscape designed for automobiles, to the neglect of other means of mobility, which has greatly contributed to our current predicament of twenty-first-century environmental (and social justice) problems. Therefore, addressing automotive transportation issues, as well as how vehicles are made and powered, is something that is vitally important to do.

This chapter examines the automobile as a material cultural artifact in order to postulate a holistically resilient evolution of vehicle design in response to global climate change and transportation mobility. As part of this exercise, I will use historical precedents and natural ecological processes to inform the objective of sustainable automotive design within a dynamically changing world. Experiments and case studies from approaches made in the built environment will also be synthesized to inform future directions for how resilient-minded automobility might function in a theoretical framework and thereby provide designers an approach for implementation. Automobility must be redesigned so that those who wish to partake in the experience now do not take away the ability from those far into the future to also do so.

Automobility and Environmentally Conscious Resilient Design

The social science-based "mobilities" paradigm was first articulated by Mimi Sheller and John Urry, referring to the exploration of things, ideas, and people in respect to broader social implications of movement.[6] Refining this approach further with regard to vehicles that can move under their own power resulted in the concept of "automobility," described by Mike Featherstone, Nigel Thrift, and John Urry as:

> The modes of autonomous, self-directed movement. The auto in the term automobile initially referred to a self-propelled vehicle (a carriage without a horse). The autonomy was not just through the motor, but the capacity for independent motorized self-steering movement freed from the confines of a rail track. The promise here is for self-steering autonomy and capacity to search out the open road or off-road, encapsulated in vehicles which afford not only speed and mobility, but act as comforting protected and enclosed private spaces, increasingly a platform for communications media, that can be enjoyed alone or in the company of significant others.[7]

As such, automobility is dynamic, complex, and functions within a systems framework, inside of which there are multiple opportunities for strategizing and implementing sustainable and resilient-minded interventions.

Little academic research addresses the specific approach of sustainable resilient design in relation to the automobile. Mintesnot G. Woldeamanuel, among other transportation planners, has touched on the topic, but within a larger, multimodal transportation planning framework.[8] Using a diversity of transport options for people, goods, and services is an essential part of a broader resilient design, but beyond that, much of how sustainable automobility should function has yet to be fleshed out. Scholars either share technological expertise on how electric and hybrid automobiles work (e.g., James Larminie and John Lowry), or provide histories of them (e.g., David A. Kirsch, Gijs Mom, Curtis D. Anderson, and Judy Anderson).[9] Environmental designers and activists, like Paul Hawken in his *Drawdown* proposal, cite electric automobiles as part of a "toolbox" of strategies for achieving environmental sustainability while meeting transportation needs. However, like the transportation planners, Hawken provides little depth on how this could be a successful approach.[10] For, as Kirsch observes in his history of electric automobiles:

> there is no such thing as an environmentally friendly automotive technology. The first automobiles, whether gasoline-, steam-, or electric-powered, represented a dramatic environmental improvement over the horse-drawn technology that they replaced. The social, financial, and environmental threats we now face as a result of our reliance on refined petroleum are not the fault of internal combustion technology per se

but of the massive expansion of the automotive transportation system. . . . Had steam or electricity succeeded in establishing an alternate technological standard and had such a system been in place today, we would still face serious (although different) social and environmental costs.[11]

Thus, swapping one set of global problems for another through the simple replacement of internal-combustion-engine automobiles with electric seems unwise, unsustainable, and nonresilient. If a future with automobility is what is desired, then the automotive industry must rethink the way vehicles are designed, made, and powered.

Returning to horse-drawn technology (or that which employs other beasts of burden) is not a viable option either, at least within the modern urbanized structure of human settlement in which more than half of all people in the world reside.[12] During the early twentieth century, it was observed that automobiles positively helped urban conditions, alleviating both the cruelty of servitude for horses and public health concerns caused by their waste.[13] While the proliferation of the automobile in the 1910s and 1920s caused the decline of the horse population due to lack of demand, the reduced animal sewage produced and improved humane treatment of animals resulted in a net environmental gain.[14] So, how does society move forward with automotive transportation if going in reverse with the technology is not a viable option? Government policies, reinforced with economic restructuring, must consider current and future projected population constraints, and what works within a multimodal system of mass transportation and walkability.

Addressing Current Problems in Order to Develop Sustainable Automobility

Resiliency is the capacity to quickly recover from difficulties. Therefore, this analysis on the sustainable redesign of automobility will begin with what needs to stop happening. There are materials and activities that undermine this resiliency objective that need to be addressed before proactive action can be taken. One widely acknowledged issue is the use of petroleum in automobiles. It is precisely because of public acknowledgment that fossil fuel emissions cause environmental harm that electric vehicles and hybrids are becoming increasingly popular. However, petroleum is also present in electric vehicles due to their materials. Even if they do not have exhaust emissions, the plastics, synthetic rubber, and metals require the burning of fossil fuels for melting and shaping. Other resource problems associated with automobiles besides petroleum concerns that have not been addressed are the frequent use of hazardous materials (such as lead, mercury, arsenic, cadmium, and beryllium), the challenge of acquiring certain materials (i.e., lithium), and the use of rare earth elements (neodymium, terbium, and dysprosium), especially in electronic components.[15] While an electric vehicle may not have tailpipe emissions, there is still a significant carbon footprint to consider from the use of plastics, synthetic rubber, electricity taken off the power grid from fossil fuel sources, and other materials derived from petroleum. Ceasing the use of hazardous materials should be a clear goal. Using toxic substances is inherently unsustainable and inhibits transportation resiliency. And yes, petroleum and its derivatives are hazardous materials. Especially problematic and rarely considered is that photovoltaic (PV) solar panels contain cadmium and lead, so the toxicity of PVC panels limits contemporary models on how the future might harvest solar energy for propulsion. Being mindful of the impacts of materials in consumer goods such as automobiles is something that our society needs to develop further (see fig. 1.1).

Fig. 1.1. While electric powered cars may not have tailpipe emissions, there is still a significant carbon footprint to consider from the use of plastics, synthetic rubber, electricity taken off the power grid from fossil fuel sources, and other things derived from petroleum. (Photo by Marion S. Trikosko. February 18, 1974. Library of Congress, Prints & Photographs Division, U.S. News & World Report Magazine Collection, LC-DIG-ppmsca-55465)

Most rare earth elements are also hazardous materials with high toxicity levels. An additional reason for avoiding them is because of the unsustainable processes involved in seeking them out, mining them, transporting ore for processing, and then refining them to levels of purity so that they can be used in contemporary electronic technologies. A significant rare earth element used in automobiles is neodymium, which is used in strong, permanent magnets and is only found in a few locations in Asia. Lithium is a hard-to-find element (technically not considered rare) and it is widely used in rechargeable batteries. Cadmium, neodymium, and lithium, among other elements, are all essential to contemporary automobiles, and those slated for design in the near future. Sufficient critical assessment of the full environmental impact of post-fossil-fuel automobility has not been conducted because engineers and consumers are so focused on tailpipe emissions.

Those interested in "green" designed vehicles have forgotten about manufacturing emissions. Journalist Bjorn Lomborg found that approximately half of the energy-related carbon dioxide emissions connected to an electric automobile's lifetime are generated as part of the production process, with the greatest issue being the lithium battery. Lithium mining and battery manufacturing is a very energy consumptive process that creates a substantial amount of greenhouse gases. Lomborg cites that for conventional internal combustion-powered automobiles, 17 percent of its lifetime carbon dioxide emissions are created during production. The manufacturing of an average automobile creates seven tons of carbon dioxide, compared to fifteen tons for an electric vehicle.[16] As a matter of comparison, larger vehicles, such as conventional sport utility vehicles (SUVs), generate about seventeen tons of carbon dioxide through their manufacturing processes. The energy, resources, and impact of the electronic components of an electric or hybrid vehicle—the *full* embodied energy of the automobile from resource extraction to disposal—have been overlooked due to the tailpipe emissions obsession. Additionally, while electric vehicles have no tailpipe emissions, they do continue to pollute if their energy comes from non-sustainable sources, and this is a common ecological footprint factor not considered as heavily as it should in the use of these automobiles.

So what, then, does an automobile without a petroleum-based fuel supply and materials, without hazardous materials, and without hard-to-find and rare earth elements look like? Electricity is still energy that can be looked to, but it is going to have to be sourced from non-fossil-fuel-based generation. Canada, France, Brazil, and Scandinavia source much of their energy from renewables, but future designs will have to modify or avoid PV solar panels that use hazardous materials and rare earth elements. There are other energy sources to consider as well, such as biofuel (biodiesel and ethanol) and the fuel cell, which will be explored more in depth later. The trickiest issues that have not even begun to be addressed regarding automobility—let alone the entire technology industry—are the intertwined problems of using certain hazardous materials and rare earth elements that are so commonly found in electronics, especially batteries, PV solar panels, and microchips. In respect to functionality, this takes original designs back to vehicles made before 1980, when automobile manufacturers began to computerize their products as well as use plastic parts.[17] Before 1980, electronic features such as lights, radio, windshield wipers, and cruise control performed without computers or microchips, and the vehicles essentially worked through mechanical systems. Contemporary vehicles—even those with conventional internal combustion engines—work on a hybridity of computer and mechanical systems. American designers do not need to oppose technologically advanced entertainment, climate control, or navigational systems based on electronics, but these systems need to be reengineered without hazardous materials or rare earth elements. This is especially the case for the increasingly anticipated autonomous driving systems and fantasized flying capabilities that automotive designers would like to have in the future.

What should be focused on in the making of automobiles are renewable resources and common earth elements. Some common earth elements such as aluminum and iron (used with carbon in steel and other common elements) and silicate or sand (used for glass) are still quasi-problematic because of the current methods of processing that depend on a high-fossil-fuel-energy input, but are at least inert or nontoxic when processing is finished. These materials can still play a role for automobiles already built, which is why the strategies to follow will be divided into two applications for preexisting vehicles and new ones to be built. Existing vehicles also have embodied energy that has already been invested in, so addressing their future role is vital. A policy example of where the embodied energy of automobiles was either ignored or forgotten was the Car Allowance Rebate System created by the American government in 2009, widely known as the "cash for clunkers" program. The program's purpose was to improve the fuel efficiency of automobiles, as well as to create an economic stimulus during a recession through new vehicle manufacturing galvanized by a cash-rebate opportunity for consumers when they traded in an old car. By 2010, more than seven hundred thousand "clunkers" were replaced by new, fuel-efficient cars, with an average improvement of 58 percent in mpg/kpl fuel economy.[18] But, there is no data that verifies that this was a net gain for the environment because the waste produced and the energy expended to make the new automobiles were not accounted for, nor the energy spent scrapping the older cars taken off the road. There is also no information about additional stresses put on places with increased mining to support new car manufacturing. Without this data, environmentally minded economists cannot respond to whether there was a net carbon emissions decrease or gain to the atmosphere through the "cash for clunkers" program or how that would contrast to an alternative approach of rehabilitating old vehicles.

For both existing and new automobiles, society will also have to challenge the industry-wide paradigm of designed obsolescence, developed by Alfred Sloan at General Motors during the 1920s.[19] All automobiles will inherently wear out their parts because mechanical things break down through friction and thermal stress, among other factors. However, as Henry Ford designed the Model T, replacement parts can and should be made durable, repairable, replaceable, and interchangeable for every make and model generation of a vehicle.[20] Indeed, the one significant technological change between the first year of Model T production in 1908 and the last in 1927 was the use of the electric starter in place of the hand-crank. This is why more than a century later, it is estimated that between fifty thousand to sixty thousand Model T Fords alone within the United States are roadworthy, let alone more elsewhere in the world.[21] Ford designed the Model T to last with reasonable regular maintenance, not for obsolescence.

Design inspiration for automobile functionality could come from nature, which is based on metabolic systems for energy and materials flow. Sometimes called biomimicry, parts and energy substances may wear out, but new ones need to be sustainably made and old ones sustainably disposed in a continuous loop of a cradle-to-cradle or upcycling framework. Every material and form of energy within the biomimicry framework is an asset for something else; there are no systematic liabilities. Biomimicry synthesizing has been conducted within built environments for thousands of years, and so the next theoretical application is to use it in automobiles. An example of built-environment biomimicry are the mud brick buildings of Aït Benhaddou (Morocco), Arg-é Bam (Iran), and Taos Pueblo (New Mexico), and the timber buildings of Kirkjubøur (Faroe Islands) and Greensted Church (England), where each have been continuously inhabited for millennia.[22] Buildings of this age can only endure when there is a culture of maintenance integrated with society, ecology, and the economy. When parts are no longer functional, they literally return to the earth and nothing toxic or hard-to-find is used. In each place, the buildings are literally integrated with their local environments and climates, creating an interdependence of natural and cultural heritage. A similar approach with transportation vehicles needs to be engineered where materials and energy requirements are in some manner synchronized with ecological processes in a symbiotic manner.

An essential paradigm shift must occur in respect to our use of materials and economy for automobility. Contemporary modern buildings and automobiles share some common underlying problems. They need to be made and designed in such a way so that their inhabitants and users, without highly sophisticated training or resources, can conduct maintenance. Historically, many small automotive manufacturing companies existed, as was the case for wagons and other vehicles pulled by horses. Using local materials and solutions, small companies were able to both build and service vehicles as needed for their customers. While this approach is antithetical to what can be produced by big companies through economies of scale, society must recognize that mass production has stressed ecological systems by using resources and generating waste at rates that the environment cannot adequately adapt to.

Rehabilitating Old Cars

The rehabilitation of old automobiles is a practice that has rarely been done, let alone for the purpose of mitigating negative environmental impacts. The earliest instance where this was conducted by an automobile manufacturer was by the Detroit Electric Car Company for its Model 97 between 1932 and 1934; however, the reasons for this were due to economic restructuring, not sustainable resiliency. From 1929 to 1934, the Detroit Electric Car Company underwent reorganization after bankruptcy due to the Stock Market Crash of 1929. During these years, the company did not have sufficient funds to mass produce new automobiles from new materials, so, as a means of making ends meet, the Detroit Electric Car Company bought back its old vehicles and renovated them with new features for market. Therefore, Detroit Electric Model 97s from 1932 to 1934 are actually older automobiles that have been rehabilitated.[23] As of this writing, Jaguar Land Rover Automotive has also recently announced that it will "restore and resell [the E-Type, made between 1961 and 1975,] to wealthy collectors through its recently established Classics division" as a fully electric vehicle.[24] The cost for the E-Type conversion by Jaguar is pricey—US$375,000—but ideally it could become a model for the development of a more environmentally minded automotive rehabilitation service, assuming that it can be made to be financially more competitive (see fig. 1.2).

More frequent is the practice of rehabilitating automobiles conducted on an individualized basis. An example from Charleston, South Carolina, is

Fig. 1.2. An example of a Detroit Electric Car from 1921. Examples such as these were refurbished by the car company as their Model 97 between 1932 and 1934. (Photo from National Photo Company Collection, Library of Congress Prints and Photographs Division, LC-DIG-npcc-21279)

a 1988 B700 Ford school bus that has been adaptively refashioned into the Lowcountry Street Grocery, "a grocery store on wheels."[25] The bus's interior includes locally grown produce, baked goods, pantry, and butcher/fish sections that serve as "a mission-driven, mobile farmers' market designed to make healthy, local food affordable" for the community, with a percentage of sales apportioned to help the area's lower income residents.[26]

A second example of environmentally friendly historic automobile rehabilitation is the 1959 Lincoln Continental owned by collector and celebrity Neil Young, who had his car modified into a biodiesel-electric hybrid.[27] Young had significant changes made to the engine, which now performs at 100 mpg (42 kpl) on biodiesel, a renewable substitute for petroleum. For its time (2007), Young's rehabilitation of his 1959 Lincoln Continental was very innovative, but this example is also reflective of societal values that are exclusively focused on tailpipe emissions. Lincoln Continentals were originally made with conventional gasoline engines that cannot use diesel or biodiesel fuel. The entire mechanical engine system had to be taken out by Young's mechanic, and a new modified diesel engine was installed with a lithium-based electrical battery hybrid system. The warning is that Frankenstein-like "Super-E cars" should be avoided because they only replicate the problems of automobility propulsion, as identified earlier by Kirsch.

One monstrous Super-E car is Bloodshed Motors's 2015 Zombie 222, a customized automobile comprised of a 1968 Ford Mustang body that has been infused "with [an] insanely powerful all electric propulsion . . . [and enhanced with] state of the art suspension and braking and embed cool new technology."[28] The company is "committed to producing the baddest, coolest, fastest vintage muscle cars in the world, all electric, all the time,"[29] and the Zombie 222 does provide that with 800 horsepower and with speeds capable of 175 mph (280 kph). The problem is that other than the exterior shell, the car is not a 1968 Ford Mustang, but something entirely different. While an exceptional demonstration of twenty-first-century electric engine technology, this is not a "green car," especially if one factors the percentage of new parts that were incorporated (particularly the massive lithium battery and electric engine). The Zombie 222 is not a resilient, sustainably designed automobile but an electric-powered wolf wearing a 1967 Ford Mustang body frame as sheep's clothing. Considering the embodied energy value of already-built automobile parts, sustainably designed, resilient, and user-friendly "eco-rods" are a future possibility; but the market for them has not yet developed. Most hot rodders are focused on horsepower and speed performance, whereas environmentally minded motorists focus on high-tech, modern, electric vehicles.

A society that has come close to developing a cultural relationship based on stewardship with the automobile is Cuba. Here, the history of the economic embargo of Cuba by the United States to constrain the Castro regime prohibited the importation of automobiles and most parts, incentivizing Cubans to considerably prolong the functioning life of their automotive resources. Cuba's car stock, though admirable for sustaining long usable life spans, does demonstrate other environmental problems with the absence of technological advancements over the past six decades, such as the lack of catalytic converters, which leads to its automobiles being highly polluting. However, the Cuban example reveals the value of maintenance knowledge. Havana tour guides proudly claim that their mechanics are more like "wizards," elevating the status of those who devote their skills to keeping something working, which is not as well appreciated in other parts of the developed world.[30] Within this framework, a repair expense does not outweigh the cost of replacement of the automobile because there is a different valuation of skilled labor and an alternative approach towards maintenance vs. replacement of materials. In comparison, automobile stewardship is fading from developed North American and European countries. The bodies of Cuban automobiles may be antique, but under the hood there is a hodgepodge of antique American, old Soviet, and contemporary parts from Japan, South Korea, and China. The "wizard's" objective was not environmentally friendly resiliency, but rather continued operation of the car.

The sustainable resiliency of the automobile will require a societal and cultural paradigm shift, on top of materials and energy processing. Since the introduction of electronics and plastics to the automobile starting in the early 1980s, manufacturing companies have made their products in a form that increasingly prohibits the average mechanically knowledgeable person from conducting service and repair work on cars. Electronic systems are evolving purposely through design obsolescence so that only a company-authorized technician with the correct software-compatible equipment can run the diagnostic program to ascertain what is not performing correctly within the vehicle. The ill performing part is designed so that it most likely cannot be repaired—it must be replaced. Today, there are automobiles being designed such that neither the owner nor a regular mechanic can change the oil because a special-made company tool is needed. Besides the issues of materials and energy power sources, this system of automobile stewardship is antithetical to resiliency.

Automobiles need to be (re)designed so that their maintenance can be conducted by the average person using locally and readily available resources to keep the mobility capability of the vehicle functioning. An example of where such a culture of automobility has emerged is among the Bush Mechanics of Australia, primarily among the Aboriginal people in the outback, where there also exists a television show on this very theme. Here, the Bush Mechanics fix flat tires by stuffing them with spinifex (a type of grass) and replace broken crankshafts with tree saplings cut to shape and held with wire, to hold it in place so that travelers can continue on to their destination.[31] Having your car break down in the Australian outback would otherwise be incredibly dangerous, which is why resilient adaptability is needed.

The Australian Bush Mechanics example illustrates that a culture of automobile maintenance that is in dialogue with the natural environment is possible, like buildings that have been inhabited continuously for centuries. With the Bush Mechanics resourcefulness framework in mind, designers can begin to envision what the 500-year-old automobile might look like. The oldest functioning automobiles are about 130 years old, and from these society can begin to assess the design shortcomings needed to be overcome so that they hypothetically could be used circa 2400 (of course respecting that automobiles made circa 1900 are usually maintained as artifacts frozen in time through extreme preservation treatments). Like the thousand-year-old building examples, the functioning centuries-old automobile would have to be an extension of its materials and energy environment. The resources needed for an automobile to function would be available within the region of use, cause no adverse effects to ecological system functions or biodiversity, and the materials and energy waste created by the vehicle would be an asset—not a liability—for the environment and local community. While technically a short-term fix regarding their contemporary automobiles, the Bush Mechanics have the right idea regarding a culture of automotive stewardship that attempts to synchronize automobility with ecological and social processes: everything you need to keep an automobile going should be naturally and readily available within close proximity to the road or your place of habitation. Automobile maintenance must be something that any average, physically capable adult could do.

Getting to this point of materials economy in respect to the automobile will take some time, so incremental steps regarding material parts will also need to be deliberated for poorly designed automobiles, with multiple approaches to consider. One entails the gradual, environmentally focused rehabilitation of a vehicle. Another is the disassembly of more problematic automobiles for reuse of their viable parts, with hazardous materials properly addressed for disposal. Nonharmful parts and mechanical systems on automobiles should evolve in such a manner that when materials wear out, they should be replaced with something that causes no adverse harm to the environment, and we would need to consider their disposal at the end of their lifecycle. Automobile makers would thus need to shift their economic objectives from one of production to that of transportation service support that enables users of vehicles to have greater environmentally minded agency in mobility.

For instance, automobiles with plastic components that cannot be replaced with something else could use biodegradable bioplastics. As an alternative material source developed on the eve of World War II, the Ford Motor Company developed a prototype automobile body made almost entirely from soybean-based bioplastic in 1941. The prototype functioned well, weighing about a thousand pounds less than its all-steel counterpart, which thus improved its fuel economy. The windows were made of transparent acrylic, which is also lighter than automotive glass and requires less energy input to make. And today, acrylic can be made from plant-based raw materials. Lighter vehicles can mitigate the destruction of collisions with less mass being involved at high velocities. With the cessation of all civilian production in 1942, followed by inexpensive petroleum after World War II when automobile manufacturing returned, Ford's use of bioplastics in automobiles never went beyond the 1941 prototype.[32] When plastics were widely introduced into automobiles in the 1980s, petroleum-based ingredients were used, despite the economic strains of the 1970s oil crisis. Acrylic is sometimes mixed with automotive body paint, but windows continue to primarily be made with glass. However, biodegradable plastics must also be used with discretion, as learned from the experience of Mercedes-Benz in the 1990s, where this material was used for wiring harnesses. In certain instances, biodegradable plastics cannot be used where extreme ranges in temperature and humidity exist from hot wires and engine parts, accelerating breakdown.[33]

Some internal combustion engine systems can be converted to greener performance. Diesel engines can be converted to biodiesel. Flexfuel engines can function on ethanol besides gasoline. The first such automobile was the Model T Ford in 1908, because of concerns that rural customers could not always obtain gasoline but could get ethanol.[34] However, depending on the age and make of an automobile, the use of alternative biofuels needs to be approached with an element of caution. Automotive engineer Hannu Jääskeläinen warns that the "use of biodiesel in existing engines may cause a number of issues related to materials compatibility, lubricating oil dilution, fuel injection equipment, and exhaust after treatment devices."[35] And just like gasoline, there are also multiple grades, qualities, and blends to biofuels that can impact the performance as well as likelihood of engine damage. This is especially an issue for homemade biodiesel, which can have quality consistency issues in contrast to commercially produced fuel. Regardless if one has a historic or modern diesel-powered automobile, avoiding these issues is important to sidestep expensive repairs and functionality issues.

Engineers will have to develop battery systems that do not use lithium, lead, or other problematic materials that are either very destructive to the environment to mine and process or are hazardous. A viable alternative are nickel-iron batteries, which are sufficiently durable in that they are expected to last more than twenty years, in contrast to lithium batteries which are only warrantied for eight. Nickel-iron batteries were used for a limited time by the Detroit Electric Car Company as an upgrade to their automobiles with lead-acid batteries during the 1910s and by the Baker Motor Vehicle Company of Cleveland, Ohio, which ceased to make cars in 1916.[36] Historic automobile collector and celebrity Jay Leno not only owns a 1909 Baker Electric Coup, but the original nickel-iron batteries are still functioning, testifying to the durability of this historic battery design and electric vehicle more than a century later.[37] Automobile users will have to wait and see how many electric or hybrid cars from 2009 will be around in 2109 with original functioning lithium batteries, but it will likely be small in number, if any.

Nickel-iron batteries are still made today and are most commonly used for off-grid renewable energy storage, such as for solar panels and windmills. They can be operated in hot temperatures, as well as overcharged and completely discharged without causing damage.[38] The downside to nickel-iron batteries is that they take longer than lead-acid or lithium batteries to recharge. However, when the Milburn Wagon Company of Toledo, Ohio, expanded its product offerings to electric automobiles in 1915, the cars were designed to have a battery exchange system. Therefore, the driver did not have to wait for recharging, and could instead pull into a service station or dealership and swap out the battery as an additional innovation in a very competitive market. Tricopian is currently in the business of offering a similar rechargeable battery service, under the name FuelRod, for electronic mobile devices so there are past and contemporary precedents.[39] By extension, a rechargeable battery system could be experimented with for electric automobiles using nickel-iron batteries in order to address the problem of a long recharge period. Moreover, the recharging facilities and infrastructure for the automotive-designed nickel-iron battery could be based off of renewable energy generation, as the battery is already used in a storage capacity. From 1915 to 1923, Milburn produced approximately four thousand electric automobiles, until General Motors bought them out and converted the plant to make internal combustion engine Buicks.[40]

Automobiles that can be powered from multiple sources enhance resiliency, especially when the energy sources can be locally or regionally produced within ecological system frameworks. Internal combustion engines (using biofuels) and hybrid electrics are what most people are familiar with. Other power contributors can use cogeneration models, including brake regeneration (which is commonly used on electric automobiles) but also possibly wind (the wind created by the speed of an automobile could be used to turn an on-board turbine for an attached auxiliary recharger). Of course, as the modifications accrue over time, the old automobiles become incrementally less "authentic," evolving into something different akin to the metaphoric George Washington's ax. While the head as well as the handle of the ax has been replaced numerous times, it is still a functional ax despite antiquarian objections that this "ax" was not truly used by George Washington. Perhaps if anonymous Jane or John Doe had used the ax instead of Washington, there would be fewer objections to its continued use. Hence why certain exceptions can be made for the more rigorous conservation of historic automobiles that have a verified provenance with a specific person or event for posterity, such as what has been documented through the National Historic Vehicle Register.[41]

Considerations for New Automobile Design

Much of what has been discussed on the rehabilitation of old automobiles can be applied to new. What must differentiate new automobiles of the future from old and contemporary ones to be adaptively reused is that, in addition to avoiding petroleum-based materials and fuels, hazardous materials, and rare earth elements, they must eschew common earth elements and materials that require high-energy inputs from fossil fuels for processing and product production, such as metal and glass. Particular automobile components made from high-energy-input materials may be impossible to avoid, so in these instances they should be used sparingly.

Historically, automobile manufacturers used regionally produced materials. For example, in 1920, the Ford Motor Company purchased approximately 313,000 acres of forestland in the upper peninsula of Michigan for producing their own timber to use in Model Ts built in Detroit. After the timber was harvested, the lumber was processed at a hydroelectric-powered sawmill near Iron Mountain, Michigan.[42] The one necessary aspect missing from this historic approach would be to use sustainable forestry practices for harvesting, which were then not yet conceived. Vehicles made from sustainably sourced local wood and other fiber materials can be a viable alternative to metal in these respects. After wooden parts come to the end of their life use, they can be composted back into nutrients for plants (assuming paints and other finishes on them are also nontoxic and biodegradable). A strategy that can be applied to already existing automobiles with metal components as they wear out is replacement with wood, especially as existing metal replacement parts become unavailable. Adaptations to enhance the safety of older automobiles can also take place during these interventions.

Using renewable, sustainably sourced materials that contain a high level of natural carbon input can provide an additional benefit of sequestering carbon taken from the atmosphere. Historically, as well as today, automobile use and manufacturing has been a major source of carbon-emission pollution, causing greenhouse-induced climate change. A net zero or carbon neutral automobile for the near future will not be sufficient. Automobiles that are carbon assets and can serve as an object of sequestering until atmospheric levels return to preindustrial normalcy are what are needed. Bamboo is a material that is very strong, light, easy to use, and durable in addition to carbon sequestering; but it is problematic outside of its native range in Asia as an invasive species. Where invasive plant species are used for material components, their production for industrial use must be managed very carefully in order to prevent ecological problems for native ecosystems.

In the future, engineers may develop technologies that could function well within automobiles and be synthesized within their material's life cycle in a cradle-to-cradle format that is nonhazardous to ecological systems. An example is carbon fiber, but as yet it has not been developed on an economically viable scale from non-petroleum-based resources.[43] Another future possibility is efficient, low-temperature fuel cells that can be made from nonhazardous materials. Presently, fuel cell technologies are in their infancy and present issues that are similar to how engineers design, make, and use batteries from hazardous materials or rare earth elements. In the end, what is needed is an automobile that can take people to where they need to go without the gambit of adverse harm.

Conclusion: Where to Go from Here?

Where to go from here depends on where society wants to be. This question addresses both a geographic inquiry as well as an ecological one. Society should want an automobile to fulfill transportation needs that walkability and mass transportation systems cannot. Automobiles in this respect should be used sparingly, as needed. This will also entail built environment rehabilitation so that it is easily possible to live, work, and enjoy most aspects of life without the automobile. This is what the world was like before the twentieth century. To paraphrase the 1903 Oldsmobile advertisement, we have seen the passing of the horse.[44] In dense urban areas, horses will not satisfy transportation needs for individualized mobility. Ever since *Homo erectus* wondered out of Africa two million years ago, mobility has been a characteristic of our species. This is not going away, but transportation planners can reallocate General Motor's strategy that automobiles can be a *want* again, and not a *need*. This is the socioeconomic framework that society must return to in an environmentally conscious, socially responsible manner. This is where sustainably designed, resilient automobility will play its role. These rehabilitated and future vehicles will be different from what is experienced today, and consumers must counterbalance the short-term material gratification that is wreaking great environmental havoc on our planet with long-term sustainable resiliency.

If sustainability is about meeting the needs of the present without compromising the needs of future generations, then you should not drive a contemporary hybrid or electric automobile. By using these vehicles in their current form, the environmental destruction that they cause will make it so that our descendants will one day not have an ecologically viable planet or the resources available to theoretically do the same. The resiliently designed automobile has to be something that could be used many generations from now and does not prevent those in the far future from developing automobility systems of their own.

NOTES

1.   Michael Shanks, "The Future of the Automotive Past—What's on the Agenda in Automotive Heritage," program book for *Driving History: Protecting Our Overlooked Automotive Heritage in the Twenty-First Century* (Allentown, PA: Historic Vehicle Association and the College of Charleston, 2016), 32.
2.   Patrick Frawley, "The Ten Dumbest Automotive Design Mistakes," *Jalopnik*, last modified April 4, 2012, https://jalopnik.com/5899054/the-ten-dumbest-automotive -design-mistakes.
3.   Daniel Tencer, "Number of Cars Worldwide Surpasses 1 Billion; Can the World Handle This Many Wheels?", *The Huffington Post Canada,* last modified February 19, 2013, http://www.huffingtonpost.ca/2011/08/23/car-population_n_934291.html.
4.   Nathaniel R. Walker, "American Crossroads: General Motors' Mid-Century Campaign to Promote Modernist Urban Design in Hometown U.S.A.," *Buildings and Landscapes: The Journal of the Vernacular Architectural Forum*, 23, no. 2 (2016): 89–115.
5.   Walker, "American Crossroads."
6.   Mimi Sheller and John Urry, "The New Mobilities Paradigm," *Environment and Planning A* 38, no. 2, (2006): 207–226.
7.   Mike Featherstone, "Automobilities: An Introduction," in *Automobilities*, ed. Mike Featherstone, Nigel Thrift, and John Urry (London: SAGE, 2005), 1–2.
8.   See Mintesnot G. Woldeamanuel, *Concepts in Urban Transportation Planning: The Quest for Mobility, Sustainability and Quality of Life* (Jefferson, NC: McFarland, 2016).
9.   James Larminie and John Lowry, *Electric Vehicle Technology Explained* (Hoboken, NJ: Wiley, 2013); David A. Kirsch, *The Electric Vehicle and the Burden of History* (New Brunswick, NJ: Rutgers University Press, 2000); Gijs Mom, *The Electric Vehicle: Technology and Expectations in the Automobile Age* (Baltimore, MD: Johns Hopkins University Press, 2013); and Curtis D. Anderson and Judy Anderson, *Electric and Hybrid Cars: A History*, 2nd ed. (Jefferson, NC: McFarland, 2010).
10.   Paul Hawken, *Drawdown: The Most Comprehensive Plan Ever Proposed to Reverse Global Warming* (New York: Penguin Putnam, 2017).
11.   Kirsch, *The Electric Vehicle and the Burden of History*, 6.
12.   Charles Clover, "Urban population to exceed 50 per cent," *The Telegraph*, last modified June 27, 2007, https://www.telegraph.co.uk/news/earth/earthnews/3298527/Urban -population-to-exceed-50-per-cent.html.
13.   Within New York City alone, according to the Sanitation Bureau of the Health Department, on the eve of the automobile transportation revolution in 1880, there resided approximately 50,000 horses that produced 100,000 tons of their own sewage waste. This would create very serious public health problems if animal-drawn vehicle dependence were brought back to cities. Even more horses would be necessary today in New York, let alone every other urban area, and the issues of animal cruelty and their

waste would be much larger in magnitude. See George Frederick Shrady and Thomas Lathrop Stedman, eds. "Medical Items and News," *The Medical Record: A Weekly Journal of Medicine and Surgery,* 19 (January 1, 1881–June 25, 1881), 280.

14. Susan D. Jones, *Valuing Animals: Veterinarians and Their Patients in Modern America* (Baltimore: Johns Hopkins University Press, 2003), 46–47.
15. Jim Motavalli, "Forget Lithium—It's Rare Earth Minerals That Are in Short Supply for EVs," *CBS News Moneywatch,* last modified June 19, 2010, https://www.cbsnews.com/news/forget-lithium-its-rare-earth-minerals-that-are-in-short-supply-for-evs.
16. Bjorn Lomborg, "Bjorn Lomborg: Green Cars Have a Dirty Little Secret," *Wall Street Journal,* last modified March 11, 2013, http://www.wsj.com/articles/SB1000142412788 7324128504578346913994914472#:JIOWYI4PFryQnA.
17. Steve Mertl, "How cars have become rolling computers," *The Globe and Mail,* last modified March 24, 2017, https://www.theglobeandmail.com/globe-drive/how-cars-have-become-rolling-computers/article29008154; and "U.S. Car Makers Adding More Aluminum, Plastic," *The New York Times,* February 5, 1981, D00018.
18. Eric Bolton, "Cash for Clunkers Wraps up with Nearly 700,000 car sales and increased fuel efficiency, U.S. Transportation Secretary LaHood declares program 'wildly successful,' " *National Highway Traffic Safety Administration,* last modified August 26, 2009, http://www.nhtsa.gov/About+NHTSA/Press+Releases/2009/Cash+for+Clunkers +Wraps+up+with+Nearly+700,000+car+sales+and+increased+fuel+efficiency,+U.S.+Tra nsportation+Secretary+LaHood+declares+program+%E2%80%9Cwildly+successful%E2 %80%9D.
19. Giles Slade, *Made to Break: Technology and Obsolescence in America* (Cambridge, MA: Harvard University Press, 2007), 29–44.
20. H. E. Weiss, *Chrysler, Ford, Durant, and Sloan: Founding Giants of the American Automotive Industry* (Jefferson, NC: McFarland, 2003), 37.
21. Lindsay Brooke, *Ford Model T: The Car That Put the World on Wheels* (MBI, 2008), 188.
22. Barry L. Stiefel and Amalia Leifeste, *Sustainable Heritage: Merging Environmental Conservation and Historic Preservation* (New York: Routledge, 2018), 143–164.
23. Anderson and Anderson, *Electric and Hybrid Cars,* 21–59.
24. Jamie Lincoln Kitman, "Jaguar's Electric E-Type Marries '60s Sex Appeal and Tomorrow's Tech," *The New York Times,* last modified September 6, 2018, https://www.nytimes.com/2018/09/06/business/jaguar-electric-e-type.html.
25. Kadence Themes and Liz Hodges, "The Bus," *Lowcountry Street,* last modified 2018, http://www.lowcountrystreetgrocery.com/the-bus.
26. Themes and Hodges, "The Bus."
27. Matt Hardigree, "Neil Young to Convert Classic Lincoln to Bio-Diesel Hybrid," *Jalopnik,* last modified November 20, 2007, http://jalopnik.com/325009/neil-young-to-convert -classic-lincoln-to-bio-diesel-hybrid.
28. Mitch Medford, "Our Mission," *Bloodshed Motors,* last modified 2013, http://www.zombie222.com/about.html.
29. Medford, "Our Mission."
30. Mireya Navarro, "Cuban Wizardry Keeps Tail Fins from Drooping," *The New York Times,* last modified June 5, 2002, https://www.nytimes.com/2002/06/05/arts/cuban -wizardry-keeps-tail-fins-from-drooping.html.
31. Vanessa Gorman, "Australian Story: David Batty Is One of the Bush Mechanics Mob," *ABC News,* last modified July 3, 2016, http://www.abc.net.au/news/2016-07-04 /david-batty-one-of-the-mob-australian-story/7561464.
32. Hawken, *Drawdown,* 168.
33. Frawley, "The Ten Dumbest Automotive Design Mistakes."
34. Richard Freudenberger, *Alcohol Fuel: A Guide to Making and Using Ethanol as a Renewable Fuel* (New York: New Society, 2009), 9.

35. Hannu Jääskeläinen, "Compatibility of Biodiesel with Petroleum Diesel Engines," *Diesel Net Technology Guide*, last modified 2010, https://www.dieselnet.com/tech/fuel _biodiesel_comp.php.
36. Anderson and Anderson, *Electric and Hybrid Cars*, 21–59.
37. Dexter Ford, "Back to the Future in a 98-Year-Old Electric Car," *The New York Times*, last modified August 5, 2007, http://www.nytimes.com/2007/08/05/automobiles /05BAKER.html?_r=0.
38. Robert U. Ayres and Richard P. McKenna, *Alternatives to the Internal Combustion Engine: Impacts on Environmental Quality* (Baltimore, MD: John Hopkins University Press), 88–91.
39. "Company Overview of Tricopian, LLC," *Bloomberg*, last modified 2018, https://www .bloomberg.com/research/stocks/private/snapshot.asp?privcapid=303568920.
40. Anderson and Anderson, *Electric and Hybrid Cars*, 42. Also see Myles Twete, "History," *Milburn Light Electrics,* last modified 2008, http://www.milburn.us/history.htm.
41. "National Historic Vehicle Register," *Historic Vehicle Association*, last modified 2018, https://www.historicvehicle.org/national-historic-vehicle-register.
42. "Ford Motor Company Iron Mountain Plant Sawmill and Power House, circa 1920," *The Henry Ford*, last modified 2018, https://www.thehenryford.org/collections-and-research /digital-collections/artifact/366487.
43. Jonathan Y. Chen, *Activated Carbon Fiber and Textiles* (Amsterdam: Elsevier/Woodhead, 2016), 53.
44. Michael W. R. Davis, *General Motors: A Photographic History* (Charleston, SC: Arcadia, 1999), 12.

CHAPTER 2

Bikes for Children, Cars for Adults: Postwar American Transportation Culture and the Legacy of Moving Images

James Longhurst

In 1984, conservative humorist P. J. O'Rourke wrote an article for the magazine *Car and Driver*, presenting an enumerated case for the abolition of bicycles from the American road. His first point was that "bicycles are childish":

> Bicycles have their proper place, and that place is under small boys delivering evening papers. Insofar as children are too short to see over the dashboards of cars . . . bicycles are suitable vehicles for them. But what are we to make of an adult in a suit and tie pedaling his way to work? Are we to assume he still delivers newspapers for a living? If not, do we want a doctor, lawyer, or business executive who plays with toys?[1]

Point 4 states simply that "Bicycles are un-American . . . too slow and impuissant for a country like ours. They belong in Czechoslovakia."[2] Bicycles, according to O'Rourke, were for children and foreigners.

While O'Rourke was a comedian, writing satire for a popular magazine, these same themes still showed up in serious policymaking throughout the twentieth century. For example, an advocate speaking in favor of urban bike trails before the United States Congress in 1967 was chastised by the committee's chair: "There was one time when I liked to bicycle also. I got that out of my system, though, in about 16 months."[3] A decade and a half later, in a hearing on federal spending for bicycle transportation, a concerned witness observed that there was a "prevailing attitude in these agencies that 'bikes are for kids.' "[4] For most of the twentieth century, mainstream culture held that riding a bicycle—either for recreation or transportation—was not appropriate behavior for American adults. That perception changed history, policy, and quite possibly our climatic future.

This chapter argues that for North America, responses to anthropogenic global climate change in the twenty-first century face challenges left by the cultural production of the twentieth: in particular, the fact that postwar culture consistently expressed the view that the bicycle is for children, while automobiles are for adults. This creates a significant problem: the "adult" choice is now the greatest contributor to climate emissions in the United States.[5]

The United States is an autocentric culture, and has been for the last seventy-five years. Particularly in the postwar period, autocentric cultural beliefs have been encoded in a variety of expressions, from films to television to music to advertising. In post–World War II bicycle safety films (theoretically meant to support bicycle use), audiences were instructed that children should ride their bikes as practice to become adult drivers. In feature-length Hollywood films, meanwhile, narratives emphasized the bicycle's value as recreation, not transportation. Automobility was associated with masculinity, independence, technological mastery, and adulthood; while bicycle usage was associated with childhood and foreign cultures. These cultural beliefs have been shaped by—and in turn have shaped—laws, policies, budgets, and the design of cities. Cultural production occurred in dialogue with changes in policy and law: as the Interstate Highway System spread and facilitated suburbanization, the Uniform Vehicle Code increasingly diminished the status of the bicycle as transportation, and street design focused almost exclusively on the automobile. Together, policy and culture locked many Americans into energy-intensive and climate-changing transportation modes.

An autocentric culture and intertwined policies complicate responses to anthropogenic climate change today. It seems unlikely, but any meaningful response to an issue considered existential by this generation is threatened by the elementary school filmstrips and B-movies of previous decades.

Scholars have written extensively about automobile culture in the US, but "there has been surprisingly little analogous work devoted to the bicycle and bicycling," according to Zack Furness.[6] While urban planning and public health professionals explore bicycles as transportation, outside of those areas, "one still finds relatively few serious engagements" with cycling.[7] Before this chapter engages in some close readings of past expressions of popular culture, a review of the limited scholarly literature is warranted.

The desire to understand the social and historical construction of mode-share—the reasons why some Americans move through their days and lives and physical space in some ways, and why others move in different ways—can be understood as one facet of what many have called the "mobility turn," or more generally "mobilities," an interdisciplinary inquiry primarily associated with sociology. Mimi Sheller and John Urry described key aspects of the mobility turn nearly two decades ago, including an understanding of automobility as a powerful, self-replicating, global phenomenon. "Automobility [is] a self-organizing autopoietic, nonlinear system," wrote Urry, "that spreads world-wide, and includes cars, car-drivers, roads, petroleum supplies and many novel objects, technologies and signs."[8] Perhaps most importantly, "the system generates the preconditions for its own self-expansion"; it expands virally over time and place.[9]

While automobility and mobility studies have themselves proliferated, what we might term as "cyclomobility" is under-examined—particularly in the US context, and very clearly within the historical discipline. Most work has been done in the fields of sociology and anthropology, and most of that has been completed by scholars in research centers outside of the United States. Historian Evan Friss observes that in the US, "bicycles have been hard to find on city streets and as subjects in library books"; literary scholars Daniel Shea and Jeremy Withers note that the extant literature "trends heavily toward sociological, geographical, and anthropological approaches," exploring neither history nor literature.[10]

But where the bicycle has been systematically examined, scholars have seen it as a signifier of multiple, conflicting meanings—available to be repurposed by successive generations, social groups, or subcultures. Withers and Shea term it a " 'floating signifier,' perpetually taking on new and varied significations," while sociologist Peter Cox calls it a "rolling signifier" with largely the same intent.[11] It is this conceptualization of the "floating signifier" that shapes much scholarship of the bicycle, including this essay. In short, the meaning of the transportation technology is contestable by the groups that do (or do not) use it; the work to encode meaning takes place within cultural discourse, and can be contradictory or seemingly capricious. Cultural anthropologist Louis Vivanco takes that concept a step further, noting that change over time matters: the question "what is a bicycle?—is closely related to the *when* of a bicycle, that is, its historical period and the diverse social and technical factors that influenced the shape and qualities of the object."[12]

Over nearly 150 years of American history, the bicycle has been associated with high society, middle-class masculinity, vitality, courtship, modernity, lawless self-endangerment, independent womanhood, advanced technology, slapstick comedy, youthful innocence, patriotic sacrifice, foreign lifestyles, childish playthings, cardiovascular health, environmental consciousness, yuppie entitlement, and millennial indulgence. As an object free to be appropriated by different groups and generations, the bicycle came to possess all these meanings, and more. This chapter focuses on the time periods that shaped the associations with childhood and foreignness.

History and Signification Before WWII

At the moment of the first appearance of the high-wheel, penny-farthing or ordinary of the 1870s in North America, the bicycle was associated with men and modernity. The bicycle was for a wealthy elite capable of affording high technology, the appropriate attire, and the leisure time to show them both as public spectacle. Historian Glen Norcliffe notes that—starting in the high-wheel era and continuing into the "Golden Age" of the safety bicycle in the 1890s—"owning a bicycle was a recognized indicator of modernity, just as having a web site is today."[13] Further, "the boom in ownership was limited to people of high social status . . . and was therefore an activity confined to the affluent, many of whom formed exclusive clubs."[14]

After the golden age bicycle fad diminished in the new century, the newly affordable bicycle was increasingly associated with children. Motorcycles and automobiles supplanted it as the height of new technology and conspicuous consumption for adults. By the interwar period, the domestic bicycle industry largely gave up on maintaining adult sales, and turned instead to children. As Vivanco puts it, "the manner in which bicycles have been sold in the U.S. has contributed to, and helped sustain, dominant American attitudes towards bicycles as children's toys."[15] Historian Robert Turpin argues strongly that a substantial part of this shift is attributable to industry marketing: "As bicycle production increased and prices fell, the bicycle industry's target market—white middle-class males—lost interest. In response, manufacturers began a series of attempts at redefining the bicycle . . . the industry's decision to begin targeting America's youth—beginning in the 1910s—had an adverse impact on adult participation in cycling."[16] The bicycle thus became the province of childhood, and policy and popular culture alike reflected this.

Prewar safety films, solely addressing children, told the audience that the bicycle was a tool for their path to adulthood: "I want to encourage every boy and girl to ride," says the uniformed police officer in the 1939 safety film *Bicycling with Complete Safety*. "It helps you grow into strong, healthy men and women."[17] The film ends with the promise that if young boys learn to ride safely, "Twenty years from now, you'll still come home to dad and mother, . . . you'll be the man they want you to be, and fellas listen, sometime you'll have a boy of your own, and you'll want him to always be careful."[18]

At the exact same time, across the United States, traffic laws were being standardized through the Uniform Vehicle Code and Model Municipal Traffic Ordinance. These laws marginalized the use of bicycles for adult transportation, and increasingly diminished the bicycle's legal status from that of a vehicle (equal to other users) to that of a plaything.[19] Except in a scattering of recreational uses, the bicycle in the United States largely became a toy for children, and seeing an adult on two wheels was an oddity.

The exception was WWII, during which adult bicycle use for transportation was encouraged by a federal rationing program dubbed the "Victory Bike." This emergency accommodation—adapting to gasoline, rubber, and metal rationing that restricted automobiles—is captured in the 1943 safety film *Points for Pedalers*: "Before the war," intones the narrator, "bicycles were used principally for recreation and pleasure . . . but today the bicycle is playing a vital part in helping to relieve America's transportation problem."[20] Unlike most such films, it shows adults in the saddle: "Men and women in all walks of life pedal smoothly and conveniently to factories and offices," says the narrator, over footage of a suit-and-hat wearing adult rider.[21] At least in wartime, the rolling signifier was briefly associated with patriotic, voluntary sacrifice.[22]

But after the war, adults volunteered to return to the automobile, and the bicycle increasingly became a prized purchase solely for children. As the *New York Times Magazine* observed in 1949, "only in the Western Hemisphere are bicycles considered something only for the kids to play with."[23] An economic think tank summarized the point in 1956: "Since adults in the United States no longer use bicycles as a means of transportation or for recreation, American machines for the past 25 years have been sold almost exclusively to boys and girls . . . Some 15-year-olds continue to ride, but social custom, especially strong among adolescents, taboos the bicycle after its user becomes eligible, usually at 16 years of age, for an automobile driver's license."[24] Historians agree with this assessment. Margaret Guroff roots the shift in signification in the changing history of the family: "As children moved from the periphery to the center of the middle-class American family, a process largely complete by the 1950s, the bicycle became an indispensable accessory for them, an emblem of parental love."[25] Frank Berto writes that the postwar bike was "used almost exclusively by children or teenagers too young to get a driver's license," while Zack Furness claims with finality that in postwar suburbia, "bikes are for kids, cars are for grownups."[26]

Postwar Educational Films

How was this signification disseminated, and what was its legacy? In postwar America, society rarely paid attention to adult bicycling, and urged children to think about the bicycle merely as practice for future driving. Vivanco argues that postwar America shaped "a deep-seated cultural framework that informs Americans' views of bicycles" into the present.[27] It was then that they started to consider bicycles "as technologically static and obsolete vehicles inferior to more 'advanced' vehicles such as motorcycles and cars." Therefore, the bike was "not suitable for serious transportation but 'less serious' pursuits like . . . child's play."[28] One form of cultural production—educational films and filmstrips— spread the message that bicycle usage was associated with a childish, dependent state, appropriate as a developmental step, but unsuitable for adults.

In countless educational films, children of the 1950s, '60s, and '70s were trained for their inevitable future as automobile drivers. Primarily, bicycle safety training of the postwar years was the domain of non-cyclists. With the League of American Wheelmen largely defunct, there was no national advocacy organization to commission or contribute to educational filmmaking or shape the message in ways that promoted cyclist rights or adult transportation. Instead, bicycle safety education was dominated by small, regional production companies that sold films to school districts or police departments. These were the same companies that made the infamous social hygiene and public health films used by schools throughout the postwar period.[29]

One of the earliest of these, a 1948 cartoon filmstrip *Bike Behavior*, demonstrates that the audience is children alone; policing their behavior in rhyming stanzas. "Boys and girls, remember these words you're hearing / leave hands free for steering!"[30] Each child in the filmstrip shows off a dangerous behavior before ending up in the hospital: "Ah, reckless youth, just having fun / a goofy boy, I know one!" The last example threatens death for a dazed victim: "Here lies . . . a wiser child . . . she could be killed, that's very true / just be sure it isn't you!"[31]

Less chillingly, many films attempted to appeal to children's attention by emphasizing bicycle riding as training for the adult responsibilities of automobile driving. *Tomorrow's Drivers* (1954), funded by the Chevrolet Dealers of America, features actor Jimmy Stewart as narrator. Bicycles here are presented in the same light as the toy cars third graders are shown driving: they are training tools for automobile-owning adults, not a viable transportation mode of their own. "And when tomorrow's drivers outgrow the small cars," intones Stewart, "safety on *two* wheels is stressed . . . in preparation for the day when *actual* driving instruction begins."[32] Similarly, *Bike Safety*, shot in 1950, showed only adolescents riding bicycles while emphasizing their future responsibility. "You are now an operator of a wheeled vehicle," declared the narrator: "You are the automobile driver of tomorrow. And good, safe bicycle riders often turn out to be the best drivers."[33] In a better-than-average example of the genre, no less a figure than Jiminy Cricket echoed this in the 1956 Disney cartoon *I'm No Fool with a Bicycle*. "Remember," instructed the conscience of a generation of children, "a bicycle is to you what a motor car is to a grown-up."[34]

Drive Your Bike (1955) reinforced the theme of bikes as automobile training. The film starts with a shot of three preteen boys in the front seat of a car, turning the wheel and bouncing along as the car sways from side to side. Eventually the camera pulls out to reveal that they are still sitting motionless in the driveway. An unidentified father figure steps to the driver's side window to ask, doubtfully, if they are *really* ready to drive. But they reassure him that they have been taught all the traffic laws at school: "We call it learning to drive our bikes. Coach tells us that we have to follow all the same traffic regulations as the cars . . . we'll be ready to drive when we're old enough."[35] *Drive Your Bike* emphasizes that growth to manhood; the purpose of bicycle riding is handed down to the boys by male role models: "That's why Coach says we should always drive our bikes like we would drive a car, and never do anything we wouldn't do if we were driving a real car." The "father" figure concludes that the boys were "learning a lot of valuable and important things that will be very useful to you when you learn how to drive a car"[36] (see fig. 2.1).

Bicycle Clown (1958), possibly the most overwrought of all the safety films, reinforces the place of bicycles as the sole province of children. Styled as a police procedural with a cast of children, an older brother investigates his brother Jimmy's (thankfully nonfatal) bike crash, visiting all of the male adults who observed his unsafe bicycling: bike shop owner, policeman, basketball coach, newspaper route supervisor. All judge Jimmy's behavior as "foolish and childish." None of the adults, it goes without saying, ride a bicycle themselves—though they all have opinions about how Jimmy rode.[37]

You and Your Bicycle, shot in 1948 and re-released in 1959, is similar in that there is no adult on a bike anywhere in the film. Repeated shots in both versions of the film are framed—rather unnervingly—through the windshield of a car that is closely following a lone child on a bike. This is what modern advocates call a "windshield perspective," alternatively termed the driver's gaze.[38]

Fig. 2.1. *Drive Your Bike* opens with a conceit repeated throughout the short educational film: clearly underage boys pretend to drive a car. They contend that learning to ride their bicycles in the same way as they will eventually drive a car prepares them for their inevitable and desirable graduation from childish bicycles to adult cars. (*Drive Your Bike* [Glendale, CA: Sullivan, 1954], 35 mm film, 10:47, from Prelinger Archives, https://archive.org/details /DriveYou1955)

Children on bikes are an "other" on the road, viewed only by adults from within their cars, never as equals. The narrator addresses the child riders: "It's difficult for a motorist to see you," making it clear that the judgmental adults are always in cars, and never on bikes (see fig. 2.2).[39]

As the floating signifier rolled into the 1960s, the educational films began appearing in color, and got a little odd, but the themes stayed constant. Arguably the strangest of all is *One Got Fat* (1963). In this parable, the bike riders are not just children, they're . . . monkey-children. Or at least ten young actors in crude monkey masks, with psychedelically strange names. Nine die or are badly injured on a ride to the park, crashing horribly after failing to follow a minor safety rule, sometimes with splatting noises involving steamrollers. The undeterred monkey-children continue on their ride after each fatality, until only one is left to eat all the picnic lunches. Only then is he revealed as a real human child and "not a monkey."[40] Much less bizarrely, 1969's *Bicycle Today, Automobile Tomorrow* flatters children by comparing them to the adult operators of exciting

Fig. 2.2. In *You and Your Bicycle*, a boy on a bike narrowly avoids a door thrown open by a careless adult, while another adult in the camera car looms behind (note the hood in the lower right). In this framing, seen throughout mid-century educational films in the US, the child is an "other," seen only through the windshield of drivers. The camera does not share the rider's perspective. (*You and Your Bicycle* [Oakland, CA: Progressive Pictures, 1948, 1959], 35 mm film, 8:59, from Prelinger Archives, https://archive.org/details/YouandYo1948)

motorized machines. The concluding lines drive home the title: "Remember, the bicycle rider of today is the automobile driver of tomorrow."[41]

The focus on the child continued into the 1970s, even after the return of adult cycling amidst the energy crisis and the arrival of affordable multi-speed bicycle. While it was now at least conceivable that adults might ride, the genre continued to primarily address children—*Peddlin' Safety* (1974) starts with a televised report of a child's bike crash, with the anchorman declaring ominously that "the child was taken to a local hospital in undetermined condition."[42] Turning off the TV, the extravagantly bell-bottomed father makes it a teachable moment: "That's why I didn't want you to take your new bicycle out onto the street until you finished your bike safety course," he instructs his daughter. "I think since we all ride bikes," he continues, including the mother, "we ought to let Colleen tell us what she's learned about bike safety," and the rest of the film recounts those safety lessons.[43]

Similarly, the General Motors-financed *I Like Bikes . . . But* from 1978 shows both adults and children on bikes, but still manages to demonstrate that bikes are childish. At ages five and ten, Lisa says "I like bikes"—but as the film shows her learning to drive, now "at fifteen, she likes bikes, but now she *loves* cars."[44] Ike the anthropomorphic cartoon bike insinuates: "When she gets her license, will she change her likes, will she still *like* bikes?"[45] Symbolically, on her first solo car outing after getting her license, Lisa backs over her own abandoned bicycle on the driveway: adult car driving bringing an end to not only bike riding, but the childish bike itself. It is just one tactic among many used to convince the audience that "safety-wise, you must realize, you *never* should trust me," as sung by Ike the self-hating bike (see fig. 2.3).[46]

Perhaps more pointedly than all the rest, *I Like Bikes . . . But* is Urry's "automobility" in action, generating the preconditions for motordom's expansion; according to an auto industry-financed film, Lisa's entrance to adulthood requires her not only to drive a car, but to come to distrust, disparage and even destroy bicycles. But all of the educational films linked bikes with childhood and cars with adulthood, and did so before a particularly susceptible audience in ways that flattered and appealed to them. The signification of childhood in the bike safety film is obvious—but was the association the same in other cultural expressions?

Hollywood Films

When it comes to feature-length dramatic films, there are not many that American bike riders would want to call their own. It is a short (and partially ignominious) list of films that have bicycles as prominent parts of the plot. The bicycle-related comedies of the silent era are largely forgotten, even with such memorable nickelodeon titles as *Naughty Grandpa and the Field Glass* (1902) and *His First Ride* (1907). Many of these incorporated bicycles as an acrobatic and comedic element, adapted from popular Vaudeville acts, as in *The Wrong Mr. Fox* (1917) and *The Paper Hangers* (1921). The films of the interwar period are more accessible, including the Frank Capra feature *Long Pants* (1927), the Carole Lombard comedy *The Bicycle Flirt* (1928), or the short comedy *Handlebars* (1933). But the most successful bicycle-centric films before the war might have been *Six Day Bike Racer* (1934) and *The Lady in Question* (1940).

The themes of these films place bicycles in relation to foreignness, childhood, courtship, or recreation. In general, the connections to courtship, recreation and leisure are established earlier in the twentieth century: closer to the golden age of bicycling use in the 1890s until World War I. While those themes continue into the twentieth century, by World War II bicycles in Hollywood feature films become a symbol of foreignness, or of arrested development.

Fig. 2.3. The short educational film that is most overtly anti-bicycle is probably *I Like Bikes . . . But* a film financed by General Motors. The ellipses in the title led to a repeated litany of complaints about the perceived dangers of bicycles from the point of view of drivers; the female protagonist likes her bike as a child, but then she "loves cars" as a young adult. Now a teenaged driver somehow in possession of that year's Chevrolet Caprice (a GM product), she immediately comes into conflict with bicycles—symbolically reversing over her own unseen bicycle, treacherously lying hidden on the driveway. (*I Like Bikes . . . But* [Lawrence, KS: Centron, 1978], 35 mm, 13:48, from A/V Geeks, https://archive.org/details/i_like_bikes)

The 1927 silent *Long Pants* epitomizes this symbolism of childhood. Barely out of short pants, slapstick star Harry Langdon portrays a small-town boy still riding his bicycle—a sign of childhood that is observed by a schoolgirl crush: "Little boys should be seen and not heard," she taunts. When a big-city flapper's chauffeured car breaks down, it takes every bicycle trick Harry knows to get her attention in this Frank Capra-directed film. The bicycle—and the shorts—stay behind when Langdon follows the girl to the big city.

A Yank at Oxford (1938), on the other hand, epitomizes the symbolism of for-eignness. There are no bicycles onscreen before the obnoxious American leaves for England; once in Oxford, practical bikes are omnipresent in the streets and in the plotline; a meet-cute happens in a bike shop, and the adult male protagonist is noteworthy for his inability to ride the right way in traffic. Shot in England, the film is filled with upright, hand-brake-equipped British roadsters ridden by adults; there are no children on bikes in the film. This is clearly a foreign culture.

The Lady in Question (1940) captures both themes. Shot on a studio lot in California, the film evokes its Paris setting partly through a constant parade of adults riding bicycles on city streets. The Hollywood feature combines courtship and drama; a young man comes in to buy a bike, and frets over whether the model he has chosen will appeal to his paramour. The bicycles used for commuting, on the shop floor, and ridden away by the two adult couples in the final scene are set dressing to establish the Parisian scene: no such things would happen in an American city.

Postwar Films: From Set Dressing to Features

For most films in the postwar era, bicycles are either components of mise-enscène, as in the prewar *The Lady in Question,* or a punch line. Either way, they occupy only small moments of screen time; but we can still extract meaning from their appearance. It is important that even in brief glimpses, the signification is clear: bikes are un-American, or for children. *A Foreign Affair* (1948), shot on location in Berlin, indicates the foreign locale partly by placing American servicemen on a tandem. *E.T. the Extraterrestrial* (1982) evokes suburban childhood through BMX bikes. *Indiana Jones and the Last Crusade* (1989) has a rack of shiny Schwinn heavyweights to symbolize the idyllic late-1930s campus of Professor Jones' college.

The bicycle was a reliable joke for Hollywood writers: in the 1963 comedy *It's a Mad Mad Mad World*, a driver accosts an adult on a bike (Jonathan Winters) literally from the driver's seat: "What's with the little kiddy bicycle, what are you, some kind of nut?" The 1987 teen romantic comedy *Can't Buy Me Love* has the teenage protagonist on a BMX bike at a stop sign; his ten-speed-mounted sidekick comments on the red sports car that pulls up next to them: "Now there's the answer: if you want to be popular, you get one of *those* [referring to the car] and you get one of *those* [the woman in the passenger seat]." The 1988 John Hughes comedy *She's Having a Baby* forces an unwilling Kevin Bacon into suburbia; driven to the edge of hallucination by the bizarre conformity of his surroundings, Bacon's character observes a cycling-mad neighbor with foreign pretensions, dramatically revealed by a slowly rising garage door. Decked out in a ridiculous aero helmet and Italian-flag jersey, the obsessive neighbor lovingly caresses his road bike before greeting Bacon with a "ciao," screaming maniacally, and pedaling away (see fig. 2.4).

Fig. 2.4. The neighbor sets off on a ride in *She's Having a Baby*. In this Hollywood feature, a brief comedic bit positions the bicycle as a ridiculous foreign affectation; the middle-aged recreational rider wearing a jersey in 7-11 racing team colors greets Kevin Bacon's disaffected suburban exile with a "Ciao!" before stroking his bike, howling in anticipation and charging off. Most of the bicycle cameos in postwar feature films are punchlines—jokes related to immaturity, childhood, foreignness, or some combination thereof. (*She's Having a Baby* [Paramount Pictures, 1988; Paramount Home Video, 2000], DVD)

Beyond these shorter cameos, *Breaking Away* (1979), *American Flyers* (1985), *Pee Wee's Big Adventure* (1985), *Quicksilver* (1986), *Rad* (1986), and *Premium Rush* (2012) all feature more screen time for bicycles. While *Pee Wee's Big Adventure* most obviously demonstrates the association with childhood, it has already received scholarly attention. Instead, this section will focus on the two bike films penned by the same writer: *Breaking Away* and *American Flyers*.

Breaking Away

Appearing in 1979, the low-budget film *Breaking Away* captured many of the contradictions of the American bicycle as it returned to prominence amid the 1970s bike boom. For cyclists in the United States—starved for cultural validation—the film was a delight, and continues to evoke fond memories for recreational riders today. But the film's themes betray the place of the bicycle in American culture. It finds dramatic tension by pitting young-adult interest in new lightweight bicycles against the mainstream conviction that bicycles are oddities for foreigners or children. For most of the characters, the bicycle conveys desirable associations with recreation, health, masculinity, and class identity. At the very same time, it is also a childish toy with no place on the road. In other words, *Breaking Away* symbolizes the conflicted nature of the 1970s bicycle boom in the United States.

The good-natured film depicts an otherwise aimless nineteen-year-old who is captivated by bicycle racing. Equipped with an imported Italian racing bike he won as a prize, Dave proceeds to remake his working-class world into an idealization of Italy. He has become an oddity in his middle American town: "He was as normal as pumpkin pie," declares a neighbor looking on from her front porch, "and now look at him." She sighs, empathizing: "His poor parents." Ignoring her, Dave embarks on an active project of Europeanization: "Buon giorno, Pappa!" he cries, and renames the cat Fellini. The cat eats from a Cinzano ashtray as Dave sings along to opera.

Most film criticism tends to focus on the class and ethnicity issues, and not the bike. Director Peter Yates, immersed in the class-conscious filmmaking of postwar Britain, always intended this: "I wanted to make a film about class distinctions in America. Coming from England, I was told they didn't exist here. But of course they do."[47] According to one critic, the bicycle and the Italian play-acting are escapes from the realities of middle-American class dynamics, where Dave and his father both have been imbued with a working-class ethic but can no longer find employment at the local quarry. The title is a play on words that is ostensibly about bikes but ultimately about class: "Breaking away applies rather to speed cycling, a form of play that looks a lot like work, an American sports solution that merely sublimates his problems," writes John Paul Russo.[48]

For Dave, his 1978 Masi Gran Criterium is from an exotic world, far away from his working class roots. The Italian frame builder Falerio Masi opened a California shop in 1972, bringing bespoke European cycles to the United States. It is this exotic foreignness that makes it possible for Dave to reimagine himself at the nearby university; the campus might not be welcoming to a working-class American, but it might have a place for the foreign exchange student he briefly pretends to be.

After nearly a century of mainstream American disinterest in the bike, and despite the 1970s bike boom, the bicycle is still foreign to this Midwest town; a lightweight racing bike doubly so. This is actually what attracts Dave. Identifying with the foreign bicycle brings him into conflict both with American identity and his working-class origins, serving as the tool for him to break away from his family and friends (see fig. 2.5). In the film, the bicycle is

Fig. 2.5. Recreational cycling is a mark of foreignness in *Breaking Away*, one of the few Hollywood feature films that is primarily about the bicycle; Dave rides his imported Masi onto the university's campus and impersonates a foreign exchange student to escape his working-class background. His Italian bike is as much a part of this costume as his bicycle-component-manufacturer cap, clumsy accent, hastily memorized phrases, and crucifix pendant. (*Breaking Away* [Twentieth Century Fox, 1979; 20th Century Fox, 2002], DVD)

exercise equipment, associated with the fitness goals of a leisure class or the wealth and privilege of the college; the climax of the film comes when Dave and his working-class friends enter the university's bike race, improbably winning it as the underdog "Cutters". Most importantly, it is still exceptional—an oddity for fitness buffs, the upwardly mobile proto-yuppies on the college campus, or the opera-obsessed; certainly not for Americans in their everyday lives. The culminating bike race on campus is not even really a competitive bicycle event—instead it is a part of a sporting weekend, with fraternity groups vying for bragging rights in juvenile competitions like tricycle races.[49]

Even as the *dénouement* places the used-car-selling father on his own bicycle (both for his health and as a sign that he has embraced his son's identity, a resolution of the film's dramatic tension), he is still a slightly ridiculous, unwelcome presence on the city street: honked at, defensive, and riding the wrong way.

What does *Breaking Away* tell us about the rolling signifier of the bicycle in American culture? After decades of disuse, and despite the bike boom of the 1970s, Americans had set their minds that cycling was for children and foreigners. For a film that evokes warm feelings in cyclists today, the message of *Breaking Away* is one of ostracism, exclusion, and a persistent inability to equate cycling with American identity.

American Flyers

Steve Tesich's screenplay for *Breaking Away* won an Oscar; but six years later, and costing millions of dollars more, his script for *American Flyers* would not have the same critical reception. A snarky footnote in Robert Hurst's guide to Colorado riding calls *American Flyers* the "fourth best out of four total bicycle racing movies."[50] Despite the difference in critical response, *Breaking Away* and *American Flyers* are quite similar. Both are movies about family more than bikes; both feature redemptive, triumphant race scenes; both have at their core a gifted young man named David. And while both offered a mainstream audience a piece of entertainment primarily about bicycling *in* America, neither successfully made the case that bicycling was anything but an oddity *for* Americans. The name, *American Flyers*, protests too much—simultaneously proclaiming its patriotism and defending bicycle racing as a valid pursuit for American men. But it also unintentionally infantilizes them; the name puns on a line of toy trains. No one flies in the movie, and the phrase itself is never uttered; the only reason to title the film *American Flyers* is to play word association with a child's toy.

The film was slight, and critics were not kind. Directed by experienced Hollywood director John Badham, *American Flyers* has more polish than the quirkily independent *Breaking Away*. But Badham's greater experience does not translate into quality: *Flyers* is calculated and bombastic where *Breaking* was charming. The opening shot is a visual joke, presenting Davey Sommers first as a cowboy—ten-gallon hat jauntily pushed back, passing by a steam boat on the wide Mississippi—only slowly pulling out to show that he is also wearing bike shorts and pumping away on a ten-speed. Soon Davey is on the road to Madison, Wisconsin with his brother Marcus, played by a young Kevin Costner.

After some vague insinuations about a possibly terminal medical condition, both Sommers brothers are entered into a road cycling race. As the first stage starts, it is time to meet a villain: extravagantly bearded and musclebound Russian cyclist Sergei Belov. Suddenly the film becomes nearly bombastic in its patriotism, fulfilling the premise of the title. The Russians are mustache-twirling villains in Soviet flag jerseys; the American national team is wearing the Stars and Stripes; and one American soon delivers an epic diatribe echoing post-Vietnam mythos. The film is jam-packed with American symbolism; Davey and his love interest spend their first night together with the TV blaring a

Fig. 2.6. *American Flyers* is drenched in bombastic patriotism from its title card to its Cold War antagonists. But nearly everything about the strategy of competitive cycling has to be explained to the American audience for this Hollywood feature film, making it clear that the bicycle is still a foreign pursuit even when cloaked in national symbols. Bicycling is portrayed as recreational and competitive, not a part of everyday transportation in cities. (*American Flyers* [Warner Bros., 1985; Warner Home Video, 1999], DVD)

montage of patriotic images over the national anthem sign-off; a space shuttle launch is broadly suggestive as they tumble into bed (see fig. 2.6).

Off screen, America was awash in patriotic symbols, both overt and misconstrued; the red, white, and blue summer of 1984 included both the Los Angeles Olympics and the release of Springsteen's "Born in the USA." *American Flyers* came out the same year as *Rambo: First Blood Part II* and *Rocky IV*, both with Soviet villains. *Rocky* features a cartoonishly muscle-bound Ivan Drago; *American Flyers* a hilariously hirsute and hulking Sergei Belov. Film critic Craig Howson made the connection explicit when the film came out: "At a time when patriotism has been assimilated back into pop culture (*a la* Springsteen, no less,) this new film offers a good ride for the price of admission."[51] The next year, *Top Gun* would fly onto American screens; *American Flyers* was like an advance scout for that blockbuster. They are both films with Cold War jingoism, shirtless men competing in close proximity, and similar plot points.

Aside from the American Muzzin's epic diatribe about the politics of Olympic boycotts that echoes post-Vietnam mythology, the patriotic message is conveyed visually—the hulking, brutish Russians juxtaposed against the wide open Colorado landscape; the repeated image of the St. Louis Gateway Arch; honest-to-goodness cowboys actually herding cattle; the omnipresent McDonald's. Despite all of this overt imagery, the bicycle itself is still foreign to the American audience. Importantly, Davey's love interest does not even seem to recognize road cycling the first time she sees it: "Hey, what the hell's that? Pony Express?"

Reflecting the foreignness of the bicycle, the biking references are made so broadly accessible that even an audience of non-cyclists could latch on. The audience might not know why Muzzin trades his team jersey for the leader's jersey, so the race leader's jersey is actually labeled "Race Leader." Before starting stage 2, an ailing Marcus Sommers delivers an introduction to racing tactics. For an American audience unfamiliar with competitive cycling, it comes at a perfect time; a simple overview of breakaway strategy and intermediate time bonuses. More racing strategy is on display at the beginning of stage 3, as Belov sends a teammate up the road to force a chase. The nameless race commentator helpfully explains the strategy. Later, Muzzin taunts Belov, explaining stage racing to an American audience: "I'm still here, Belov . . . Only I'm not behind you, I'm really two seconds ahead . . . *you* know why you won the Olympics: because I wasn't there! But now I'm here! Only I'm not here, I'm two seconds ahead!" It all comes down to the finish line, but not in a way that would intuitively make sense to a non-cycling audience; Muzzin still has an eleven-second lead on Davey from the previous two stages. Davey has to win on a time gap, a concept without direct comparisons in other American sports; the director takes pains to explain the concept through a commentator's voiceover.

American Flyers is not a good film. Most of its pleasures come from campiness and melodrama, not from timeless imagery or craftsmanship. It is emotionally manipulative and maudlin rather than moving. Furthermore, the bicycling in *American Flyers* is almost solely about exercise, recreation, and competition; it is not transportation. Neither is the bicycle an inhabitant of the city in this film. Davey does not follow the rules of the road; he is on sidewalks and in elevators in the opening scene, and the race takes place on both sides of the double yellow line, outside of the normal rules of traffic.

Taking the challenge of cultural anthropologist Luis Vivanco to heart, we need to consider the way that this film conceives of the rolling signifier.[52] The bicycle itself—either as a physical object or as a cultural construct—is not the subject of the film in the same way it is in *Breaking Away*. In *American Flyers*, they are props, or vehicles of competition. They are not the subject of the film, and the camera spends more time in close-ups on the actors' faces, or wide panoramas with bikes in the foreground. Biking's status as an American subculture is not really discussed at any point.

This might be a film where the results of the 1970s "bike boom" in adult cycling should be visible, but they do not seem to be here; bicycles in this film are not tools of urban transportation, or components of an environmentally conscious lifestyle, or a choice for avoiding expensive gasoline. Probably the only real clue offered by the film to the meaning of the bicycling in the 1980s is the efforts needed to explain—or elide—race strategy and everyday concerns. Bicycling as a sport is foreign to the audience. But bicycling as transportation also seems foreign to the filmmakers. The only woman who rides a bike in the film (and the only bike ridden for transportation) is a comedic gag; a senior citizen pilots her trike disapprovingly past Davey in the opening scenes.

Judging from the film, reasons to ride in the 1980s might include extreme aerobic conditioning or cut-throat competitiveness, but not everyday transportation. The trailer for the film highlights competition, camaraderie, and adrenaline. Here, the *when* of the bicycle—contemporaneous with the cardiovascular and aerobic fitness fads of the early '80s—makes the bicycle a piece of exercise equipment.

Neither *Breaking Away* nor *American Flyers* offered adult bicycling as a valid identity for Americans. It was an abnormal, extreme, or foreign subculture. The filmmaker's efforts to make bicycling understandable to an American audience demonstrate that bicycling was an excluded subculture in the 1980s. But a bigger sign of the exclusion is *American Flyers*' lack of success. Ultimately forgettable, it had neither the critical nor cult following of *Breaking Away*, and few bicycle-themed films followed.[53]

Conclusion

Since the 1990s, the USEPA has prepared an annual report of greenhouse gases. The draft "Inventory of U.S. Greenhouse Gas Emissions and Sinks," finalized in 2018, marked a milestone when "emissions from transportation activities, in aggregate, accounted for the largest portion (28.5 percent) of total U.S. greenhouse gas emissions." In 2016, for the first time in the sixteen-year history of the report, the transportation sector of the economy became the largest contributor to climate emissions in the United States—larger than commercial, industrial, and electricity production.[54] Not only is transportation now the greatest contributor to climate emissions, but it is also one of the most overlooked solutions: recent research shows that "living car-free" was one of "four recommended actions that are of substantial magnitude throughout the developed world"; all four of these high-impact practices, including finding ways to get around in the modern world without a car, were rarely recommended in textbooks or supporting literature.[55] There appears to be a bicycle-shaped blind spot; daily bicycle transportation is not conceivable as a way of life for adults in North America.

This essay suggests that the inability of Americans to conceive of the bicycle as a response to catastrophic global climate change lies in the cultural production of twentieth-century automobility. By the new millennium, childhood and foreignness had become the dominant meanings of the bicycle. Either way, the bike was rarely portrayed as being used by American adults navigating their daily lives. Politicians, planners, and the police took that assumption with them as they shaped the cities in which we live today.

This is a preliminary exploration of the rolling signifier in one medium. The work of labelling bicycles as foreign and juvenile also took place on the small screen as well as the large; the Andy Griffith Show marked a visitor as British by showcasing his bicycle touring in "Andy's English Valet" (1963). *I Love Lucy* (1951–57) only put the protagonists on bicycles when they travelled to Italy. In the late '80s primetime drama *thirtysomething*, actor Peter Horton's college professor is presented as self-indulgent and immature, partly signified by his persistent use of a ten-speed bicycle for transportation. And the bicycle's role in young adult literature might help explain why, even in a youth-obsessed culture, appropriation of the bicycle by adults was somehow not possible.

Though the history of popular culture elucidates the difficulty in advancing the bicycle as a transportation solution for the twenty-first century, all hope is not lost. In fact, our understanding of the bicycle as floating signifier is cause for hope: as with any such linkage, the association with childhood is not indelible. Even P. J. O'Rourke's satirical essay for *Car and Driver* could be taken positively; the fact that a comedian wrote an outrageous claim meant that the cultural association had to be constantly made, remade, and defended. As time passes, the meaning of the bicycle may change, given new economic or political pressures, or the growing realities of anthropogenic climate change. Perhaps in the twenty-second century, the bicycle may be for far-seeing adults, and the automobile for children.

NOTES

1. P. J. O'Rourke, "A Cool and Logical Analysis of the Bicycle Menace and an Examination of the Actions Necessary to License, Regulate, or Abolish Entirely This Dreadful Peril on Our Roads," *Car and Driver*, June 1984, 64–5. Cf. O'Rourke, "Dear Urban Cyclists: Go Play in Traffic," *Wall Street Journal*, April 2, 2011, C3.
2. O'Rourke, "A Cool and Logical Analysis."
3. *Nationwide Trails System Hearings on H.R. 4865, and Related Bills*. 90th Cong. 144 (1967) (responses to statement of Keith Kingbay, League of American Wheelmen).
4. *Federal Aid Highway Act of 1981: Hearings Before the Subcommittee on Transportation of the Committee on Environment and Public Works*, 97th Cong. 396 (1981) (statement of David G. Burwell, National Wildlife Federation).

5. Environmental Protection Agency, *Inventory of U.S. Greenhouse Gas Emissions and Sinks, 1990–2016*, EPA 430-R-18-003 (Washington, DC: GPO, 2018), ES-23–27, www.epa.gov/ghgemissions/inventory-us-greenhouse-gas-emissions-and-sinks.
6. Zack Furness, "Foreword," in *Culture on Two Wheels: The Bicycle in Literature and Film*, ed. Jeremy Withers and Daniel P. Shea (Lincoln: University of Nebraska Press, 2016), xi.
7. Furness, "Forward," xi.
8. John Urry, "The 'System' of Automobility," *Theory, Culture & Society* 21 (2004): 27.
9. Urry, "The 'System' of Automobility," 27.
10. Evan Friss, "Writing Bicycles: The Historiography of Cycling in the United States," *Mobility in History* 6 (2015), 127–133; Jeremey Withers and Daniel Shea, "Introduction," in *Culture on Two Wheels: The Bicycle in Literature and Film*, ed. Jeremy Withers and Daniel P. Shea (Lincoln: University of Nebraska Press, 2016), 2.
11. Withers and Shea, "Introduction," 2.
12. Luis A. Vivanco, *Reconsidering the Bicycle: An Anthropological Perspective on a New (Old) Thing* (New York: Routledge, 2013), 25.
13. Glen Norcliffe, *The Ride to Modernity: The Bicycle in Canada, 1869–1900* (Toronto: University of Toronto Press, 2001), 32.
14. Norcliffe, *The Ride to Modernity*, 32.
15. Vivanco, *Reconsidering the Bicycle*, 50.
16. Robert J. Turpin, " 'Our Best Bet is the Boy': A Cultural History of Bicycle Marketing and Consumption in the United States, 1880–1960," (PhD diss., University of Kentucky, 2013), 7.
17. *Bicycling with Complete Safety* (Bell & Howell, 1939), film, 8:54, from Internet Archive, https://archive.org/details/0935BicyclingWithCompleteSafety.
18. *Bicycling with Complete Safety*.
19. James Longhurst, *Bike Battles: A History of Sharing the American Road* (Seattle: University of Washington, 2015), 80–119.
20. *Points for Pedalers*, (Aetna Life Company, 1943), film, 11:13, from Periscope Film, https://www.youtube.com/watch?v=XzFMv-eIS7s.
21. *Points for Pedalers*.
22. James Longhurst, "Reconsidering the Victory Bike in World War II: Federal Transportation Policy, History, and Bicycle Commuting in America," *Transportation Research Record* 2672 (December 1, 2018), 29–37.
23. Quote from Foster Hailey, "Bicycles Built for Millions," *New York Times Magazine*, October 16, 1949, 78–9; David V. Herlihy, *Bicycle: The History* (New Haven: Yale University Press, 2004), 336.
24. Percy Bidwell, *What the Tariff Means to American Industries* (New York: Council on Foreign Relations, 1956), 70.
25. Margaret Guroff, *The Mechanical Horse: How the Bicycle Reshaped American Life* (Austin: University of Texas Press, 2016), 114.
26. Frank Berto, *The Dancing Chain: History and Development of the Derailleur Bicycle*, 4th ed. (San Francisco: Cycle Publishing/Van der Plas, 2014), 179, 199; Zack Furness, *One Less Car: Bicycling and the Politics of Automobility* (Philadelphia: Temple University Press, 2010), 115.
27. Vivanco, *Reconsidering the Bicycle*, 25–6.
28. Vivanco, *Reconsidering the Bicycle*, 25–6.
29. Devin Orgeron, Marsha Orgeron, and Dan Streible, eds., *Learning with the Lights Off: Educational Film in the United States* (New York: Oxford University Press, 2012), 9–11; Geoff Alexander, *Academic Films for the Classroom: A History* (Jefferson, NC: McFarland, 2010), 5–10. Many of these films have been preserved by the Prelinger Archives, https://archive.org.
30. *Bike Behavior* (Burbank, CA: Cathedral Films, 1948), filmstrip. This rare filmstrip was briefly available online but has since been removed; some copies are catalogued at

libraries across the United States, including in the collection of the Connecticut State Library.

31. *Bike Behavior.*
32. *Tomorrow's Drivers* (Jam Handy, 1954), film, 10:58, from Internet Archive, https://archive .org/details/Tomorrow1954.
33. *Bike Safety* (Lawrence, KS: Centron, 1950), film, 9:48, from Internet Archive, https:// archive.org/details/bicycle_safety.
34. *I'm No Fool with a Bicycle, with Jiminy Cricket* (Walt Disney Pictures, 1956). See also Furness, *One Less Car*, 115–117.
35. *Drive Your Bike* (Glendale, CA: Sullivan, 1954); from Internet Archive, https://archive .org/details/DriveYou1955.
36. *Drive Your Bike.*
37. *Bicycle Clown* (Glendora, CA: Sid Davis, 1958), film, 1:44, https://www.youtube.com /watch?v=Cg_ni72fhls&list=PLEB312C58DFC25F1F.
38. Longhurst, *Bike Battles*, 170.
39. *You and Your Bicycle* (Oakland, CA: Progressive Pictures, 1948, 1959), film, 8:58, from Internet Archive, https://archive.org/details/YouandYo1948.
40. *One Got Fat* (Interlude Films, 1963), film, 14:47, from Internet Archive, https://archive .org/details/OneGotFa1963.
41. *Bicycle Today, Automobile Tomorrow* (Inglewood, CA: Sid Davis, 1969), film, 10:08, https:// www.youtube.com/watch?v=oqpNqoumVcA.
42. *Peddlin' Safety* (Richmond, VA: Virginia Department of Education, 1974), film, 13:53, from Internet Archive, https://archive.org/details/PeddlinSafety.
43. *Peddlin' Safety.*
44. *I Like Bikes . . . But* (Lawrence, KS: Centron, 1978), film, 13:48, from Internet Archive, https://archive.org/details/i_like_bikes.
45. *I Like Bikes . . . But.*
46. *I Like Bikes . . . But.*
47. Quoted in Al Auster, "Review: Breaking Away by Peter Yates, Steve Tesich," *Cinéaste* 10 (Winter 1979–80), 48–49.
48. John Paul Russo, "Italian American Filmmakers: No Deal on Madonna Street," *Italian Americana* 13 (Winter 1995), 6.
49. John Schwarb, *The Little 500: The Story of the World's Greatest College Weekend* (Bloomington: Indiana University Press, 1999).
50. Robert Hurst, *Road Biking Colorado's Front Range: A Guide to the Greatest Bike Rides from Colorado Springs to Fort Collins* (Guilford, CT: Globe Pequot, 2005), 153. Hurst included European films in his top four. See also K. Edgington, Thomas Erskine, and James M. Welsh, *Encyclopedia of Sports Films* (Lanham, MD: Rowman & Littlefield, 2005), 13–15.
51. Craig Howson, "American Flyers," (Arizona) *Courier* (December 20, 1985), 10.
52. Vivanco, *Reconsidering the Bicycle.*
53. Jeroen Heijmans and Bill Mallon, *The Historical Dictionary of Cycling* (Lanham, MD: Rowman & Littlefield, 2011), 20.
54. Environmental Protection Agency, *Inventory of U.S. Greenhouse Gas Emissions and Sinks*, Fig ES-14 (Washington, DC: EPA, 2018).
55. Seth Wynes and Kimberly A. Nicholas, "The Climate Mitigation Gap: Education and Government Recommendations Miss the Most Effective Individual Actions," *Environmental Research Letters* 12 (July 12, 2017), https://doi.org/10.1088/1748-9326/aa7541.

CHAPTER 3

E-Scooters and the Urban Micromobility Revolution

Matthew C. Swanson

Los Angeles and the car. The city and its automobile infrastructure have become so imbricated that clichés like "Everybody drives in LA" are treated as incontrovertible facts. Naturally, however, there is truth in the cliché; the car is still king in Los Angeles. In fact, the car's reign over this city is despotic, affording little room for alternative modes of transportation. Outside of certain dense, well-connected areas, moving without a car means accepting longer travel times: it is not uncommon for a five-mile trip to take twice as long by public transit as by car when there is light traffic. This leads the majority of Angelenos to commute as single drivers in automobiles. According to the US Census Bureau, 72.3 percent of Los Angeles County residents drove to work alone, which is close to the national average of 76.4 percent.[1] Couple this with the estimated 7.7 million registered vehicles in Los Angeles County in 2017, and it's easy to estimate that over 5 million cars are being driven around Los Angeles County every single day, which amounts to a large carbon footprint. According to the Environmental Protection Agency, of all the sources of greenhouse gas emission in the United States, the transportation sector generates the largest share at 28.5 percent in 2016, of which 90 percent of the fuel was petroleum based.[2]

There are, however, signs that Angelenos are eager for a change in transportation infrastructure. The passage of local ballot initiatives Measure R in 2008 and Measure M in 2016, which raised sales taxes in Los Angeles County with the explicit purpose of funding for public transit, demonstrated that Angelenos are willing to tax themselves to fund alternatives to the automobile. The downside is that these new light rail and subway lines take years (and billions of dollars) to construct. Furthermore, Los Angeles is a massive city, totaling approximately 469 square miles of land, which means that many people's residences will remain far from their nearest transit stop. Solving the first-mile, last-mile problem will be especially crucial for any efforts to decarbonize this city. That is why micromobility matters, here and in many other American cities.

Los Angeles is ground zero for a new shared mode of transit service called electric scooters, or e-scooters, which are one part of a larger micromobility revolution around the United States. The first and largest of these e-scooter companies, Bird, is headquartered in the Los Angeles metropolitan area. Can this nascent mode of transportation improve infrastructure in an automobile-centric metropolis while reducing the city's sizable carbon footprint? Beginning with a brief investigation of the 1930 Olmsted-Bartholomew Report, which reimagined Los Angeles' transportation infrastructure but ultimately was not adopted, this essay will discuss transportation infrastructure reforms that could facilitate decarbonization. In particular, I will investigate the potential of the recent e-scooter boom in Los Angeles to effect larger changes in the city's transportation infrastructure and environment.

Pleasureway Parks and the Car

The 1930 Olmsted-Bartholomew Report for the Los Angeles Area, which envisioned a Los Angeles replete with green space and parks, never became reality, but it now functions as an imaginative exercise for new generations of planners. As we look back to its recommendations, which featured a mix of short-sighted and prescient arguments, we should ask ourselves what can be revived and what needs to be revised. The report made the case for a comprehensive, coordinated system of large parks with connecting parkways, neighborhood playgrounds, and regional recreation areas, including public beaches all along the coast. In the midst of a mushrooming population and urban creep into nature, the report sought to integrate natural and urban systems in a more fluid way. However, for all its positive aspects, the Olmsted-Bartholomew plan's over-reliance on the automobile is one of its major weaknesses.

Central to the Olmsted-Bartholomew Report was its proposed system of parkways, which the report called the most urgently needed facet of the plan.[3] Parkways, as envisioned by Olmsted and Bartholomew, would be scenic, tree-lined roads that would connect parks and turn them into nodes in a larger network of public space and nature. In this vision of the city, an Angeleno could experience an uninterrupted, pleasurable journey through nature via car, driving from park to park through corridors bounded by trees. Pleasure was one of the main affective tools employed by Olmsted and Bartholomew (they used the terms "parkway" and "pleasureway parks" interchangeably), and it did not apply exclusively to the destination of travel. In their assessment, navigating this network of easily accessible, tree-lined arteries would be a pleasurable experience in and of itself:

> Such a system should be so distributed that no home will be more than a few miles from some part of it; and should be so designed that, having reached any part of it, one may drive within the system for pleasure, and *with* pleasure, for many miles under thoroughly agreeable conditions and in pleasant surroundings. Free from interruption of ordinary urban and suburban conditions, driving there may be either wholly for the pleasure of such driving or, more generally, it may be over the pleasantest if not always the shortest route to some other recreational objective.[4]

The focus on the affective response to the experience of driving gives us an insight into Americans' transportation habits today and why they have been reticent to give up cars. As the Olmsted-Bartholomew Report describes them, the pleasureways do indeed sound pleasant and enjoyable to drive; however, the conditions for such a positive affective experience of driving are frustrated in contemporary cities by various factors like congestion. The pleasure described in the report is predicated upon a pair of assumptions: the absence of traffic that could interrupt the flow through the parkway and universal access to cars. Interrogating the former reveals a lack of prescience on the part of Olmsted and Bartholomew; interrogating the latter points to a lack of inclusion.

If a smooth flow of traffic on the parkway is crucial to pleasure from the drive, then congestion is the bête noire. In their defense, Olmsted and Bartholomew were aware of how quickly the city's population was growing, and it is possible that their plan, if it had been implemented, would have alleviated traffic concerns for a time. However, it is debatable whether they could have foreseen how much more the region and its number of cars would continue to grow from the 1950s onward. The aggregate length of proposed parkway routes was 440 miles, which they believed would be sufficient to preserve traffic flows through the region.[5] But there are 650 miles of freeway in Los Angeles today, approximately 50 percent more than the 440 miles of proposed parkway routes in the Olmsted-Bartholomew Report.[6] Even with these hundreds of miles of freeway, the city experiences serious traffic congestion across the region on a daily basis. It is known now that as cities increase in size, traffic congestion increases even more. The relationship between a city's population and its traffic congestion is not linear but superlinear: Traffic congestion increases at a rate of 15 percent above a directly proportional, one-to-one relationship.[7] Even if those tree-lined parkways had been built, today they would be clogged with traffic, effectively eliminating most if not all of the pleasure derived from their use. As Olmsted and Bartholomew recognized, "for increasingly frequent periods the primary highways are congested to a degree which makes the so-called pleasure trip anything but pleasurable, except to those who can enjoy any conditions so long as they sit in an automobile."[8]

Olmsted and Bartholomew tailored their plan to Los Angeles' automobile infrastructure because they believed that the car was the future of Southern California, but they did not clearly address how people without a car would be able to navigate the pleasureways. In 1930 there were 806,264 registered automobiles in Los Angeles County.[9] Meanwhile, according to 1930 census data, the population of Los Angeles County was 2,208,492, which illustrates the disparity between the number of car owners and the number of residents. In light of this data, it can easily be inferred that poorer residents, including many who belonged to racial minorities, could not afford to own a car and thus would have been less able to enjoy the full benefit of parkways or large nature preserves farther from the city center. This situation was not helped by the lack of public transit development in the report: "It is doubtful, in view of the wide use of the automobile for transportation and pleasure, whether any considerable extensions will be made in street-car facilities."[10] Again, Olmsted and Bartholomew fell back on pleasure and the automobile, ignoring the possibility of alternative low-cost modes of mobility.

They argued that their plan would work only insofar as the city would provide motorways on a scale unforeseen in the past; otherwise the "friction of distance will gradually press it back toward the familiar and deplorable metropolitan conditions obtaining in older cities, where population and land values are crowded into much smaller areas."[11] One of the great ironies of the report is that Los Angeles later did build freeways on an unprecedented scale (even more miles than the report suggested), but the "friction of distance" happened in spite of and because of the transformative effect of the automobile, whose infrastructure destroyed neighborhood fabrics and enabled sprawl that pushed populations farther apart. Not only did car culture cause the carbon footprint of cities like Los Angeles to skyrocket, it powered population displacement and reified people's separation from nature.

The best way to recuperate the more promising dimensions of the Olmsted-Bartholomew Report today is through an urban political ecology approach by

"[asking] questions about who produces what kind of sociological configura-
tions for whom."[12] Because the plan centered on automobile ownership, it was
geared toward whites who had the capital to afford cars. That means that in the
report's vision of a better LA, those without a car would be less able to engage
with and derive enjoyment from nature. Although the demographic disparities
of automobile ownership between whites and nonwhites or between socioeconomic classes may not be as pronounced as it was in 1930, the problem of
unequal access to environmental benefits—and unequal distribution of environmental harm—persists in cities today.

So the question is how a twenty-first-century Olmsted-Bartholomew-style
transportation reconfiguration could combine with a reduction in Los Angeles'
carbon footprint. This will require a multipronged approach with major
changes at the infrastructural level—expanding the Metro system, road diets
(a technique in transportation planning whereby the number of car lanes on
a street is reduced in order to create room for other systemic improvements),
and the effective management of micromobility options to close the gaps between Metro stops and thereby reduce our dependence on fossil fuel vehicles.

E-Scooters and the Micromobility Revolution

Temporary changes in urban traffic patterns can help Angelenos reconceive
how they move around the city. CicLAvia, a twice-a-year event in which miles
of streets are closed to cars and taken over by cyclists, functions as such an
"ephemeral intervention," "a temporary demonstration of how the city might
function and feel with a radically redesigned transportation infrastructure."[13]
Such interventions can be effective tools to help citizens imagine alternative
infrastructures and develop a different sense of time and distance: "For many
participants, CicLAvia radically alters their mental map of LA. Normally,
Angelenos perceive their city in terms of time and aggravation, not space and
mobility. The distance between two points is not about absolute mileage but
instead is measured by the time necessary to get to the destination, as well
as the emotional energy expended. CicLAvia makes part of the city suddenly
feel intimate and pedestrian-scaled."[14]

Paley and Berman compile testimonies from participants of the first
CicLAvia who say that the experience also makes the city feel smaller and
more navigable: "We're alone in our cars. We pass above whole neighborhoods
on freeways and never actually see them. Today, I've seen buildings I never
took the time to lay eyes on before. Today gave people a chance to just slow
down and it connected the neighborhoods to the city in a new way. That's

important."[15] Not only is cycling a carbon-neutral means of locomotion, it also increases our engagement with our surroundings and deepens the pleasure we derive from nature and its connection to the built environment.

While ephemeral interventions like CicLAvia serve as useful tools for imagining alternative infrastructures and transportation cultures, concrete changes in mobility are also underway. In his essay "Back to the Future in Transportation Planning," Marlon G. Boarnet looks at the return of older forms of transportation that are experiencing a resurgence in Los Angeles. For the past two centuries, transportation planning has been tied to the development of new technologies that lowered the cost of transportation over greater distances—walking to buggies to streetcars to automobiles to interstate freeways—but we have been stuck in the same mode for over fifty years, which now leads to a shift to "older" modes such as bicycles and streetcars as well as to local demonstrations of "Neighborhood Electric Vehicles."[16] This shift to "older" modes of transportation is coterminous with a revolution in micromobility: using smaller, less energy-intensive vehicles to traverse short distances at the local level. As Alissa Walker points out, what we witness today is actually the second micromobility revolution; early twentieth-century city streets contained a multitude of different types of vehicles propelled by humans, horses, and motors—including motorized scooters—sharing city streets in relative harmony and safety.[17] Although the first micromobility revolution lost to automobiles, which now dominate American streets while crowding everything else into slivers of sidewalk (and possibly a few narrow bike lanes that often must negotiate a space that also includes parked cars and cars making turns), the second micromobility revolution has reason for greater optimism.

One of the newest, most exciting developments in local urban transportation, and the vehicle that has animated the second micromobility revolution, is the e-scooter—publicly shared, dockless, electric-powered scooters that are activated by a smartphone app. Although Boarnet's essay predates the advent of Bird and Lime e-scooters, they would fit neatly into the model of "Neighborhood Electric Vehicles" because their speed is capped at fifteen miles per hour, and they are primarily used for short trips of two miles or less. Despite the micromobility revolution including more vehicles than just e-scooters, they have gripped the public imagination in a way that dockless bikes have not, and they have enjoyed an unprecedentedly rapid adoption rate among urban residents. Prior data indicates that 2 to 3 percent of the population over eighteen years old in metropolitan areas had used the car-sharing service Zipcar in 2013, approximately twelve years after this company launched service; by contrast, in 2018 e-scooter sharing services had been available for less than twelve months and had already experienced an average adoption rate of 3.6 percent across major cities.[18] The meteoric rise of the e-scooter in Los Angeles and other cities across the United States provides a fascinating opportunity to restructure urban transportation networks and to aid in decarbonization efforts, if properly deployed and cultivated. Granted, the limited range of these electric-powered scooters prevents them from being a panacea, but in combination with a more ubiquitous, reliable Metro system as well as "complete streets" that have protected lanes for single-passenger modes of transit, strategically placed e-scooters and the micromobility revolution they form part of could generate a sea change in the way people navigate cities.

Of course, there are some obstacles that the e-scooter will need to clear before it can be considered a viable solution to the problems outlined in this essay. The subsequent sections of this essay will discuss three potential challenges for e-scooter acceptance and success in cities—safety, urban scale, and perception among minority and lower-income populations—followed by a discussion of their potential contribution to decarbonization. Given that e-scooters are such a new phenomenon, having mushroomed in 2018, there is not yet much literature or research on them. But some 2018 studies in Charlotte, Portland, and Washington D.C. could provide insights that are also useful for Los Angeles and other cities around the country. The City of Charlotte's Department of Transportation released a report on e-scooter and dockless bikeshare usage in the city in 2018. Charlotte is one of the few cities that has both dockless bikes and dockless e-scooters, and the city, unlike most others, requires companies to give them rideshare data. The report showed that Charlotte residents took 726,077 trips on e-scooters between May and December 2018 compared to 265,526 trips on bikeshares between November 2017 and December 2018, and looking exclusively at the month of December 2018, e-scooter users took 82,532 trips versus 3,312 trips for bikeshare users.[19] In addition, the average e-scooter trip was roughly twice as long as the average bikeshare trip during the study period—1.7 miles versus 0.9 miles. This data suggests that not only are e-scooters more popular than bikeshares when both are available, they are preferred for longer trips. The total trips taken by e-scooters are nearly three times as many as the number of total trips taken by bikeshares, but we must keep in mind that e-scooters were not introduced to Charlotte until six months after bikeshares were. Looking just at the month of December 2018, e-scooter trips far outstrip bikeshare trips by a factor of almost twenty-five. This suggests that once e-scooters arrived, Charlotte residents strongly preferred to use them over bikeshares. Of course, this city is only one data point, and it does not include any demographic information such as the socioeconomic or racial makeup of Charlotte e-scooter users. However, it suggests a promising future for e-scooters, which is corroborated by data from Portland, Oregon.

The Portland study counted 700,369 trips taken on e-scooters during the four-month study period.[20] It utilized a broad range of data sources that included availability, data from the e-scooter companies on availability, trips, collision, and complaints; injury reports to the Portland Police Department; emergency room and urgent care data; e-scooter user surveys; as well as separate focus groups for the Black community, people with disabilities, and residents of East Portland (an area of Portland that is not as well served by public transit). This enabled the study to collect more demographic, safety, and decarbonization data than the Charlotte study. For this reason, I shall return to the Portland study a few times throughout this essay.

E-Scooter Safety on City Streets

In order for cities to fully embrace e-scooters, they must be convinced that they are a safe means of getting around. Questions of the safety of this new mode of transit can be divided into two categories: safety of the e-scooter rider and safety of pedestrians. Although the former should be the most important issue of safety, the latter receives a disproportionate amount of media attention. It is not difficult to find people who complain about the behavior of irresponsible e-scooter riders—the way they recklessly ride on sidewalks and almost run into pedestrians, or the way they park scooters in the middle of walkways. However, the first study at UCLA on the public health impact of injuries associated with e-scooter use indicated that 92 percent of the 249 reported injuries were to riders, not pedestrians.[21] The Portland study corroborates this with only 3 percent of emergency room visits during the study period involving pedestrians.[22] Although one could conclude from these studies that e-scooters are unviable and unsafe—the 40 percent head injury incidence is troubling and should be taken seriously as part of a larger conversation on helmet safety—there are limitations to the data collected from the study. For one, the studies don't indicate the circumstances that led to each emergency room visit. Some of the injuries to e-scooter riders may have resulted from evasive actions to avoid collisions with people or cars, which then caused the scooter riders to lose balance and fall. Furthermore, the UCLA study's authors acknowledge that one of its major limitations was that they could not evaluate how better infrastructure and urban planning could reduce injuries. For example, did the majority of injuries occur in areas where there were no bike lanes? Without more data regarding the location of the incidents, we can't write off e-scooters as too dangerous to operate.

One may ask why cities do not replace e-scooters with an expanded bike-share program. A legitimate proposal, but sometimes it is necessary to avoid the physical exertion of pedaling a bicycle, depending on attire, physical health, or ability. So cities must provide options that cater to various needs and demands. In addition, Populus, a mobility data platform that seeks to foster better relationships between cities and private mobility operators, has found more parity between female and male adopters of e-scooters (3.2 percent versus 4.4 percent) compared to female and male adopters of bikeshare programs (12 percent versus 21 percent), which they hypothesize may be due to women's perceptions about the safety of the two modes of transportation.[23] It is possible that women may feel safer riding e-scooters than bicycles because they are easier to maneuver on sidewalks—even though that is not what most cities want—which points back to the core problem that riding e-scooters on streets is perceived as too dangerous. In fact, the number of cyclists who visited emergency rooms during the Portland study period was 429 compared to the 176 from e-scooter riders.[24] And the same safety concerns surrounding e-scooters, such as helmet usage and fatal collisions with cars, apply to bicycle riders; in most states it is not illegal for adults to ride without a helmet, and many urban streets do not separate cars from other vehicles on wheels.

Because most American cities have not revised their street designs since the ascendency of the automobile, they remain unwelcoming and risky for cyclists and e-scooter users. Consequently, those who oppose e-scooters absolve the behavior of motorists and obfuscate the poor design of streets that make e-scooter riders feel unsafe sharing the road. To best ensure the safety of all micromobility users and to make the second micromobility revolution a success, cities need to wrest control from cars and restructure their streets and curbs. We must build infrastructure that will allow micromobility to flourish, which means affording riders enough protection from vehicles that could otherwise mangle or kill them. To date, in spite of the rising number of emergency room trips, there have been only three reported fatalities involving e-scooters, and two of those resulted from the e-scooter rider being struck by an automobile.[25] So even though injuries from falling off an e-scooter or colliding with a pedestrian should not be discounted, cars still present the greatest mortality risk to riders, cyclists, and pedestrians.

It is now widely accepted that the best way to influence a driver's behavior is by changing the design of streets to keep them physically and visually narrow.[26] Another more recent term for this sort of street redesign is "road diet," which would replace one lane for automobiles in each direction with ubiquitous scooter/bike lanes. Because scooters are capped at speeds of fifteen miles per hour, they are a natural fit for sharing bike lanes with cyclists. To further ensure safety, these lanes would ideally be protected from cars by bollards or other barriers. And what's good for the scooter is good for the pedestrian and cyclist, because ameliorating the current paucity of bike lanes around much of Los Angeles would keep e-scooter riders from sharing sidewalks with pedestrians. In fact, road diets coupled with an expansion of micromobility options may reduce the total number of traffic fatalities, since traffic fatality rates heavily depend on the number of automobiles and automobile vehicle miles traveled per capita.[27] So if better infrastructure makes micromobility safe and inviting, and if more people start to replace car trips—34 percent of Portland e-scooter riders during the study period stated that they replaced car trips with e-scooter trips—then e-scooters may contribute to a reduction in automobile fatalities.[28] By instituting road diets that shrink the number of car lanes and expand the space for non-motorists, not only would cities make their streets instantly more inviting to e-scooter riders as well as all carbon neutral forms of mobility, they could also reduce serious injuries and fatalities.

Micromobility and Urban Scale

Scale remains one of the major problems in building any sort of large transportation network, and this is no different for micromobility options. Because of their top speed of fifteen miles per hour and dependence on battery power, e-scooters have a limited range. Until their batteries improve significantly, e-scooters are not an optimal means for regularly traversing distances of more than five miles. The good news is that data collected by the US Department of Transportation on one-way household trips that used a single privately operated vehicle in 2018 showed that 59.4 percent of vehicle trips were less than six miles.[29] Furthermore, Populus' analysis of the most recent national transportation data reveals that 45 percent of trips made in the United States are three miles or less, and 78 percent of those trips were made by personal vehicle.[30] These figures show that even if e-scooters are only used for trips under five miles, they still have the potential to replace millions of trips within cities each year. And by supplementing short e-scooter rides with public transit, they can then start to replace automobile trips longer than five miles. In fact, e-scooter companies readily admit that they see themselves as primarily a solution to the first-mile, last-mile problem of public transit—the difficulty in getting to and from a transit hub to one's final destination. The Populus report shows that e-scooter riders tend to view them in the same way, using them in conjunction with public transit: "Based on data from over 7,000 people in major U.S. cities, a majority of people (70 percent) view e-scooters positively: they expand transportation options, enable a car-free lifestyle, are a convenient replacement for short trips in a personal vehicle or ride-hailing service, and are a complement to public transit."[31] Although it predates the e-scooter arrival, a 2016 report by the Transit Cooperative Research Program corroborates the correlation between micromobility with frequent public transit use, lower rates of car ownership, and reduced transportation spending.[32] Thus, micromobility must be seen as one component of a larger multimodal solution, including an expanded Metro system that is either grade-separated from automobile traffic or at least given priority over cars at intersections. This can be achieved by signal prioritization for trains over cars, dedicated bus lanes, and even congestion pricing in crowded areas in order to nudge individuals to drive less and use transit more.

Expanded e-scooter infrastructure at the neighborhood level would also help address the problem of scale, especially because it is much less costly to install compared to any other mode of transit. Setting up a few dozen e-scooters at the neighborhood level plus some new bike lanes costs a city far less than constructing a subway or light rail line through the same neighborhood. In Spain, the city of Seville, at a modest cost of 32 million euros, created eighty kilometers of bike lanes in eighteen months while repurposing five thousand parking spaces.[33] Manuel Calvo, the architect of the Plan de la Bicicleta de Sevilla, estimates that the cost of this infrastructure improvement would have yielded only five or six kilometers of highway. He further points out that the Seville bike network serves more daily trips than the city's metro line, which cost 800 million euros to construct. Of course, this does not discount the importance of a well-functioning, wide-reaching public transit system in a sprawling metropolitan area. Seville is not a perfect analogue for Los Angeles, which has a land area nine times larger and a population over five times larger. It would not be feasible for Los Angeles to only invest in bike lanes and then expect people to travel thirty miles solely by bike or e-scooter. We should think of trains as the major arteries of a circulatory system, pumping large volumes of citizens far and wide, and of microtransit use on dedicated bike lanes as the many smaller capillaries that shuttle smaller volumes of people into the larger arteries. Focusing on greatly expanding the number of "capillaries" around transit stops, parks, residential neighborhoods, and other destinations is cost-effective and reduces the scale problem. As Seville has shown, creating new "capillaries" is a fiscal bargain, and in Los Angeles, it would compound the effectiveness and benefits of e-scooters at the local level.

Perception of E-Scooters among Minority and Low-Income Populations

Finally, perception of this new technology in underserved communities remains a concern. In fact, some would argue that the car is still the best way for economically disadvantaged groups to increase their urban mobility, but the fact remains that to purchase, operate, insure, and maintain a car still costs far more than to use a combination of micromobility and public transit. So it would make sense to bring e-scooters to traditionally underserved neighborhoods and transit deserts, but in Los Angeles that has not yet happened. The majority of e-scooters are situated around Santa Monica and the Westside (areas that have a white majority population and higher than average median household incomes), although occasionally a user may ride one all the way to downtown or even East LA (an area with 96 percent Latinx population, the highest percentage of any neighborhood in the city, and below average median household incomes), where they are regarded with wary curiosity. Eric Huerta, a mobility activist in East LA, argues that right now, e-scooters are associated with "tech bros" and tourists rather than locals in his local community.[34] In order to appeal to underserved communities, e-scooter companies will have to work hard to dispel negative associations with "techies" and gentrification, two related forces that threaten some low-income communities. Despite the potential threat to his community, Huerta is cautiously optimistic about the possibility for e-scooters to help people get around.

In addition, the Populus study offers some promising insights for e-scooters in underserved communities. In this study of Washington D.C., public support for micromobility services such as e-scooters is highest among lower income groups: 72 percent of people with annual incomes below $25,000 and 75 percent of people with annual incomes between $25,000 and $50,000 expressed positive views.[35] The findings of the Portland study are consistent with the Washington study: 74 percent of Portland residents of color and 66 percent of residents with annual incomes below $30,000 view e-scooters positively.[36]

The Populus study collected data on micromobility transit use in the Washington D.C. area to see how dockless vehicles have addressed transit equity concerns. Two findings from this study are noteworthy. First, by creating an index to measure the average distance to the nearest vehicle for each location in the city, Populus compared dockless vehicles like e-scooters to the city's established docked bikeshare locations. It found that dockless vehicles are more accessible across the entire city, including in traditionally underserved areas, and that the network distance to a dockless vehicle is shorter than for the existing docked bikeshare system, even though the fleet of docked vehicles is much larger than that of dockless vehicles.[37] So even though there are fewer dockless vehicles in the city, their untethered nature adapts them better to the needs of low-income areas. The second noteworthy finding from the study is that African Americans in Washington D.C. adopted dockless services over traditional bikeshares at a significantly higher ratio than white residents of D.C. In fact, the ratio of adoption of dockless vehicles to docked vehicles was 2.6:1 among African Americans versus 1.2:1 among Whites.[38] When given the opportunity to use them, African Americans in D.C. show a much stronger preference for dockless options like e-scooters. These two findings suggest that e-scooters do have a high potential to be successful among urban racial minorities and in underserved areas. This will be put to the test in Los Angeles in 2019, when Bird is scheduled to roll out a full pilot program for the city, which will include more scooters in Central and East Los Angeles.

One major caveat for the adoption of e-scooters by black users is the fear of racial profiling. Several members of the black focus group in the Portland study stated that "the overall threat of an escalating incident outweighed the desire to try e-scooters."[39] In order for e-scooters to be more widely adopted and accepted in communities of color, scooter companies and cities need to work to counteract incidences of police officers enforcing riding laws more harshly on people of color, which can lead to violent and deadly escalations. And to reiterate an earlier point, cities should work to expand bike lanes so that black e-scooter users can't be profiled for minor offenses like riding on sidewalks. Otherwise, it is vital that e-scooter companies and cities work closely with communities of color to carefully control the introduction of these vehicles so that it's not simply another case of entrepreneurs claiming public space and forcing their product into it. If local communities are not given a say, then the e-scooter can potentially become an agent of gentrification.

E-Scooters and Decarbonization

So far I have shown that e-scooters are viable solutions for short trips around a city and that they can be a useful tool for making mobility more egalitarian. Can they also contribute to the reduction of urban carbon footprints? One might think that because they run on electric motors powered by rechargeable batteries, e-scooters must be much more environmentally friendly than internal combustion engine vehicles. They are—but with some qualifications. The first concerns the source of the electricity that charges the e-scooters: "If your city gets most of its power from a coal or natural gas-fired power plant, that means your scoot around the neighborhood has a positive carbon footprint."[40] At the national level, electricity production ranks only slightly below transportation in terms of greenhouse gas emissions (28.4 percent), so switching to electric vehicles will not solve the problem in and of itself; they are only as clean as the source of their electricity.[41] As of 2016, the Los Angeles Department of Water and Power derives 19 percent of its power from coal and 34 percent from natural gas, but it is working toward complete divestment from coal by 2025.[42] Unfortunately, achieving complete decarbonization by divesting from natural gas will take longer. The LADWP plans to implement incremental reductions in its power derived from natural gas, from 34 percent in 2016 to 21 percent in 2036.[43] Still, this is encouraging, and Los Angeles' progress may be bolstered by California's goal of getting 100 percent of its electricity from renewable sources by 2045, and with Los Angeles Mayor Eric Garcetti abandoning plans to spend billions of dollars to rebuild three natural gas plants along the coast, the city may be able to expedite the timetable for complete energy sector decarbonization.[44] This means that as time goes on, electric vehicles will continue to become more environmentally friendly and should consequently comprise a greater share of vehicle miles traveled.

The second consideration is the type of transportation being displaced: "If you're scooting instead of walking, then the ride has a higher environmental cost. But if you're replacing a car ride, then it has an environmental benefit since an e-scooter uses a tiny fraction of the energy consumed by a car."[45] Furthermore, if the convenience of having an e-scooter nearby convinces somebody to make a trip that they didn't need to make, this also results in a net positive in emissions. However, when used primarily as a solution to public transit's first-mile, last-mile problem, e-scooters definitely lower a city's carbon output, especially if people choose e-scooters over a car ride to a transit stop. Although the Portland study could not definitively claim that e-scooters contribute to a reduction in climate pollution, it does estimate that the 801,887 miles traveled by e-scooters during the study period "replaced approximately 301,856 vehicle miles that would have been traveled in single occupancy vehicles and other shared vehicle trips."[46] The study then goes on to estimate how much e-scooters contribute to decarbonization: "Using the U.S. Environmental Protection Agency's average CO_2 emissions per vehicle mile, we estimate that during the pilot, e-scooters prevented automobiles from emitting approximately 122 metric tons of CO_2, equivalent to removing nearly 27 average passenger vehicles from the road for a year."[47] Of course, these are just estimates, and as the study acknowledges, whether survey respondents would behave in accordance with their responses is uncertain. Also, the study lacks "data about emissions associated with the e-scooter companies' supply chains, manufacturing processes, charging and deployment operations, frequency of scooter replacement, their waste stream, or more."[48] Without data on the companies' practices or the source of the electricity that is charging the e-scooters, we cannot definitively say to what extent e-scooters support decarbonization efforts. In sum, the carbon output of e-scooters is relative to how they are being used and how they're being charged, so our use of them must be strategic to shrink our emissions.

To facilitate the strategic use of e-scooters in a sprawling city like Los Angeles, a multimodal, integrated, inclusive solution is necessary. For one thing, e-scooters should be incorporated even more closely into the LA Metro network. The city needs to ensure a steady supply of e-scooters adjacent to and within a two-mile radius of all Metro rail stops, which would also ensure proximity to many bus stops. Furthermore, Los Angeles Metro should work with e-scooter companies to allow payment through the TAP card, Metro's electronic ticketing payment method for rides on buses and rail lines, which would make it easier for people to seamlessly transition between the two modes of transportation. It would also be helpful for e-scooter companies to offer discounted rates for low-income users.

The last two parts of an intermodal solution are road diets to shrink the amount of street space reserved for cars and transition to electricity from 100 percent renewable sources. Certainly, the former is the most controversial part of the plan for a city so dependent on cars, but it is a necessary one. It is simply too inexpensive to be a single driver in Los Angeles right now. The Department of Energy has established that as gasoline prices drop, vehicle miles traveled increase.[49] Any successful effort to decarbonize will require driving to become more expensive, whether by increasing fuel prices or by congestion charges as implemented in cities such as London. With the increased revenue from these sources, cities can expedite investment in public transit and micromobility solutions. Finally, switching to electric trains, trucks, cars, and scooters will not help us reach a zero carbon future if we are still generating electricity from coal and other fossil fuels. All of the facets of this integrated solution can help cities like Los Angeles lower its carbon footprint, and while some of the proposed solutions are more costly or time-intensive to achieve, micromobility options and expanded bike lanes are eminently achievable and can jumpstart the effort to total transportation decarbonization.

Conclusion

The Olmsted-Bartholomew plan, though never adopted, remains a productive thought experiment for reimagining Los Angeles transportation and access to nature. I have outlined the groundwork here for a new kind of urban O-B plan that decenters the automobile and promotes micromobility options like e-scooters. This new vision turns streets into sites of resistance against the hegemony of the automobile that keeps us tethered to fossil fuels. Of course, with a city the size of Los Angeles, the e-scooter or bicycle alone cannot effect change at the macro level. Any sort of large-scale reconfiguration of our transportation infrastructure that would decarbonize the city must be multi-pronged, including major increases in public transit lines, protected lanes for slower modes of transportation, and micromobility options to address the first-mile, last-mile problem at the neighborhood level. The implementation of this multimodal solution, in addition to helping decarbonize the city, would make transportation around the city more egalitarian, reducing the cost and travel time for residents of lower income neighborhoods to access more distant locales. As an ancillary benefit, it would facilitate environmentally friendly access to nature in and around the city. Locals and visitors to a city with a climate like Los Angeles will always be drawn to its outdoor recreation spaces, and for most of them, the most convenient way to access nature in the city right now, whether at the beach or the hiking trails, is via automobile. An expansive network of micromobility and public transit would reduce the carbon footprint we exert in order to get to nature, thereby redeeming the aspiration of the 1930 O-B plan to facilitate access to nature while ameliorating the plan's carbon dependency.

Los Angeles has a tremendous opportunity right now for consciously choosing alternative modes of urban transportation that overcome the city's car-centric philosophy and articulate a new political vision of a greener, more affordable, more accessible, and more enjoyable city. If Los Angeles can successfully harness the micromobility revolution for its progress toward decarbonized transportation, it will serve as a model for many other cities around the globe.

NOTES

1. "Census Bureau Reports 471,000 Workers Commute into Los Angeles County, Calif., Each Day," United States Census Bureau, March 5, 2013, https://www.census.gov /newsroom/press-releases/2013/cb13-r13.html.
2. US EPA, "Sources of Greenhouse Gas Emissions," Overviews and Factsheets, last modified 2018, https://www.epa.gov/ghgemissions/sources-greenhouse-gas-emissions.

3. Greg Hise and William Francis Deverell, *Eden by Design: The 1930 Olmsted-Bartholomew Plan for the Los Angeles Region* (Berkeley: University of California Press, 2000), 193.

4. Hise and Deverell, 95. Italics in original.

5. Hise and Deverell, 194.

6. "Freeways and Highways in Los Angeles County, California," accessed October 29, 2018, http://www.laalmanac.com/transport/tr26.php.

7. Luis Bettencourt and Geoffrey West, "A Unified Theory of Urban Living," *Nature* 467 (October 20, 2010): 912–13, https://doi.org/10.1038/467912a.

8. Hise and Deverell, *Eden by Design*, 111.

9. Matt Novak, "Nobody Walks in L.A.: The Rise of Cars and the Monorails That Never Were," Smithsonian, accessed October 26, 2018, https://www.smithsonianmag.com/history/nobody-walks-in-la-the-rise-of-cars-and-the-monorails-that-never-were-43267593.

10. Hise and Deverell, *Eden by Design*, 117.

11. Hise and Deverell, 109.

12. Nik Heynen, Maria Kaika, and Erik Swyngedouw, "Urban Political Ecology: Politicizing the Production of Urban Natures," in *In the Nature of Cities : Urban Political Ecology and the Politics of Urban Metabolism*, ed. Nik Heynen, Maria Kaika, and Erik Swyngedouw (New York: Routledge, 2006), 2.

13. Aaron Paley and Amanda Berman, "Systemic Change Through CicLAvia," in *Planning Los Angeles*, ed. David C. Sloane (American Planning Association, 2012), 180.

14. Paley and Berman, 182.

15. Paley and Berman, 186.

16. Marlon G. Boarnet, "Back to the Future in Transportation Planning," in *Planning Los Angeles*, ed. David C. Sloane (American Planning Association, 2012), 147–61.

17. Alissa Walker, "Don't Ban Scooters. Redesign Streets," Curbed, July 13, 2018, https://www.curbed.com/word-on-the-street/2018/7/13/17246060/scooters-uber-lyft-bird-lime-streets.

18. Populus, "The Micromobility Revolution: The Introduction and Adoption of Electric Scooters in the United States," July 2018, 8, https://www.populus.ai/micro-mobility-2018-july.

19. "City of Charlotte Shared Mobility Program," City of Charlotte Government, accessed February 9, 2019, https://charlottenc.gov.

20. Portland Bureau of Transportation, "2018 E-Scooter Findings Report" January 15, 2019, 6, https://www.portlandoregon.gov/transportation/78431.

21. Tarak K. Trivedi et al., "Injuries Associated With Standing Electric Scooter Use," *JAMA Network Open* 2, no. 1 (January 25, 2019): e187381–e187381, https://doi.org/10.1001/jamanetworkopen.2018.7381.

22. Portland Bureau of Transportation, "2018 E-Scooter Findings Report," 22.

23. Populus, "The Micromobility Revolution," 13.

24. Portland Bureau of Transportation, "2018 E-Scooter Findings Report," 22.

25. Cindy Widner, "Austin Electric-Scooter Fatality, One of First in Nation, Sheds Light on Injury Reporting," Curbed Austin, February 6, 2019, https://austin.curbed.com/2019/2/6/18214119/austin-electric-scooter-death-fatalities-injuries.

26. Dan Burden, "Cities, Streets, and Cars," in *Cities and Cars: A Handbook of Best Practices*, ed. Roger L. Kemp (London: McFarland, 2007), 9–10.

27. Hamed Ahangari, Carol Atkinson-Palombo, and Norman W. Garrick, "Automobile-Dependency as a Barrier to Vision Zero, Evidence from the States in the USA," *Accident Analysis & Prevention* 107 (October 2017): 77–85, https://doi.org/10.1016/j.aap.2017.07.012.

28. Portland Bureau of Transportation, "2018 E-Scooter Findings Report," 22.

29. "FOTW #1042, August 13, 2018: In 2017 Nearly 60% of All Vehicle Trips Were Less

Than Six Miles," Energy.gov, accessed March 25, 2019, https://www.energy.gov/eere
  vehicles/articles/fotw-1042-august-13-2018-2017-nearly-60-all-vehicle-trips-were-less
  -six-miles.

30. Populus, "The Micromobility Revolution," 4.
31. Populus, "The Micromobility Revolution," 3.
32. Sharon Feigon, Colin Murphy, and Transportation Research Board, "Shared Mobility
    and the Transformation of Public Transit," Transit Cooperative Research Program,
    2016, 7, http://www.nap.edu/catalog.php?record_id=23607.
33. Michael Andersen, "Six Secrets From the Planner of Sevilla's Lightning Bike Network,"
    Streetsblog USA (blog), May 7, 2018, https://usa.streetsblog.org/2018/05/07/six
    -secrets-from-the-planner-of-sevillas-lightning-bike-network.
34. Kai Ryssdal, "The Problem with Scooters," December 5, 2018, in *Marketplace*, podcast,
    http://www.marketplace.org/shows/marketplace/12052018.
35. Populus, "The Micromobility Revolution," 15.
36. Portland Bureau of Transportation, "2018 E-Scooter Findings Report," 6.
37. Populus, "Measuring Equitable Access to New Mobility: A Case Study of Shared Bikes
    and Electric Scooters," November 2018, 5, https://www.populus.ai/news/measuring
    -equity-dockless.
38. Populus, "Measuring Equitable Access to New Mobility," 7.
39. Portland Bureau of Transportation, "2018 E-Scooter Findings Report," 25.
40. Umair Irfan, "Electric Scooters' Sudden Invasion of American Cities, Explained," Vox,
    August 27, 2018, https://www.vox.com/2018/8/27/17676670/electric-scooter-rental
    -bird-lime-skip-spin-cities.
41. US EPA, "Sources of Greenhouse Gas Emissions."
42. Los Angeles Department of Water and Power, "Briefing Book 2017–18," August 2017),
    7, 9, https://s3-us-west-2.amazonaws.com/ladwp-jtti/wp-content/uploads/sites/3
    /2017/09/08143247/Briefing-Book-Rolling-PDF.pdf.
43. Los Angeles Department of Water and Power, "Briefing Book 2017–18," 9.
44. Sammy Roth, "Los Angeles Ditches Plan to Invest Billions in Fossil Fuels, Mayor Eric
    Garcetti Says," *Los Angeles Times*, February 11, 2019, https://www.latimes.com
    /business/la-fi-garcetti-los-angeles-gas-plants-20190211-story.html.
45. Irfan, "Electric Scooters' Sudden Invasion."
46. Portland Bureau of Transportation, "2018 E-Scooter Findings Report," 27.
47. Portland Bureau of Transportation, "2018 E-Scooter Findings Report," 27.
48. Portland Bureau of Transportation, "2018 E-Scooter Findings Report," 28.
49. "FOTW #1024, April 9, 2018: Changes in Vehicle Miles of Travel Often Mirror Gasoline
    Price Changes," Energy.gov, https://www.energy.gov/eere/vehicles/articles/fotw-1024
    -april-9-2018-changes-vehicle-miles-travel-often-mirror-gasoline.

Part II

Car Cultures

CHAPTER 4

"Carbolization": Cars, Carbon Emissions, and the Global Discipline of Automobility

Gordon M. Sayre

Futurama and the Imperialism of Automobility

The most popular attraction at the 1939–40 World's Fair in New York City was Futurama, an exhibit sponsored by General Motors and conceived and built by the theatrical and industrial designer Norman Bel Geddes, who elaborated upon it in his book *Magic Motorways* (1940). Futurama consisted of a huge diorama or architectural model covering around an acre of floor space inside the exhibit hall, a miniature landscape of America in 1960. Visitors were treated to industrialized farms, dams, and power plants, airports with model planes, and, most important for the sponsor and designer, superhighways such as had not yet been built anywhere in the world apart from a few short segments in Nazi Germany and in coastal US cities, including the Arroyo Seco Parkway in Los Angeles. The superhighways in Futurama featured tiny cars, some of them moving along the lanes, among the only moving parts in the diorama. To view the exhibit visitors rode in seats mounted on a conveyor belt, looking down at the diorama through windows while listening to a recorded narration synchronized to the progress of the moving seats. The ride lasted eighteen minutes and the belt accommodated almost six hundred passengers at a time, but nonetheless long queues formed, and on some days more than thirty thousand visitors rode it.[1] To enhance the experience, Bel Geddes created at the exit from the building an illusion of emerging into the model, and thus into the future. As E. L. Doctorow depicted it in his novel *World's Fair* (1985):

And then the amazing thing was that at the end you saw a particular model street intersection and the show was over . . . you came out into the sun and you were standing on precisely the corner you had just seen, the future was right where you were standing and what was small had become big, the scale had enlarged and you were no longer looking down at it, but standing in it, on this corner of the future, right here in the World's Fair.[2]

Fair or unfair, that future is now, and I argue that at Futurama, the prototypical (post)modern subject ceased to be an ambulatory human and became instead a driver or passenger in a car. Futurama's design for industrial and transportation infrastructure was hugely successful and helped make modern societies dependent on automobility. This occurred first in the US with the Interstate Highway System, and soon after in Western Europe, Canada, and Australia, then in the wealthier nations of Asia, and more recently in Latin America, Africa, and around the globe. As more cars are sold and as expressway infrastructure continues to be built in the most populous nations of the developing world—India, China, Indonesia, Nigeria, and Brazil (on track to be the first, second, fourth, fifth, and sixth most populous by 2030)—the combined threats of carbon emissions, climate change, and growing fleets of cars pose a grave danger to the earth's atmosphere and environment. I propose a word for this threat: *carbolization*, a blend of car, carbon, and globalization. This chapter aims to place this concept in the terminology used by social theorists of automobility, and then describe the difficulties of mitigating the several trends and problems combined in the term.

The landscape, or motorscape, that Futurama depicted as being twenty years ahead was not entirely prescient of what transpired by 1960. With regard to its aesthetic details, the art deco and brutalist styles of the buildings, and the huge scale of the towers and plazas in the model, were created only in a few major cities, and the personal aircraft that were to take off and land atop the skyscrapers never got off the ground. And, as David Gelernter noted in his oral history of the 1939 New York World's Fair, "One thing the world of tomorrow didn't have was churches, and their absence was noted with disapproval. For the 1940 season hundreds were added, and a university."[3]

The Futurama exhibit was created by General Motors, and the World's Fair also featured exhibits by Ford and Chrysler in neighboring pavilions, and thus it is tempting to see it as an instance of corporate manipulation of politics and opinion. The car industry and oil industry stood to benefit from a road construction program funded by taxpayers, and in 1930 three-quarters of the world's cars were built and more than 90 percent of the world's oil was pumped in the US.[4] However, Paul Mason Fotsch in a perceptive article about the Futurama exhibit concludes: "By not directly promoting General Motors cars, the vision it creates of an automobile-dominated world is made to seem natural and not something sponsored by a car company. The text that is heard through the speakers during the tour pretends to be simply information but is actually an advertisement for GM cars and cars in general."[5]

General Motors had surpassed Ford to take the largest share of the US car market in 1927 when Ford discontinued the Model T and shut down its Detroit factories to retool for production of the new Model A. During the Great Depression, GM continued to build market share amid a 75 percent decline in overall US sales volume from 1929 to 1932. Futurama was a publicity coup for GM, and Alfred P. Sloan, the CEO who helped make it the largest, most profitable company in the world, was a marketing genius. However, unlike Henry Ford in the 1910s, Sloan emphasized profit margins over market share, in part because he believed if GM's share rose too far above 50 percent, antitrust authorities might seek to break up the company.[6]

Shortly after the Fair opened, World War II broke out. When the United States entered the war, much of Detroit's industrial resources were diverted toward producing military trucks, ships, airplanes, and other materiel, but in the late 1940s pent-up demand and worldwide growth led Detroit to huge profits selling new cars with increasingly flamboyant designs. It was the halcyon period for American auto industry, unhindered by concerns about pollution and waste, and with only faint protests about rising traffic fatalities. But whereas many Americans follow the industry and feel nostalgic about the cars of the 1950s, fewer know the history of the road system that together with the cars constitute the system of automobility (see fig. 4.1).[7]

Magic Motorways is important to read today because in projecting the world of 1960 as portrayed in Futurama (of which the book includes many photos), Bel Geddes also anticipated self-driving cars, and promised solutions to the safety and congestion problems that still plague the world's roads today. The cars on the superhighways in Futurama were to be guided by automatic controls that enabled them to travel at high speeds without danger of collisions. In the 2010s, as this technology has again captured media and popular fascination, the cars are referred to as "driverless cars" or "autonomous vehicles" (often abbreviated as AVs). They are being commercialized by Uber and other companies for use as taxis in urban areas, and are touted as freeing commuters from the tedium, stress, and dangers of driving. In Geddes' book, however, the busy commuter was treated not as a pampered customer, but rather as a weak cog in need of discipline or correction:

> Human beings, even when at the wheel, are prone to talk, wave to their friends, make love, day dream, listen to the radio, stare at striking billboards, light cigarettes, take chances. . . . With the changes in the car, will the driver too be changed? . . . These cars of 1960 and the highways on which they drive will have in them devices which will correct the faults of human beings as drivers. They will prevent the driver from committing errors. They will aid him in passing through intersections without slowing down or causing anyone else to do so and without endangering himself or others.[8]

In the totalitarian design and paternalist rhetoric of Bel Geddes, the driver's dependence upon the car was entrenched by superhighways even as the competence of the drivers to guide the cars they had purchased was cast in doubt by the conditions these highways created.

Social theorists of automobility, such as John Urry, write of "path-dependence" in transport planning. In "Inhabiting the Car," one of his many articles on the topic, Urry described "two interdependent features of automobility: the car is immensely flexible *and* wholly coercive." Not only drivers are coerced, the entire society is disciplined by automobility, which "coerces people into an intense flexibility. It forces people to juggle tiny fragments of time so as to deal with the temporal and spatial constraints that it itself generates."[9] Moreover, as Fotsch points out, in a society where a car is essential for travel to and from work, a worker's time commuting and the wages spent buying and maintaining a car amount to uncompensated labor.[10] The discipline and dependence of automobility have been astonishingly successful, because the postmodern driver-subject regards the car as essential:

> In a 1975 survey, 71 percent said that a car was essential for them to live "the good life," a higher percentage than any element of American life except home ownership, a happy marriage, and having children. But by 1991 the figure had risen to 75 percent, making cars more important to us than children, who were bumped to a sad fourth place. While some argue that this simply reflects an ever-rising consumer ethos, it also shows that the car is the king of all commodities we desire.[11]

Fig. 4.1. Aerial view of skyscrapers and expressways in model for Shell Oil Company by Norman Bel Geddes. (Photo by Richard Garrison. Wikimedia Commons, https://commons .wikimedia.org/wiki/File:Shell_Oil_City_of_Tomorrow_model_c._1936-37.jpg)

Whatever the constituents of a good life might be, Americans and other humans continue to produce both more children and more cars. As cities grow more sprawling and populous and more roads are built, residents in these cities expect to drive rather than use other transport modes, and it becomes nearly impossible to redesign infrastructure and redirect daily habits so as to undo "a transportation monoculture that's unsustainable."[12]

The superhighway infrastructure of modern urbanism is unsustainable not only for its waste of energy and space, but also for the social tensions it exacerbates between the rich and the poor, and between those with cars and those without. These tensions were subtly referenced in a short film depicting Futurama, entitled *To New Horizons* (1940). A stentorian voice-over told viewers that the city of 1960 "has been redesigned around a highly developed, modern transportation system," and added a clue to the changes that had been made in the forties and fifties: "On all express city thoroughfares the rights of way have been so routed as to displace outmoded business sections, and undesirable slum areas whenever possible."[13] The agenda for automobility and urban renewal involved displacing the industrial laborers and people of color who worked in and lived near the urban factories of the major US cities of the period, such as New York City, Buffalo, and Detroit.

The story of urban renewal and accompanying racial segregation in US cities has been told by other scholars.[14] I wish to focus here on the poorly recognized, unfairly distributed, yet direct impacts of cars and driving. Air pollution from cars; deaths, injuries and medical costs from car crashes; the time and resources lost to drivers due to traffic congestion—these all are among the externalities of automobility. Economist Richard Porter defines the concept: "Almost all our automobile problems arise from the car's generation of external costs. When we get into our cars, we are prepared to pay the private costs of driving. But we ignore the external costs which, when added to the private costs, make the social cost of driving extremely high."[15]

Anthropologist Daniel Miller, editor of a collection of essays entitled *Car Cultures*, writes, "Much of the literature on externalities has now become an attempt to generate a larger audit of the car in terms not so much of financial costs but of environmental, social, and ecological 'costs.'"[16] In economics, an externality is a cost or risk entailed in a product or behavior that is not paid by the persons using the product, but instead imposed upon others. Auto insurance and fuel taxes don't come close to covering the external costs that a car driver imposes on the pedestrians, lungs, and other travelers using the roads built for cars, and thus automobility is heavily subsidized by the state. Carbolization emphasizes how cars and automobility create externalities that extend to the entire atmosphere and thus are imposed upon all the earth's living beings. According to the 2014 IPCC report, in 2010 about 14 percent of worldwide carbon emissions come from transport, and in North America the figure exceeds 25 percent. According to a 2006 report from the Environmental Defense Fund, "The United States has 5% of the world's population and 30% of the world's automobiles, but it contributes 45% of the world's automotive CO_2 emissions."[17]

The problem of carbolization and the potential solutions to it are related in a dialectical manner. On the one hand, carbolization is autotelic, self-perpetuating, or path dependent, and therefore difficult to reverse. It is fostered by neoliberal capitalism and its totalizing impulses. On the other hand, the flexible coercion of automobility does inspire some resistance. In the US, in the past quarter century, many large cities have seen a reversal of the white flight and general depopulation of the urban cores that began in the 1950s and 1960s with urban renewal and superhighway construction. A few cities have even begun to dismantle expressways or (more expensive still) bury them in tunnels, so as to reclaim the land devoted to cars, and reconnect neighborhoods separated by highways. Many cities in Western Europe, and more recently in the US and Canada, have developed bike-share systems and built extensive networks of bike lanes. Thus, carbolization eventually produces a desire to limit cars and expressways, to restore or cultivate the communal urban pleasures that cars destroy, and to restrain the enormous CO_2 emissions from cars. Unfortunately, the cumulative effects of carbon pollution upon temperatures and sea levels are likely to overwhelm these nascent efforts to address and reverse carbolization.

China: A Twenty-First-Century Futurama

The pace of growth of automobility and carbolization in China has been astonishing. In the 1980s, the state prohibited private ownership of cars. By 2009, the number of registered cars, buses, vans, and trucks on the roads in China reached sixty-two million (still only about a third of the number in the US), and in the following year, as the US was mired in recession, China became the largest manufacturer and the largest market for new automobiles. In 2009–10, China also became the nation with the largest share of worldwide carbon dioxide emissions. Some estimate that the size of the car and truck fleet there will exceed five hundred million by 2050.[18]

Before the 1949 Communist Revolution, Beijing, then known in English as Peking, built a ring of trolley lines around its historic core, the Forbidden City. After the revolution, Mao Zedong's regime collectivized property, and cars and trucks were not available for ownership by individuals, but the nation needed industrial forms of transport for its enormous population. In 1949 Chairman Mao endorsed the Flying Pigeon bicycle, produced by the Changho Works factory in Tianjin, near Peking, as a national icon, a symbol of the successful Chinese citizen. Into the 1990s, the streets of Peking and other Chinese cities were filled with bicycles, and internal combustion engines were limited for the most part to buses, trucks, trollies, tractors, military vehicles, and trains. Bicycle journalist Dan Koeppel observes: "The Flying Pigeon was the single most popular mechanized vehicle on the planet, becoming so ubiquitous that Deng Xiaoping—the post-Mao leader who launched China's economic reforms in the 1970s—defined prosperity as 'a Pigeon in every household.' "[19] Such prosperity was controlled by the state, and an official license was required to own a Flying Pigeon. Half a billion of these bicycles are still in use in China, but they are increasingly pushed aside by millions of cars that restrict the travel of bicycles and imperil their riders. In Peking, a second ring road was begun in the 1960s, 32.7 kilometers long, and completed in 1992. Individuals began to buy their own cars in the 1990s, and China quickly began a freeway construction frenzy: a sixth Beijing ring road, 187.6 kilometers long, was completed in 2009 and a seventh, more than a thousand kilometers long and connecting with nearby cities Heibei and Tianjin, is under construction now.[20]

The twenty-year promise of Futurama, of transport and energy industries that would transform a nation from a land of rural farmers into a land of power plants, transmission lines, expressways, and skyscrapers, was fully realized in China between roughly 1990 and 2010. The seven ring roads of Beijing are evocative of the nationwide statistics that from 2000 to 2006 the miles of express highways in China more than tripled, and the number of cars more than quadrupled. Yet even then China had fewer than four cars per one hundred people, whereas the US had eighty. If it ever reaches the same rate of car ownership as in the US, China alone will have a billion cars.

The fleet of privately owned cars and trucks has also grown quickly during the last forty years in India, Brazil, and many nations in Africa and East Asia. I focus on China not because it is uniquely responsible for carbolization, but because, as a centrally planned economy, it provokes the question of whether, why, and to what degree Chinese leaders sought to emulate the infrastructure of automobility that had been promoted by the Futurama exhibit and built in the United States and elsewhere. With no training as a Sinologist, I cannot hope to answer those questions in detail. Instead, I argue that the momentum of carbolization is driven by desires that Chinese people of all social levels have embraced, just as enthusiastically as people in the US and other regions: the sense that cars bring mobility and mobility brings freedom, the status consciousness of drivers and their urge to display their cars, and the belief in the automobile industry as a nationalist priority and key to economic growth.

Koeppel, in reporting from China in 2006 for a story on the Flying Pigeon bicycle, wrote: "China isn't China. It is America, just after World War II . . . In our culture then—and in China now—the car isn't just transportation. It's the foundation upon which a middle class is built."[21] Peter Hessler, author of several books about China and a correspondent for *The New Yorker*, in 2005 visited the engineers and executives of Chery, one of several Chinese companies that aspired to export its cars, and also interviewed Zhang Chunxian, China's minister of communications, who when asked about the purpose of the new roads, "mentioned Condoleezza Rice's visit to the People's Republic in July, 2004. According to Zhang, Rice told a Chinese official that she had fond memories from her childhood of vacations spent travelling in the family car. 'She said those trips helped her love the United States,' Zhang explained. 'By building expressways, we can boost the auto industry, but that's only a small part of it.' "[22] Popular desires coincided with industrial policy, and Chinese leaders perceived, by studying the industry elsewhere in the world, that auto assembly plants employ large numbers of workers at higher wages than the textile, toy, electronics, and other consumer goods factories that comprised most of China's exports and most of the products sold at Walmart or Target. After the collapse of the Soviet Union, the Czech Republic and Slovakia welcomed the construction of many automotive factories; the latter produces six hundred thousand units a year. In 1994, Chinese economic policy makers declared automobiles a "pillar industry" that would stimulate industrial and economic expansion.[23] They must have seen how the German automobile industry was able to recover after the devastation of WWII, and by the 1970s was selling Mercedes and BMW models at higher prices and higher profits than its competitors. Japanese automakers followed the same formula, and in the late 1980s created new brands—Lexus from Toyota, Acura from Honda, and Infiniti from Nissan—and successfully competed with the German brands for market share in the United States, which was then the world's largest by a wide margin. Korean automakers Hyundai and Kia (which since 2015 have an interlocking ownership structure) are trying to repeat the pattern, and Chinese companies would like to do the same.

The automotive industry is not merely a source of wealth and growth, it is a source of national pride and identity. Just as medium-sized countries often have a national airline, many countries also want to have an auto industry and to export its products. Plans to export a Chinese-brand car to the United States and Canada have been announced several times since 2009, and still have not occurred, but the goal remains a priority for Chinese leaders. Ted Conover, for his book *The Routes of Man,* visited China and joined a week-long road trip with a motoring club in order to document the giddy excitement of Chinese drivers. He also spoke with "leading automotive journalist" Li Anding, who had "a palpable sense of pride" as he drove his car: "It meant China was finally entering the world stage and participating fully in human progress. It had the additional meaning of something long denied that could finally be acquired . . . the right to buy cars . . . Driving is our right." [24]

I review this history of the auto industry in order to show that carbolization is not a consequence of neoliberal or neocolonial capitalism. The seductive appeals of the car and the highway have infected people under many political ideologies, and although the competing interests of motorists, bicyclists, and transit riders have set off a mini culture war in the US and Canada, "It is one of the perversities of the era that, in the political arena, bikes and trolleys are deemed 'liberal,' while cars are 'conservative' even though in real life all political persuasions use these various modes of travel equally." [25]

In China, the privilege of automobility was first promised to the party elite and to the managers of state-owned companies, who notoriously came to flaunt their status in chauffer-driven black Audi sedans. As the number of cars and freeways in the country has grown so quickly, however, the privilege of the Audi sedan has become less valuable, and the rich elites have sent their children abroad to be educated in the US or Australia, where they can buy Audis and BMWs at much lower prices than in China, and drive them faster on less crowded highways. [26] The current Chinese dictator Xi Jinping, as part of his faux-populist anticorruption campaigns, has discouraged the spread of black Audis among the apparatchiks, and yet the elite have guarded the status of their imported cars, in part by imposing tariffs and policies making it harder for others to buy prestige import cars. Most recently, we see China imposing daily driving bans, limiting traffic to cars with certain license plate numbers, and slapping tariffs on replacement parts for imported brands. [27] These efforts have had little success at reducing traffic congestion, for Chinese drivers use creative means to defy them.

Leftist social theorists have diagnosed some of the symptoms of carbolization, even as the phenomenon now defies the ideological conclusions they often drew from it. The New Left intellectual André Gorz, a close associate of Herbert Marcuse and Jean-Paul Sartre, observed: "The automobile is the paradoxical example of a luxury object that has been devalued by its own spread." He added: "If everyone can have luxury, no one gets any advantages from it. On the contrary, everyone diddles, cheats, and frustrates everyone else, and is diddled, cheated, and frustrated in return."[28] Whereas many American ideologues since Henry Ford have promoted the idea that the car is an engine of democracy, even of egalitarian virtues, Gorz called the bluff by pointing out: first, that ubiquity of car ownership creates such congestion and pollution that motorists no longer enjoy the mobility they felt they were promised; and second, that class distinction was the ideology of the car from the start. Once working people dutifully bought cars, "They had been promised a bourgeois privilege, they had gone into debt to acquire it, and now they saw that everyone else could also get one. What good is a privilege if everyone can have it?"[29]

Gorz in 1973 did not perceive the problem of CO_2 emissions, but his Marxist theory of automobility nonetheless foretold the quandaries of carbolization. The dream of Futurama promised fast cars, cheap gasoline, and superhighways for bourgeois Americans, but when the dream spread to the rest of the world, the promise was betrayed, because the externalities of automobility—congestion, pollution, the waste of resources, and now greenhouse gas emissions—came to affect the entire globe. As Gorz observed, the transportation advantage afforded by a bicycle, unlike a car, continues to benefit the consumer even if bicycles are available to everyone.

In the United States and Europe, the bicycle began as a luxury product in the 1880s and created a fad among sporting and leisure classes. Many of the engineering and manufacturing techniques developed for bicycles, "lightweight steel tubing, wire spokes, chain and shaft drives, drop forging, adjustable ball bearings and roller bearings, the free-wheel clutch, differential and variable gears, single tube pneumatic tires, reliable brakes, acetylene lamps and dynamos for electric lights," were carried over to the automobile industry within twenty years.[30] And ironically, the lobbying campaigns of bicyclists or "wheelmen" for improved roads on which to ride their machines created conditions that helped nurture the market for cars. A century later, only a few avid cycling history enthusiasts are familiar with this history, and only a few cities have adopted policies and traffic designs that encourage citizens to eschew cars and travel by bicycle instead. Where this has occurred, however, it is evidence of the dialectical nature of carbolization, which pushes automobility to such extremes that those suffering its ills seek to resist it.

Again, it is in China, with its own distinct history of bicycling, that this dialectic becomes most visible today. Two reports from the New York Times serve to document the evolution. On December 6, 2002, correspondent Joseph Kahn reported:

China has spent billions of dollars to convert Shanghai's European-style warren of row houses and winding lanes into a Jetsonian vision of modernity. Elevated expressways now weave through a forest of glass and metal. Arching suspension bridges and their on-ramps spiral over the Art Deco facades of colonial-era waterfront banks . . .

The city has so far banned bicycles on 54 major roads and made no provision for people to ride or carry bikes across the Huangpu River to Pudong, the city's new financial and industrial center . . .

Big round signs showing a bike with a red slash through the middle warn riders away from many intersections. Traffic police dole out five-yuan fines (60 cents) to violators.[31]

At that time, the Chinese authorities considered bicycles to be backward and unbefitting a major global financial center. But thirteen years later, pollution and congestion in China had already reached crisis proportions, prompting an effort to restore the role of bicycles:

Today, only 12 percent of commuters in Beijing pedal to work, compared with 38 percent in 2000, according to government data . . .

But now, facing concerns about pollution, Beijing worries that too many people have abandoned the bicycle, and it hopes to reverse course . . .

China's capital, often choked by motorized vehicles, is eager to encourage more commuters to return to two wheels. It wants to increase the proportion of commuters who use bikes to 18 percent by 2020, according to city transportation officials.[32]

Carbolization, Emissions, and Regulations

How or why did drivers not predict carbolization, not foresee the dangers of their dependence upon automobility? This section examines how the regulation of automobile emissions and efficiency have succeeded at mitigating air pollution in most cities of North America and Europe, but failed to stanch the growth of carbolization. Auto tailpipe emission standards began in the 1960s in the United States, but the problem of pollution was perceived much earlier. Even around 1900, when the automobile was a novelty luxury product purchased by the rich for conspicuous consumption, the externalities of auto emissions were already an issue. At first, tailpipe emissions were perceived as a "smoke" problem akin to the smokestacks of factories and coal-fired boilers.

Even amidst the smog crisis in the Los Angeles basin in the 1940s and 1950s, local authorities were reluctant to accept the finding that cars, not factories, were the major source of smog. As historian Tom McCarthy describes it: "The last thing Southern California wanted to hear was that using automobiles caused the problem. Many people never accepted this explanation. Faced with changing their behavior—by driving less—or installing emission control technology on their cars to deal with the chemical causes of smog, Southern Californians turned their eyes toward Detroit."[33]

The response to smog in Los Angeles, which first reached crisis levels in 1943, can also be explained in part by Futurama. In Bel Geddes' *Magic Motorways*, the car was celebrated as a pastoral tool, as a way to move residential neighborhoods away from the smoke and grime of urban industry (and, though this was often left unstated, away from poor immigrants and people of color). This is why many of the earliest superhighways in New York and Los Angeles were and are called "parkways." Hence, many drivers were incredulous when told that the car was the cause of Los Angeles' air pollution. However, California scientists like CalTech chemist Arie J. Haagen-Smit, and politicians, including Kenneth Hahn, began a long struggle with auto manufacturers, who at first resisted emissions limits out of a political principle, then responded with engineering innovations that enabled them to meet ever more stringent regulations. California instituted emissions controls in 1964, inspired by evidence that General Motors had conspired with Chrysler and Ford to deliberately withhold installing positive crankcase ventilation or PCV valves on its cars. Emissions control measures, including catalytic converters, PCV valves, and reformulated no-lead gasoline have been a great success, notwithstanding cheating as with the Volkswagen diesel emissions scandal that came to light in 2015. The exhaust stream from a modern car engine is sometimes cleaner than the ambient air in polluted cities. And because politicians have been able to impose mandates on car manufacturers to build cleaner burning engines, these changes remain virtually invisible to the driver, who continues to cruise the path-dependent lanes of automobility.

In the United States, automobile emission controls, safety features, and fuel economy have all been regulated through legal mandates imposed upon the design and technologies of the cars, and although the auto industry has generally resisted the implementation of these regulations, it eventually has complied, and in many cases has later admitted that the federal regulatory regime benefitted the industry in its public relations and in competing with European and Japanese competitors (who have been forced to respond to regulators in those markets).

Carbon dioxide emissions, however, are an inevitable by-product of combustion and cannot be reduced with devices like a catalytic converter. The
Environmental Defense Fund estimates that the CO_2 directly released from a car
motor amounts to 19.4 pounds per gallon of gasoline.[34] Thus carbon dioxide as a
major greenhouse gas has shifted the ground rules of emissions control on cars.
The existing regulations were designed to address the health danger to people
in the immediate area who breathed the unburned volatile organic compounds,
particulates, ozone, and oxides of nitrogen that made up the catchall term smog.
They succeeded because engineers found means to modify the cars that clog the
largest cities and the most problematic regions for smog, such as the Los Angeles
basin. But the public health threats of smog are now disconnected from the
global effects of climate change. Any and all burning of fossil fuels contributes
to greenhouse gas emissions, and only by reducing the amount of hydrocarbon
fuels burned by cars can regulators address the threat of global warming.

Unfortunately, the fuel efficiency of cars has failed to match the rapid improvements in pollution controls since the 1970s. The Model T Ford, which
comprised a third of the cars on the road in the US in 1913, weighed just 1,200
pounds and was powered by a 20-horsepower engine that averaged 28.5 mpg.
The Model T's exhaust was highly toxic. But as a contributor to carbon dioxide
emissions, it was less offensive than the average car on US roads today, which
weighs about three times as much, has an engine many times more powerful,
and, therefore, is a less efficient consumer of hydrocarbon fuels in spite of all
the engineering advances of the past century. In 2004, average miles per gallon
was 24.7 for all US cars, and in 1973 it was 11.3.

The regime that regulates vehicle efficiency is called the Corporate Average
Fuel Economy or CAFE, instituted in the United States by the Energy Policy
and Conservation Act, signed by President Richard Nixon in December 1975.
Like the emissions regulations instituted a decade earlier, the laws have
avoided forcing any mandates on consumers or drivers of cars, but instead
relied on automakers to develop engineering solutions. Burning hydrocarbons
is essential to the internal combustion engine automobile, gasoline prices have
remained near the levels they were in the age of the Model T, and consumers have not chosen to buy cars that are smaller, lighter, and more efficient.
What's more, the CAFE regulations have developed loopholes that allow manufacturers to manipulate their average. Regulators in the United States created
a special category for light trucks, which need to meet a CAFE standard of just
21.5 mpg. Automakers responded by designing more and more cars, including
Sport Utility Vehicles, to fit the "light truck" category, and by successfully marketing SUVs to buyers who have no need for a 4WD off-road machine.

The CAFE law is a potentially effective framework, and could be amended and improved to address the problem of carbolization. In 2015, regulations issued by the Obama administration set a new goal of 54.5 mpg for the CAFE by 2025, but in 2017 the Trump administration announced plans to lift these regulations. And even if the previous CAFE standards remain in force, hybrid and electric vehicles, the best hope for urgent and drastic reductions in CO_2 emissions from cars, earn credits under the law which allow manufacturers to calculate this small share of vehicles as far more efficient than they really are, offsetting many of the trucks and SUVs that earn the highest profits. Thus, we see in today's new car market that nearly every automaker offers at least a few electric and hybrid models, of which they intend to sell only a very small number, enough to meet their CAFE target. *Green Car Reports*, quoting Ward's Auto News, reported a total of 1.2 billion cars in 2014, and estimated that carbon emissions of this fleet would have to be cut by 80 percent to stabilize global CO_2 levels.[35]

A consequence of this focus on regulating the machine, not the addictive behavior or the infrastructure that sustains dependence on the privately owned car, is that most drivers continue to expect technological solutions to pollution externalities, and do not expect to have to change their transportation habits. Drivers are rarely forced, or even encouraged, to change their driving behavior in order to meet clean air or carbon emissions goals. They may be invited to drive clean-burning cars, or to pay more for fuel, but rarely are they forced to leave the car behind and use a different mode of transport. Even in authoritarian states like China, efforts to limit driving, such as by rationing road space through calendar day driving bans and license plate registration lotteries, have a mixed record, largely because those in power have mixed motives. The elites want cars and want to display their power through their cars, and yet they share many of the externalities of congestion and pollution, and of road collisions.

So what is needed to counter the threat of carbolization? The effects of Futurama need to be reversed; the notion of the driver, or car-driver hybrid, as the prototypical subject of modernity, must be abandoned, and the ambulatory human re-enfranchised.

A 2012 study recruited 1,136 US adults to wear pedometers and found that on average they walked 5,117 steps per day, about half the distance recorded in studies on residents of Australia and Switzerland. Moreover, from 1980 to 2012 the share of US workers who commuted by walking fell from 5.6 percent to 2.8 percent, while the share using bicycles held steady at 0.6 percent.[36] Muscle-powered transportation—walking, bicycling, skateboarding, or scootering—needs to be at the center of any plan to address carbolization, for two reasons: First, because pedestrian travel and lively street life is the key to improving liveability, not only of the megacities where more and more people in all parts of the world will live in the twenty-first century, but in small towns as well. Neighborhoods with pedestrians are safer, and humans who walk more are healthier. Second, because any public transit system can succeed in reducing congestion and pollution only if its users are ready and able to walk to and from the nearest station or stop. This is what transport planners call the "last mile problem." It can be addressed by making walking habitual again, and by encouraging the use of small and efficient "last mile vehicles" including bicycles or electric scooters.

Even Futurama's modernist cities did not entirely ignore pedestrians, after all. The diorama included bridges and sidewalks elevated above street level, in order to increase the lanes of traffic and prevent the dangers of walking across streets. As E. L. Doctorow's young narrator of his autobiographical novel reported of his visit to Futurama: "In the cities of the future, pedestrian bridges connected the buildings and highways were sunken on tracks below them. No one would get run over in this futuristic world."[37] But the model failed to convey how future pedestrians would enjoy walking above the noisy polluting cars, and this aspect of Bel Geddes' design has also proven unsuccessful (see fig. 4.2).

If planners place the ambulatory human at the core of their work, it will also lead to more efficient transport at all levels. The most seductive futurist dream of the moment is the autonomous vehicle, which monopolistic corporations, including Apple, Google, and Uber are promoting as a magic solution to urban congestion and pollution problems. The fantasy is particularly seductive to a generation of consumers habituated to ordering up all manner of goods and services on their smart phones. If an autonomous Uber taxi can be summoned to the curb and deliver a passenger anywhere in the city, then walking even as far as the nearest bus stop seems obsolete. Indeed, there is ample evidence that bus ridership is declining in cities where ride-hailing services are most prevalent. And these same cities, led by New York City and San Francisco, have seen congestion not improve but worsen. Whereas urban drivers of their own cars had been encouraged to use public transit or muscle-powered movement due to the shortage of parking spaces, the ride-hailing services now place stress upon use of a space that cannot easily recoup payment: the curbside from which every ride-hail passenger expects to be picked up and dropped off. The specter of idling, circling, polluting autonomous limousines haunts the world's richest cities.

Fig. 4.2. View of GM auditorium and elevated walkways over cars. (The General Motors Auditorium at Futurama, 1939. Photo by Richard Garrison. Wikimedia Commons, https://commons.wikimedia.org/wiki/File:Street_intersection_Futurama.jpg)

Conclusion

Carbolization is a major threat to our planet, as automobility is spreading faster than ever, and the number of cars is forecast to rise from 1.2 billion to 2 billion within the next twenty years. The worst effects of congestion and pollution will be felt in the megacities of the developing world. Sao Paolo, Jakarta, Lagos, and Beijing already know these problems, and many other cities will soon experience them. Because the threat of a warming climate is global, and that of rising sea levels affects the coasts where many of these cities are located, many nonurban dwellers among the more than six hundred million humans who live below thirty feet above sea level will also feel indirect consequences by 2050.[38] One source of hope is that the outsized political power of the largest, most polluted cities will likely drive the regulatory environment in the next several decades. Residents there may see the futility of a car monoculture, and the lowering costs of battery powered vehicles may lead to the development of electric bikes, scooters, and cars that can inspire a new futuristic vision for a cleaner, more human urban design.

NOTES

1. Paul Mason Fotsch, "The Building of a Superhighway Future at the New York World's Fair," *Cultural Critique* 48, no. 1 (2001): 65, 84.
2. E. L. Doctorow, *World's Fair* (New York: Random House, 1985), 253.
3. David Gelernter, *1939: The Lost World of the Fair* (New York: Free Press, 1995).
4. Daniel Sperling and Deborah Gordon, *Two Billion Cars: Driving toward Sustainability* (Oxford: Oxford University Press, 2009), 113.
5. Fotsch, "The Building of a Superhighway," 83.
6. Tom McCarthy, *Auto Mania: Cars, Consumers, and the Environment* (New Haven: Yale University Press, 2007), 92; James M. Rubenstein, *Making and Selling Cars: Innovation and Change in the U.S. Automotive Industry* (Baltimore: Johns Hopkins University Press, 2001), 209.
7. Among the many studies of the concept of automobility, I recommend Michael Featherstone, Nigel Thrift, and John Urry, eds., *Automobilities* (London: SAGE, 2005); Jörg Beckmann, "Automobility—A Social Problem and Theoretical Concept," *Environment and Planning D: Society and Space* 19 (2001): 593–607; John Urry, "The 'System' of Automobility," *Theory, Culture & Society* 21 (2004): 25–39.
8. Norman Bel Geddes, *Magic Motorways* (New York: Random House, 1940), 48, 56.
9. John Urry, "Inhabiting the Car," *Sociological Review* 54 (2006): 19, 20.
10. Fotsch, "The Building of a Superhighway," 90–91.
11. Catherine Lutz and Anne Lutz Fernandez, *Carjacked: The Culture of the Automobile and Its Effect on Our Lives* (New York: Palgrave Macmillan, 2010), 4.
12. Sperling and Gordon, *Two Billion Cars*, 13–14. Sperling and Gordon add: "Even in places where fuel is costly, transit service outstanding, and population density high—as in much of Europe—cars account for 80 percent of travel." They call this the "Gas-Guzzler Monoculture," a useful analogy to industrialized agriculture and foodways.
13. *To New Horizons*, (General Motors, 1940), film, 23:00, https://www.youtube.com /watch?v=aIu6DTbYnog.
14. The classic study is Jane Jacobs, *The Death and Life of Great American Cities* (New York: Random House), 1961. For more recent studies, see Dolores Hayden, *Building Suburbia, Green Fields and Urban Growth, 1820–2000* (New York: Pantheon Books, 2003), 162–175; and Mary E. Triece, *Urban Renewal and Resistance: Race, Space, and Resistance in the Late Twentieth to the Early Twenty-First Century* (Lanham, MD: Lexington Books, 2016).
15. Richard C. Porter, *Economics at the Wheel: The Costs of Cars and Drivers* (San Diego: Academic Press, 1999), 3.

16. Daniel Miller, *Car Cultures* (Oxford: Berg, 2001), 14.
17. Ralph Sims et al., "Transport," in *Climate Change 2014: Mitigation of Climate Change, Contribution of Working Group III to the Fifth Assessment Report of the Intergovernmental Panel on Climate Change 2014,* 608, https://www.ipcc.ch/report/ar5/wg3/; John DeCicco and Freda Fung, *Global Warming on the Road: The Climate Impact of America's Automobiles* (New York: Environmental Defense, 2006), iv, https://www.edf.org/sites/default /files/5301_Globalwarmingontheroad_0.pdf.
18. Sperling and Gordon, *Two Billion Cars,* 205–216.
19. Dan Koeppel, "Flight of the Pigeon," *Bicycling* (January/February 2007), 60–67.
20. "Put a Ring on It," *South China Morning Post,* International Edition, August 12, 2014.
21. Koeppel, "Flight of the Pigeon," 65. For more about Koeppel and other bicycling activists in Sao Paolo and Los Angeles see the film *Bikes vs. Cars* (2015), directed by Swedish documentarian Fredrik Gertten.
22. Peter Hessler, "An Upstart Automaker Targets the American Market," *The New Yorker* September 26, 2005, https://www.newyorker.com/magazine/2005/09/26/car-town.
23. Sperling and Gordon, *Two Billion Cars,* 212.
24. Ted Conover, *The Routes of Man: How Roads are Changing the World and the Way We Live Today* (New York: Vintage, 2010), 229.
25. Edward Humes, *Door to Door: The Magnificent, Maddening, Mysterious World of Transportation* (New York: Harper Collins, 2016), 254.
26. The trend has been highly visible in my hometown of Eugene, Oregon, around the campus of the University of Oregon. See Diane Dietz, "Bringing the Bling: College Students are flocking from China, many of them wealthy," *The Register Guard,* Eugene, Oregon, February 24, 2014.
27. Owen Guo, "Want to Drive in Beijing? Good Luck in License Plate Lottery." *The New York Times,* July 28, 2016.
28. André Gorz, "l'Idéologie sociale de la bagnole," *Le Sauvage,* September/October 1973, trans. by Patsy Vigderman and Jonathan Cloud as "The Social Ideology of the Motorcar" in *Ecology as Politics* (Boston: South End Press, 1980), 69–71. André Gorz was the *nom de plume* of the Austrian-born Gerhart Hirsch, 1923–2007: "L'automobile offre l'exemple d'un objet de luxe qui a été dévalorisé par sa propre diffusion. . . . si tout le monde accède au luxe, plus personne n'en tire d'avantages; au contraire: tout le monde roule, frustre et dépossède les autres et est roulé, frustré et dépossédé par eux."
29. Gorz, "The Social Ideology of the Motorcar," 72: "On leur avait promis un privilège de bourgeois; ils s'étaient endetté pour y avoir accès et voici qu'il s'apercevaient que tout le monde y accédait en même temps. Mais qu'est-ce qu'un privilège si tout le monde y accède?"
30. Pryor Dodge, *The Bicycle* (Paris: Flammarion, 1996), 152.
31. Joseph Kahn, "Shanghai Journal: Today's China, in a Rush, Has No Time for Bikes," *The New York Times,* September 6, 2002.
32. Owen Guo, "Beijing Journal: A City Choking on Cars Hopes Commuters Will Return to Two Wheels," *The New York Times,* November 11, 2015.
33. McCarthy, *Auto Mania,* 122. See also James Flink, *The Automobile Age* (Cambridge, MA: MIT Press, 1990), 384–390.
34. Many respond to this fact by asking how the carbon dioxide emissions can weigh more than the gasoline itself, at six to seven pounds per gallon: "The answer is, when gasoline is burned, the carbon in it (which has an atomic weight of 12) is combined with two atoms of oxygen (which each have an atomic weight of 16) to form CO_2 (which has a molecular weight of 44). After adjusting for the hydrogen in the fuel (which gets combusted into water), the CO_2 released when gasoline is burned weighs about 3.14 times as much as the gasoline itself" (DeCicco and Fung, *Global Warming on the Road,* 2006, p. 27 n. 12).

35. John Voelcker, "1.2 Billion Vehicles on World's Roads Now, 2 Billion By 2035: Report" *Green Car Reports*, greencarreports.com, July 29, 2014.

36. Brian McKenzie, *Modes Less Traveled—Bicycling and Walking to Work in the United States: 2008–2012* (American Community Survey Reports, U.S. Census Bureau, May 2014), quoted in Edward Humes, *Door to Door*, 302.

37. Doctorow, *World's Fair*, 252.

38. Gordon McGranahan, Deborah Balk, and Bridget Anderson, "The Rising Tide: Assessing the Risks of Climate Change and Human Settlements in Low Elevation Coastal Zones," *Environment & Urbanization* 19, no. 1 (2007): 17–38.

CHAPTER 5

Hydrocarbon Enslavement and Fantasies of Freedom

Patrick D. Murphy

Transportation's contributions to anthropogenic climate change cannot be measured at the tailpipe alone. All too frequently discussions appear touting electric vehicles, for example, as a solution to the unsustainability and destructive effects of private vehicular transportation. Yet, the switch to electric cars and trucks over the next few decades will do little to reduce the carbon wedge represented by the 1.2 billion vehicles on the world's roads, a number estimated to rise to at least 2 billion in less than twenty years.[1] The rosiest projections of electric car sales estimate that they will account for only 15 percent of cars on the road by 2040.[2] Why is there not more discussion, instead, of the environmental necessity of eliminating personal vehicles fueled, directly or indirectly, by hydrocarbons as part of the drastic efforts required to avoid a 1.5 degree centigrade planetary warming? A powerful cultural imaginary renders a car-free world almost impossible to imagine much less realize.

Fantasies of freedom abound in popular culture and political ideologies, no more so than in advertising and media portrayals of the automobile. In 2002 United States senators, such as Bond, Lott, and Mikulski, famously opposed raising light vehicle miles-per-gallon requirements on the basis of freedom of choice for "soccer moms" to keep buying minivans.[3] During NFL playoff games in January 2019, Toyota aired a commercial comparing its Tacoma pickup truck to a wild horse breaking free of its corral in order to avoid being domesticated.[4]

Upward mobility and becoming "middle class" in the world has become indistinguishable from the automobile, which serves as the key symbol for demonstrating achievement of that status, a status that allegedly means not simply economic security but freedom of choice on a daily basis in myriad small ways. If middle class is too low for one's aspirations, luxury car commercials, including by Lincoln, Volvo, Lexus, Mercedes, and Cadillac, portray an even more elevated exurban lifestyle..

Thus, powerful cultural forces are at work militating against the abandonment of the individual private mode of transportation, which is a crucial factor in the continued self-destructive human reliance on hydrocarbons. Whether those are consumed in the form of gasoline and diesel fuel or the coal and natural gas that produce the bulk of the world's electricity, our current use trajectory will have us exceeding atmospheric carbon goals and any chance of mitigating global warming. The car has come to be perceived as a vehicle of freedom with this car culture imaginary shaping decisions not only about transportation, but also living spaces, eating habits, and even body weight.

The sacrosanct status of the personal car has become so entrenched that in the Princeton "Stabilization Wedges" proposal elimination of cars is not even considered. There fifteen wedges are introduced with a combination of eight of them needing to be implemented to keep eight billion tons of carbon out of the atmosphere per year between now and 2060. The efficiency proposals for cars only call for reducing their carbon footprint by (1) doubling the fuel efficiency of two billion cars and (2) reducing by half the number of car miles driven.[5] Why allow the number of cars on the road to nearly double? Even should fuel efficiency be doubled for all two billion cars, which is doubtful, fuel consumption would be at the same rate as today with a billion vehicles.

Creating the Car Culture Imaginary

If it did not begin with it, the drive toward the establishment of car culture in the United States certainly accelerated with the development of the automobile assembly line by Henry Ford. In December of 1913, the first Model T rolled off the Ford assembly line ushering in a new era of automobile affordability.[6] Less than a decade later, the United States decennial census indicated that more Americans lived in cities than in rural areas.[7] Urbanization and automobile ownership rapidly expanded hand in hand.

It was Ford's stated goal to build a "motor car for the great multitude" with the goal that "when I'm through about everybody will have one."[8] Indeed, with the price of the Model T falling from $850 to $300 between 1908 and 1925, and a manufacturing worker's wages nearly $1,300 annually, buying a Model T then was equivalent to buying the cheapest cars on the market today. It is no wonder that by the summer of 1924 Ford had produced ten million Model Ts.[9] In 1925 it is estimated that there was approximately one car per every two households in the United States. Today, that figure is totally upended with fewer than 9 percent of households without a car. It is particularly striking that this ratio of ownership went from approximately one car for every three people in 1960 to the one for every two ratio by 2008.[10] In many suburban households, the practice appears to be one vehicle for every family member of driving age. Indeed, Subaru likes to tout the handing down of its cars to teenagers because the parents have purchased a new one.[11]

Back in the 1920s, light trucks were exclusively work vehicles and that notion largely held true into the 1950s, especially since the first crew cab that could actually hold a family did not appear until 1957 when International Harvester debuted one. Even then, it was for "crew" and not for hauling the wife and kids. Indeed, it wasn't until 1983 with Chevrolet's introduction of extended cab models that the family truck became a common sight.[12] The impetus, though, for this shift to trucks as people movers did not arise from a need for mixed-use vehicles, but rather as a means for circumventing the CAFE fuel efficiency standards first enacted in 1975 and which only applied to "cars." Standards for light trucks were not introduced until 1978.[13]

Light trucks are held to less strict fuel economy standards than automobiles. Minivans replaced station wagons because they were initially built on a truck chassis and so were classified as trucks, and similarly with SUVs. For automakers, this cultivation of consumer desire for gas guzzlers was necessitated by the benefits of the bottom line. Small car sales have simply never brought in the revenue to be had by selling luxuriously outfitted pickups and SUVs. While global car companies continue to offer subcompact cars and mini trucks in some markets of the world, they have phased them out or withheld them from sale in the United States.[14]

Rise of the Suburb and Drive-Thru Everything with Supersizing

Christopher Wells in *Car Country* provides a detailed explanation of the rise of suburbia after World War II in the United States.[15] Here I will highlight just a few of his key points and instead focus on an issue that arises after the historical scope of his analysis, which terminates in the late 1950s: the drive-thru everything of American life. With Bluetooth and Wi-Fi readily available, along with fully reclining bucket seats, telecommuters would only need a toilet to live and work entirely in their cars. Products can be delivered, groceries picked up curbside, and, if living in Florida, attend the Daytona Beach drive-in church, or if in Michigan, its Grand Rapids relative.[16]

Visions of the suburb built around an auto-centered infrastructure, according to Wells in Part IV of *Car Country*, were being developed and promoted as early as the 1930s, but their full realization had to wait until after the Korean War. Designs for suburban tracts had already been developed and the necessity to situate workers near newly built, large-scale military materials factories, such as the Joliet Army Ammunition Plant (JAAP) built in 1940, provided experience in slapping up hundreds of identical houses and duplexes for the influx of thousands of civilian employees. The JAAP covered fourteen square miles with over eleven hundred buildings surrounded by small farm towns.[17] In one of these, for example, Wilmington, Illinois, where I grew up, entire neighborhoods were built from scratch, and after World War II the houses were sold off by lottery.

The peacetime prosperity of the 1950s coupled with the rental housing shortage after 1945 provided both a clientele with the money to become homeowners and their need to find adequate living space for their rapidly growing families, those children known today as "baby boomers." Further, converting assembly lines from the manufacturing of military equipment to the production of consumer goods, especially automobiles, necessitated persuading everyone they should own a car and other durable goods.

Buying cars on credit had already been a long established practice by the 1950s, with General Motors' first foray into it in 1919 requiring a 35 percent down payment and a one-year payoff.[18] By 1930, it is estimated that two-thirds of new cars were being bought on credit.[19] Thus, the rise of automobile ownership also contributed to the cultural concept of being perpetually in debt. Credit card companies have created the perverse perspective that being in debt is a form of freedom because people can then buy what they really cannot afford.

From the flop of Ford's 1928 installment purchase plan for Model Ts,[20] much like layaway purchasing at department stores, the pay-as-you-go concept of buying what a person could afford was gradually replaced in American culture by the pay-as-much-as-your-credit-cards-will-allow mentality. As a result, the freedom to practice relentlessly immediate gratification has become a hallmark of car culture. It is the freedom to maintain a drive-thru life mentality dependent on car ownership and hydrocarbon consumption with its attendant release of carbon emissions from millions of cars idling in line to get a latte, make a bank deposit, or drop off dry cleaning.

In the 2018 essay "Cupholders Are Everywhere," Nancy A. Nichols remarks: "Although it might be hard to imagine now, eating and drinking in cars was next to impossible." Starting with her dismay that the 2019 seven-passenger Subaru Ascent SUV has nineteen cupholders, she reviews the history of this once rare but now ubiquitous accessory. She points out that it did not become fashionable to eat in one's car until the 1950s advent of drive-in restaurants, but even then the car was parked. "Things began to change during the late 1960s and 1970s," Nichols claims, because "the suburbs grew" creating the modern commute with the car "a place in its own right." Nevertheless, cupholders were an add-on item until Chrysler made them standard in a minivan in 1984. The place of the cupholder in the car culture imaginary has become so important, notes Nichols, that in 2007 a survey indicated that its number was more important for choosing a new vehicle than fuel efficiency information.[21] In 2014, McDonald's even aired an ad in which a young man shops for a used car while drinking a McCafé. He glances in at each car negatively shaking his head until he finds one that has a cupholder just the right size for his disposable coffee cup and says "perfect."[22]

Eating in the car went from the convenience of remaining in one's seat while food was served by a carhop to eating while struggling through the morning commute. Eating and drinking while riding in a car has become so important to people that the Tesla S was roundly criticized for lacking rear cupholders.[23] Driving, eating, and drinking have ceased to be separate activities but have become a fusion of continuous consumption of food and hydrocarbon. According to Jacqueline Botterill's research, "over 80 percent of North Americans regularly eat in the car."[24]

But the universal necessity of owning a car for eating junk food while driving was not the only outgrowth of expanded car sales in the 1950s and the development of various service industries to support car culture. The rise of the drive-in theater was another form of this drive-thru car culture. As with the visions for suburbia, the first drive-in theatre opened in 1933. By 1958 the number of such theaters had peaked at a little over four thousand.[25] Of course, today many vehicles, especially minivans, come with their own TV screens. As with eating, then, one need not stop the car to view a movie now.

Interestingly enough, Richard Hollingshead developed his idea for such a theater as a result of his mother being morbidly obese and unable to fit into a theater seat.[26] While it might be fortuitous that his mother's weight problem led to his invention, the expansion of obesity is not a mere correlation with the rise of car culture, but part of a feedback loop. As Americans shifted their employment increasingly from agriculture and other forms of manual labor to sedentary desk jobs, they also decreased the amount of walking they did on a daily basis and their use of public transportation. Precisely when postindustrial labor became less and less physically demanding, so too did drive-thru purchasing and car commuting reduce the amount of exercise people obtained through normal daily activity.

Car culture, then, produces not only dangerous levels of CO_2 emissions, exacerbating global warming, but also dangerous levels of body weight, not only in the United States but anywhere else that it takes hold. China is a case in point. Although private ownership of cars was not encouraged until 1994, the number of cars on the road in China has risen from fewer than twelve million in 2007 to two hundred million by 2017, a nearly eighteen-fold increase, producing ten of the world's twenty-five most congested cities.[27] At the same time, the rise in obesity in China has paralleled this stunningly rapid embrace of car culture. As a 2006 epidemiology study out of the Chinese Academy of Medical Sciences noted, "Coinciding with China's continuing modernisation are reductions in physical activity and labour intensity in both urban and rural areas. People are expending less energy on traditional forms of transportation, such as walking and cycling."[28] The study points to car ownership as the key factor in this change.

As of 2018, China had the largest number of obese children in the world, and two major contributing factors are the rise in the consumption of western-style junk food and a drastic decrease in the number of children who walk or bicycle to school.[29] Worldwide, car culture along with "the increasingly sedentary lifestyle created by the computer and other innovation is requiring escalating expenditure in the health care system and in the health and fitness industry to compensate for lifestyles that are incompatible with human biology."[30]

The recent Lancet Commission Report, "The Global Syndemic of Obesity, Undernutrition, and Climate Change," explains that the three key terms of the report's title "constitute a syndemic, or synergy of epidemics, because they co-occur in time and place, interact with each other to produce complex sequelae, and share common underlying societal drivers."[31] The report states unequivocally that car culture is a disaster for both the environment and individual health and well-being:

> Car use has been associated with an increased risk of obesity, and changes in commuting from cars to active or public transportation have been associated with reductions in BMI. Furthermore, reduction in carbon dioxide emissions through reduced motor vehicle use and increased active travel (e.g., bicycling or walking) exceeds the reduction in greenhouse-gas emissions that could be expected from increased use of lower emission motor vehicles. Transportation systems and community designs that support active transportation, reduced car use, and access to healthful foods are triple-duty actions for The Global Syndemic.[32]

There is an additional negative feedback loop at work in terms of increased carbon emissions. More time commuting and driving in general[33] has led to a higher intake of fast food, with a significant portion of ingredients being beef and dairy products. Cattle, being ruminants, are a major source of methane gas.[34] Thus, the diet of a car culture that seeks convenience foods that can be eaten "on the go" further contributes to global warming by sitting in traffic scarfing up a quarter pounder after having idled for an indefinite period of time placing an order and then waiting for it to be popped out the drive-thru window.

Many environmental planners call for reducing the car-centered suburbs and building up people-centered urban areas to address both climate change and the transition to a post-carbon socioeconomic system. In *Urban Ecologies*, Christopher Schliephake comments on Edward Glaeser's *The Triumph of the City* that it "strikes a more optimistic tone that is shared by other ecologists and environmentalists who hold that cities are more sustainable when they are more dense and tightly packed, relying on public transportation instead of excessive car driving and less energy consumption due to the urban climate."[35] Similarly, Jorgen Randers writes in *2052*:

> The trend toward more urbanization will be strengthened by climate change in two ways. First, per capita greenhouse gas emissions are lower for megacity dwellers than for people living in the periphery, because of the reduced need for personal travel. The climate cost of shipping huge quantities of food and water to the city is lower than the climate cost of long commutes from rural homes to city work. Second, it is cheaper (per person) to defend one megacity against the vagaries of extreme weather than to protect many individual settlements spread throughout the countryside.[36]

The Role of Cinema and Television in the Promotion of Car Culture and Its Attendant Hydrocarbon Enslavement

The consolidation of any dominant cultural imaginary requires a significant role to be played by the entertainment industry and the literary arts. While literature predates the rise of car culture by thousands of years, the film industry and the auto industry developed simultaneously in the 1890s. It is no wonder, then, that cars have figured prominently in motion pictures ever since the first car chase appeared in the 1903 silent film *Runaway Match*.[37] In that film the romantic couple successfully elopes when the car of the pursuing father of the bride breaks down as he chases after them. And while numerous movies with car chases do have the hero as a police officer, spy, or secret agent, they also frequently portray positively a criminal, bad boy, or rebel.

A key component of the allure of the automobile, then, is this underlying element of rebelliousness, of rule breaking, of wielding technology in defiance of the established order. This notion is perhaps best exemplified by the commercial Isuzu ran during the 1992 Olympics in which a child is being told by a teacher to "stay within the lines" when coloring, but she does not. The ad then cuts to the girl as a young woman driving her bright orange Rodeo, the same color as her hair, off road in a rapturous frenzy.[38]

Bootleggers as heroes, for example, have been a common feature of films that include car chases, such as the 1958 *Thunder Road*, starring Robert Mitchum, or the 1977 *Smokey and the Bandit*, starring Burt Reynolds.[39] Such lawbreakers are often perceived as scofflaws rather than outlaws. Yet, outright criminals, especially if they are seeking revenge or carrying out a vendetta, are also portrayed as heroes, such as the car thieves in *Gone in 60 Seconds* and *The Italian Job*, or a getaway driver as in *The Transporter* (2002) or the eponymous *Baby Driver*.[40] Although often the gangsters of film in the 1930s and 1940s ended up dead or imprisoned at the end of their films, such as James Cagney in *White Heat* (1949),[41] they nevertheless are cheered on through much of the movie as they elude law enforcement's best efforts to rein them in. The bad boy hero is perhaps no better exemplified than Danny Zuko played by John Travolta in *Grease*, who wins his car race in the LA river against a cheating low life and, of course, wins the heart of the onlooking love interest, played by Olivia Newton John. The popularity of the fast-driving hero (or antihero) has led to an entire franchise built around the macho, muscle-car driving heroes of *Fast and Furious*.[42]

While the representations of cars are crucial to the inculcation of a car culture mentality, how the alleged benefits of car ownership are portrayed in entertainment media is just as critical. Key among all such benefits is the rise of the suburb. Indeed, in "How TV Predicted America's Moves from City to 'Burbs and Back Again,'" authors Christopher and Lisa Leinberger take up this very issue. They argue that in the late 1940s and early 1950s, TV sitcoms tended to use the "walkable urban" as a primary setting, citing *The Honeymooners*, which aired from 1951–57, as their prime example.[43] The classic Christmas film, *It's a Wonderful Life*, is set in a small town, but with the same "walkable urban" emphasis as a bigger city.[44] The foreshadowing of the rise of suburbia, though, appears in the film in the form of Mr. Bailey's planned affordable housing development, which is intended to draw people from the squalid rentals owned by the film's antagonist.

In television sitcoms, the move to the suburbs as a more desirable place to live was well underway a decade after Bailey celebrated family, friends, and community. *I Love Lucy* may represent the most significant reflector and promoter of this shift when in its sixth season, episode 15, airing in 1957, Lucy decides the family should buy a house in Connecticut and become a suburban family.[45] Other shows of the time were set in the suburbs from the start, such as *The Adventures of Ozzie and Harriet* (1952–66) and *Leave It to Beaver* (1957–63).[46] *The Dick Van Dyke Show* (1961–66) used New Rochelle as its setting, a commuter community connected to New York City by rail.[47] Except for three episodes of its entire run, the show was shot before a live studio audience. As a result, Rob's commute was never included in the series. The most perilous part of his daily grind seemed to be the challenge of coming home each day without tripping over the living room ottoman. Housewife Laura had the car at her disposal and, as a result, a 1964 episode is able to be built around the challenge of Laura informing Rob that the car he adores, although rarely drives, has been scratched while parked somewhere.[48]

None of these shows portray the need to eat in one's car because of long commute times or traffic jams, but they do identify the pleasures of food with car ownership through the idyllic treatment of the drive-in restaurant. Even the futuristic cartoon series *The Jetsons* (1962–63) presumed that the drive-in would survive into the age of living off-world as represented by "The Spaceburger Drive-in."[49] Although there were some drive-up food stands on rural roadways prior to World War II, the contemporary drive-in and drive-thru restaurants are a postwar phenomenon and parallel the rise of the suburb. In-N-Out burgers opened in Baldwin Park, California, in 1948, the same year that McDonald's provides the walk-up window for ordering. Smaller chains appear throughout the 1950s and 1960s, and McDonald's finally establishes the drive-thru window in the mid-1970s.[50] The drive-up grocery pickup lanes that have sprouted up at Walmart, Kroger's, and other grocery chains are the logical outcome of a desire to conduct every form of business without opening a car door.

But more than just good family fun, the drive-in and the car it requires for service have been associated with teenage freedom and rites of passage. There is Arnold's in *Happy Days*, the Frosty Palace in the film *Thunder Road*, and Mel's in *American Graffiti*.[51] The drive-in offered the promise of boys and girls being able to meet without the watchful eyes of their parents. And, if the stars and hormones aligned, then the auto could become a trysting wagon as the nubile youths motored off to lover's lane or some other secluded spot.

In *That '70s Show*, the teen stars, for instance, get caught having sex in the back of the family station wagon in one episode.[52] *The Blob,* with Steve McQueen in his first starring role, opens with him kissing his love interest while sitting in his convertible out in the countryside, which enables them to see the alien come crashing to earth.[53] Sexual activity in cars is featured in films from major motion pictures, like *Titanic,* to politically themed films, such as *Gattaca,* to low budget road trips, such as *Dirty Girl.*[54] Movies are so replete with car sex scenes that websites rate the best ones and various surveys have been conducted about car sex. "Smooching in Sedans: Exploring How Often Americans Hook Up in a Vehicle" appears on the website driving-tests. org. It provides data from a survey of a thousand people across three generations, concluding that approximately 84 percent of respondents engaged in some kind of sexual activity in a car, including oral sex and intercourse.[55] *Cosmopolitan* magazine, of course, has over the years published how-to articles on car sex. Such activity reflects, among other aspects, the tendency in car culture toward the impulsive behavior of immediate gratification and the illusion that the automobile is both a personal space, rather than a public location, and a safe place, despite the obvious correlation between reckless types of driving, such as driving under the influence, excessive speeding, and street racing, with high traffic-related death rates.

The automobile is inaccurately portrayed as a relatively safe haven for drivers in comparison to public transportation in the media, and perceived as such by drivers. These representations promote the fantasy that driving gives people control over their destinies and their safety, allaying the anxiety and fears that come with someone else being at the helm of any other form of transport. Thus, while film and television series have gradually turned a critical lens on suburban life as not the idyll Lucy or Rob believed it be, they nevertheless have continued to present driving, whether as commute or escape, as a better alternative than urban living reliant on public transportation.

Many tourists visiting New York and other cities with rapid transit avoid riding the subway due to fear of bodily harm. That same attitude, however, does not seem to apply when traveling abroad, particularly in Europe or Japan, where Americans are seen relying extensively on trains, light rail, and subways to get around London, Paris, Amsterdam, or Berlin. This fear arises from exaggerated representations of American public transit violence in films and television shows.

Entertainment media highlight subway violence out of proportion to its actual occurrence, such as the murder of Ally's mother in *Remember Me,* a film set just prior to 9/11 in New York, or the rape of the young woman in the recent Keanu Reeves movie *Exposed.*[56] Such fear is reflected, for instance, in the attitudes of millennials who prefer ridesharing to public transit because those ridesharing are perceived to be a more homogenous group and, therefore, supposedly less likely to commit violent acts.[57] Also, heightened anxiety is expressed by riders whenever there is a violent subway or light-rail crime, despite their relative rarity.[58]

Statistics, however, do not bear out these fears. Taking public transit of any kind is far less likely to lead to death or injury than commuting by car by several magnitudes.[59] Thus, here the power of the cinematic imaginary to prejudice people against public transit in favor of maintaining the freedom fantasies of car culture is readily on display. In order to maintain this skewed perception, Americans practice what I have labeled elsewhere as DIM: Discrete Incident Mentality.[60] A drunk driver killing a family by hitting them head on, a distracted commuter who has spilled coffee all over his lap T-boning another driver at an intersection, or a deadly multicar pile-up in dense fog are all treated as unlucky events. In contrast, public transportation violence is perceived as endemic and systemic, despite its relatively low frequency of occurrence. Women in the United States, for example, are seven times more likely to be murdered by someone they know than they are by a stranger in any location, and approximately 80 percent of rape victims know the person assaulting them.[61]

Part of this gap in comprehension about driving versus taking the subway comes from the notion that driving is a necessity and so the risks attendant upon it are simply a given of having mobility freedom. Xenophobia also plays a role. People who are different are more likely to be perceived as a threat than people who are the same or similar, even though, again, for female homicide the reverse holds true.

Studies show that any increase in the use of ridesharing services is coming at the expense of public transit ridership rather than reducing car miles driven.[62] Investments of auto companies such as GM and BMW-Daimler in ridesharing platforms have been analyzed as a recognition that in the future there will be fewer individuals owning their own cars and praised as a means for reducing the carbon footprint of motor transport by reducing solo trips and keeping vehicles in service more continuously throughout the day.[63] Such claims ignore that most ridesharing is currently used on the weekends, in the evenings, or one-way destinations, such as airports, and not during rush hour windows when the highest number of cars are on the road, with 76 percent of Americans driving alone to work.[64] Rather, such investment in ridesharing represents a half-measure designed to perpetuate car culture in opposition to government investment in public mass-transit expansion.

The Future as More of the Same or Different

Realist fiction is for the most part of little help in envisioning an alternative to car culture because it must depict the necessity of addressing anthropogenic climate change. As Indian novelist Amitav Ghosh has noted, "fiction that deals with climate change is almost by definition not of the kind that is taken seriously by serious literary journals: the mere mention of the subject is often enough to relegate a novel or a short story to the genre of science fiction."[65] Further, addressing climate change requires challenging a fundamental belief of the cultural imaginary: "Climate change poses a powerful challenge to what is perhaps the single most important political conception of the modern era: the idea of freedom."[66]

As Ghosh notes, science fiction is the one genre that ought to offer opportunities for envisioning an alternative cultural paradigm. Yet here, too, lack of vision tends to overwhelm vision. Too often future cities are overflowing with electric cars, hovercrafts, or some other private passenger vehicle that does nothing to challenge car culture as such. A case in point is Kim Stanley Robinson's *New York 2140*. There, in a partially submerged Manhattan, the wealthy zip around in their private hydrofoils complaining about traffic on the waterways and the challenges of parking in New York, as exemplified by one of the novel's narrators, Franklin, the financial day trader.[67]

Other novels, however, have challenged car culture and offered alternative visions of a climate change, post-hydrocarbon future. The oldest of these is actually Ernest Callenbach's *Ecotopia*, published in 1975, long before much attention was given to climate change.[68] In 1981, Callenbach published the prequel, *Ecotopia Emerging*, that explains the rise of the separatist party and the principles on which its founders based the formation of the ecotopian state, carved out of Northern California and the Pacific Northwest.[69] Before treating these together, though, another novel published just after *Ecotopia* is worthy of consideration. In 1977, popular novelist and journalist Arthur Herzog published *Heat*.[70] The plot of the novel is predicated on abrupt climate change raising global temperatures, with the hero of the novel, a scientific crisis researcher, struggling to get his own governmental organization and American politicians to understand what is happening and to act swiftly and with sufficient magnitude to address the problem. The first half of the novel basically sets up the crisis for readers to bring them up to speed on the climate change research conducted in the 1970s. Most of the rest of the next hundred pages are devoted to initiating responses, including geoengineering. But the most important part of the novel consists of the few pages devoted to social reorganization to limit energy consumption and driving: "Unnecessary driving was forbidden, along with all frivolous consumption of energy. . . . Why not have neighborhood automobiles, cooperatively owned. . . . There should be more emphasis on public than on private property. . . . The public was encouraged to use bicycles."[71] It is clear at novel's end that, although geoengineering in the form of reflective satellites has allayed the immediate crisis, consumer society and car culture will not be making a comeback.

Callenbach espoused similar values in the writing of his two novels, and, indeed, Herzog may have been influenced by *Ecotopia* in writing up the social transformation he depicts at the end of *Heat*. *Ecotopia* follows journalist Will Weston from New York as he visits isolationist Ecotopia nineteen years after its secession from the United States. The narrative consists of Weston's journal entries and his official newspaper posts. Only a few pages in, Weston notes that the taxi bringing him to the border at Lake Tahoe "required a special dispensation to allow an internal combustion engine to pass their sacred portals"; while in San Francisco, Ecotopians rely on "electric taxis, minibuses, and delivery carts" fueled mainly by solar energy, as well as a national electric railway system and a copious number of bicycles to get around.[72] Suburban sprawl has been eliminated. In short, Callenbach envisioned an urban and rural society knit together by solar power transportation and a strong sense of community, sustainability, and personal responsibility, all of which are anathema to car culture as such.

But if climate change was not already a major concern, why the need to abandon car culture and suburbia? Car culture has developed around a machine for which fuel must be found, rather than starting with a renewable source of energy, such as Callenbach's preferred solar power, as the basis for designing a sustainable society. Callenbach makes it clear that though his vision of an ecotopia in the early 1970s was not initiated by concerns over climate change but rather a basic environmental sustainability orientation, by 1981, global warming was front and center, as evidenced by the italicized historical insert that mentions "a 'greenhouse effect.' "[73] Further, peak oil theory appears in another such insert, which concludes: " 'Thus, like a lumbering dinosaur unable to face the fact that the climate had changed, daydreaming of the better pasturage of yesteryear, oil-hungry America lurched toward some unseen economic catastrophe.' "[74]

In *Ecotopia Emerging*, as the new Survivalist Party forms its goals, a key statement becomes "no private cars": "The private automobile system of transportation was the most costly, in energy and dollar terms, that the world had ever seen . . . and no technical fix was going to stop it."[75] Quickly, the party leaders realize: "The decline of the automobile would, in fact, necessitate a wholesale rebuilding of American communities."[76] In a rather humorous conversation, a small group discusses the problem of weaning men, specifically, from their cars because "the car embodies phallic power." Therefore, the group concludes that there will be a need for "car-kicking clinics . . . so they don't need a car's power to feel all right."[77]

Callenbach wrote much of *Ecotopia Emerging* with an eye toward what he sensed would be the antienvironmental attitudes of the Reagan years, which began the same year as the novel was published. As radical as it and *Ecotopia* were, many of the aspects of the two have come to pass in less socially comprehensive forms, such as the rapid expansion of renewable energy. But the question in both novels of whether compromise is possible keeps arising and the Survivalist Party invariably rejects it. Are there half measures that will suffice to limit the impacts of climate change without abandoning car culture and the machines that drive it?

Any Car Remains a Climate Changer

Trailing in the wake of Tesla, automakers around the world from General Motors to the Volkswagen Group to Geely are rushing to develop electric cars and autonomous driving vehicles. Although touted by many organizations, such as the Safe Climate Campaign, some governments, such as the Chinese, and the industry itself as "clean" vehicles that will reduce the impact of personal vehicles on climate change by reducing CO_2 emissions, they will actually not accomplish that goal. Rather, the emphasis on electric cars, SUVs, and light trucks both reflects and reinforces the freedom fantasies that have catapulted the personally owned automobile into its position as the hallmark of middle- and upper-class status. Although they will reduce the obvious air pollution of smog shrouded cities, they will not help avoid the fateful global warming that the IPCC reports and other studies portray as a threshold that the world dare not cross.

A rapid increase in the number of electric light vehicles on the world's roads will necessitate an equally sharp increase in electricity production. There is no evidence to suggest that any significant part of the world currently enjoys excess electricity capacity or that any country is adding capacity sufficient to enable a rapid mandatory transition to electric vehicles. The five largest car markets in the world, accounting for over three-fourths of all light vehicles purchased, are China, the US, India, Germany, and Japan.[78] They also rank first, second, third, fourth, and sixth in terms of coal consumption for electricity generation.[79] Even if all countries, and not just these five, phased out coal-fired power plants by 2050, that would be too little too late in terms of the amount of CO_2 they will be pumping into the atmosphere over the next thirty years.

Ultimately, all of the projections about hydrocarbon emission reductions from increased sales of electric cars only counts as a reduction from what the same number of new gasoline powered cars on the road would produce. Electric cars will form part of the projected doubling of vehicles on the road, not an actual substitution for existing cars. Unless governments mandate the scrapping of cars traded in when a consumer purchases an electric one—a highly unlikely legislative act—those used cars will just be resold to other buyers and the working poor at home or exported to other countries in Asia and Africa. Global used car exports constitute a thriving market in countries such as Uganda, where sixteen-year-old cars are being imported with an expectation they will be driven for another twenty. And in Kenya 99 percent of the cars imported for sale are used ones from Japan and Europe.[80]

Conclusion

Anthropogenic climate change is being propelled by a variety of factors not entirely limited to hydrocarbon consumption, such as methane releases from enormous herds of meat cattle and deforestation for grazing and farming. Nevertheless, the global expansion of American-initiated car culture has increased the role of transportation, particularly that of individually owned cars and light trucks, in the production and release of CO_2 and other greenhouse gases more rapidly than any other identifiable factor. Additionally, the hydrocarbon enslavement specific to private vehicle ownership permeates other aspects of daily life and the generation and maintenance of deleterious cultural values.

A rapid and significant addressing of anthropogenic causes of climate change, therefore, requires a fundamental reconfiguration of American demographics, lifestyle choices, and attitudes toward transportation, and by extension those same aspects of all other countries that have embraced the values and behaviors stemming from an autocentric culture. Not only is there needed a rapid upscaling of the new urbanism that advocates thriving city centers, carfree zones, and walkable neighborhoods, but also a realignment of the spatial relationships between living spaces, commercial locations, and business and manufacturing workplaces. As the permaculture activist David Holmgren has noted, "There is a desperate need to recast energy descent as a positive process that can free people from the strictures and dysfunctions of growth economics and consumer culture."[81]

The car culture imaginary continues to propel people and many institutions to seek solutions that are at best only half measures unlikely to address adequately the severity of global warming and the role of personally owned vehicles in anthropogenically induced climate change. It remains so powerful and becomes more globally powerful as car culture is embraced in one country after another, that many people find the enormous swarm of vehicles in *Minority Report* and the fairy tale of traffic-jam-free roads by means of autonomous vehicles believable.[82] In contrast, few people can envision a sustainable cultural imaginary that, instead of punishing them by taking something away— "they want to take away your cars" warned President Trump in El Paso[83]—will reward people psychologically, socially, health-wise, and economically by enabling them to avoid the worst environmental disasters caused by anthropogenic climate change.

NOTES

1. Daniel Sperling and Deborah Gordon, "Two Billion Cars: Transforming Culture," *TR News* 259 (November/December, 2008), 3–9, https://onlinepubs.trb.org/onlinepubs /trnews/trnews259billioncars.pdf.
2. Matt Egan, "No Peak in Oil Demand Yet, Despite Electric Cars," *CNN Business*, March 11, 2019, https://www.cnn.com/2019/03/11/investing/peak-oil-demand-electric-cars-iea /index.html.
3. David E. Rosenbaum, "Senate Deletes Higher Mileage Standard in Energy Bill," March 14, 2002, *The New York Times*, https://www.nytimes.com/2002/03/14/us/senate-deletes -higher-mileage-standard-in-energy-bill.html.
4. Toyota TV Commercial, "The Untameables," featuring Don Swayze, Ad ID: 1834566, last airing January 11, 2019, https://www.ispot.tv/ad/dTqw/toyota-the-untameables.
5. "Stabilization Wedges," Princeton University Carbon Mitigation Initiative, accessed February 20, 2019, http://cmi.princeton.edu/wedges.
6. History.com Editors, "Ford's Assembly Line Starts Rolling," last modified November 23, 2019, www.history.com/this-day-in-history/fords-assembly-line-starts-rolling.
7. "Urban and Rural Areas," last modified December 17, 2019, www.census.gov/history /www/programs/geography/urban_and_rural_areas.html.
8. For quotes from Henry Ford, see www.thehenryford.org/collections-and-research /digital-resources/popular-topics/henry-ford-quotes.
9. History.com Editors, "Ford's Assembly Line Starts Rolling."
10. Shuling Tang, "History of the Automobile: Ownership per Household in U.S.," last modified September 9, 2016, https://en.wikibooks.org/wiki/Transportation _Deployment_Casebook/History_of_the_Automobile:_Ownership_per_Household _in_U.S. See also, Mary Gormandy White, "Car Ownership Statistics," accessed March 3, 2019, cars.lovetoknow.com/Car_Ownership_Statistics; and, "What percentage of U.S. households own a car?" accessed March 3, 2019, https://www.quora.com/What -percentage-of-U-S-households-own-a-car.
11. 2018 Subaru Forester TV Commercial, "Making Memories," song by Gregory Alan

Isakov, Ad ID: 1701700, last airing March 3, 2018, https://www.ispot.tv/ad/wiJd/2018 -subaru-forester-making-memories-song-by-gregory-alan-isakov.

12. John Linden, "History of the Pickup Truck," 2019, www.carcovers.com/resources /history-of-the-pickup-truck.html.

13. For 1973 CAFE standards, see Union of Concerned Scientists, "A Brief History of U.S. Fuel Efficiency Standards," December 6, 2017, https://www.ucsusa.org/clean-vehicles /fuel-efficiency/fuel-economy-basics.html. Also, see "Corporate Average Fuel Economy (CAFE) Standards," August 27, 2014, www.transportation.gov/mission/sustainability /corporate-average-fuel-economy-cafe-standards.

14. "7 Ford Pickup Trucks America Never Got: Utes, Mini-Utes, Bakkies and Long-Wheelbase Duallies That Ford Never Sold Here," August 24, 2015, https://autoweek .com/article/classic-cars/7-ford-pickup-trucks-america-never-got. Also, see Tom Appel, "Forbidden Fruit: 5 Small Pickup Trucks Americans Can't Buy," July 13, 2015, http:// blog.consumerguide.com/forbidden-fruit-5-small-pickup-trucks-americans-cant-buy.

15. Christopher Wells, *Car Country: An Environmental History* (Seattle: University of Washington Press, 2012).

16. Daytona Beach Drive-in Christian Church, Disciples of Christ, accessed March 1, 2019, http://www.driveinchurch.net/; Woodland Drive-in Church, accessed March 1, 2019, https://driveinchurchgr.org/.

17. Joliet Army Ammunition Plant, accessed March 7, 2019, cumulis.epa.gov/supercpad /cursites/csitinfo.cfm?id=0501179; also, accessed March 7, 2019, www.fs.usda.gov /detail/midewin/learning/history-culture/?cid=stelprdb5155180.

18. Jeff Gitien, "History of the Auto Lending Industry," October 18, 2017, https://lendedu .com/blog/history-of-auto-lending-industry.

19. Gitien.

20. Gitien.

21. Nancy A. Nichols, "Cupholders Are Everywhere," April 22, 2018, www.theatlantic.com /technology/archive/2018/04/cupholders-are-everywhere/558545.

22. McDonald's McCafé TV Commercial, "Car Shopping," Ad ID: 1130025, last airing December 29, 2014, www.ispot.tv/ad/7jH0/mcdonalds-mccaf-car-shopping.

23. Nichols, "Cupholders Are Everywhere"; see also, Matthew Debord, "Tesla Finally Fixed This Important Design Flaw: Its Cupholders," *Slate*, February 24, 2016, https://slate .com/business/2016/02/tesla-solves-glaring-cupholders-problem.html.

24. Jacqueline Botterill, "Mobile Eating: A Cultural Perspective," *International Review of Social Science Research* 7, no. 2 (2017): 71.

25. Robin T. Reid, "The History of the Drive-in Movie Theater," May 27, 2018, www .smithsonianmag.com/arts-culture/the-history-of-the-drive-in-movie-theater -51331221.

26. Reid.

27. Sarah Zheng, "China Now Has over 300 Million Vehicles . . . That's Almost America's Total Population," *South China Morning Post*, April 19, 2017, updated July 20, 2018, www.scmp.com/news/china/economy/article/2088876/chinas-more-300-million -vehicles-drive-pollution-congestion.

28. Yangfeng Wu, "Overweight and Obesity in China: The Once Lean Giant has a Weight Problem that is Increasing Rapidly," *BMJ* 333 (7564): 362–363, https://doi.org /10.1136/bmj.333.7564.362; www.ncbi.nlm.nih.gov/pmc/articles/PMC1550451.

29. Pinghui Zhang, "China has largest number of obese children in world, study says: Mainland also ranks second behind the United States for number of obese adults, international research reports," *South China Morning Post*, June 13, 2017, updated, July 20, 2018, www.scmp.com/news/china/society/article/2098042/china-has-largest -number-obese-children-world-says-study.

30. David Holmgren, *Future Scenarios: How Communities Can Adapt to Peak Oil and Climate Change* (White River Junction, VT: Chelsea Green, 2009), 21.

31. Boyd A. Swinburn, et al., "The Global Syndemic of Obesity, Undernutrition, and Climate Change: *The Lancet* Commission Report," *The Lancet* 393 (February 23, 2019), 791.

32. Swinburn, 810.

33. Elizabeth Kneebone and Natalie Holmes, "The Growing Distance Between People and Jobs in Metropolitan America," *Brookings*, March 2015, 1–25, https://www.brookings .edu/wp-content/uploads/2016/07/Srvy_JobsProximity.pdf; Patrick Sisson, "High housing costs and long commutes drive more workers to sleep in cars," March 6, 2018, www.curbed.com/2018/3/6/17082570/affordable-housing-commute-rent-apartment; also, see Gabriela Saldiva, "Stuck in Traffic? You're Not Alone. New Data Show American Commute Times Are Longer," NPR, September 20, 2018, www.npr.org/2018/09/20 /650061560/stuck-in-traffic-youre-not-alone-new-data-show-american-commute-times -are-longer.

34. "Emissions of Greenhouse Gases in the U.S.," U.S. Energy Information Administration, March 31, 2011, www.eia.gov/environment/emissions/ghg_report/ghg_methane.php; Kendra Pierre-Louis, "Your Burning Climate Question: Meat and Global Warming," *The New York Times*, January 25, 2018, http://www.nytimes.com/2018/01/25/cows-global -warming.html.

35. Christopher Schliephake, *Urban Ecologies: City Space, Material Agency, and Environmental Politics in Contemporary Culture* (Lanham, MD: Lexington Books, 2015), 40–41, n. 4.

36. Jorgen Randers, *2052: A Global Forecast for the Next Forty Years* (White River, VT: Chelsea Green, 2012), 170.

37. *Runaway Match*, directed by Alfred Collins, Gaumont British Picture Corporation, 1903, film, www.youtube.com/watch?v=CteD9ROdtKs.

38. Isuzu Rodeo Commercial, August 1992, accessed March 2, 2019, www.youtube.com /watch?v=DrIVJaryqA0.

39. *Thunder Road*, directed by Arthur Ripley, performed by Robert Mitchum and Gene Barry, D.R.M. Productions, 1958, film; *Smokey and the Bandit*, directed by Hal Needham, performed by Burt Reynolds and Sally Field, Universal Pictures, 1977, film.

40. *Gone in 60 Seconds*, directed by Dominic Sena, performed by Nicholas Cage and Angelina Jolie, Touchstone Pictures, 2000, film; *The Italian Job*, directed by F. Gary Gray, performed by Donald Sutherland, Mark Wahlberg, and Charlize Theron, Paramount Pictures, 2003; *The Transporter*, directed by Louis Leterrier and Corey Yuen, performed by Jason Statham and Qi Shu, EuropaCorp, 2002, film; *Baby Driver*, directed by Edgar Wright, performed by Ansel Elgort, John Bernthal, and Jon Hamm, TriStar Pictures, 2017, film.

41. *White Heat*, directed by Raoul Walsh, performed by James Cagney and Virginia Mayo, Warner Bros., 1949, film.

42. *Grease*, directed by Randall Kleiser, performed by John Travolta and Olivia Newton-John, Paramount Pictures, 1978, film. The *Fast and The Furious*, directed by Rob Cohen, performed by Vin Diesel and Paul Walker, Universal Pictures, 2001, film, plus at least eight sequels and various spinoffs.

43. Christopher and Lisa Leinberger, "How TV Predicted America's Moves from City to 'Burbs and Back Again,'" Nextcity.org, June 6, 2014, http://nextcity.org/daily/entry /tv-shows-cities-suburbs-moving-america; *The Honeymooners*, 1955–56, Jackie Gleason Enterprises and Paramount Television, TV series.

44. *It's a Wonderful Life*, directed by Frank Capra, performed by Jimmy Stewart and Donna Reed, Liberty Films, 1946, film.

45. *I Love Lucy*, "Lucy Wants to Move to the Country," Season 6, Episode 15, CBS, aired January 28, 1957, Desilu Productions, written by Madelyn Davis, et al.

46. *The Adventures of Ozzie and Harriet*, ABC, 1952–66, Stage Five Productions, TV series; *Leave It to Beaver*, 1957, CBS, 1958–1963, ABC, Gomalco Productions, TV series.
47. *The Dick Van Dyke Show*, CBS, 1961–66, Calvada Productions, TV series.
48. *The Dick Van Dyke Show*, "Scratch My Car and Die," CBS, Season 3, Episode 26, aired March 25, 1964, Calvada Productions, written by John Whedon.
49. *The Jetsons*, "A Date with Jet Screamer," Season 1, Episode 2, ABC, aired September 30, 1962, Hanna-Barbera.
50. Nate Barksdale, "Fries with That? A Brief History of Drive-Thru Dining," History.com, last modified August 22, 2018, www.history.com/news/fries-with-that-a-brief-history -of-drive-thru-dining; "You Won't Believe Where McDonald's Opened Its First Drive- Thru," *AZ Central*, August 29, 2016, updated September 1, 2016, www.azcentral.com /story/travel/arizona/2016/08/29/mcdonalds-first-drive-through-sierra-vista-arizona /88009974.
51. *Happy Days*, ABC, 1974–84, Henderson Productions, TV series; *American Graffiti*, directed by George Lucas, written by Lucas et al., Universal Pictures, 1973, film.
52. *That '70s Show*, "Parents Find Out," Season 2, Episode 19, directed by David Trainer, CBS, aired March 7, 2000, Carsey-Warner Company, TV series.
53. *The Blob*, directed by Irvin S. Yeaworth Jr. and Russell S. Doughton Jr., performed by Steve McQueen and Aneta Coursaut, Tonylyn Productions, 1958, film.
54. *Titanic*, directed by James Cameron, performed by Leonardo DiCaprio and Kate Winslet, Twentieth Century Fox, 1997, film; *Gattaca*, directed by Andrew Niccol, performed by Ethan Hawke and Uma Thurman, Columbia Pictures, 1997, film; *Dirty Girl*, directed by Abe Sylvia, performed by Juno Temple and Jeremy Dozier, The Weinstein Company, 2010, film.
55. "Smooching in Sedans: Exploring How Often Americans Hook Up in a Vehicle," last modified January 30, 2019, https://driving-tests.org/smooching-in-sedans. See also, C. Struckman-Johnson et al., "Sexual Behavior in Parked Cars Reported by Midwestern College Men and Women," *Journal of Sex Research* 54, no. 8 (2017): 1064–76, www.ncbi .nlm.nih.gov/pubmed/27634060.
56. *Remember Me*, directed by Allen Coulter, performed by Robert Pattinson and Emilie de Ravin, Summit Entertainment, 2010, film; *Exposed*, directed by Gee Malik Linton, performed by Keanu Reeves and Ana de Armas, Company Films, 2016, film.
57. National Academies of Sciences, Engineering, and Medicine, *Understanding Changes in Demographics, Preferences, and Markets for Public Transportation* (Washington, D.C.: National Academies Press, 2018), 21.
58. Mike Snyder, "Perceived Link Between Transit, Crime Tough to Dispel," *Houston Chronicle* July 20, 2017, www.houstonchronicle.com/news/columnists/greater-houston /article/Perceived-link-between-transit-crime-tough-to-11303477.php.
59. Paul Mackie, "Transit Is 10-Times Safer Than Driving—and Makes Communities Safer, Says New APTA Report," September 8, 2016, mobilitylab.org/2016/09/08/transit-10 -times-safer-driving-makes-communities-safer-says-new-apta-report/; American Public Transit Association, *The Hidden Traffic Safety Solution: Public Transportation*, September 2016, www.apta.com/resources/reportsandpublications/Documents/APTA-Hidden -Traffic-Safety-Solution-Public-Transportation.pdf.
60. Patrick D. Murphy, "Challenges to Developing a Long-Term Environmental Perspective: PAN and DIM," in *Routledge Handbook of Ecocriticism and Environmental Communication*, ed. Scott Slovic, Swarnalatha Rangarajan, and Vidya Sarveswaran (New York: Routledge, 2019), 167–174.
61. Olga Khazan, "Nearly Half of All Murdered Women Are Killed by Romantic Partners," *The Atlantic*, July 20, 2017, www.theatlantic.com/health/archive/2017/07/homicides -women/534306; Kathryn Casteel, Julia Wolfe, and Mai Nguyen, "What We Know

About Victims of Sexual Assault in America," *FiveThirtyEight*, January 2, 2018, https://projects.fivethirtyeight.com/sexual-assault-victims.

62. National Academies of Sciences, Engineering, and Medicine, *Broadening Understanding of the Interplay Among Public Transit, Shared Mobility, and Personal Automobiles* (Washington, D.C.: National Academies Press, 2018).

63. "General Motors Invests in Ride Sharing: Is This the Future of Automakers?" *Forbes*, January 6, 2016, www.forbes.com/sites/greatspeculations/2016/01/06/general-motors-invests-in-ride-sharing-is-this-the-future-of-automakers/#629c03644f5b; Charles Riley, "Rivals BMW and Daimler Are Spending $1 Billion (Together) on the Future of Transportation," CNN Business, February 22, 2019, www.cnn.com/2019/02/22/business/daimler-bmw-mobility/index.html.

64. Adle Tomer, "America's Commuting Choices: 5 Major Takeaways from 2016 Census Data," Brookings, October 3, 2017, www.brookings.edu/blog/the-avenue/2017/10/03/americans-commuting-choices-5-major-takeaways-from-2016-census-data.

65. Amitav Ghosh, *The Great Derangement: Climate Change and the Unthinkable* (Chicago: University of Chicago Press, 2016), 7.

66. Ghosh, 119.

67. Kim Stanley Robinson, *New York 2140* (New York: Orbit Books, 2017), 16–21.

68. Ernest Callenbach, *Ecotopia* (1975; New York: Bantam, 1977).

69. Ernest Callenbach, *Ecotopia Emerging* (Berkeley: Banyan Tree, 1981).

70. Arthur Herzog, *Heat* (1977; New York: Signet, 1978).

71. Herzog, 186.

72. Callenbach, *Ecotopia*, 7, 15.

73. Callenbach, *Ecotopia Emerging*, 6.

74. Callenbach, *Ecotopia Emerging*, 11, italics in original.

75. Callenbach, *Ecotopia Emerging*, 35.

76. Callenbach, *Ecotopia Emerging*, 68.

77. Callenbach, *Ecotopia Emerging*, 151.

78. "Top Ten Largest Car Markets in the World," *China Daily*, August 13, 2018, http://www.chinadaily.com.cn/a/201808/13/WS5b70bac4a310add14f385474_6.html.

79. UN Environment Programme, *Emissions Gap Report 2019*, November 2019, https://wedocs.unep.org/bitstream/handle/20.500.11822/30797/EGR2019.pdf. See also "Coal Consumption by Country," Worldometer, https://www.worldometers.info/coal/coal-consumption-by-country/.

80. Sophie Edwards, "Developed Countries 'Exporting Pollution' by Trading Second-Hand Vehicles to Poorer Countries, Experts Say," Devex January 26, 2017, 2019, www.devex.com/news/developed-countries-exporting-pollution-by-trading-second-hand-vehicles-to-poorer-countries-experts-say-89457.

81. Holmgren, *Future Scenarios*, 29.

82. *Minority Report*, directed by Steven Spielberg, performed by Tom Cruise and Colin Farrell, Twentieth Century Fox, 2002, film.

83. Christina Wilkie, "Trump: Democrats Want to Take Away Your Car and Ban Cows," CNBC February 12, 2019, www.cnbc.com/2019/02/12/trump-targets-alexandria-ocasio-cortez-green-new-deal-in-campaign-speech.html.

CHAPTER 6

Suicide Machines: Bruce Springsteen, Ballard, and Broken Heroes on a Last Chance Power Drive

David LaRocca

The main title of this chapter contains more than a double entendre: we are aware of automobiles as a way to die, intentionally or not (and so driving can sometimes seem dangerous enough to simply feel like a "suicide mission"); and no doubt, there are people who are "reckless" drivers—an adjective that contains much irony; and, in the context of the concerns of the present volume, the automobile-as-object-of-nonrenewable-resource-consumption-and-pollution becomes an emblem of global climatic destruction (incrementally, we appear collectively to be driving our way to extinction). In the remarks that follow, I aim to direct attention to the imaginative landscape of driving—in particular, as we find it in music, literature, and film. In these realms of song, story, and cinema, we encounter raw emotion, mythic power, and dynamic interrelationships of cultural forms and norms (for example, in terms of gender, sexuality, late-capitalist consumer culture, and the constitution of individual identity in relation to broad, anonymous social structures and strictures). For special focus, I have selected the music of Bruce Springsteen—especially song lyrics from the 1970s, the heyday of the muscle car, a "last chance power drive" before the arrival of the cheap, economical imports from Japan and Germany; J. G. Ballard's controversial novel *Crash* (also from the seventies, published in 1973) depicting symphorophilia, primarily expressed by variations of car-crash sexual fetishism; and, lastly, the film adaptation of Ballard's book, made by David Cronenberg in 1996.[1] By means of close analysis of some lines of lyrics, passages of fiction, and cinematic scenes, I hope to provide a complement to the other studies in this volume—in particular, by dwelling on some ways in which the invention of conceptual and emotional relationships to automobility (as revealed in these bold, influential, and indelible cultural artifacts) may have inadvertently "driven us" to destruction. The current, and increasingly dire, environmental crisis feels like humanity's greatest accident. Is this a love affair we can shake or transform, or will we perish—*crash*—because of the romantic intensity of our infatuation? I look to Springsteen, Ballard, and Cronenberg to illuminate the contours of our passion so that we might reflect further on our own, individual and collective, relationship to the means and machines of automobility.

Though hailing from different generations and locales (Depression-era Shanghai for Ballard [b. 1930; relocating to England in 1945] and postwar New Jersey for Springsteen [b. 1949]), the works of art of most interest here emerge from the early 1970s. Ballard's *Crash* is published the same year—1973—as Springsteen released two studio albums: *Greetings from Asbury Park, NJ* and *The Wild, the Innocent & the E Street Shuffle*. We might even have evidence for a shared gestalt across the Atlantic and across the generations, since, at that time, no matter your age, there is a confluence of factors that everyone shared. Among them, the 1970s had the highest number of traffic fatalities (before and since); in *Unsafe at Any Speed* (1965), Ralph Nader was the leading voice admonishing us to increase car safety in the face of striking evidence of vehicular dangers. Hence the shared salience of cars-as-a-mortal-threat. Meanwhile, a film such as George Lucas' *American Graffiti* (*also* from 1973 but set in 1962) depicts the romance and glamour of an era—the first of its kind—in which children grew up owning their own cars (or at least driving them); yet the denouement of that film, like so many others of that time, features the tragic consequences of life on the road. Other touchstones, in this regard, might include: *Bullitt* (1968, dir., Peter Yates), *The French Connection* (1971, dir., William Friedkin), *Badlands* (1973, dir., Terrence Malick), *The Sugarland Express* (1974, dir., Steven Spielberg), and *The Night the Lights Went Out in Georgia* (1981, dir., Ronald F. Maxwell). Moreover, adding to a further sense of the era, taken from our present-day vantage, we can look back to see a time defined by an emerging ecological awareness (Earth Day was first celebrated in 1970 in the immediate wake of the Apollo lunar orbit that revealed a tiny blue planet "rising" in a vast expanse of deep space), the severity of a major oil crisis (again, the worst before and since), not to mention the state of radical art in avant-garde and punk cultures, along with the emerging dynamics of sexual liberation for both heterosexuals and homosexuals.

Songs of the Open Road: Springsteen

The cover of Bruce Springsteen's autobiography, *Born to Run* (2016), shows him in Frank Stefanko's photograph from 1978, leaning on the prominent twin front headlights of Springsteen's 1960 Chevrolet Corvette. Springsteen shoots the camera a casual glance, with a slightly furrowed brow—comfortable and relaxed perhaps because he is being backed by his powerful metal pony. Maybe all humans must look this way when leaning on—that is, relying upon—our personal machine pets; cars have been a form of armor coupled with an advertisement. They present a picture of who we think we are, or who we want to be, and all the while intimate that we drivers are safe in the seat—and moreover, in control of the wheel. These are descriptions that bear some truth, but when drawn out in the convulsive, churning sounds of a questing, romantic voice—say, in the songs of Bruce Springsteen—they become exaggerations, call them dreams and nightmares.

For a man who, in the years before this photograph was taken, had been singing about the way cars get you out of town *or* leave you trapped in it (if the powerful engine makes you free, the clunker leaves you stranded), this is an image of someone with a sought-after, much-desired prize. His songs of desperate lovers and loners have, as the photograph attests, yielded fame and glory for this troubadour with a stunning black Corvette. While Springsteen, by 1978, had the wherewithal to leave New Jersey for good, it turns out he planted his roots not far from his familiar routes; despite finding wealth and fame, he remained a loyal, local denizen of the familiar ground, living permanently just a few miles from where he began. A wide distance *psychologically*, he will tell you, from the troubled, tattered streets of Freehold to the posh grounds of Colts Neck and Rumson. Yet, it is precisely these literal truths that make it easier for us to think of Bruce Springsteen, the songwriter, as providing a prominent, influential, and enduring mythic image of the American road, and even more so, of those who would choose to ride upon it—hunting or haunting, as the case may be.

While the 1978 photograph and Springsteen's 2016 autobiography of exception perspicuity, vigor, and vulnerability provide orientation, it is to the specific phrases and lines from his songs—that have shaped a generation, indeed now generations of listeners—that I wish to turn our attention. In the vernacular of Springsteen's written work as a lyricist, cars are among the most prominent thematic characters, right alongside working-class men and often-elusive, always-compelling women. In an otherwise straightforward heteronormative setup, the car complicates things, turning a romantic affair into a three-way drama. The car either helps the man scoop up his girl and take to the road, or it provides the means for a solo getaway; the car obeys him or betrays him; the car is a settled home or it is unmoored; it provides a way to measure the achievements of domestic life and to escape them.

Beginning to collect an inventory of pertinent songs, we could list "Born to Run" and "Thunder Road" (*Born to Run*, 1975), "Racing in the Street" and "Something in the Night" (*Darkness on the Edge of Town*, 1978), "Cadillac Ranch," "Stolen Car," and "Wreck on the Highway" (*The River*, 1980), "Highway Patrolman," "Open All Night," "State Trooper," and "Used Cars" (*Nebraska*, 1982), "Pink Cadillac" (non-album B-side of "Dancing in the Dark," 1984); "Valentine's Day" (*Tunnel of Love*, 1987), "Highway 29" (*The Ghost of Tom Joad*, 1995), "Car Wash" (*Tracks*, 1998), "Last to Die" (*Magic*, 2007), and most recently, "Hitch Hikin'," "The Wayfarer," and "Drive Fast (The Stuntman)" (*Western Stars*, 2019), among scores of others. This cursory list shows, even in a quick gesture, how essential meditations on automobiles—their forms, their movements, their intimate roles in people's lives and imaginations—are to Springsteen's oeuvre. While the titles alone often confirm their membership, or give a clue to it, it is rather in the lyrics themselves that we find the true contours of Springsteen's creative coupling of man, woman, car, and road—along with their kindred emotional registers: sex, freedom, power, and dreams (and their inverted correlates: failed romance, being tied down, feeling disenfranchised [impotent!], and suffering broken dreams [lost, stranded, dissipated, idle]). Since the appointed purpose of these notes is to explore resonances between Springsteen, Ballard, and Cronenberg (and owing to space constraints), I will not rehearse claims and extended observations made in many fine studies about Springsteen's songbook.[2] The point on the present occasion, then, is to read for the artful repetition of iconic imagery—that is, variations on broad, but bold themes—a revelation made possible by close, careful reading of specific texts. To thematize the exploration in anticipation of Ballard and Cronenberg, I offer an analysis of selected lyrics under subheads meant to capture a few of the resonant signature elements of Springsteen's corpus.

Figurations: Drivers, Dreams, and Dames

Drawing inspiration from our subject, let's take a brisk, critical tour of some Springsteen song lyrics, here radically reduced in scope so that we might catch a glimpse—moving fast as we must—to read for the lusters and glean a few salient themes. In "Rosalita (Come Out Tonight)" (*The Wild, The Innocent & The*

E Street Shuffle, 1973), the narrator appeals to a father's hope for his daughter's well-being, offers some braggadocio about a new record deal and some fresh cash in his pocket, and aims to make good on his affections. His fate, as for many others in the mythopoesis of the mid-Atlantic, is tied to his car's: "And my tires were slashed and I almost crashed, but the Lord had mercy / And my machine, she's a dud, out stuck in the mud somewhere in the swamps of Jersey." Romance and the road are regular partners, as in "Jungleland" (*Born to Run*, 1975): "And the Magic Rat drove his sleek machine over the Jersey state line / Barefoot girl sitting on the hood of a Dodge."

As we continue the tour through lyrics from the seventies, Springsteen revels in revealing mechanical details—"I got a sixty-nine Chevy with a 396, Fuelie heads and a Hurst on the floor." But his narrator goes further to personify the powerful creature: "she's waiting"; "me and my partner Sonny built her straight out of scratch" ("Racing in the Street," *Darkness on the Edge of Town*, 1978). A similar pattern of taking stock of stock cars and what adventures—what dares and daring rides—await was seen early on in *Greetings from Asbury Park, NJ* (1973), where we meet that "pure American brother, dull-eyed and empty-faced" who "races Sundays in Jersey / in a Chevy stock super eight." And when Jimmy the Saint isn't riding and racing, he "leans on the hood telling racing stories" ("Lost in the Flood"). As with the characters we find in films of this era—say, debut films by Terrence Malick (*Badlands*) and Steven Spielberg (*The Sugarland Express*), and George Lucas' *American Graffiti*—Springsteen's boys and girls live in and among cars. The machines are not just mechanical extensions of themselves, but also a primary conditioning agent for their emotional and mental lives, a spiritual partner for sussing out what is possible in life and in love—and what may lie forever beyond the horizon of possibility. In this time, cars played a significant concept-determining role in the lives of the young. Perhaps they still do at present, but for different reasons: then, for the exploration of freedoms and pleasures, whereas today they are totems of the ecological crisis of the Anthropocene (complicating and compromising any pleasure that might be had by virtue of a droning insistence on the implicit political, economic, and moral relationship one has to global climate change).

On *Greetings*, the propulsive ratio of cars and booze in wild, dark Jersey nights continues in "Spirit in the Night," where romantic match-ups are interrupted by fellows "all duded up for Saturday night," and arriving with an invitation to the lake. Wild Billy has booze and a plan, "so let's try it." On *The Wild, The Innocent & The E Street Shuffle*, from the same year, the car models continue to stack up and upgrade—from Dodge to Chevy to Cadillac—as in "New York City Serenade": where Billy (Wild Billy?) enjoys the company of Diamond Jackie, and the two set out to "boogaloo down Broadway / And come back home with the loot."

And when it is time to get out of New Jersey, the car is the partner Springsteen calls upon again and again, from "Thunder Road"—when he tells Mary to "climb in" as he is "pulling out of here to win"—to "Goin' Cali" (1991) where the voices in his head are replaced by the voices of friends who say "come on out West," where he is told "it's a place where a man can really feel his success," so he packs up, says his good-byes, "and when the dirty work was done / He turned his wheels into the fading sun." Springsteen's thematic coupling of cars and consciousness—whether the intensity of young love or the onset of world-weary depression in later years, when dreams are faded, forsaken, or squandered—continues up to the present day in *Western Stars* (2019) and its eponymous companion film (2019, dir. Springsteen and frequent Springsteen collaborator, Thom Zimny). In addition to a range of car-driver types (a "gearhead" feels like a throwback to earlier, familiar figures), we encounter a hitchhiker, a wayfarer, a truck driver, and various incarnations of the restless vagabond whose default setting is onwardness—behind the wheel ("I take my El Camino, throw my saddle in and go") or looking for wheels ("Thumb stuck out as I go").[3]

In Springsteen's latest work, his Jersey-sensibilities continue to be transfixed by the American West (as a place and as a concept), while his expression of dreams and defeats remain very much "on the road." "It's the same old cliché," he sings on "The Wayfarer," "slippin' from town to town," and yet, there is much truth and revelation in cliché. Imagining a well-worn car stuntman for the movies—who as a nineteen year-old was "king of the dirt down at the Remington draw," and "liked the pedal and didn't mind the wall"—the chorus repeats: "Drive fast, fall hard . . . Don't worry about tomorrow, don't mind the scars / Just drive fast, fall hard" ("Drive Fast [The Stuntman]"). And as we will see in higher relief in Ballard and Cronenberg's *Crash* (where the blending of man and machine is a dominant theme), Springsteen's depiction of his all-too-human hero harkens back to the way he used to describe the mechanics of cars: "I've got two pins in my ankle . . . a steel rod in my leg, but it walks me home."

Romance: Deferred and Made

The late actor and comedian Robin Williams' Elmer Fudd–inspired version of "Fire" (single, 1977) may be more famous than Springsteen's own, but it suffices to distill the car's role as romantic catalyst. The moving car is the first layer of seduction, the playing radio layers another. There is an indication that her consent is not forthcoming, but we are told that when the two kiss, it's "fire." On the innuendo-infused track "I'm Going Down" (*Born in the USA*, 1984), two lovers share a bench seat and the fraught negotiations of another case of mismatched desire. Sitting in a car outside her house, he makes a move (with what he calls "heat"), but she makes it clear that he is "way out of bounds." When fevers were a better fit, as when "Me and Crazy Janey was making love in the dirt, singing our birthday songs," the harmonies were real: "Together we moved like spirits in the night (all night)" ("Spirit in the Night," *Greetings from Asbury Park, NJ*, 1973). And endurance—of performance and passion—recur in "Prove It All Night" (*Darkness on the Edge of Town*, 1978), when the fellow has been "working real hard trying to get my hands clean . . . To buy you a gold ring and a pretty dress of blue." (Four decades later, though, the blue dress is replaced by "that little blue pill"—an admission of loss laced with a hope for recuperation ["Western Stars," *Western Stars*, 2019]).

In "Seaside Bar Song" (1973), the formula finds its rhythm, where Billy (still Billy!), has a Chevy (a '40 coupe deluxe with chrome wheels and a "stick shift (hey!)"), luring us into further (sexualized) anthropomorphisms: "give[s] her gas, pop[s] the clutch." The fellow calls out for a partner in the vein of creepy incest that used to (still does?) excite: "Hey girl, you wanna ride in Daddy's Cadillac?" The boy narrates the obvious—something about a "a pretty girl on a sweet summer night that gets this boy excited." But it may be the road itself that is the best partner for settling nerves, since "the highway is alive tonight," and on it—with it—there is no need to be scared. In time, the radio finally playing "something you can move to," the narrator finds a calmer companion, once poised—like the car they drive—to "cut loose your drive power."

Dreams: Made and Deferred

Most of the time, the driver of Springsteen's cars is a dreamer—aspiring to some measure of greatness, certainly freedom from inherited constraints: on the road, in the front (or back) seat, and looking out to the horizon ("Love and glory goin' 'round and 'round" ["The Wayfarer," *Western Stars*, 2019]). The wheel itself reveals a paradox in Springsteen, as it does elsewhere—for as it can take you away, out of town, it can also, as it were, turn in place, forever returning you to where you started out from: for each who can say "My wheels are hissin' up the highway / Spinning 'round and 'round" ("The Wayfarer"), there is another who never leaves the city limits.

Making dreams is, as we all know, especially as we age, so different from realizing them; and in Springsteen's world, it often doesn't take that long for a dream to be made and then deferred—or worse, lost altogether. Even as the car proved the crux of a teenage courtship, we hear: "Then I got Mary pregnant / And man, that was all she wrote / And for my nineteenth birthday I got a union card and a wedding coat" ("The River," *The River*, 1980). Our hero is trapped in a place and in a marriage and the car will not take him anywhere of note: "We went down to the courthouse / And the judge put it all to rest / No wedding day smiles, no walk down the aisle / No flowers, no wedding dress." By contrast, just a few years earlier, in "Jungleland" (*Born to Run*, 1975), there was still an onward fervor, a lust for life that didn't seem troubled by matrimony or the drudgery of the nine-to-five: "Beneath the city two hearts beat, soul engines running through a night so tender / In a bedroom locked, in whispers of soft refusal and then surrender." Or again, in "Prove It All Night" (*Darkness on the Edge of Town*, 1978), the dreams are real, still unrealized, but also threatened by reality. A person's "hunger"—that drives one on, and that draws others near or repels them further—is the force that figures desire and the hopes that give shape to visions. Dreams are there to tempt us forward, but just the same, they dissipate as we do. The boy tells the girl, "you want it, you take it, you pay the price." These are tragic dreamers, always on the road—coming and going, always looking.

Like so much in Springsteen's catalogue, we seem to follow characters and types, familiar people whose lives we pass, as on a highway, as encountered at a pit stop or in a roadside bar ("It's the same sad story" ["The Wayfarer," *Western Stars*, 2019]). And when we hear their stories, we must be prepared for heartbreak, quietly kept pain, and behaviors meant to offset their frustration and hurt: "Now some guys they just give up living and start dying little by little, piece by piece / Some guys come home from work and wash up and go racing in the street" ("Racing in the Street," *Darkness on the Edge of Town*, 1978). Racing on those same streets, in another vignette on the same register, we find our hero has found a "little girl" who was partner to "this dude from L.A.," driving a Camaro. Now, a few years later, "She sits on the porch of her daddy's house . . . all her pretty dreams are torn." Yet, against the dissipation, we are told that "For all the shut-down strangers and hot rod angels rumbling through this promised land / Tonight my baby and me we're gonna ride to the sea and wash these sins off our hands" ("Racing in the Street," *Darkness on the Edge of Town*, 1978). Springsteen's intimate knowledge of Catholicism not only provides a sense of cosmic force—something one might have to fight against, if also one that might bless the revolt—but also offers a language with which to express the achievement of dreams, or the limitations that make their realization compromised or worse, impossible.

When we ride together, as we learned earlier, the road holds promise not fear: "The highway is alive tonight so baby do not be frightened" ("Seaside Bar Song," 1973), but when solo, "living on the edge of the world," "this turnpike sure is spooky at night when you're all alone." ("Living on the Edge of the World," bootleg 1979). The second song is kindred and a kind of precursor to "Open All Night," from *Nebraska* (1982), where our driver meets Wanda who works at Route 60's Bob's Big Boy Fried Chicken, and seems to tell her all about the enticements of his ride: with a "carburetor, baby, cleaned and checked," "a new clutch plate and a new set of shocks," and "her line blown out she's humming like a turbojet." The car is ready for Wanda, as is its driver. And soon enough, attention to the car's qualities shifts to those of the woman he wishes to woo, with a map nearby, heading to "scrap metal hill." But it cannot last as the car falters ("oil pressure's sinking fast") and its driver calls out "deliver me from nowhere."

As this critical survey of Springsteen lyrics winds up, I wish to emphasize lines from "The River" (*The River*, 1980), invoked above, where we have an apotheosis of form and sentiment: where the car, the body of a desirable woman, and the status of memories and dreams is invoked. A river in Woody Guthrie's hands would be an analogue of the highway (just below an "endless skyway"), but for Springsteen, the river may be barren—a dusty dead end. The dreamer here remembers riding in his brother's car, "Her body tan and wet down at the reservoir / At night on them banks I'd lie awake / And pull her close just to feel each breath she'd take." But time has passed and we don't know how much, memories "come back to haunt me / they haunt me like a curse," and remind us what was hoped for and what was never achieved: "Is a dream a lie if it don't come true / Or is it something worse"?

If "The River" coalesces essential attributes of Springsteen's romantic figuration of men, women, and their cars, "Jungleland" (*Born to Run*, 1975) prognosticates a more generic human fate, and does so with a radical intensity, where "the street's on fire," a spectacle of a "real death waltz between what's flesh and what's fantasy." But the poets and troubadours, a company fit for Springsteen himself, come up short: "In the quick of the night they reach for their moment and try to make an honest stand / But they wind up wounded, not even dead, tonight in Jungleland." These lines from "Jungleland" could serve as an epigraph to J. G. Ballard's *Crash*, published in 1973—the same year as *Greetings from Asbury Park, NJ* and *The Wild, The Innocent & the E-Street Shuffle* were released and only a couple years before *Born to Run*. Deciphering

"what's flesh and what's fantasy" is at the core of the novel, and for that con-
founding combination, so is the nature of being "wounded, not even dead."

Literary *Crash*: Ballard

As we turn to Ballard's *Crash*, and later Cronenberg's film of the same title,
the techno-industrial pornography of those works may have us looking back
upon Springsteen with something of a lament that we had not applied a sufficiently intense focus on what might be deemed the euphemistic—and thus
wonderfully rich psychoanalytic content—of the lyrics, since with Ballard the
cliché man/machine dualism reaches new heights of postmodern kitsch and
does so with bravado and without an accompanying admission of shame. Even
a quick glance over Springsteen's lyrics—filled as they are with references to a
"stick shift (hey!)," "a pink Cadillac," etc.—will have our attention (re)turned
to phallic and pudendal significance.

Let us dwell on a fairly rudimentary, but perhaps sufficient for our purposes, definition of pornography—namely, as that which is aimed to produce
or elicit sexual arousal. In this nomenclature, "porn" is a kind of conceptual
prefix, a modifier meant to signal the nature of what follows (hence, porn
film, porn star). A secondary use has become broadly popular in contemporary
culture meaning an excessive, perhaps irresistible desire for something—and
in these instances, porn amplifies the preceding word (as in cabin porn, food
porn, disaster porn). As we cast about for analogies and homologies, associations with the word "porn"—even in a lexicographical sense—do most of the
work, as among them we find: sexy, smut, vulgarity, offense, indecency, impro-
priety, obscenity, profanity, lewd, salacious, erotica, dirtiness, filth, scatology,
prurience, abomination, immoral, and (the easily mistaken double entendre)
curse. The range is impressive: everything from sexual expressiveness to moral
judgment, from religiously-inflected condemnation to the physiology of the
libido and the body (as it must, involving fluids and fecal matter). Again, all
that Jersey blood, sweat, grease, sun-tan lotion, and motor oil we heard about
in Springsteen songs calls out for its pornographic credentials. As we turn to
Ballard's take on cars, we may pause to ponder the etymology of *porn*, with its
protocapitalist sense of the prostitute (Gr. *porne*), and thus the act of selling
(Gr. *pernanai,* to sell), and not to be missed, the ways in which such transac-
tions involve "trafficking." Pornography, then, is a certain "writing" (Gr. *gra-
phein,* to write), or depiction of, the sexually explicit.

What, then, is the scandal of J. G. Ballard's *Crash*, written by none other
than the author of the much-beloved semi-autobiographical novel *Empire*

of the Sun (1984), later made into a celebrated, eponymous film by Steven Spielberg (1987) and starring a young Christian Bale? It is the young Jim ("Jamie Graham," by way of Ballard's own J. G.) who captions the aerial attack by P-51 Mustangs on his Japanese prisoner of war camp with "the Cadillac of the skies."[4] Cars are on young Jim's mind even under these dire conditions. The scandal, then, in the seventies, might be the unmatched way in which Ballard turns the car into a sex toy. But he goes further, he also makes the sex toy into an instrument of injury, even death. Eros and Thanatos are coupled and coupling. From our vantage, entering the third decade of the new millennium, these scandals seem quaint, provincial, since the continued and expansive use of cars has now been shown to imperil the earth as such, or at least, the inhabitation of the planet by organic life forms. Cars have driven us to the point of extinction.

Ballard has called our participation in driving a "pandemic cataclysm," and as such Zadie Smith glosses his sentiment by saying that "the death-drive, Thanatos, is not what drivers secretly feel, it's what driving explicitly *is*."[5] And yet, what motivates that existential condition is the pulsing directive of Eros, hence the abundant instances in which cars are surrogates and mediators for human sexuality. As Smith says: "The real shock of *Crash* is not that people have sex in or near cars, but that technology has entered into even our most intimate human relations. Not man-as-technology-forming but technology-as-man-forming."[6] In short, cars are needed for the embodied gratifications of flesh-and-bone people.

It is now a commonplace in stories of computer-human relationships— from E. M. Forster's *The Machine Stops* (1909) to filmic depictions in Kubrick's *Dr. Strangelove* (1964) and *2001: A Space Odyssey* (1968) and onward to *The Matrix* (1999) and much else—that humans risk giving up control to their digital overloads. The specter has only magnified in the age of Web 2.0. Cars, that is, old-fashioned cars, with their combustion engines and gasoline and oil, seem antique, hardly worth our worry—since, of course, cars are now increasingly merely computers with wheels. The age of IoT has dawned. Looking back to Ballard, *with* Ballard, from our present moment is useful since it may remind, or perhaps reframe, how we got to this point. Smith tells us how Ballard "invert[s] the power-balance between people and technology, which in turn deprives his characters of things like interiority and individual agency. They seem mass-produced, just like the things they make and buy."[7] As cars shift to an increasing autonomy, and moreover, when they are "unfixable" by garage mechanics, but instead need software updates from "the cloud," the transition will be complete: humans will be entirely alienated from the product and the process of owning it. Any lingering fantasies, any tempting narratives of empowerment and control, will be dashed.

Why, though, does Ballard willingly describe *Crash* as the first "pornographic novel about technology"? To speak of the "sexual explicitness" of technology would (should?) seem a category mistake—even if we have a well-honed habit of describing cars in anthropomorphized sexual terms (as having hips, lips, guts, muscles, eyes, a rear, etc.). Smith claims, "it can be shocking to be forced to look at the fond and familiar with this degree of clinical precision," say, cars-as-instruments-of-pleasure-*and*-injury; but, as she emphasizes, "Ballard was in the business of taking what seems 'natural'—what seems normal, familiar, and rational—and revealing its psychopathology."[8] Smith, like many other readers, describes Ballard's talent as, in part, a "gift for defamiliarization."[9] It is at the point where defamiliarization meets the automobile, in *Crash*, that we encounter the "pornography of technology." What is a car really for? What, after Smith, indeed after Wittgenstein, are we meant to understand not as its meaning but as its use?[10]

In Springsteen's lyrics, we are tempted to think that the hero's heteronormative dreams are legitimate—a desire for a woman, a few bucks, a drink, and the open road, etc.—but they are so often predicated on the having and using of a car. As Smith notes: "Ballard reminds us that dreams are often perverse."[11] And the surprising (Freudian?) outcome of such a claim turns us anew to the pornography of technology. What do we want from it and why? In *Crash*, what we find is a certain allegory of desire recalibrated from its everyday status as inert fact and attuned, instead, to a creative register; in short, the novel moves us away from being a spectator-driver (who steers the car, and tries to avoid the worst fate—a crash) into an agent-driver (who dreams of the best possible crash, and then, almost beyond belief, *rehearses* it—that is, crashes on purpose). The "erotic tenderness" of Vaughn, who "dreamed of dying at the moment of her orgasm," provides characteristic expression of Smith's notion of "technology-as-man-forming."[12] We should add: "man-forming" until it is man-destroying (individually, then collectively). The first line of the novel may as well have been the last: "Vaughn died yesterday in his last car-crash."[13]

While the dangers of driving would make for a facile injunction (our own pleas to one another to "drive safely" seem magical spells cast, with hope against hope), Ballard's postulation is that in car crashes—indeed, in the wounds they create—lay "the keys to a new sexuality born from a perverse technology."[14] Cars as perverse? And if so, how does that deviancy relate to human sexuality? Given Vaughn's obsession with the erotics of car-crashes, he can himself be catalogued as a symphorophiliac (a "lover of misfortune")—one for whom sexual arousal involves staging or watching tragedy; thus, symphorophilia is primarily expressed by variations of car-crash sexual fetishism.[15] The car's perverting force is a function of its status as an object of desire—and as a means for sexual expression; the very definition of a fetish requires that a human develop an erotic fixation on a nonliving object or nongenital body part.[16]

Cinematic *Crash:* Cronenberg

What does David Cronenberg contribute to our experience of *Crash*? Perhaps most obviously, but also most pointedly, two perceptual aspects that a novel must deny (for formal reasons) and cinema can express (for formal reasons): motion and sound. Given their impact on human experience, how fitting that cars and movies share these traits. Where Ballard must give us description, Cronenberg renders with unflinching immediacy the visceral and kinetic experience of cars in motion, their sounds *in extremis*, along with the bodies driving and along for the ride. Indeed, cinema and automobile, which enjoyed infancy together in the last decades of the nineteenth century, and came into full form and global domination in the twentieth century, are an uncanny set of twins: they are all about speed, motion, and sound. Not surprisingly, cinema has taken the car as a figure worthy of attention, and/or has made the car a means for making films ("the tracking shot" has its origins in locomotive language, but the "traveling shot" seems to broaden the scope to include the road). These technological pairings are complemented by cultural ones: "Around the deaths of James Dean and Albert Camus, Jayne Mansfield, and John Kennedy," we read in Ballard's prose, "[Vaughn] had woven elaborate fantasies."[17] From Grace Kelly to Princess Diana, from Jackson Pollack to Paul Walker, the celebrity car fatality has become another tragic myth of the technological recent past and present. These crashes do not occur on film; they are, instead, an epiphenomenon of the seventh art. The salience of this specific death is magnified by celebrity; it becomes an emblem, and its salience abides longer than most other similar catastrophes. Owing to our narcissism, we (individually and collectively) fear for our own lives behind the wheel, for "if celebrities can die, then surely I can die."

Ballard's descriptive power is, as some literary critics are wont to say, "cinematic," but in what sense? Not just the forensic diction that provides such a visceral image, but also the rhythm of the syntax—the way the two drive on, move along, as in this passage, where Ballard (the narrator) calls to mind his first accident with his wife, Catherine:

Catherine vomited over my seat. This pool of vomit with its clots of blood like liquid rubies, as viscous and discreet as everything produced by Catherine, still contains for me the essence of the erotic delirium of the car-crash, more exciting than her own rectal and vaginal mucus, as refined as the excrement of a fairy queen, or the miniscule globes of liquid that formed beside the bubbles of her contact lenses. In this magic pool, lifting from her throat like a rare discharge of fluid from the mouth of a remote and mysterious shrine, I saw my own reflection, a mirror of blood, semen, and vomit, distilled from a mouth whose contours only a few minutes before had drawn steadily against my penis.[18]

While seeming so much at odds—flesh and metal—the body and the machine, somehow especially in Ballard's perception, continue their mutual emplacement:

The brief avalanche of dissolving talc that fell across her eyes as I moved my lips across their lids contained all the melancholy of this derelict vehicle, its leaking engine oil and radiator coolant.[19]

The volumes of Helen's thighs pressing against my hips, her left fist buried in my shoulder, her mouth grasping at my own, the shape and moisture of her anus as I stroked it with my ring finger, were each overlaid by the inventories of a benevolent technology—the moulded binnacle of the instrument dials, the jutting carapace of the steering column shroud, the extravagant pistol grip of the handbrake. I felt the warm vinyl of the seat beside me, and then stroked the damp aisle of Helen's perineum. . . . The plastic laminates around me, the colour of washed anthracite, were the same tones as her pubic hairs parted at the vestibule of her vulva. The passenger compartment enclosed us like a machine generating from our sexual art an homunculus of blood, semen and engine coolant.[20]

Published in 1973, it can read like a psychosexual extrapolation of 1930s Henry Miller—in Ballard's words, a "strange and perverse dream" in the form of a "mildly pornographic novel."[21] One may be distracted by a perceived and aggrandized vulgarity that makes the entire literary—and thereafter cinematic—project moot. It's pornographic! It's smut! Or, at least, unflinchingly graphic erotica. As Lars Svendsen tells us: "The reaction of one reader in Ballard's publishing house was symptomatic: 'This author is beyond psychiatric help. Do Not Publish!' "[22] (Likewise, along with an R-rating, the MPAA anointed a separate cut of Cronenberg's film with an NC-17 rating, one of the surest signs of extreme prejudice and fear of explicit content in Hollywood.[23]) Looking for an etiology of such expressiveness, such medical-ized acuity, perhaps we can figure our protagonist as suffering from some variant of obsessive compulsive disorder (OCD), and Ballard the novelist as finding a way to poetize the pathology, as in this line, which cannily couples fixations with the organic and the mechanical, the fluids of the human body and the fluids of the machines we use: "When had they last bathed their geni-talia, did small grains of faecal matter still cling to their anuses as they pre-scribed some antibiotic for a streptococcal throat, did the odour of illicit sex acts infest their underwear as they drove home from the hospital, the traces of smegma and vaginal mucus on their hands marrying with the splashed engine coolant of unexpected car-crashes?"[24] One reaches for a way to ac-count for such literary inventions. Perhaps "avant-garde porno-tech erotica"?

Funnily enough, it may be the sober sayings of the late Roger Ebert, indel-ible sage of Midwestern sentiments, that set us straight on all this: "Now of course there is no connection between eroticism and automobile accidents. . . . *Crash* is about characters entranced by a sexual fetish that, in fact, no one has."[25] Ebert's jarring diagnostic confidence—in the midst of his positive, four-and-a-half-star review—will leave us wondering what to do with Ballard *and* Cronenberg: "Cronenberg has made a movie that is pornographic in form, but not in result. Take out the cars, the scars, the crutches and scabs and wounds, and substitute the usual props of sex films, and you'd have a porno movie. But *Crash* is anything but pornographic: it's about the human mind, about the way we grow enslaved by the particular things that turn us on, and forgive ourselves our trespasses."[26] Despite the debated transgressiveness of the ob-jects of Ballard's prose, the work's literary merit seems unimpeachable and its invitation to cinematic representation irrepressibly tempting. Is pornography art?[27] Is the auteur's "challenging, courageous, original" take on sexual obses-sion in company with low-grade San Fernando Valley porno videos?[28] We seem returned to (perhaps, as we must, in the wake of Clement Greenberg's endur-ing statement on) the relationship between avant-garde and kitsch.[29] If this is a distinction that contemporary culture has absorbed, modernism seems to confirm that we are now well-lost of the high and low of art. That may be the case, and yet it would seem that sexual explicitness remains a condition for scandal at whatever level, and thus preserves the debate over the criteria that would place a work under the mantle of art.

I mention the cultural circumstances of the reception of literature, in part, to emphasize what Cronenberg offers, at once, to our reading of Ballard and also to our thinking about the "erotic delirium"—indeed, the erotic sublime. There *is* an erotic sublime on display because these fetishistic scenarios involve *perceived* terror (hence the longing, the lust, the threat).[30] Yet, *delirium* is perhaps the better term since the fear is justified—these cars crash; the human vulnerability to injury and death is not a synecdoche for desire but its literalized fulfillment.

In writing about Springsteen's lyrics above, I attended to the text as a literary and cultural critic might, leaving aside any mention of his (actual, not metaphorical) *voice*. Springsteen's biography lends a unique credence to the viability of his poetry, including his sonic fictions—the characters, places, narratives, themes, and doppelgängers that populate his work—and the sound of his voice conveys a tremendous amount of the feeling one might derive from that poetry. Now, as we have Ballard's novel in hand, we turn to Cronenberg to ask what his cinematic "treatment" of that prose fiction might have done. Among the many fascinating aspects of this adaptation from page to screen, I wish to emphasize Cronenberg's alertness to the *performativity* within the narrative of novel—the way, for example, that Ballard in his prose, and the character Ballard in his thoughts, give expression to metafiction *and* metacinema. (And not just as a gimmick or afterthought brought on by the fact that Cronenberg makes Ballard a film producer; in the novel, James produces television commercials—including ones for cars, such as Ford's "new sports car range"[31]).

When Ballard (the character) is remembering his first accident, he says: "For a moment I felt that we were the principal actors at the climax of some grim drama in an unrehearsed theatre of technology, involving these crushed machines, the dead man destroyed in their collision, and the hundreds of drivers waiting beside the stage with their head-lamps blazing."[32] Ballard (the character) reframes the scene of the car-crash as "a scene"—or "a set"—as if it were a movie or a stage-play. In the novel, this analogy must be something the reader imagines, while in Cronenberg's film (with Ballard's prose close at hand), we see the uncanny way in which that momentary feeling has come to pass: we, the audience of *cinéastes* are, in fact, rubberneckers! James Spader (as James Ballard) and Holly Hunter (as Helen Remington) are "the principal actors" providing a choreographed version of what, for us viewers, is a perpetual "unrehearsed theatre of technology"—life on the open road, on "this machine landscape," is forever exposed to risks of our own creation and those of untold, unknown others.[33]

Ballard, in the novel, like Ballard the novelist, is keenly aware of the way driving is *choreographed*; the leitmotif of "rehearsal" (and the "unrehearsed," as above) is recurrently invoked: "[These minor car accidents] are rather like rehearsals. When we've all rehearsed our separate parts the real thing will begin."[34] In following the rules of the road, the system flows with speed and some grace; it is only in those moments of transgression (lane crossing, verging, veering, etc.) that the "death waltz" begins. Ballard (the character) is haunted by the "stylization of the terrible events that had involved us," the way cars and roads and people all appear orchestrated to perform their roles—not just the safe driving, but the accidents too.[35] These also seem planned, part of the overall design. And yet, as we continue to drive without seeming alarm at the prospect of such demise, we share Ballard's sober assessment from the stretcher: "Already I felt isolated from the reality of this accident."[36]

What, then, is the *reality* of the film *Crash*? And how are we, as audience members, as drivers, to understand our relationship not just to the characters but also to their cars and car-accidents—"aware that the interlocked radiator grilles of our cars formed the model of an inescapable and perverse union between us," a "growing sense of a new junction between my own body and the automobile," "faded hair spilling through the chromium spokes of the steering wheel"?[37] A reply comes in the form of associations conjured by the reading and screening of *Crash*, namely, that they seem to generate the same kind of intellectual and emotional frisson felt in reading Nabokov's *Lolita* (1955) and watching Tarantino's *Death Proof* (2007). The radically transgressive nature of these artworks—with their reflections on the twinned experiences of cars and sexuality—instigate a cataloguing of sins (adultery, incest) and fears (sudden death by vehicular assault). In *Lolita* the car is a character, a means for a road trip that prolongs the affair; in *Death Proof*, the car occasions the *ballet* of death (severed limbs flying artfully in the air), an unexpected contrast to the (androgynous) muscle cars that populate the film. With Cronenberg's *Crash*, though, the car is a synecdoche for (mostly) heterosexual longing, loss, and unarticulated grief. Like the novel, the film encourages a straightforward (straight? clinical?) realism so that the perversity of its images, commentary, and socially transgressive movements can make their fullest impact on the audience.

The pacing and tone of the film can feel staged (an attribute befitting an awareness that James is a film producer; we see movie sets, for example, within the movie). And the dialogue and acting, likewise, can arrive with a cool detachment (Catherine's delivery is especially mannered—her "mock-grief was a mere stylization of a gesture"[38]—calling to mind Antonioni's muse, Monica Vitti, gorgeous, but largely affectless, vacant even; Stanley Cavell has described those works as revealing "the absence of not merely feeling, but of so much as the effort to explain that absence"[39]). Ballard's prose likewise turns a glossary of otherwise clinical terms into names worthy of causing sexual arousal: smegma, mucus, membrane, cellulose, perineum, natal cleft, nasolabial fold, vagal, cavernosa, patella, musculature, orifice, the "tender fossas" of her iliac.[40] A medical doctor uses such words to prosecute her duties; for Ballard, they are the proper analogues of the names of car parts and automobile attributes: chromium, metallized, binnacle, switch, treadle, plate, panel, grille. As if Ballard had invented a recipe for his techno-eroticism, one need only bring the two glossaries together—mix them in artful ways—to achieve his distinctive literary style.[41] Cronenberg undertakes a similar coupling but does so (must do so!) in motion pictures, and so the cinematography is often measured—slowly tracking or zooming—to allow for a similar kind of focalized look, indeed, a stare (thereby providing a cinematic frame for our collective *schaulust*, a "lust of the eyes"). This coupling of lexicons reinforces the way Ballard describes himself as perceiving the "sexual possibilities of everything around me," and how "the elements of new technologies"—in the hospital, in cars, in airplanes, and elsewhere—"linked our affections."[42] Here Ballard finds kindred forms in "their barely concealed genitalia and the engine nacelles of giant aircraft."[43] Cronenberg's mandate as a filmmaker for such conjunctions, then, would be realized when he could sexualize such objects (planes, cars, hospital equipment, etc.) by photographic and sonic means. For Ballard the erotic fantasist and fetishist, the film would have to reflect the "metallized excitements of our shared dreams of technology."[44]

Iain Sinclair is more emphatic in assessing a contrast between Ballard the novelist and Cronenberg the filmmaker. In this "post-mortem," Sinclair says, "the prose is urgent, swarming with a maggoty life that runs counter to the cryogenic elegance of Cronenberg's translation."[45] Cronenberg's *Crash*, then is not a "faithful" rendering of the novel, but instead, as Sinclair writes, "belongs to its own time"—that is, the 1990s.[46] In fact, *Crash* (the film) sits at the midpoint between the publishing of *Crash* (the novel) and the present day. For our purposes, then, Cronenberg's *Crash* becomes a way for us to study how these themes—of life with automobility—persist, but also transform over time. We can ask ourselves how much Sinclair's assessment of life circa 1996 holds up for us today:

> [The film] belongs to a climate of pre-millennial boredom. It's a novella of the last days. It has to run for ever, hours and hours of road footage, centuries of sex without fertility or climax. It's a chamber work from the era of Clintonian telephone adultery (where the participants fall asleep). I want to see *all* the out-takes, the wet dawn motorways,

the yawning, shivering actors. That's the vision that has been tapped. Post-surveillance anti-drama. The death of excitement. A riposte to Hollywood's mega-budget prostitution of the senses. We have to learn to endure boredom to the point where egoless enlightenment can be achieved.[47]

Sinclair's cultural studies approach to "climate" takes us away from the film and the novel to something like the conditions under which both can be encountered. In fact, strains of the noted characteristics persist and have become more pronounced on film; consider the continuing evolution of slow cinema, essay films, and transcendental cinema as variations of "anti-drama" in pursuit of a moment of revelation. Indeed, Cronenberg's formalism—offering a "necrophile masque"—may make a reader of the novel wonder what a "faithful" adaptation would look and sound like.[48] Indeed, promiscuity seems inbred to the novel, as if deviance from it were the right of any adaption. For one thing, how would we account for the novel's narrator, James Ballard and the tone of his relentless, unselfconscious first-person narration? But the question of point of contact may be even more salient, and turn us around, or rather turn us back, since, obviously, I am writing about Ballard (and Cronenberg and Springsteen) from the present day—now nearing a half-century since these texts under discussion began to emerge. The very preoccupations of this volume frame my approach to the selected material, and place us (i.e., the contributors) in a position to mount instances of ecocritical writing in an antipastoral mode. In this way, we are continuing—by critical, philosophical means—the work expressed in song, story, and cinema.[49]

Conclusion: From Porno-Tech Delirium to Pre-Apocalyptic Prostitution

In the sixties, Jean-Luc Godard, a signature figure of the Nouvelle Vague, offered a striking meditation on the (perhaps unwitting or unconscious) link between capitalistic consumption and, yes, prostitution. In his film *2 or 3 Things I Know About Her* (*2 ou 3 choses que je sais d'elle*, 1967), Godard offers a vision of (with the etymology still in mind) porno-capitalism. As Amy Taubin writes: "Godard saw [the film] as an opportunity to explore a subject always on his mind—prostitution, and not only the actuality of it but as a metaphor encompassing all exchanges involving labor, money, and power in capitalism."[50] As customers of consumables, we are (all?) subject to the odd sense that *we* are being bought and sold (e.g., the way jobs pay us for our time, the proceeds from which we use to buy more products, and so on in the so-called "hedonic treadmill"[51]). In his distinctive way, Godard makes his protagonist duplicate—Juliette Janson is played by Marina Vlady—so that he can make an actual (fictional) prostitute into a (nonfictional) figure of the alienated Western bourgeoisie. "*2 or 3 Things* depicts the violation of both the city and Juliette," writes Taubin, and in this tandem, accentuates the way *what* we buy and own may come to own us and worse, destroy us (exhibit A: the automobile). The two or three things we *might* know about such characters—as well as ourselves (what *do* I know about myself?)—is part of Godard's provocation, since the film is always already asking such questions. Godard's film, a half-century on, remains generative for thinking about our emotional and erotic relationship to (our) bodies and the objects we presume to own.

Our thinking above about Catherine (in *Crash*) in company with Monica Vitti, and now with Juliette Janson and the actress Marina Vlady, underline how it is men—in all of these cases—who write these characters, these fictions, make these films, etc. While Godard may be lauded for his insights, his "inventiveness, and no one can ignore his facility," we might wish to join Cavell in noting where we find such "inventiveness compromised."[52] Thinking about how these women are characterized in literature and on screen, Cavell's registration of critique seems especially apt: "By taking a subject with no character, from whose person he has removed personhood, a subject incapable of accepting or rejecting anything," Godard has *himself* created "the condition of prostitution, and of advertisement."[53] His moral and political condemnation of consumer culture (including the "manhandling" of women) does not seem to breach his own capacities for *self*-criticism. Cavell's way of taking Godard to task doesn't eviscerate the potency of Godard's commentary, but instead further enriches it with irony and a philosophically minded humility.

Even as Godard turned his camera on women (perhaps who did not assume their complicity in the irony just noted), the song lyrics written by Springsteen often seem to be a decades-long lamentation over the failure of capitalism to satisfy the young, yearning heart (of both women and men). According to Springsteen's instances of folk poetry, the dispossessed masses of the lower-middle class—from the fifties to the present day—have had to cling to the few precious objects they choose to care for, cars preeminent among them, and, thus the dreams (broken or not) and values (achievable or not) that have attached themselves to the car (as icon, as myth).

According to Roger Ebert, as noted earlier, there is no such condition as symphorophilia, and though we might doubt his credentials as a psychiatrist, much less a theorist of human sexuality, as critics, we could all be on solid ground to wonder after the confluence of sex, cars, injury, and death; with Springsteen and Ballard, fresh in mind, we have distinctive and contemporaneous images of this amalgamation. From across an ocean, in two different countries, from staggered generations, these writers come to conclusions that reflect their times, places, and preoccupations—and yet are, nevertheless (and surprisingly, uncannily), pertinent to one another. Together, Springsteen and Ballard provide a useful heuristic for assessing the significance of the automobile in the daily lives of late twentieth and early-twenty-first century people, all of whom must contend with lives and landscapes shaped by its topography-defining presence and undeniable ubiquity.

Among several productive points of overlap, we might emphasize that Ballard and Springsteen both regard eroticism as activated—and sustained—by *transgression*. Indeed, the valences of "discharge" become pronounced in their company: given the quotations above, Ballard's obsession with bodily and vehicular fluids is apparent; meanwhile Springsteen's cars often serve as an accomplice to the release of sexual frustration (the backseat) or as a means for fleeing from it (the getaway). As a mobile signifier in its own right, "transgression" points to the "going across" of borders, lines, and territories.[54] These can be physical spaces, but more often they are mental. In Ballard's novel and Springsteen lyrics, we recurrently find out how erotic desire is primarily cognitive—dependent mostly on imagination, that is, on desire, longing, and dreaming (not so much in the Freudian sense, as in "having dreams" of some future). In this sense, the body is in the service of the mind's erotic demands; the body is an intermediary between bodies, be they made of flesh or steel. Not surprisingly, when erotic desire is frustrated—by conventions, by normative pressure, by prudery, by lack of imagination, by cowardice, by "the Man"—the pain can be severe. For Springsteen, this pain comes in the form of "broken dreams"; for Ballard, it is literalized in broken bodies—and as *wounds* (remembering here that "trauma" derives from the Greek for wound, while *traum* in German translates as dream). Yet, while a typical Springsteen hero may dwell in his misfortune, feeling it as a fate worthy of fury, Ballard eroticizes forms of trauma: the wound itself is transformed into an object of desire. In *Crash*, the open wound is but another bit of flesh to fetishize.

As Ballard (the character) begins to make love with Gabrielle, a woman partially paralyzed by a car crash, things proceed in unconventional ways, as when he begins to explore her wounds—and comes to think of his own: "As I unshackled the left leg brace and ran my fingers along the deep buckle groove, the corrugated skin felt hot and tender, more than the membrane of a vagina. This depraved orifice, the invagination of a sexual organ still in the embryonic stages of its evolution, reminded me of the small wounds on my own body, which still carried the contours of the instrument panel and controls."[55] A concentrated exploration of surface—where human flesh collides with "a tour de force of technology and kinaesthetic systems"[56]—culminates, somewhat logically, if again unconventionally: "My first orgasm, within the deep wound on her thigh, jolted my semen along this channel, irrigating its corrugated ditch. Holding the semen in her hand, she wiped it against the silver controls of the clutch treadle."[57] Feeling bashful, let me have Ballard the narrator take up the position of hermeneutician: "Each of her deformities became a potent metaphor for the excitements of a new violence. Her body, with its angular contours, its unexpected junctions of mucous membrane and hairline, detrusor muscle and erectile tissue, was a ripening anthology of perverse possibilities."[58] (Can we take a moment to appreciate how capable Ballard is as a novelist *and* as a cultural diagnostician—even for a malady that apparently does not exist?!) Gabrielle provides not just these wounds (that can be transformed into sites of sexual excitement) but also the ferrovitreous elements to fulfill the coupling of man and machine—in effect, to achieve what Ballard calls a "metal dream."[59]

What remains, then, to consider—in this perhaps unlikely coupling of Ballard and Springsteen—is how pleasure (perhaps especially sexual pleasure) and torment are both (primarily) "in the head," not the body. We create dreams ("broken" ones or "metal" ones), have fantasies that enliven or enervate, satisfy or destroy. In "Thunder Road" (*Born to Run*, 1975), heterosexual eroticism is choreographed with cars, with personal memory, and we are forced to remember how dreams shape our perception of desire—how there is "magic in the night": The non-hero of this melodrama calls out to Mary to "climb in" since they inhabit a "town full of losers," and he is "pulling out of here to win." He acknowledges "your lovers," and later, "all the boys you sent away," and in this finds himself haunted by their violence, their effect on her: "They scream your name at night in the street / Your graduation gown lies in rags at their feet." In all this turmoil of dreams and desires, seductions and summoning, there is eroticism mixed with trauma, and the palpable sense that the erotic arises as an antidote to death—whether of dreams, the spirit, or our bodies.

Coupled with the sexual energy of the scene—a suitor coaxing Mary to join him—there is also a Springsteen specialty: braiding signs of religious redemption with the symbology of the open road. From Woody Guthrie's "Will Rogers Highway" to Bob Dylan's *Highway 61 Revisited*, the American "ribbon of highway" "from sea to shining sea" has, of course, been celebrated for its liberatory potential—and no doubt, in song and novel, its literary fecundity.

In Springsteen's classic song "Thunder Road," he turns up the dial on salvation, where a girl like Mary will "waste [her] summer praying in vain for a savior to rise from these streets." Our rider declines to name himself such a savior, countering with the fact the only redemption he offers is "beneath this dirty hood." And maybe they are both not as good as they want to be, so they might as well "trade in these wings on some wheels." But where are they headed? To hell? No: "Heaven's waiting down the tracks." And as we see in the recent pop film adaptation of such ideas, *Blinded by the Light* (2019, dir. Gurinder Chadha), Springsteen's own iconography as an artist is tied up with not just the description of hallowed highways but the giving of a hope that "these two lanes will take us anywhere." For it is only with his hope, on the road, that one could fathom riding out "to case the promised land"—a wonderful edge of criminality and transgression finishing off the plea to Mary. *Take* my hand, *take* us anywhere, and now *take* the promised land—that is, *case* it. For the pursuit of happiness—driving your way in its direction, it would seem, demands a willingness to assume control: to get in, to gun it, and to steer.

Part of the subtitle of the chapter derives from a Springsteen lyric. And in invoking "Broken Heroes on a Last Chance Power Drive," I have meant to underscore how each of these encounters with popular culture—in music, novel, and cinema—provides a portrait of a hero (or heroine) who has seen his (or her) dreams compromised or otherwise dissipated, all the while "gunnin' that bitch loaded to blastin' point." In fact, Springsteen's father, Doug—a depressive who never told his son that he loved him—packed up his car and drove West from New Jersey to California to front his own "last chance."[60] With one car-load of belongings, and nothing more than a dream to get out of town, he drove West to a promised land far beyond the Jersey shore—driving "as if the miles could repair."[61]

The myth of the "last chance" has stoked and broken many a dream—the sense that "it's now or never"—yet as we continue to face grave admonitions from climate scientists about the "breaking point" and "the point of no return," we seem intent on a headlong pursuit of the "death waltz," heading for what Ballard calls, punningly, "autogeddon."[62] We, members of the human species, circa 2020, *we* are "broken heroes on a last chance power drive" mightily equipped with our individual and collective "suicide machines." In late capitalism, we seem at last to have arrived at a time when, despite or because of our addictive, expansive consumerism, there is paradoxically "nothing left that you could sell" ("Lost in the Flood," *Greetings from Asbury Park, NJ*, 1973). We are tired, we are spent. Instead of the glories of the open road—the desert sunrises, the mountain sunsets—there is "just junk all across the horizon, a real highwayman's farewell." As we say adieu to the age of the combustion engine—indeed, Volvo has already stopped making gas-only engines, and Mercedes-Benz announced it would soon cease their manufacture—the gesture can feel like a confirmation of a new era, that we will stem the tide in time. But then many environmental signs suggest we are too late. If we are already lost in the flood, we too will start asking: "Hey kid, you think that's oil? / Man, that ain't oil, that's blood" ("Lost in the Flood," *Greetings from Asbury Park, NJ,* 1973).

The Biblical resonance of being "lost in the flood" is now joined by the climate-science literalness of newly impeded coastlines (including the Jersey shore), pressing us with accelerating urgency to the question of our love affair with cars, with oil, that is, with blood—the passions that circulate in it, that culminate in its coursings, that release when the body is broken. What has for more than a century been a tool for conveyance, then an object of desire, and also something used to fulfill other desires, is now, at last, the subject of our most vital concern: our very existence. As the *New York Times* gamely inscribes new headlines week after week, month after month, detailing the extent of the devastation already achieved—and all that is predicted to come—life goes on, or seems to. Cars are still on the road. Gas is cheap. Auto-advertising is ubiquitous. We must be delusional, and suffer, as the behavioral economists and psychologists tell us, from an impairment in believing the future will arrive and that we should prepare for it.

Dystopian films of future apocalypse—from *The Omega Man* to *Mad Max* to *I Am Legend*—all feature prominently the survival of a car that is used as a means of survival for our survivor-hero. Springsteen, Ballard, and Cronenberg complicate these fantasies of survival-after-the-fact. They turn us back upon the psycho-geography (and -pathology) of everyday life, where we discover (if we are lucky!) how our attempts at pleasure and satisfaction are caught up with the causes of our pain and defeat.

One of the terrors of working on this chapter emerged from sharing a genuine sense of Dr. Helen Remington's sentiment: "After this sort of thing," a car-crash, "how do people manage to look at a car, let alone drive one?"[63] The rhetorical question is complemented by Ballard (again, the character), struggling to rise from his hospital bed after the accident that killed Helen's husband:

> After being bombarded endlessly by road-safety propaganda it was almost a relief to find myself in an actual accident. Like everyone else bludgeoned by these billboard harangues and television films of

imaginary accidents, I had felt a vague sense of unease that the grue-
some climax of my life was being rehearsed years in advance, and would
take place on some highway or road junction known only to the makers
of these films. At times, I had even speculated on the kind of traffic
accident in which I would die.[64]

In recent years, it seems that this nightmare of a hyper-specific death-
lying-in-wait, a kind of traffic fatality-fatalism, and its attendant anticipatory
grief, has been coupled with the grander nightmare of impending species
death. If the science holds, and our behaviors remain undeterred by the
reports, we should admit that we are *all* on a last chance power drive, trying
as we might to decide if we will slow down or (perversely) simply speed up
toward our doom—as we "[ride] headfirst into a hurricane and [disappear]
into a point" ("Lost in the Flood").

For these conclusions, we may encounter some pushback from a techno-
optimist who says our future, and survival, lies with electric cars and autonomous (i.e., "driverless") cars. In this scenario, there will be little-to-no polluting
emissions, and likewise very few, if any, accidents, injuries, and casualties;
from reckless to wreck-free, the "car crash" will become an anachronistic way
to die, like some medieval disease now eradicated. (But there will still be traffic
jams—and they may be worse![65]) If such a picture proves true, our survival
will be our reward. But one wonders about our psychological and even psychosexual relationship to driving—the shift must be as significant as from
on-foot to on-horse to in-car. We are, at last in a position to judge "if we can
see the inward change in men," as Eugene Morgan (Joseph Cotton) said in *The
Magnificent Ambersons*.[66] We have seen the change. And for that insight—propelled in part by the expressiveness of "Bruce!" and Ballard—we appear poised
to call the experiment with combustion at an end, that is, to enter a "post-
driving" experience of mobility. Intriguingly, Ballard anticipates this state-of-
affairs, and its attendant state-of-mind, when his character, James, borrows
a car from the studio. Even after he drives the car off the film set, James has
the persisting "notion that the car was still being used as part of an imaginary
event."[67] In a post-emission/post-casualty world of autonomous cars, driving
itself may become fetishized anew as nostalgia is coupled with some compen-
satory technology—perhaps VR and AR and immersive realms in which "dangerous" driving is a function of a purely hypothetical reality. By technological
means, symphorophilia will find new ways of expressiveness. Whether "erotic
delirium"—and the agency that feels empowered to dream "the metal dream"
while driving—can survive as well remains to be seen.

NOTES

1. For quick identification and differentiation, let me note that Cronenberg's *Crash* (1996) is not to be confused with the high melodrama of Oscar winner for Best Picture *Crash* (2004), written and directed by Paul Haggis. Earlier still, there is Harley Cokeliss' *Crash!* (1970), which is based on Ballard's *The Atrocity Exhibition* (1970) and, intriguingly, carried this title before Ballard himself published the novel *Crash* in 1973.

2. Louis P. Masur, *Runaway Dream: Born to Run and Bruce Spingsteen's American Vision* (New York: Bloomsbury, 2009); Roxanne Harde and Irwin Streight, eds., *Reading the Boss: Interdisciplinary Approaches to the Works of Bruce Springsteen,* (Lanham: Lexington Books, 2010); David Garrett Izzo, ed., *Bruce Springsteen and the American Soul: Essays on the Songs Influence of a Cultural Icon* (London: McFarland, 2011); Mark Bernhard, Kenneth Womack, and Jerry Zolten, eds., *Bruce Springsteen, Cultural Studies, and the Runaway American Dream* (Burlington: Ashgate, 2012); Donald L. Deardorff II, *Bruce Springsteen: American Poet and Prophet* (Lanham: The Scarecrow Press, 2014).

3. "Gearhead" and "Thumb stuck out as I go" come from "Hitch Hikin'," while "I take my El Camino, throw my saddle in and go" is drawn from the title track, "Western Stars" (*Western Stars*, 2019). Indeed, the hitchhiker's description of a "Gearhead in a souped-up '72" should call to mind an inventory of such figures depicted especially in Springsteen's lyrics from the '70s.

4. "Cadillac of the skies" is likely screenwriter Tom Stoppard's reading of Ballard's phrase "Cadillac of air combat" in the novel, J. G. Ballard, *Crash* (1973; New York: Picador, 2014), 151.

5. Zadie Smith, "On *Crash*," *The New York Review of Books*, July 10, 2014, nybooks.com.

6. Smith's *New York Review of Books* piece "On *Crash*" was reprinted as a preface to a reissue of Ballard's novel (2014), xi.

7. Smith, xiii.

8. Smith, ix.

9. Smith, ix.

10. Smith, xiii.

11. Smith, xv.

12. Ballard, *Crash*, xii, 2–3.

13. Ballard, 1.

14. Ballard, 7.

15. See John Money, "Paraphilias: Phenomenology and Classification," *American Journal of Psychotherapy* 38, no. 2 (1984): 164–78. Paraphilia is the term, in the *DSM-5*, that has replaced sexual perversion and sexual deviation; it is understood as including sexual fetishism.

16. See American Psychiatric Association, ed., "Fetishistic Disorder," in *Diagnostic and Statistical Manual of Mental Disorders,* 5th ed. (Washington, DC: APA, 2013), 700.

17. Ballard, *Crash*, 9.

18. Ballard, 10.

19. Ballard, 68.

20. Ballard, 69.

21. Ballard, 57, 59.

22. Lars Svendsen, *A Philosophy of Boredom*, trans. John Irons (London: Reaktion Books, 2005), 82. First published as *Kjedsomhetens filosofi* (1999).

23. Martin Barker, Jane Arthurs, and Ramaswami Harindranath. *The Crash Controversy: Censorship Campaigns and Film Reception* (New York: Wallflower Press, 2001).

24. Ballard, *Crash*, 20–21.

25. Roger Ebert, review of *Crash*, March 21, 1997, https://www.rogerebert.com/reviews/crash-1997.
26. Ebert.
27. See Linda Williams, *Hard Core: Power, Pleasure, and the "Frenzy of the Visible"* (Berkeley: University of California Press, 1989); Linda Williams, ed., *Porn Studies* (Durham: Duke University Press, 2004); and Linda Williams, *Screening Sex* (Durham: Duke University Press, 2008).
28. Ebert.
29. See Clement Greenberg, "Avant-Garde and Kitsch" (1939) in *Art and Culture: Critical Essays* (Boston: Beacon Press, 1961). Will Self said Ballard was "the last great English avatar of the avant-garde."
30. For reflections on the humanistic sublime, see my " 'Profoundly Unreconciled to Nature': Ecstatic Truth and the Humanistic Sublime in Werner Herzog's War Films," in *The Philosophy of War Films*, ed. David LaRocca (Lexington: University Press of Kentucky, 2014), 437–82.
31. Ballard, *Crash*, 27.
32. Ballard, 15.
33. Ballard, 44.
34. Ballard, 41.
35. Ballard, 15.
36. Ballard, 17.
37. Ballard, 17, 45, 52.
38. Ballard, 28.
39. Cavell, *The World Viewed: Reflections on the Ontology of Film*, expanded ed. (1971; Cambridge: Harvard University Press, 1979), 96.
40. Ballard, *Crash*, 165.
41. For more on Ballard's style and how, in particular, it finds its way *out* of its literary origins, specifically, how Ballard's *Crash* is "taken up and transformed through its adaptation into philosophy and film: Jean Baudrillard's *Simulacra and Simulation* (1994) and David Cronenberg's *Crash* (Canada, 1996)," see Catherine Constable, "Theory as Style: Adapting *Crash* via Baudrillard and Cronenberg," in *New Takes in Film-Philosophy*, ed. Havi Carel and Greg Tuck (New York: Palgrave Macmillan, 2011), 135–53.
42. Ballard, *Crash*, 21, 23.
43. Ballard, 32.
44. Ballard, 32.
45. Iain Sinclair, *Crash: David Cronenberg's Post-Mortem on J. G. Ballard's "Trajectory of Fate"* (London: BFI, 1999), 43.
46. Sinclair, 57.
47. Sinclair, 57.
48. Sinclair, 57.
49. See also my chapter "Hunger in the Heart of Nature: Werner Herzog's Anti-Sentimental Dispatches from the American Wilderness (Reflections on *Grizzly Man*)," in *Dark Nature: Anti-Pastoral Essays in American Literature and Culture*, ed. Richard J. Schneider (Lanham: Lexington Books, 2016); and my review of Susan McWilliams Barndt's *The American Road Trip and American Political Thought*, in *The Review of Politics* 81, no. 3 (2019): 529–32, https://doi.org/10.1017/S0034670519000159.
50. Amy Taubin, "The Whole and Its Parts," an essay in the insert accompanying Criterion DVD #482, *2 ou 3 choses que je sais d'elle* (1967), 87 min, color.
51. The notion of the "hedonic treadmill" can be found in modern theorists such as P. Brickman and D. Campbell, "Hedonic Relativism and Planning the Good Society," in *Adaptation-level Theory*, ed. M. H. Apley (New York: Academic Press, 1971), 287–302.

The cyclical, ceaseless nature of the image finds fine form much earlier, though, in Robert Burton: "A true saying it is, *Desire hath no rest*, is infinite in itself, endless; and as one calls it, a perpetual rack, or horse-mill, according to Austin, still going round as in a ring," *The Anatomy of Melancholy* (1621).

52. Cavell, *The World Viewed*, 99.
53. Cavell, 99.
54. For more on the *trans-* prefix and its deployment in philosophy, literature, cultural studies, and political theory, see David LaRocca and Ricardo Miguel-Alfonso, eds., *A Power to Translate the World: New Essays on Emerson and International Culture* (Lebanon, NH: Dartmouth College Press, 2015).
55. Ballard, *Crash*, 162. The scene with James and Gabrielle, and her wounds, is referenced at 01:16:00 in Cronenberg's film.
56. Ballard, *Crash*, 163.
57. Ballard, 163.
58. Ballard, 161.
59. Ballard, 163.
60. Bruce Springsteen, *Born to Run* (New York: Simon and Schuster, 2016), 109.
61. Springsteen, 112.
62. "Jungleland"; Ballard, *Crash*, 41.
63. Ballard, *Crash*, 60.
64. Ballard, 30–31.
65. John Markoff, "Urban Planning Guru Says Driverless Cars Won't Fix Congestion," *The New York Times*, October 27, 2018, nytimes.com.
66. In *The Magnificent Ambersons* (1942, dir. Orson Welles), Eugene Morgan (Joseph Cotton) offers some pertinent remarks at 00:41:43, including an admission: "I'm not sure George is wrong about automobiles. With all their speed forward, they may be a step backward in civilization. . . . And I think men's minds are going to be changed in subtle ways because of automobiles. . . . May be that in ten or twenty years from now—if we can see the inward change in men by that time—I shouldn't be able to defend the gasoline engine, but would have to agree with George."
67. Ballard, *Crash*, 49.

CHAPTER 7

Remainders of the Fossil Regime: Automobility Regression in Three Post-Apocalyptic Novels

Brent Ryan Bellamy

The space of the future is a smooth and neoliberal space, where passengers move as freely as goods and capital.

> —Karen Pinkus, "On Climate, Cars, and Literary Theory"

The cultural expression of energy is brought home by the historiographical thought experiments of post-apocalyptic stories.[1] Most post-apocalyptic novels offer energy revelation by way of reducing the possibilities for the future. In particular, such tales restrict (auto)mobility and the high-speed transportation of both goods and people around the globe, focusing instead on a locale or region traversable by slower modes of travel. Unlike the vision of a neoliberal future molded around smooth, technology-driven transportation, as described in the epigraph by Karen Pinkus, post-apocalyptic stories subtract fossil fuels from social life thereby revealing the absolute reliance of the modern subject on such fuels, their by-products, and the habits they encouraged. As subjects of "petroculture," especially those of us situated in developed countries, we have come to expect a smoothness of conveyance to our destinations, on the one hand, and the reliable delivery of goods to us at home, on the other.[2] Post-apocalyptic texts interrupt this connection. They imagine how characters might respond to new strains on travel and limited access to goods, and they project future possibilities for the remainders of petromodernity. Such novels administer a litmus test for survivability and adaptive potential in the form of post-apocalyptic plots.[3]

The reduction of the scale and complexity of contemporary social life to its imagined core conflicts and contradictions unsurprisingly produces an awareness of energy concerns that has, until quite recently, remained largely absent in the field of cultural production more broadly. Given the infrastructural failure that post-apocalyptic stories typically assume, their characters appear in a world in which aspects of contemporary life, such as automobility, exist only as distant memories or rare luxuries, assuming they have not been forgotten entirely or been ramped into some violent spectacle of a fossil-fueled battle royal amid the rubble-strewn wastes.[4] More likely in post-apocalyptic scenarios are futures of scarcity, where the goods and services that required shipments from afar or energy and communications infrastructures will be available no longer: absent a steady supply of fuel, lines of supply are severed, networks of communication and the attendant sense of social connectivity evaporate, gears seize and foods rot, the productivity of all labor is radically constrained.[5]

Post-apocalyptic novels that take the question of fuel sources and energy infrastructures into their calculations of character survival perform a useful form of speculative reasoning. Whether suspicious of the fossil regime or nostalgic for the explosive potentials of oil's energic burst (and how could one not feel a little of each?), these texts offer critical lessons about the legacies of fossil fuels and their impact on modern life. What becomes clear in examining this archive is that post-apocalyptic novels develop more compelling scenarios when they imagine what a life without electricity might look like, as opposed to prophesying the end of oil in particular. These energy apocalypse novels better represent both the inertial necessity of energy for modernity and the profound impacts of a life not *just* without oil, but *also* without extraction and refinement teams, distribution networks, maintenance crews, and technocrats of energy infrastructure. By imagining what has vanished from an imagined future, post-apocalyptic novels draw attention to what exists in the present.

As early as the 1960s post-apocalyptic scenarios were considering the impacts of a loss of petroleum and electricity on daily life. Pat Frank's *Alas, Babylon* (1959), for instance, is set in the town of Fort Repose, FL. The book dramatizes the isolation of such a town during the nationwide Red Alert: "Like most small towns, Fort Repose's food and drug supply was dependent upon daily or thrice weekly deliveries from warehouses in the larger cities. Each day trucks replenished its filling stations. For all other merchandise, it was dependent upon shipments by mail, express, and highway freight, from jobbers and manufacturers elsewhere."[6] Even in 1959, before just-in-time production and the green revolution, small towns and urban centers relied on industrial agriculture.[7] Frank's novel traces the enchainment from stores' shelves and fueling stations' reservoirs through delivery fleets and drivers back to implied warehouses and gasoline refineries. What the post-apocalyptic story does that other fictions do not is to shock awareness of energy into being through a focused, subtractive gesture. The disappearance of items from store shelves or, rather, their lack of replenishment, signals the fossil-fueled character of their logistics.

Frank does not stop there. Using the focal point of Fort Repose as a figure for what must be going on elsewhere across the United States, *Alas, Babylon* runs a thought experiment premised on removing the supply chains that keep any given town or city fed and fueled: "With the Red Alert, all these services halted and at once. Like thousands of towns and villages not directly seared by war, Fort Repose became an island. . . . Its inhabitants would have to subsist on whatever was already within its boundaries, plus what they might scrounge from the countryside."[8] The importance of transportation, and what has since become known as "logistics," is striking in Frank's description of how Fort Repose "became like an island."[9] What might be presumed to be a constantly stable and plentiful supply of food in the supermarket or petrol at the gas pump is under constant movement—goods are sold or thrown out, gasoline is pumped into vehicles and then burned. One of Frank's characters realizes that "one thing he certainly should have foreseen . . . was the loss of electricity."[10] This realization seems obvious in retrospect, but rather than stocking nonperishable foods, the characters gather fruits and meats.

The post-apocalyptic story, in adhering to a reality effect, can make evident the obvious, though unrealized truth:

> Even had Orlando escaped, the electricity would have died within a few weeks or months. Electricity was created by burning fuel oil in the Orlando plants. When the oil ran out, it could not be replenished during the chaos of war. There was no longer a rail system, or rail centers, nor were tankers plying the coasts on missions of civilian supply. . . . Even those sections of the country which escaped destruction entirely would not long have lights. Their power would last only as long as fuel stocks on hand.[11]

In narrative form, posing the question of how a town might go about living through the aftermath of a nuclear attack, the text also addresses an unremarked upon feature of daily life. The petrocapitalist reliance on the ceaseless circulation of commodities generates a population and social infrastructure that is profoundly unprepared for any kind of catastrophic situation and particularly ill-equipped for the nuclear crisis imagined by Frank.

Subsequent post-apocalyptic novels would include the disappearance of fuel as part of their thought experiments. In the 1990s, Octavia E. Butler's *Parable of the Sower* (1993) makes similar gestures to the ones found in Frank's novel. Butler's scarcity-wracked United States of 2024 is one where massive social and cultural changes have taken place, yet such changes have no single source; rather, decline and enclosure characterize this future. Butler reveals the lack of transportation before sharing the animating conceit of the protagonist: Lauren Oya Olamina has a drug induced condition known as hyperempathy. In *Parable*, automobiles cease working as gasoline gets put to other uses. "To the adults," Olamina writes in the journal entry dated Sunday, July 21, 2024, "going outside to a real church was like stepping back into the good old days when there were churches all over the place and too many lights and gasoline was for fueling cars and tracks instead of for torching things."[12] The conjunctive rhythm of this sentence accounts for the loss of old habits, in this case they are not Olamina's and belong instead to her elders' thoughts. They equate burning gasoline in the internal combustion engine with bounty and imagine this arrangement is the way things ought to be. Along these lines, Olamina adds: "They never miss a chance to relive the good old days or to tell kids how great it's going to be when the country gets back on its feet and good times come back."[13] Butler ominously suggests of her storyworld not that the gasoline has run out or stopped being refined and distributed but rather that it has been put to more violent, immediate uses. The lack of automobiles becomes important again later in *Parable of the Sower* as Olamina travels away from her walled community of Robledo in search of a place to found a new homestead.

Before this journey, Butler includes other important references to the waning of automobility. In the journal entry dated Saturday, March 29, 2025, Olamina writes, "The Moss rabbit house is a converted three-car garage added to the property in the 1980s according to Dad. *It's hard to believe any household once had three cars, and gas fueled cars at that.* But I remember the old garage before Richard Moss converted it. It was huge with three black oil spots on the floor where three cars had once been housed."[14] Those three spots signify the absent presence of fossil-fueled automobility and the relations that it supported. For adults in Butler's storyworld, those three stains indicate a lost wealth that might someday return. To Olamina and others of her generation, they signal a difficulty to understand the remains of the fossil regime now erased by an economic-decline induced transition away from fossil-fueled logistics.

In the analyses that follow, I look specifically to futures of scarcity and futures depicted as oil-poor. After the energy apocalypse the neat routines of middle-class life have been rendered near impossible to maintain: working late most weeknights, running the weekend's errands, enjoying a meal with friends, and so on. The deep-seated patterns of considerations imprinted upon the petro-modern subject remain in place. Some characters still behave as though the lights will come back on or the shipments of food will begin to arrive once more. These behaviors reveal in negative what a life lived in energy abundance is like, and, in having that sort of life stripped away, one can begin to see the profound inequalities that structure it. Reading post-apocalyptic novels with *energy* in mind means attending to the presence of abundant energy, the effects of having it, and strategies for coping *with* it just as much as for coping without it.[15] I analyze three recent novels that feature a regression of automobility: Emily St. John Mandel's *Station Eleven* (2014), Peter Heller's *The Dog Stars* (2012), and John Varley's *Slow Apocalypse* (2012).[16]

Station Eleven: Energy's Apocalypse

Emily St. John Mandel's *Station Eleven* captures a feeling of *power*lessness so acutely that, if only for a moment, the full gravity of losing power is fully conveyed to the reader. Twenty years after the "Georgia Flu" has massively reduced the world population, a character flips a light switch:

> Kirsten closed her eyes for just a second as she flipped the light switch. Naturally nothing happened, but as always in these moments she found herself straining to remember what it had been like when this motion had worked: walk into a room, flip a switch and the room floods with light. The trouble was she wasn't sure if she remembered or only imagined remembering this.[17]

This passage implies that the expectation that something might happen as a character flips a switch is *un*natural. It connects grasping for the light to a memory that cannot be accessed, yet this feeling is one Kristen has attempted to reach before. She attempts to access what Patricia Yaeger has called "the touch-a-switch-and-it's-light magic of electrical power," and all she can find are her own uncertainties.[18] In the novel, it has been twenty years since the power failed. Though it thinks explicitly about energy, the novel omits the cause of energy failure. It invites assumptions about what has taken place. At least that is the assumption I make about the status of energy infrastructure in this novel. A disease ravaged the population of North America and perhaps little could be done to get the dams, nuclear power plants, and the coal furnaces running once more.

The narrative recounts the experiences of several characters before, during, and after a disease outbreak devastates North America, alternating between multiple moments—a lead up to the outbreak, immediately following it, and a moment twenty years later. The novel moves between the past in LA, year zero in Toronto, and year twenty in the Great Lakes region and the Severn City airport. In year zero, an emergency medical technician named Jeevan Chaudhary holes up with his brother to wait out the collapse brought about by the disease. In year twenty, the focus jumps back and forth. One group makes a home in the airport, using the space provided and the food stored to get themselves on their feet.[19] A character in the group founds a Museum of Civilization to commemorate the past, accepting MP3 players, magazines, and other items for the collection. As Diletta De Cristofaro makes clear, this Museum elegizes the "bygone hyper-globalized world" in a way that ultimately refuses "to paint the old world as worthy of a destruction."[20] Kirsten Raymonde is part of another group: an orchestra and theatre troupe that continues to tour the Great Lakes region. They take every opportunity to explore the ruins of modernity, such as houses, old schools, and so on.

Raymonde's encounters defamiliarize spaces and actions habitual for most readers—from the routine of flipping a light switch to that of going to school. The structures are still in place, but instead of producing electrical effects and orchestrating social activities, these remainders have been repurposed either as useful in new ways or as startling reminders of the technological thrust of human culture. The strain of remembering slips between certainty and fancy, and it signals the principal work that the post-apocalyptic mode does in relation to thinking about energy: it allows for the imaginary subtraction of energy's use. Even the half-remembered, half-forgotten ways energy used to touch the lives of characters living in the wake of societal collapse face this reduction, marking all the more strongly the bizarre, yet normalized ways that modern humans interact with energy on a daily basis.

In a revelation remarkably similar to the one experienced by one of Frank's characters in *Alas, Babylon*, one of Mandel's characters realizes the human-motive power that is required to keep a city moving. I quote at length:

> On silent afternoons in his brother's apartment, Jeevan found himself thinking about how human the city is, how human everything is. We bemoaned the impersonality of the modern world, but that was a lie, it seemed to him; it had never been impersonal at all. There had always been a massive delicate infrastructure of people, all of them working

unnoticed around us, and when people stop going to work, the entire operation grinds to a halt. No one delivers fuel to the gas stations or the airports. Cars are stranded. Airplanes cannot fly. Trucks remain at their points of origin. Food never reaches the cities; grocery stores close. Businesses are locked and then looted. No one comes to work at the power plants or the substations, no one removes fallen trees from electrical lines.[21]

Characters caught in post-apocalyptic stories often have this revelation, it seems. Of course, it also attempts to produce this awareness for readers as well. Frank's work nurtured a preparedness movement in the United States with his elaboration of what practical steps could be taken to ready oneself for a nuclear strike. Mandel does not outline a program for survival here, so much as reproduce the profound insight that despite the illusion of a dearth of work, so many must labor every day to make sure people in the city can move, are fed, clothed, and warm. It is not too much of a stretch to equate Mandel's work here and other post-apocalyptic writers with producing a kind of organic Marxism. The passage above so clearly highlights the secret of the commodity: it is human labor that Chaudhary discovers in his musing. That it takes a rupture, even an imagined one, of the steadily moving, fossil-fueled city signals both the way oil as a motive force has become hidden in plain sight and the efficacy of imagined scenarios to make such facts plainly visible once more.

Distinct from the above considerations of automobility regression, post-apocalyptic novels also lament other things lost after the catastrophe. Early in *Station Eleven*, Mandel takes an entire chapter to list places one can no longer go and things one can no longer do, mapping in the manner of making an itinerary:

No more diving into pools of chlorinated water lit green from below. No more ball games played out under floodlights. No more porch lights with moths fluttering on summer nights. No more trains running under the surface of cities on the dazzling power of the electric third rail. No more cities. No more films, except rarely, except with a generator drowning out half the dialogue, and only then for the first little while until the fuel for the generators ran out, because automobile gas goes stale after two or three years. Aviation gas lasts longer, but it was difficult to come by.[22]

The order of things in Mandel's list is worth considering. The list transitions from the heady days of summer—swimming pools, baseball, and warm nights—to public transport; the list's theme hangs on a thread of electric power. Mandell's list expands from concrete immediacy to increasingly abstract and general phenomena: "No more cities." The real loss here is dissimilar from that explored by Chaudhary or by Pat Frank's characters in *Alas, Babylon*. Here, it is the petrocultural experiences of modernity that Mandel's list begins to mourn.

The second burst of Mandel's list cleaves to the theme of energy for entertainment: "No more screens shining in the half-light as people raise their phones above the crowd to take photographs of concert stages. No more concert stages lit by candy-coloured halogens, no more electronic, punk, electric guitars."[23] The list is associative and grounded in a location: the concert hall. The specificity of the references to "electronic, punk, and electric guitars" informs the reader that this list could only be Raymonde's if it was someone else's first, as Raymonde was too young to hold memories of such things. Automobility regression entails the development of a keen sense of nostalgia for the things a younger generation never even had the chance to experience. The occasion of the novel itself provides Mandel an opportunity to process the significance of a loss of power in the way it might come to shape intergenerational relationships and give rise to new energy cultures.

As much as these losses communicate, it is the central paragraph of Mandel's litany that stands out as most crucial to the project of figuring post-apocalyptic survival: "No more flight. No more towns glimpsed from the sky through airplane windows, points of glimmering light; no more looking down from thirty thousand feet and imagining the lives lit up by those lights at that moment. No more airplanes, no more requests to put your tray table in its upright and locked position." It is not the loss of connection that troubles the litany's speaker most. It is rather the experience of flying itself. The list captures affective, embodied experience of being on a plane, even though one of its central characters struggled to recall flipping a light switch.[24] The speaker interrupts themselves, "but no, that wasn't true, there were still airplanes here and there. They stood dormant on runways and in hangers. They collected snow on their wings. In the cold months, they were ideal for food storage. In summer the ones near orchards were filled with trays of fruit that dehydrated in the heat. Teenagers snuck into them to have sex. Rust blossomed and streaked."[25] The speaker here must be either a narrator, who exists outside the time of the storyworld, or one of the characters that transform the Port Severn Airport into a livable community. A whole group of survivors hole up in an airport, using the airplanes exactly as described in the above passage.

Once used to convey passengers around the world, they now serve the more mundane purpose as climate controlled, or at least, private spaces close to home, yet far enough to make them useful. This group of survivors not only make use of one of the most profoundly liminal and alienating spaces of modernity, but they also found a museum dedicated to memorializing petroculture.

Subtracting oil is not like removing any other commodity from the story-world. That difference only becomes visible in stories, such as post-apocalyptic ones, where oil is gone and, as it turns out, with it goes just about everything else.[26] If energy input is measured in the form of how oil fuels infrastructures, the development of machinery, and everyday life, the very materials of Mandel's lists, then the traces of the energy regime are right there on the surface as surely as are the remainders of capital in post-apocalyptic fiction. Critic of the post-apocalypse Briohny Doyle argues that such remainders "form the substance of the postapocalyptic imagination."[27] I argue that by subtracting oil from the story-world, post-apocalyptic storytelling, such as Mandel's, moves beyond positive claims about the social meaning of oil and begins to imagine a reduced future that simultaneously addresses the deep energy commitments of the real-world present and hints at the possibilities for a post-petrol future. *Station Eleven* envisions a world where the detritus of late capitalism has not vanished. Instead the physical traces of an energy regime, such as the light switch in the above passage, mark the spaces of Mandel's book as useless reminders of half-forgotten memories. The touring group of performers has even converted the cabs of old cars into sleighs to be pulled along with them. The remainders of the fossil regime persist as either half-forgotten memories or in the repurposing of old objects for new ends. *Station Eleven* effectively communicates the loss of the fossil regime precisely because it does not take oil as its object. It sets out to tell a story leading to and flowing from the massively fatal Georgia Flu. Rather than imagining whether good life will be possible without oil, it subtracts the energy regime by necessity. Without the people in place to maintain the system, attend to the infrastructure, and monitor the pipelines and reactors, these systems simply break. *Station Eleven* offers itself as a novel useful for thinking about energy, precisely because it takes other stories as its focus—the exploration of abandoned homes, the litany of lost experiences, or the people who make a home out of an airport.

Fuel as Resource for *The Dog Stars*

In Peter Heller's novel *The Dog Stars*, the protagonist lives at a small air field, which he describes as a superb place to live, given the post-apocalyptic conditions:

On a big creek, check. So water, check. Anyone who read anything knew, too, that it was a model for sustainable power, check. Every house with panels and the FBO run mostly on wind. Check. FBO means Fixed Base Operator. Could've just said the Folks Who Run the Airport. If they knew what was coming they wouldn't have complicated things that much.[28]

Hig is a knowledgeable pilot: he understands the short life span of unleaded gasoline, where to find the freshest airplane fuel, and how to best extend its shelf life. At one point, he imagines that the supply will last him as long as he needs, thinking to himself: "In ten years the additive will no longer keep the fuel fresh enough. In ten years I'll be done with all this. Maybe."[29] The novel accounts for the continued use of fossil-fueled vehicles in a thoughtful way, which is not to say that it is energy-focused. Rather, it constructs its concern about fossil fuels as background ambience. Here, fuel-concern registers through an older sense of economy (as in household accounting). Unlike *Station Eleven*, *The Dog Stars* considers fuel as resource.

The book fluctuates between the punchy internal dialogue of the character and something approaching metacommentary. The book's aphoristic form makes this distinction clear: it does not have chapters, as such; instead sections are separated by an asterisk. A section could be a sentence, a paragraph, or longer. Hig often thinks in short bursts of rhetorical glee: "I still got a mild kick out of free gas."[30] In accretion, this mode transforms, becoming a more involved rationalization of the post-apocalyptic scenario. These thoughts still belong to Hig but offer a more complete picture of the storyworld—an airplane pilot survives the apocalypse, lives on an air field, and has an airplane with plenty of fuel.

The novel blends post-apocalyptic tropes with explanatory information about fuel. In a sense, it provides a kind of post-apocalyptic energy literacy. "I fuel up. The pump runs off its own solar panel. Used to use a battery and inverter but the battery died so I wired it directly to the inverter and now can only fuel up if the sun is shining which it is. I have a hand pump if I need it, but it's a pain." Hig has access to three kinds of energy: stored, solar, and kinetic. His work is taxing, but ultimately enjoyable. He climbs a step-ladder to fill the tanks "through capped intakes at the top of each wing." He complains, "it's a real pain to be on the ground and pump and keep track of the fuel level which is checked by climbing up and looking straight down into the bladder through the fill hole." He can fuel up his ride, but the procedure requires focus. Though he can "estimate and get it close," it is "easier just to stand up there and pull the trigger on the pump hose and hear the reassuring electric hum and the clicking of the numbers rolling on the meter like filling up a car used to be."[31] In filling up the plane's tank, Hig expresses nostalgia for the easy of automated pumps and electric sensors. Doing things by hand and eye is challenging. Ultimately, he communicates his own expertise and capacity as a pilot in the face of automobility regression.

Hig interrupts such nostalgic longing. He notes the fuel's shelf-life, "Plenty of gas still out in the world but problem is the auto gas went stale and bad a year or two after. 100 low lead, which I burn, is stable something like ten years." In this way, Hig shares his intimate knowledge of how to treat a fossil-fueled machine and how much longer he has until the fuel runs out. He continues, "I expect to lose it one of these days. I can add PRI [fuel stabilizer] and nurse it along for ten more years probably. Then I'll have to look for jet fuel which is kerosene and lasts for basically ever. I know where it is, the closest. I know that right now I'm the only one alive who knows, or at least knows how to get it out." But, Hig's ruminations in the passage are not entirely for the sake of energy literacy, they also play on the convention of the post-apocalyptic mode; for instance, Hig raises risky propositions, resource wars, and the dangerous lengths one will go to for fuel: "Every time I land at Rocky Mountains Airport I feel vulnerable in ways I never do at other stops. It's too big. A big old jetport with scores of buildings, hangars, sheds and the pumps and the steel fill plates out in the open."[32] The fuel situation at the Hig's air strip recalls the past way of doing things, and, as Hig struggles with awkwardly fueling his plane, he forecasts the future fortunes of his fuel supply.

Each trip to scout their small territory is limited by the amount of fuel required to get home again safely, by a point of no return, by a limit beyond which Hig cannot go. *The Dog Stars* does not stop at that limit. On one of his trips around the perimeter, Hig intercepts the briefest signal from a distant control tower. It is choppy and cuts out, but leaves him in a slowly mounting dilemma, indeed it takes a full three years before he decides to act. The novel realizes the question of whether he should investigate this message, trading in his life of repeated tasks and his companion Bangley's insistence that he not get lost in "Recreating" to chase this ghostly faint signal of a new, different situation.[33] Hig's conundrum, in the novel, echoes decisions long ago made by the implied necessities of capital: to continue on short excursions to gather more supplies or to take the chance on a long-haul flight chasing an alien signal to see if there is another way of living?

For all its consideration of fuel as resource, *The Dog Stars* concludes by offering a standard conclusion to its post-apocalyptic plot. Hig follows the signal and finds love, and he must use his cunning and ingenuity along the way. This novel does not end up imagining a future energy transition, so much as it bears witness to one man processing the trauma and depression of surviving the love of his life and then the death of his dog. Loss is sad, true, but *The Dog Stars* offers little more than that fact. Its relation to energy is still imagined in much the same way as Robinson Crusoe. It tracks energy in the form of the records. Unlike Crusoe, Hig attends to airplane fuel rather than driftwood and foodstuffs. The book's post-apocalyptic conceit raises questions about energy as resource, and encourages the view that with the right knowledge, training, and equipment the right person could continue to fly in a world where fossil fuel extraction, refinement, and distribution has come to a standstill.

Slow Apocalypse in Energy's Absence

As with the characters in Mandel's and Heller's novels, those in John Varley's *Slow Apocalypse* must consistently check if their old habits and patterns of movement make sense. After holing up in their suburb, the central characters set out to discover if Los Angeles, once the land of highways and automobility, is passable in the aftermath of a massive earthquake. Varley's protagonist Dave Marshall thinks to himself, "the map is not the terrain."[34] His discovery that many of LA's landmark buildings are absent or destroyed after a massive earthquake rocks the city seems to prove him correct. Moreover, the community militias make previously traversable roadways impassable with barricades. The ease of movement that motor vehicles granted vanishes along with highway maintenance crews, traffic cops, and drive-thru restaurants. *Slow Apocalypse* narrativizes the process of checking each no-longer usable feature of modern life like so many blocked or dead-end streets. Late in the novel, Dave Marshall, his wife Karen, daughter Addison, and daughter's horse Ranger join with Dave's others to escape LA. They manage it at a slow crawl in an escalade and two retrofitted Mad-Max-type vehicles: a U-Haul truck and a school bus each equipped with a wood-chip burning engine and book-stuffed armor plating.[35]

The hook for the plot of *Slow Apocalypse* catches on Marshall's role as a Hollywood screen writer. This fact that renders him woefully underprepared for the events of the novel, even if it is also what gives the chance to prepare for the worst. At the novel's opening, Marshall is doing research for a sci-fi thriller when a retired military man who warns him of a top-secret scientifically manufactured super virus capable of rendering the world's oil reserves inert.[36] The single science-fiction story element is also what causes the breakdown of modern life. The virus itself first appears as a Hollywood plot hook, described by an old military man, but it turns out to be true. The virus is a literary conceit in the truest sense then: if readers can accept it, the rest of the story follows. The camera eye of the novel itself, set in motion by the event of the petroleum virus, does not reveal any more than Dave Marshall can see or describe. Instead the novel stages a geopolitical event that it then tracks through the particular senses of a character caught in Los Angeles. On the surface, the apocalyptic event that rocks Los Angeles is an earthquake, yet Marshall has insider information and so the reader knows that the quake is a result of the solidification of oil reserves.

With multiple touchstones in the post-apocalyptic tradition, *Slow Apocalypse* reads like an amalgamation of *Ill Wind* (1995), by Kevin J. Anderson and Doug Beason, and Albert Brooks' *Twenty Thirty* (2011), and ends like James Howard Kunstler's *World Made by Hand* (2008).[37] Its recombinant storyworld takes on the remainders of an LA remade by the narrative act of world destroying, of previous apocalyptic plots, and of variant approaches to questions of both the subtraction of *oil* and the consideration of *energy* after the apocalyptic event. T. S. Miller writes a review of the novel for *Strange Horizons* and makes an astute point: "At this point in the universal saturation of all forms of culture with apocalypse, it can be exceedingly difficult to produce an end of the world that we haven't already seen before."[38] The synthesis provided by the novel, however, offers a better vantage on the working of the genre itself, and, I would argue, its entanglement with the cultural logic of the fossil regime. In the same review, Miller writes, *Slow Apocalypse* "narrates the gradual diminishment of the world, the forced reduction of modern globalized society to a collection of impossibly distant localities."[39] The novel not only forcibly removes oil from the storyworld causing literal and figurative shockwaves, but it also tracks the profoundly isolating effect that both the earth's tectonic upheaval and reduced vehicle availability can have. Before this point gets lost, I think that both of Miller's observations of Varley's book are telling of the same phenomena: the fossil regime and its culture of transport both enables and produces a cultural milieu wherein the stories we tell are multiple and appear varied, yet closer inspection reveals a repetition compulsion in both the arena of travel and the domain of narrative. More work has yet to be done on the correspondence drawn in Varley's storyworld between an "end of the world we haven't seen before" and the "forced reduction of modernized global society to a collection of impossibly distant localities." The lived experience of such a transformed social and political space will prove profoundly unique and challenging when compared to the suburban experience of Marshall and his family.

The repeated narrative act of subtracting oil and the fossil regime from imagined futures emphasizes the longevity and tenacity of oil's modernizing promise. In Mandel's and Heller's attempts to imagine what an energy-scarce future would be like, I still find a world of abundance. Whether food, art, culture, and community, or not-yet-stale airplane fuel, these novels do not capture the scarcity of food and resources imagined by Varley. *Slow Apocalypse* demonstrates that it is increasingly difficult to produce a sight-yet-unseen end-of-the-world story, not because of its generic remainders and plot repetitions, but because its city-street verisimilitude and refugee-crisis imaginary present a near-future extrapolation founded in a real world that does not seem to need destruction of oil reserves to threaten collapse.

The post-apocalyptic imaginary is one that can be tied to the cultural horizons of capital once it has become entirely reliant on fossil-fuels. In "A Short History of Energy Cultures: Or, the Marriage of Catastrophe and Exuberance," Fredrick Buell engages scarcity thinking as a possibly revelatory way of imagining oil culture's current dominance: "Oil's possible collapse, as imagined today, provides both motivation and a heuristic for asking many interesting questions about oil's relationships with culture, in both the past and the present."[40] Drawing on environmental sociologist William Catton's work, Fredrick Buell forms his argument around twin poles: "Fossil-fuel culture can be, in short, described as an 'age of *exuberance*'—an age which is also, given the dwindling finitude of the resources it increasingly makes social life dependent on, haunted by *catastrophe*."[41] Buell tracks a nuanced unfolding of the fossil regime between these two poles of exuberance and catastrophe. As he explains, they do not describe discrete periods; rather, they are coeval: "Exuberance and catastrophe materialized as historically specific forms of capitalist triumph and oppression, of environmental domination and destruction, and of human liberation and psychic and bodily oppression."[42] This view of the present entangles the raw potential and unbridled destructiveness supplied by oil's electric burn.[43] The dance between the two moments will always entail experience of the dominant's opposite. No moment of exuberance without catastrophe and vice versa.

Oil, on Buell's account, fuels a cultural vision of reality through the entwinned logics of catastrophe and exuberance, which, in my account, take on the role of the two percussive narrative beats found in post-apocalyptic writing. Buell nicely posits their connection. Through his dialectic of exuberance and catastrophe, Buell presents two variants of a reactionary logic. These are not different periods in the history of fossil-fueled capitalism. These modes should not be thought of as phases that follow on each other's heels. Instead they hew closer to what Adorno and Horkheimer identified as the dialectic of enlightenment—socialism and barbarism all in one. Each moment provided by oil's liquid energy—driving a car on a freeway, getting an ultrasound in a doctor's office, or eating food shipped from the other side of the planet—is mirrored by the misery of oil—not only by gushers and pipeline bursts, but also by the blanket of CO_2 warming the planet and the conflicts for control of oil fields and refineries. Buell offers an analytic for critical interpretation that attends to the impacts of oil *within* cultural texts. Apocalypse, revelation, and their aftermath are just as entwinned and have just as much a chance of repeating.

Alas, *Babylon, Parable of the Sower, Station Eleven, The Dog Stars*, and *Slow Apocalypse* stage complex relations to energy as a regime. Frank imagines what happens to Fort Repose not after the bomb strikes, but once it has become "like an island" cut off from the shipment of goods and delivery of electric energy. Butler imagines the United States in a steep economic decline that has forced many to fend for themselves in a world where gasoline is no longer the cheap, subsidized commodity it is in the real world. Mandel extrapolates the embodied feelings of living in a world without energy except in half-glimpsed memories. Heller's novel usefully considers fuel as resource but in doing so loses sight of the energy regime itself. Varley combines elements of Mandel's storyworld with Heller's attention to transportation. He imagines stop-gap solutions to the loss of automobility at the same time as he maps the changing terrain of Los Angeles. The fuel innovation and preparedness of the protagonist serve to protect his family from the fate suffered by the masses—forced into camps, crowded onto boats, shipped to an unknown future.

Varley's energy apocalypse reveals a guiding fantasy at the heart of the post-apocalyptic mode: that the masses of real-world refugees, forced out of their homes by the state, economic decline, war, and climate change, would simply disappear in the world-destroying apocalyptic event. In *Station Eleven* one group of people take shelter in the airport, yet there is enough room for each of them. In *The Dog Stars* any figures approaching the hanger are dealt with, gruesomely and at a distance, by Bangley. In *Slow Apocalypse*, as in *Parable of the Sower*, the refugees do not disappear. The hungry wander the streets, the thirsty congregate in buildings hollowed out by depression, and the tired keep watch in shifts. After a showdown with some bikers who were terrorizing a mountain town, David Marshall and his crew eventually settle there. Yet, the fact of the refugee crowded boats seems to be forgotten by the novel's end. Massive refugee populations, incredible armies of the unemployed and unemployable—this is a social problem raised by Varley's book, but it is not one that the narrative itself can resolve. As many people as the fossil-fueled energy system can support in this golden era of energy abundance, there are still many outside in the dark.

NOTES

I would like to thank Tatiana Prorokova-Konrad and the team at West Virginia University Press and to acknowledge that this chapter comes out of a forthcoming, book-length study from Wesleyan University Press, *Remainders of the American Century: Post-Apocalyptic Novels in the Age of US Decline*. An early version of this chapter was given as a lecture to the classes of Marija Cetinic at the University of Amsterdam.

Epigraph. Karen Pinkus, "On Climate, Cars, and Literary Theory," *Technology and Culture* 49, no. 4 (2008): 1007, 1002–9, https://doi.org/10.1353/tech.0.0161.

1. I use the turn of phrase *post-apocalyptic* to name a mode of writing and to acknowledge that the events described in such writing take place after a massively destructive event that reveals some fundamental truth and anticipates the rise of a new social order. I use the term *apocalypse* in both the popular and the etymological senses, following Lois Parkinson Zamora, who complains of the abuse and misunderstanding surrounding the term: "The word is almost always used as a synonym for disaster or the end of the world, rather than a synonym for revelation, and a vision of radical renewal coming out of the destruction." Lois Parkinson Zamora, "*Regression and Apocalypse: Studies in North American Literary Expressionism*, and *In a Dark Time: The Apocalyptic Temper in the American Novel of the Nuclear Age* (Review)," *MFS Modern Fiction Studies* 37, no. 2 (1991): 276–77, https://doi.org/10.1353/mfs.0.0297.

2. I use the term *petroculture* to capture the cultural and social dimension of fossil-fuel use. The term names a wide ambit of concerns, intended to enclose both the unconscious of energy production, distribution, and consumption themselves, and the profound impact these processes exert on cultural production, social norms, and humanity's creative capacity to think and enact variant futures. In "Oil in an American Imaginary," *New Formations* 69 (Winter 2009), Peter Hitchcock argues that "in general, oil dependency is not just an economic attachment but appears as a kind of cognitive compulsion that mightily prohibits alternatives to its utility as a commodity and as an array of cultural signifiers" (82). For further writing on what has been described as "an energy unconscious," see Stephanie LeMenager, *Living Oil: Petroleum Culture in the American Century* (Oxford: Oxford University Press, 2014); Graeme Macdonald, "Improbability Drives: The Energy of SF" *Strange Horizons*, February 15, 2016, http://strangehorizons .com/non-fiction/articles/improbability-drives-the-energy-of-sf; Vivason Soni, "Energy," in *Fueling Culture: 101 Words for Energy and Environment*, ed. Imre Szeman, Jennifer Wenzel, and Patricia Yaeger (New York: Fordham University Press, 2017), 132–35; Patricia Yaeger, "Editor's Column: Literature in the Ages of Wood, Tallow, Coal, Whale-Oil, Gasoline, Atomic Power and Other Energy Sources," *Publication of the Modern Literary Association* 126, no. 2 (2011): 305–10.

3. My treatment of the post-apocalyptic mode departs slightly from the work of others considering it as a genre. Cf. Heather J. Hicks, *The Post-Apocalyptic Novel in the Twenty-First Century: Modernity beyond Salvage* (New York: Palgrave Macmillan, 2016), 2. Hicks treats the post-apocalyptic novels "as an alternative to postmodern formal experimentation, these texts use the conventions of post-apocalyptic genre fiction to interrogate the category of modernity." Meanwhile, Barbara Gurr argues that "post-apocalyptic narratives ask us to consider what it means to be truly human, particularly

in the context of survival horror and genocide, by testing not only our physical survival skills, but also our values, our morals, and our beliefs." Barbara Anne Gurr, ed., *Race, Gender, and Sexuality in Post-Apocalyptic TV and Film* (New York: Palgrave Macmillan, 2015), 1. For a discussion of genre and mode, see Veronica Hollinger, "Genre vs. Mode," in *The Oxford Handbook of Science Fiction*, ed. Rob Latham (Oxford: Oxford University Press, 2014), 139–51; and Marie-Laure Ryan, "Mode," in *Routledge Encyclopedia of Narrative Theory* (New York: Routledge, 2005), 315–16.

4. See Roger Zelazny, *Damnation Alley* (New York: J. Boylston, 2015) or George Miller's Mad Max films.
5. For a discussion of real-world energy infrastructures under threat, see Gretchen Bakke, *The Grid: The Fraying Wires Between Americans and Our Energy Future* (New York: Bloomsbury, 2016).
6. Pat Frank, *Alas, Babylon* (New York: Harper, 2005), 117.
7. For just-in-time production, see David Harvey, *The Condition of Postmodernity: An Inquiry into the Conditions of Cultural Change* (London: Wiley, 1992) and Jeffrey Nealon, *Post-Postmodernism* (Stanford: Stanford University Press, 2012). For green revolution, see Fredric Jameson, "Periodizing the 60s," in *Ideologies of Theory* (New York: Verso, 2008), 483–515.
8. Frank, *Alas, Babylon*, 117.
9. See Deborah Cowen, *The Deadly Life of Logistics: Mapping Violence in Global Trade* (Minneapolis: University of Minnesota Press, 2014).
10. Frank, *Babylon*, 151.
11. Frank, 151.
12. Octavia E. Butler, *Parable of the Sower* (New York: Grand Central, 2000), 8.
13. Butler, 8.
14. Butler, 73, my italics.
15. Graeme Macdonald has identified a consistent tendency of energy-speculative futures: "Consciously or otherwise, it is significant that the fictions of future energy-scarce scenarios contain salient caution about an almost-post-carbon future of 'alternatives' that does not necessarily herald a renewables utopia." Crucially, he argues that "in doing so they reveal the *nature* of any society as bound-up with a specific energy mode and particular system of social power." Graeme Macdonald, "Research Note: The Resources of Culture," *Reviews in Cultural Theory* 4, no. 2 (2013): 1–24, 14, italics in original.
16. Automobility regression is meant to play with the Library of Congress subject heading "Regression (Civilization)," which was used to classify certain early post-apocalyptic texts.
17. Emily St. John Mandel, *Station Eleven* (Toronto: Harper Avenue, 2014), 150.
18. Yaeger, "Editor's Column," 309.
19. Typically located outside of the city core, the entrances are all controlled at ground level and elevated for a view in the waiting lounge. There is plenty of washroom space and wide concourse halls. There are many food preparation areas as well. It makes sense, depending on the particular apocalyptic event, for a story to be set there.
20. Diletta De Cristofaro, "Critical Temporalities: Station Eleven and the Contemporary Post-Apocalyptic Novel," *Open Library of Humanities* 4, no. 2 (2018): 37, http://doi.org/10.16995/olh.206.
21. Mandel, *Station Eleven*, 178.
22. Mandel, 31.
23. Mandel, 31.
24. Chaudhary, too, struggles with remembering the light switches no longer function: "There was a stupid moment or two when he stood near the front door, flipping the light switches. On/off, on/off." Mandel, *Station Eleven*, 178.
25. Mandel, 178.

26. For further discussion of this difference, see Amitav Ghosh, "Petrofiction: The Oil Encounter and the Novel," in *Incendiary Circumstances* (Boston: Houghton Mifflin, 1992), 138–51.

27. Briohny Doyle, "The Postapocalyptic Imagination," *Thesis Eleven* 131, no. 1 (December 2015): 101, 99–113, https://doi.org/10.1177/0725513615613460.

28. Peter Heller, *The Dog Stars* (New York: Alfred A. Knopf, 2012), 9.

29. Heller, 10.

30. Heller, 152.

31. Heller, 74.

32. Heller, 74.

33. Heller, 56. This bind in the novel raises precisely the very material problematic of fossil fuels, what David McDermott Hughes calls oil's missed utopian moment, meaning that instead of building suburbs, automobiles, and highway infrastructure, energy-laden reserves of oil could have been used to ensure a renewable-energy future. David McDermott Hughes, *Energy Without Conscience* (Durham, NC: Duke University Press, 2017).

34. John Varley, *Slow Apocalypse* (New York: Ace Books, 2012), 190.

35. Varley's novel stands out for its inclusion of bicycles as a primary mode of transportation. It has always struck me as odd that more post-apocalyptic novels did not feature bicycles as a reliable form of transportation. Kim Stanley Robinson's ecotopian novel *Pacific Edge* (1990) features cyclists prominently and Octavia E. Butler's *Parable of the Sower* opens with a bicycle ride, but there is no reason why post-apocalyptic texts besides these do not include this mode of transport more often. Mountain bikes, especially, would be useful for any terrain, they are easy to learn how to maintain, and, presumably depending on one's location, bike shops and thus spare parts are abundantly available. If there is anything that seems science-fictional about Varley's post-apocalyptic foray, it has to be the wood-chip engines, and yet the concept has been proven to work. The YouTube channel Engineer775 Practical Preppers posted a video in 2011 titled "The Wood Gas Generator Runs the Whole Farm!" that features this description: "Running our entire place off of gasified white oak chunks and running the gas into a 1972-25Kw Onan 30 EK genset through a simple homemade carburetor," https://www.youtube.com/watch?v=yYGKn12Weu4. Wood-fired combustion is a real technology, and it seems that some preppers are very interested in it. It goes without saying that Engineer775 was fortunate to have a homestead, the gear, the practical knowledge, and the time to pull off this level of private engineering. Essentially, a gasoline engine can be retrofitted to run off of wood gas by installing a hopper and wood burner with the fumes directed into the combustion engine. They are not as powerful as a gas-powered engine, but they work.

36. *Slow Apocalypse* is Dave Marshall's writing. It is part journal, part manuscript; readers discover in the epilogue that they have been reading a character's first-hand account all along.

37. Designed to clean up a massive oil spill, a microbe dubbed "Prometheus" devours not just oil but all petroleum products, casting humanity into a civilization regression in *Ill Wind* (*Slow Apocalypse* is also derived from the classic monster-trope of "the blob" in SF and comes about in the same mad-scientist, runaway-invention kind of way). In a post-cancer United States, Los Angeles suffers a major earthquake but the US government—financially destitute as they are—cannot respond in *Twenty Thirty*. Finally, in the post-oil *World Made by Hand*, when upstate New York has been cut off from communication not only with the rest of the world but also with the next state over, a small town becomes a hub of activity and its denizens work together to subsist and to survive.

38. T. S. Miller, "*Slow Apocalypse* by John Varley," *Strange Horizons* (January 28, 2013).
39. Miller, "*Slow Apocalypse*."
40. "Oil has become an obsessive point of reference in and clear determinant over the daily lives of many, either victimizing them directly and cruelly as with Shell in Nigeria, or Texaco in Ecuador, or making them increasingly feel that their developed-world normalities are a shaky house of cards." Fredrick Buell, "A Short History of Oil Cultures: Or, the Marriage of Catastrophe and Exuberance," in *Oil Culture*, ed. Ross Barrett and Daniel Worden (Minneapolis: University of Minnesota Press, 2014), 69–88, 70.
41. Buell, "A Short History," 71; my emphasis. William Catton posits that "today mankind is locked into stealing ravenously from the future," situating a coming catastrophe as the consequence of the good times had in the present. William Catton, *Overshoot: The Ecological Basis of Revolutionary Change* (Urbana: University of Illinois Press, 1982), 3.
42. Buell, "A Short History," 74.
43. Buell mentions several post-apocalyptic novels in passing as he concludes his analysis, including Butler's *Parable of the Sower* and *Xenogenesis Trilogy* (1987–1989), Kazuo Ishiguro's *Never Let Me Go* (2005), McCarthy's *The Road* (2006), Sarah Hall's *The Carhullan Army* (2007), James Howard Kunstler's *World Made by Hand* (2008), and Andreas Eschbach's *Ausgebrannt* (2007). Buell, "A Short History," 82–83.

Part III

Film, Energy, and Climate Change

CHAPTER 8

Intermodal Aesthetics and the Otherwise of Cargo

Megan Hayes and Jeff Diamanti

In 2009, container ships were responsible for 90 percent of global trade in manufactured goods, and the globe's ninety-thousand active ships consumed 7.29 million barrels of oil equivalent fuel per day.[1] Yet intermodal shipping has evaded international regulations on environmental impact during the period in which it came to dominate global trade. Neither the Intergovernmental Panel on Climate Change (IPCC) nor the United Nations Conference on Trade and Development (UNCTAD) have meaningful policy or oversight dedicated to the shipping industry—only a string of nonbinding recommendations and statements of concern. This is despite the industry's astonishing consumption of fossil fuels relative to other forms of transportation, and in spite of that consumption occurring in some of the most sensitive environments on the planet.[2]

Intermodal shipping relies predominantly on low-grade bunker fuel distilled from diesel because of the material and economic advantages it provides to heavy load shipments. And while the International Maritime Organization (IMO) has technically monitored the pollution from maritime vessels following the 1973 signing of the International Convention for the Prevention of Pollution from Ships (MARPOL), intermodal shipping has continued to rely on ever increasing quantities of bunker fuel to power globalization. Bunker fuel is so central to the shape of post-1970s commerce that energy historian Vaclav Smil describes the diesel engine powering intermodal shipping as one of two "prime movers of globalization," though the lion's share of attention, environmental discourse, and regulation has been directed to gasoline-based engines on land and in the sky.[3] This elemental asymmetry in what since the first IPCC report in 1990 has been a preoccupation with air over water in the scientific and conceptual apparatus of climate change extends through the technical, cultural, and political discourses responsible for advancing concern for climate. From measures of the depleting ozone layer in the stratosphere since the 1970s, to tropospheric radiative forcing that first dominated IPCC reports on aerosols and other greenhouse gases in the 1990s, the atmospheric has organized research, policy, and the politics of metaphor at the same time that the planet's hydrosphere and its ecology has borne a kind of forgotten responsibility for anthropogenic climate change.[4] Our argument here is that intermodal shipping containers formalize an aesthetic of postindustrial capitalism in its very shape, function, and optical modality: a way of seeing the world and its ecologies in order to make good on the drives of capital, and hence also a way of rendering certain ecologies optically invisible and ecologically forgettable. We call this way of seeing *intermodal aesthetics* and it will be the purpose of this chapter to characterize its intimacy with and indifference to the concerns of climate.

Intermodal aesthetics are not immune to environmental degradation—boxes rust and hulls peel, just as salinity and airstreams enter into the calculation of cost and circulation time—and yet the primacy of interchangeability abstracts both content and context into the logic of turnover time. This matters for the industry's relationship to policy for two reasons. First, oceans have borne the weight of advanced globalization in the form of the logistics revolution during which time seaborne trade quadrupled from eight thousand billion tonne-miles in 1968 to thirty-two thousand billion tonne-miles in 2008.[5] Second, the National Oceanic and Atmospheric Administration (NOAA) estimates that since the beginning of the industrial era oceans have "absorbed some 525 billion tons of CO_2 from the atmosphere, presently around 22 million tons a day."[6] As a result, acidification of the oceans has increased by roughly 30 percent over the past two centuries, for which there is no comparable acidification event for the last fifty-five million years.[7] This dramatic shift in ocean chemistry has an array of strange and devastating effects on marine life, such as the inability of fish to navigate and shelled creatures to build their homes, with attempts to disentangle further effects from the simultaneous stresses faced by the ocean—such as those of massive algae blooms—the object of recent scientific enquiry.[8] So while the sea is the medium of intermodal aesthetics, it remains a medium, never fully figuring as what Melody Jue, following George Canguilhem, calls the oceanic milieu—an ecology of elements, agents, bodies, processes, temperatures, and materialities.[9] This is for two reasons at once: the dominance of anthropocentric modes of figuring pollution using the human lung as the dispositif of environmental regulation, on the one hand, and the marginalized status of the effects of diesel from maritime trade on marine biologies across the planet on the other. In these modes of figuring oceans, globalization is what happens on the water, while the stuff that happens beneath it involves planetary feedback loops only very recently visible and thinkable from within the scientific and political apparatus of global warming.

The enlivening of the sea on the back of the postwar shipping boom makes thinking in the interstices of these two oppositions incumbent upon any discipline, politics, or practice concerned with political ecology: the hydrospheric versus the atmospheric, and the grids of globalization versus the interpermeations of planetary life. Which is to say that under the sea, globalization looks and feels a lot different than the grid that cuts across its surface during the era in which the atmospheric organized our coming to consciousness of anthropogenic climate change, not just because the hydrospheric consists of a kind of epistemological darkness, but also because the regulatory apparatus responsible for thinking about the political *ecology* of maritime economics (UNCTAD and the IMO alike) has until very recently been a touch hydrophobic.[10]

If the sea had been forgotten from dominant narratives, concepts, and concerns of the late twentieth and early twenty-first centuries, then its genre of return across recent scientific research, policy, cultural anthropology, and visual culture will of necessity put pressure on the spatial distinction between globalization and planetarity, even if the distinction remains. Along with this question of periodization and axis, however, is a secondary claim: that pressure on the distinction does not turn it into a contradiction, much less resolve it, in part because what is still missing is an institutional form of looking that sees planetarity and globalization as mutually embedded concerns for and of the sea. In the in-between space of these genres of return—the global grid on the one hand, and the planetary hydrosphere on the other—sit the three visual mediations of water that make up this essay's analytic focus, simply for the interventions they collectively supply to an archive that has been unable, or unwilling, to think these oppositions conjointly. In the absence of an intergovernmental concert of concern for oceans both above and below their surfaces, cultural modes of perceiving, understanding, and attuning to the hydrospheric help bear the responsibility of remembering that which, by definition, must remain forgotten amidst the tectonics of planetarity and globalization.[11]

First, the figure of the cargo ship, in Noël Burch and Allan Sekula's *The Forgotten Space* (2010), cuts through maritime space, reconstituting it as globalism's grid. Second, Lucien Castaing-Taylor and Véréna Paravel's *Leviathan* (2012) holds onto the boat as an anchor point around which one is flung while disorientation builds amidst a waterlogged grid made visual through novel camera technologies available in the early 2010s. Finally, we follow a rogue vessel wandering in the aftermath of an imagined civilizational breakdown in the fifth episode of Shezad Dawood's ongoing *Leviathan Cycle* (2017–). In this chapter, we read these three films as aesthetic and conceptual interventions into the antinomy of political economy and political ecology. These interventions press upon capital's abstraction of maritime space—by way of the cargo ship and its largely unregulated labor and environmental envelope—until it starts to rub up against a paradoxically enlivened marine biology afloat in the toxic trails of the shipping industry's estimated one billion tons of greenhouse gas emissions between 2007–2012.[12]

In thinking the two sides of this antinomy together—the political economy of capital and the uncounted space of what Elizabeth Povinelli terms "the otherwise"—we seek to bridge the gap between two parallel fields of research.[13] By capsizing our axis of orientation to the ship, we bring environmental/energy humanities into dialogue with new/historical materialism. To do so we build on recent work on feminist trans-corporeality and posthumanism by Stacy Alaimo and Astrida Neimanis in order to reposition the political ecology of intermodal shipping.[14] In particular, we are interested in drawing out the theoretical, political, and environmental concepts made available in the archive assembled by these three visual interventions in order to figure the largely uncounted contributions to the increasingly toxic composition of what Neimanis calls the planetary hydrocommons—a commons, to be sure, both because it remains *res communis* and because what is common to all living bodies is their internal immersion in water. The petrocultural grid of globalization charted by the shipping industry's rapid expansion in the postwar era here dissolves into the planetary world of water, or what Povinelli has recently termed the threshold to late liberal reason.[15] Our contention is that a critical vocabulary able to see the ship from the sea up, instead of the sky down, is indispensable to any critique of energy and climate in turn, and that a reorientation to the vantage point of this vocabulary begins in the in-between of *The Forgotten Space* and both Dawood's and Castaing-Taylor and Paravel's *Leviathan*. This is because the cargo ship sits centrally between both the political economy and political ecology of hydro- and biospheric processes, interpermeating both pairs every day and with increasing severity as emissions continue to pour into the hydrologic cycle, diesel swirls summon the deepest parts of the ocean, and the volume of trade continues to surge unchallenged.

Seaways

The soulless, standardized box that is the shipping container, Marc Levinson argues, is the thing that sets globalization in motion, shrinking the globe and expanding economies; its regularity, rigidity, and anonymity bracing what is a nearly seamless global system built upon containerization.[16] Critically, the intermodality of this system allows for linear progression, fluid horizontal movement, and the bypassing of that which is not in aid of growth and unimpeded free-trade. It has become a kind of headless monster of capitalism's facility with maritime space, but not a monster you would ever encounter in its depths. Instead, intermodal shipping is a *monstrous abstraction* of materiality, turning all bodies, fabrics, substances, elements, and relations into cargo and commodity. Even empty space itself comes with a price.

It is precisely this momentum that *The Forgotten Space* butts up against, the "essay film" manifesting as an assembly of neglected frictions across infrastructure spaces of the globe. The film's declared project is to address what lies in the wake of containerization by stacking stories across scale—a failed attempt at providing toads with safe passage in their migration under railroad tracks; a tent city nestled between two railway lines at the Alameda Corridor; and the absurdity of the Korean and Indonesian crew on a ship that never sails near North America eating richly subsidized Californian rice (while Korean rice farmers go bankrupt). Just as momentum builds, the film halts, pivots, and peels back another layer again, its agitated, recursive style intervening in a homogenous global space of fluid linearity. In the tangential gathering of the film, time is repeatedly scratched over in a thickening present of equally significant infrastructural contradictions.

The Forgotten Space grows out of Allan Sekula's larger project of "critical realism," and most immediately from his photographic series *Fish Story* (1989–95). Sekula is seeking the recuperation of art—the photograph, most immediately—from a "mystified, vaporous, and ahistorical realm," and its reclamation "as a discourse anchored in concrete social relations."[17] By this he means to recall the commitment to making available a kind of cartography of the present through which a divided and alienated social could rediscover relationality in the service of what Georg Lukács, in the original formulation of *social* realism, imagined would be necessary for triggering and maintaining social revolution. In this way, Sekula long stood out from the late 1970s onward for his resolutely socialist commitment to a documentary and photographic realism oriented by labor relations in a rapidly globalized world, since the commitment to both realism and labor relations in those same years largely disappeared from the cultural compass of postmodernism.

The common thread of contestation through Sekula's practice is an opposition to abstraction; to a reading of form within a perimeter at the loss of contingency. It is in aid of this greater project that *The Forgotten Space* stacks infrastructure spaces and their contradictions, and it is what is at stake in Sekula's insistence on working in "sequence" rather than "series."[18] The repetition of seriality gestures toward a certain endlessness, which in turn implies fundamentally uniform and fungible parts. The sequence, in contrast, is anchored in specificity: each part takes up its own space as it maps out a present in which every image tethers the rest, thus posing a problem to the abstraction produced by logistics. *The Forgotten Space* as stack becomes an ethical response to the present, in which the camera frame attempts to render sequentially the complexity of space through time in a manner adequate to that of the lived conditions of the world.

As conceptual apparatus, the stack provides a logic for an alternate spatial rendering of the world through an aesthetic procedure that shrinks the distance between an international and largely impersonal division of labor in different sectors implicated by maritime trade. We become bored in solidarity with operators and maintenance crew in Hong Kong; frustrated with the exploited truck drivers of America; livid for the standing reserve of labor growing at the edges of logistical landscapes in Los Angeles, not just for their living conditions, but for the toxicity that surges through all the bodies that *The Forgotten Space* stacks. Insofar as we move through these spaces with the box, following the global grid coordinated by various ports, the stacking of stories and scenes of violence on the working and immiserated body becomes an affordance of seeing with, as opposed to against, the intermodal. Even as the scales of trade and means of circulation threaten to overwhelm the film's focalization of globalization through intermodal aesthetics, living labor will turn out over and over to defer any fully automated and posthuman circulatory system across capitalism's grid.

But here the promise of labor that *The Forgotten Space* recalls remains contingent precisely on the intermodal aesthetics capable of stacking in the first place; the stack doubling as a vista onto both the forgotten labor and the means of abstraction necessary for the reproduction of globalization's turnover time. These means are not only found containerized in ports, but also computationally stacked in the digital architecture underwriting the logistics revolution. This second, "accidental megastructure" of the stack, as proposed by Benjamin

Bratton, interweaves the continental, urban, and perceptual scales, perforating certain borders and introducing others.[19] The container, whilst stackable, remains fundamentally atomistic, encouraging individual components to take flight to faraway sites of consumption. Bratton's conception of a stack, while still modular, has a different temporality: components are fundamentally part of a whole by way of their messy simultaneity. It is through this globally contemporaneous stacking that *The Forgotten Space* accumulates, building a kind of meshwork, its interruption of linearity carving out the globe as grid.

And yet, while *The Forgotten Space* remembers a political ecology that both fulfills and is shed in the wake of the ship's journey through the infrastructure space of globalization, it stops before peeling back to a broader ecology still. In a film suggesting that the violence incurred by "the evils of productivist, 'globalized' capitalism"[20] may be understood by addressing the sea, it seems strange to not encounter the violence done to the sea itself. Whilst the space which is forgotten is ostensibly maritime, the film remains stubbornly buoyant: this global grid never breaks below the surface, seemingly unable to enter into the question of the ecological otherwise of cargo, hesitant before its toxic wake. What about the ocean as such, as more than a fluid, flat surface? What of the hydrospheric, and the complexities of its more-than-human ecologies? In terms of the ocean's figuration, the film employs a rather frugal aesthetic, extending only as deep as extractive potential permits. The stacking, then, becomes a continual omission, a building of erasure, and in this way the ocean is constituted as globalism's grid alone.

The globe, Gayatri Spivak argues, is on our computers: "No one lives there."[21] In this sense it is in the genre of an abstract ball, a "gridwork of electronic capital."[22] Her proposition is that such an abstract globe be overwritten by planet. The veracity of planetarity lies in its resistance to neat contrast with globality, in the inability of saying "the planet, on the other hand."[23] Which is to say, planetarity unnerves the rationalization of the earth into a mode of ownership, returning it to the grounds for alterity—what Povinelli, echoing Spivak's proposition, calls *the otherwise* of late liberal reason. *The Forgotten Space* tracks the logistical spaces created, but made invisible by, globality, turning the intermodal into a paradoxical kind of object: the means of globalization, and a situated mode of seeing its stacked contradictions as well. But even the film cannot flip the box upside down to see what its modality is designed to excise from calculation: the very ecology that lubricates intermodal mobility and absorbs its hidden costs. The camera is focalized through the ship as an environment, and we know this because each chapter returns us to the stable frame atop the ship's cabin. We must plunge down below the deck—beyond even the physical limits of the ship that reaches deep down beneath the ocean's surface. Doing so will get us closer to the otherwise of cargo, even if it is made available without the feelgood resolution of so many environmental documentaries looking to raise awareness, since the planetarity that exists in the milieu of the sea involves for Spivak an "underived intuition . . . not susceptible to the subject's grasp."[24]

Toward the Otherwise of Cargo

A jump down below the deck requires first and foremost a technical grasping that Lucien Castaing-Taylor and Véréna Paravel introduce by attaching GoPro cameras to different appendages of a fishing vessel off the coast of New England. The effect is dizzying and disorienting for the viewer. The GoPro allows the frame to synchronize to the bounciness of the boat and the blurred threshold of above and below water. This ship is not the ship of cargo, however, but one of the thousands that pull the contents out from the sea before that content gets formed into the intermodal. In this way *Leviathan* doubles as an aesthetic viewpoint of the camera *held,* as it were, by the vessel's chains, anchor, and nets, instead of a cameraman, as well as a zooming into the constitutive industries sharing space with the intermodal at sea. And this sharing space matters because the fishing industry predates intermodal shipping by centuries, even if its calculus is wholly reconstituted by the globalization of cargo. It is here, with this ultra-modern medium of filmmaking, that we see the uneven temporalities of the sea and the intermodal breaking with the gridwork of modernism.

For modernism, the grid functioned aesthetically to abstract that which lay below. In Rosalind Krauss' rendering, the modernist grid is not a point of arrival at an absolute beginning, but instead a veiling figure atop the originary object.[25] It abstracts, doubles, and binds surface. Its meshwork is both a protection against intrusion from the outside and a silencing of surface in the negation of any preceding origin. Inherently without center, the grid becomes a medium of sameness, grounding a mode of repeatability that smooths the landscape into one of lateral continuity. This modernist grid prefigures the grid of globalization, and the tyranny of abstraction that comes with optimization in the sphere of exchange. In opposition to a certain pull of abstraction as pure aesthetic disinterest, this abstraction of the globe is resolute: you can't look at a logistics map and see dead fish—that would be the concrete piercing back through the abstract, and a return to origin. In the gridwork of Krauss' modernism, there is just more capital. But by *holding on* or grasping for the full range of viewpoints embodied by the fishing vessel, *Leviathan* lets the figure of the fish—both living and dead, commodity and excess—pierce through the grid of modernism.

By throwing the camera overboard, the frames gathered by *Leviathan* get the gridwork wet, dragging the camera through the threshold of hydro- and atmosphere so that what you hear and what you see is a medium-specific grasping (and gasping) for air. The film begins at night in a frenzied scene of reeling in a net, but it takes a long time before we can begin to situate ourselves on the gear of the worker who anchors us. Diegetic sound overwhelms the visual: forceful waves; clanking chains; the spooling of nets; the flopping around of fish, slapping against one another on deck (see fig. 8.1). A muffled voice starts issuing directions to a coworker who is having trouble disentangling a bright yellow chain. The net, chain, pulley, boat, and worker are knotted to the milieu of the sea. The workers take their positions and watch as the net spools, stopping periodically to prevent further knotting. Even though the apparatus of the boat is highly mechanized—powered by the same fossil fuels as the cargo ships that will take up where this one leaves off—pulling the stuff of cargo out from the sea is not passive, but hyperactive. The relative and provisional

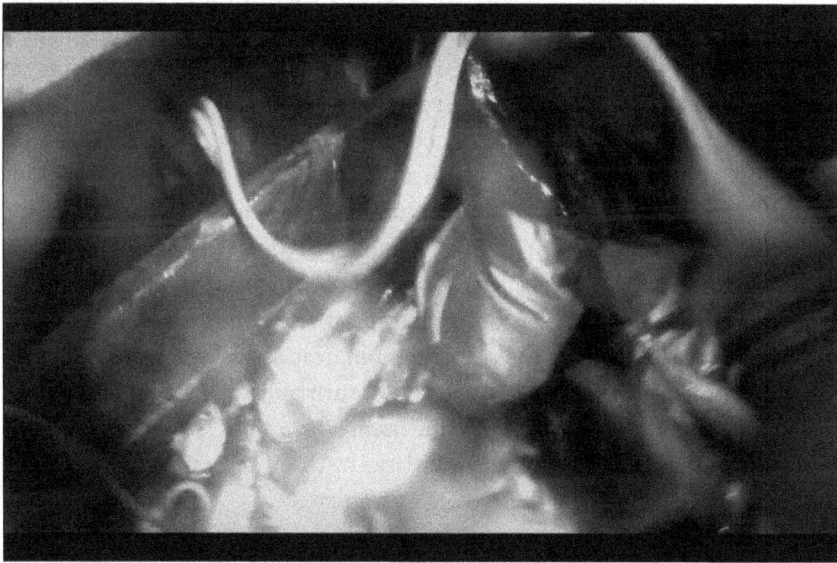

Fig. 8.1. Worker standing in fish (Castaing-Taylor and Paravel, dir., *Leviathan*, 2012).

stillness of the frame is the stillness of the body to whom our camera view-point is attached, which jerks back and forth from the wake of the ship to the colleagues aggressively fighting against both wet rope and a bobbing boat. But this is not a human viewpoint, even though we begin stuck to a human body. The viewpoint is one that follows the various appendages of the boat as it reaches into the water and pulls bodies out. The condition of workers does not go unnoticed, but it is not the concern of a camera that can be stuck to any surface, wet or dry.

By midway, it is clear that *Leviathan* will be an extended exercise in using the ship as a platform for the frame of the camera, utilizing every line that grasps at the water. The gaze of the camera plunges us into environments that would drown, suffocate, or freeze the human. And the effect of this plunging is awful. Fish flop at the feet of workers, but they are not abjected by a camera that holds them in a still frame from above. Instead we lay sidewise with the fish, watching hands and hooks reach down to convert life into cargo, chopping off gills and gutting them before sorting their flesh into various boxes. The camera's indifference to human handling makes proximate the *grasping* at the sea and the *processing* of commodities that sits at the threshold of planetarity and globalism. *Leviathan* tracks the translation of the one into the other *in situ*. At a crucial moment in the film we realize that this deck is an ensemble of value production, where laboring bodies crisscross with a living milieu that is drawn into the grid of the intermodal. We learn, in other words, that the destination of this scene's contents weighs like a kind of spectral presence. Lingering on the eyes of an exhausted and precarious worker and the severed head of a fish (see fig. 8.2), we see this weight embodied in the concrete. This is hard work and the price is paid by a range of bodies.

But the camera plunges back into the sea before long. The accumulated images of the film, mingling behind the eyes, become fuel for an extended relationality—the relinquishment of the role of cinematographer pictures a more radically democratic concept of the social as seabirds' circle in wait of a meal, and starfish navigate the turbidity of marine snow. As a result, the grid which had collapsed spatiality gets soggy, in turn pulling different stakes into focus. The question of how to image the human on a global scale, but as multi-ply contingent, is slowly submerged, assisted by the literalization of rising seas made possible by throwing the camera overboard.

The elemental shift that occurs when one thinks from the ocean might help to warp the epistemological bounds recalled by the inherent unthinkabil-ity of Spivak's planetarity. Melody Jue, considering the medium specificity of thought, has something similar in mind when she asks "under what conditions

Fig. 8.2. Fish head on boat (Castaing-Taylor and Paravel, dir., *Leviathan*, 2012).

have terrestrial knowledge structures evolved, and how would they appear radically different in an aqueous environment"?[26] If the hydrosphere is to cut through an atmospheric hegemony, and if the planetary is to flood the global, a certain watery awakening must occur. Astrida Neimanis suggests that this happens by way of a phenomenological attunement to our already fundamental bodily wetness. The tributaries that make up the genealogy of Neimanis' thought—a phenomenology born of Maurice Merleau-Ponty, the rhizomatics of Deleuze and Guattari, and the French *écriture féminine* of the late twentieth century—flow as a feminist posthuman phenomenology that seeks to challenge an epistemological phallogocentrism by way of acknowledging life's intrinsically hydrological cycle. This cycle exists formatively (not without disavowal) in the constant watery interpermeations between the embodied self and the material of the world. We are both created and sustained in and by water, by what is swallowed, excreted, absorbed, gestated, and wept, and are crucially redefined as a "we" in the meantime. For Neimanis, "our wet matters are in constant process of intake, transformation, and exchange."[27] To recognize the wetness of one's embodiment is to get in the way of a body as individually coherent, and as having a firm perimeter: that is, the liberal humanist body. Such "discrete individualism" is, as Neimanis puts it, "a rather dry, if convenient, myth."[28]

But, as Spivak's planetarity attests, water's alterity "contains us as much as it flings us away."[29] This knowing of water is predicated on water's ontological *unknowability*, be they waters within or beyond our epidermal perimeter. It is a relinquishment of sovereignty into a more-than-human hydrocommons, necessitated by the presumed difficulty of outthinking the weight of the ocean. A dive into the epistemological darkness of the hydrospheric might exert a kind of hydraulic pressure on thought; a pressure to start configuring a politics, and regulatory apparatus that knows how to breathe underwater, in order to feel the urgency of, for instance, an increasing ambient acidity, which—if you are a pteropod—also means an imminent and terrifying dissolve.

Leviathan Cycle for a Dissolving Grid

Dawood's *Leviathan Cycle* signals in its name a mythological genealogy reanimated by the warming waters of climate change. Thomas Hobbes' *Leviathan* (1651) famously figured the sovereign head of the commonwealth at the top of a monstrous body politic whose civil peace it guaranteed. Hobbes' warning in the wake of the English Civil War (1642–52) came in the form of natural philosophy of political form, where the material interests of competing subjects promised perpetual war of the strong against the weak until an absolute figure settled and transformed the "war of all against all" into the legal fabric of the commonwealth. Hobbes' figuration of the body politic as this monster thus translates the latent danger of the sea into the potential for civil breakdown in the wake of the sovereign state. Even as the liberal political theory that would in time redefine the relationship between the social contract and the state amidst the French revolution *dethroned* Leviathan, the imprint of this originary figure on modern statecraft would remain latent in the cultural imaginary of the sea.

By episode 5 of *Leviathan*, the state has dissolved in the wake of a vaguely termed cataclysm event with which episode 1 opens. Characters have come in and out of focus through each of the fifteen-to-twenty-five-minute episodes as the camera wanders around the beaches and buildings where human and nonhuman life now share the camera's attention after the melodrama of the viewer's present is imagined as expired. From the UK through to Paris, Venice, the beaches of Morocco, and finally the port of Rotterdam, *Leviathan* folds the ruins of sovereignty into a landscape whose mood remains distinct from human voice, but none the less active because of it. The growing impact of nonhuman animals, plastic debris, rocks, and the vegetation is marked as ascendant by jump cuts to an archival viewpoint where the bodies of whales and fish are dragged up into the production line of global capitalism, made passive and inert at the cusp of their becoming cargo. In episode 5, for instance, the cargo ship captained by the episode's titular character, "Ismael," *wants* to focalize the narrative, but cannot because footage drawn from the National Film Board of Canada and Eye Filmmuseum in the Netherlands (see fig. 8.3) jumps us around diegetically from one side to the other of the *Leviathan*'s opening event. Dawood's films are intermodal dissolves where archival past and lived present blend boundaries, in turn troubling the distinction between them and the categories of bodies that register on screen. Faint echoes of the sovereign state remain in the embodied discourse of the ship's captain—Ismael literalizes the power of the sovereign by submitting Ben from episodes 1–4 to sexual submission and eventually obedience—but it is now radically restricted in place. No longer extended or extendable across territories of land, the residue of the state seeks refuge on the cargo ship.

State boundaries find themselves replaced by elemental ones as the grid dissolves beneath this lost tribe at sea. The terrestrial—though watery—human bodies are contained atop the ocean, set apart from the waters below by the bulk of the cargo ship. Yet they are also bodies being undone, the stability of their "terra firma presumptions"[30] disintegrating in the midst of this unknown

Fig. 8.3. Archival footage of cod fishery (Shezad Dawood, "Ismael," 2019).

future that has been threaded through concerns of marine conservation, migration, and mental health. For Alaimo, such an undoing comes from an encounter with a very material ethics of trans-corporeality which stresses the intermeshing of, and movement between, substances of the human and the more-than-human world. Trans-corporeality is both descriptive and prescriptive, since it understands the environment not as separate, inert, or empty but rather as interior to and continuous with all bodies.[31] The dissolve Alaimo is speaking from is that of the sea creatures who, in acidifying seawater, are no longer able to draw upon the calcium carbonate necessary to build their shells—a rather apocalyptic figuration invoking a certain bodily vulnerability. Our protagonist, Ben, is indeed exposed, his flesh laid bare and human exceptionalism violently displaced. The human once more becomes matter amongst an ever-cyclical reorganization of matter, carrion of the gods, or at least of Ismael (formerly George).

Thinking with the ecodelic possibilities of this shell on acid, Alaimo marks the contemporary moment as one in need of material immersion over transcendence. Immersion is both descriptive and analytic for Alaimo: it details the practice of engagement with the material embeddedness of the subject as body, exposed as it is to differential flows and forces eroding and remaking it in time and place. Thinking with a dissolution of bearings and certainty becomes a way out of the mess arrived at in an epistemological framework of totalizing confidence. In a changed world—be that of anthropogenic climate change, or a post-cataclysmic *Leviathan*—the human is no longer safely ensconced, set against a backdrop of world. Instead, *Leviathan's* characters have become little more than barnacles clinging to the body of a dead whale. The elemental border is the whales' demise as they approach humanity at the surface, becoming prey by way of their lingering mammalian need for air. But as humanity pillaged the seas, so it pillaged itself, "and the humanity that we held so dear was a corrupted thing."[32] The reckoning with self as the stuff of the material world finds itself to be an emergent otherwise when the world in which it is situated has turned its back to the hubris of (a certain mode) of humanity. This ship is emptied of cargo, and the human drama of its interior spaces becomes only loosely anchored to the sovereignty of self that the cycle more generally has been imagining back into the dissolve of the sea. This dissolution of self feels familiar in the experience of *Leviathan* when it seems as though all one can grab hold of is either a fragmentary descent into madness, or some new and calming attachment to the landscape in which this descent unfolds—but which is not itself in a state of madness. It bears repeating, in other words, that the narratology of madness in *Leviathan* does not immediately translate into a madness shared beyond the human. The mood of the cycle suggests otherwise.

It's not that the wake of state-sanctioned sovereignties means all bodies on the planet become coequal with flesh, brought back to the material entanglements from which they originate. That entanglement was already radically unequal in distribution, and the future tense of our present that *Leviathan* imagines for us is one where that unequal distribution has been intensified. The otherwise of cargo in the cycle—the milieu of bodies and elements that come back to the foreground of the cycle's mise-en-scène—is also in a condition of dissolve. But they have been for some time; the archive confirms as much. The difference is that the human's plunge into the same economy of dissolve is reason enough to freak out and grab hold of whatever might delay dissolve. Holding onto the ship proves tempting, but in our reading of episode five, the ship is also a violent reminder and remainder of the unnerving proximity of the sovereign and the flesh, so only a provisionally stable object. And for Eric L. Santner in his rereading of the problem of *reading* flesh in the annals of psychoanalysis and governmentality, "this visceral yet somehow virtual dimension of the flesh that begins to haunt everyday life in modernity needs to be grasped . . . as the royal remains, the residues of the substance of the king's sublime body that has, in the age of popular sovereignty, entered into the life of the people without ever fully being able to find its proper locus or fully binding *Verfassung*."[33] The flesh cannot become a constitution of the polis—a fully binding *Verfassung*—but it begins in the era of popular sovereignty to *constitute* power. This paradox or differential animates so many anxieties about the body in Santner's reading. The remains of the sovereign get distributed across the flesh of the polis in this genealogy, so that attention to the flesh proves promising and disorienting for Freud and Lacan, and the primary locus for biopolitical formation in Foucault, but never as the final cause of this or that symptom. As a residue, the flesh bears a certain responsibility—it is both responsive and formative to the distributions of power's tensions—already dissolving the leviathan of premodern sovereignty into its biophysical constitution. Stripped of the apparatus of state power, or at the very least in the process of being stripped from it, *Leviathan* couples the dissolve of the sovereign's body down into the hydrological scene of a landscape newly enlivened by the otherwise of late capitalism.

Our argument all along has been that even though intermodal aesthetics has accelerated an abstraction of materiality into the calculus of capital and its global grid, the intermodal is also emerging as a focal point for a number of scenes of dissolve in the wake of Smil's prime movers of globalization.

The ship charts the grid, but the milieu of its environment has become enlivened as concept and concern of a specifically hydrological phrasing to climate change. The intermodal names the movability across a wide range of landscapes, and it implies containerization but does not specify to what end. Here we are thinking of visual culture, and the frame of the camera in particular, through the lens of the intermodal—that is, as a kind of container that passes through environments and gathers them as subjects, objects, and the otherwise of a given *mise en scène*—both because of the camera's injunction to form, and its proximity to the industrial network from which the name originates.[34]

The intermodal therefore helps to bring together varied stresses on the general materiality differently phrased across much of the work in the environmental humanities responsive to the work of Bruno Latour, Donna Haraway, and Karen Barad. Dethroning the human as the exclusive locus of agency in the animation of the world has meant phrasing materiality in the language of political form. The question that has occupied this chapter is sensitive to such phrasing, but is nevertheless eager to specify how an intermodal organization of matter at the threshold of capital's logistical grid and the otherwise of cargo *matters*. What makes the intermodal a strategic designation is that it gathers without pretense of retaining any conceptual distance from the thresholds of economy and ecology. We are trying to keep both in focus, even if they begin to blur. The intermodal is our way into the water because it floats around in this interstice, helping to focalize the irreducibility (but persisting intimacy) of planetarity and globality. Intermodal aesthetics are thus both a way of tracing political form without essentializing or even preferring material properties, and a way of figuring ourselves into a political orientation with the otherwise of cargo—the multiplicity of species, qualities, elements, and extents of ecology that are both invisible to the calculus of globalization, and rub up against its underbelly and its toxic trails. Maybe we don't need less intermodal aesthetics; maybe we need more.

NOTES

1. Paul Evans, "Big Polluters," New Atlas, April 24, 2009, https://newatlas.com/shipping-pollution/11526.
2. The Paris Climate Agreement drafted in late 2015 famously made no mention of maritime trade.
3. Vaclav Smil, *Prime Movers of Globalization* (Cambridge, MA: MIT Press, 2010).
4. The sea was never forgotten entirely, especially in the canon of ecological thought. Rachel Carson's *The Sea Around Us* (1951), for instance, takes the sea as primary to all other ecological concerns of twentieth-century industrial society. The point is, instead, that how it was remembered and figured was always through a kind focal point that

somehow missed or forgot the political ecology of twentieth-century trade (i.e., the intermodal).

5. "World Seaborne Trade," International Chamber of Shipping, http://www.ics-shipping .org/shipping-facts/shipping-and-world-trade/world-seaborne-trade.

6. "Ocean Acidification," Ocean Portal, Smithsonian's National Museum of Natural History, December 18, 2018, https://ocean.si.edu/ocean-life/invertebrates/ocean -acidification.

7. Lesley Evans Ogden, "Marine Life on Acid: Predicting Future Biodiversity in Our Changing Oceans," *BioScience* 63, no. 5 (May 2013): 322–328.

8. Ulf Riebesell, et al., "Toxic Algal Bloom Induced by Ocean Acidification Disrupts the Pelagic Food Web," *Nature Climate Change* 8 (2018): 1082–1086.

9. Melody Jue, "Vampire Squid Media," *Grey Room* 57 (Fall 2014): 82–105.

10. Sandra Laville, "UN shipping agency accused of secrecy over maritime pollution," *The Guardian,* November 20, 2018, https://www.theguardian.com/environment/2018 /nov/20/international-maritime-organization-transparency-international.

11. We here build on insights offered by Cecilia Chen, Janine MacLeod, and Astrida Neimanis in their introduction to *Thinking with Water* (Montreal: McGill-Queen's University Press, 2013) regarding the cultural materiality through which concepts and relations to water come to matter, precisely in the absence of this transnational concert of concern we mention here.

12. T. W. P. Smith et al., *Third IMO Greenhouse Gas Study 2014* (London: International Maritime Organization, 2015), http://www.imo.org/en/OurWork/Environment PollutionPrevention/AirPollution/Documents/Third%20Greenhouse%20Gas%20Study /GHG3%20Executive%20Summary%20and%20Report.pdf.

13. Elizabeth A Povinelli, "Routes/Worlds," *e-flux* 27 (September 2011), https://www.e-flux .com/journal/27/67991/routes-worlds.

14. Stacy Alaimo, *Exposed: Environmental Politics and Pleasures in Posthuman Times* (Minneapolis: University of Minnesota Press, 2016); Astrida Neimanis, *Bodies of Water* (London: Bloomsbury, 2017).

15. Elizabeth A Povinelli, *Geontologies: A Requiem to Late Liberalism* (Durham, NC: Duke University Press, 2016).

16. Marc Levinson, *The Box: How the Shipping Container Made the World Smaller and the World Economy Bigger* (Princeton: Princeton University Press, 2016).

17. Allan Sekula, "Dismantling Modernism, Reinventing Documentary (Notes on the Politics of Representation)," *The Massachusetts Review* 19, no. 4 (Winter 1978): 859.

18. Allan Sekula, "Dismantling Modernism, Reinventing Documentary (Notes on the Politics of Representation)," in *Dismal Science: Photo Works 1972–1996*, ed. Debra Risberg, (Illinois State University, 1999), 249.

19. Benjamin H Bratton, *The Stack: On Software and Sovereignty* (Cambridge, MA: MIT Press, 2015): 5.

20. Noël Burch, "Essay Film," Notes on The Forgotten Space, 2010, http://www.the forgottenspace.net/static/notes.html.

21. Gayatri Chakravorty Spivak, *Death of a Discipline* (New York: Columbia University Press, 2003): 72.

22. Spivak, 72.

23. Spivak, 72.

24. Gayatri Chakravorty Spivak, "Planetarity," *Paragraph* 38, no. 2 (2015): 292.

25. Rosalind E. Krauss, *The Originality of the Avant Garde and Other Modernist Myths* (Cambridge, MA: MIT Press, 1986): 7.

26. Jue, "Vampire Squid Media," 85.

27. Neimanis, *Bodies of Water*, 2.

28. Neimanis, 2.

29. Spivak, *Death of a Discipline*, 73.
30. Stacy Alaimo, "Jellyfish Science, Jellyfish Aesthetics: Posthuman Reconfigurations of the Sensible," *Thinking with Water,* ed. by Cecilia Chen, Janine MacLeod, and Astrida Neimanis (Montreal: McGill-Queens University Press, 2013), 153.
31. Stacy Alaimo, *Bodily Natures: Science, Environment, and the Material Self* (Bloomington: Indiana University Press, 2010), 2.
32. Shezad Dawood, *Leviathan,* "Ismael" (2018), https://leviathan-cycle.com/information/.
33. Eric L. Santner, "The Royal Remains: The People's Two Bodies and the Endgames of Sovereignty," in *Sovereignty in Ruins*, ed. George Edmondson and Klaus Mladek (Durham: Duke University Press, 2017), 206.
34. For more on the industrial origins of cinematic visuality, see Jonathan Beller, *The Cinematic Mode of Production* (Hanover: Dartmouth College Press, 2006).

CHAPTER 9

Nature Guarding "Her Treasures" in Oil Comedies: The Case of *Local Hero* and *Fubar: Balls to the Wall*

Robin L. Murray and Joseph K. Heumann

Near the opening of *Local Hero* a promotional video reviewed at a Knox Energy company board meeting in Houston, Texas, exclaims, "Nature guards her treasures jealously. Just a decade ago, these fields were beyond our reach. We didn't have the technology. Today a Knox engineer will tell you that he might need a little time, but he'll get the oil. He knows a little time is all that we have left."[1] The video is played for comic effect, with the company's owner and board president Mr. Happer (Burt Lancaster) dozing off in the dimly lit room, adding his snores to the documentary voiceover. But the claims in the video also point to the environmental bent of the film. The gross-out comedy *Fubar: Balls to the Wall* makes a similar point. Early on, Tron (Andrew Sparacino) warns the film's heroes Terry (David Lawrence) and Dean (Paul Spence) who seek riches in the tar sands of Alberta, Canada, "The Mac, she's a cruel mistress, and she will freeze you, if you don't love her, the way we all love her up here. We are the Mac . . . are you the Mac?"[2] Instead of arguing that oil and its natural environment can "mix," can share an equally beneficial interdependent relationship, *Local Hero* and *Fubar: Balls to the Wall* construct the relationship between nature and the oil industry as adversarial. To "get the oil," Knox engineers or Canada's oil field workers must defeat nature rather than live with it communally.

Film has always had a complicated relationship with oil, seeing it as a source of spectacular effects, a comedic prop for gags and pratfalls, as well as a more serious plot source. An oil-smeared face and slide across an oil slick bring out the laughs in films from Buster Keaton's *The Paleface* to *Boom Town*, *All Dogs Go to Heaven*, and *The Son of Rambow*.[3] The gag gains an antifeminist edge in *Oklahoma Crude*, when an oil-smeared Lena (Faye Dunaway) succumbs to her mercenary would-be lover Mase (George C. Scott).[4] Mase's earlier pratfalls into puddles of oil merely add to the humor in what could be a more complex look at the oil industry. Yet despite how, as Stephanie LeMenager suggests, oil's "biophysical properties have caused it to be associated with the comic 'lower bodily stratum,' in Mikhail Bakhtin's phrase," we wondered if comic films might better address oil as the "shit and sex" of entertainment and reveal the stink behind the flare.[5] As we noted in our book *Film and Everyday Eco-Disasters*, many documentary and fictional films claim the oil and fishing industries can work interdependently once appropriate safety precautions are in place.[6] By drawing on comic tropes, individual and communal stories and a productive nostalgia, we assert the oil comedies *Local Hero* and *Fubar: Balls to the Wall* begin to expose the smell. Instead of suggesting oil and the environment around it can live interdependently, *Local Hero* and *Fubar: Balls to the Walls* reveal the real costs of oil extraction to both human and nonhuman nature.

Redefining Eco-Comedy and the Comic Eco-Hero in *Local Hero*

Responding to the ongoing success of Scotland's offshore oil and gas development after the oil embargoes of 1973 and 1979, *Local Hero* tells a "big oil story" focusing on Knox CEO Happer's goal to build an enormous oil refinery in remote Ferness Bay, Scotland (see fig. 9.1). To quickly secure the property rights Happer sends chief negotiator Mac (Peter Riegert) to the remote Scottish village and bay. Things fall apart immediately. Greedy villagers, eccentric beachcomber Ben Knox (Fulton Mackay), webbed-toed oceanographer Marina (Jenny Seagrove), and Happer himself complicate the deal, turning a tragic premise into eco-comedy. Although the eco-disaster is presented through models and verbal rhetoric rather than spectacular visions of oil's cost, most contemporary viewers would recognize the environmental issues broached in *Local Hero*. Bill Forsyth's comments on the 2008 DVD release of *Local Hero* emphasize possible ecological implications of the film. According to Forsyth, "The environmental message in the film was very soft . . . what I call soft-core environmentalism."[7] Despite this blatant admission of even a low-key environmental message in *Local Hero*, much of the research about the film highlights its reinforcement (or disruption) of what McArthur and Meir call "the Scottish Discursive Unconscious," a tendency "to represent Scotland

Fig. 9.1. *Local Hero* presents eco-disaster through models and verbal rhetoric rather than spectacular visions of oil's cost, but most contemporary viewers would recognize the environmental issues broached in the film. (*Local Hero*, written and directed by Bill Forsyth [Enigma Productions, 1983], film)

and Scottish people in the regressive terms of tartanry and kailyardism," stereotypical representations that place the country and its people outside the global economic and political community.[8]

Some scholarship, however, does examine the environmental issues addressed by *Local Hero*. Jonathan Murray declares, "Despite being so given over to enraptured representation of Nature," *Local Hero* suggests that "human creativity is severely limited in its ability to imbue such images with any meaningful degree of accuracy or complexity."[9] Dorothy J. Howell argues that the movie's core theme "can be broadly characterized as environmental stewardship."[10] Murray suggests that Ben's reaction to the community's attempts to sell out also point out a strong environmental message. Ben "sees the beach as a resource to be exploited for more sustainable financial benefit, explaining, 'I'm still working the place myself. It's my living. It supports me.' " Our reading of *Local Hero* connects with this research but sees this environmentalist discourse amplified by multiple elements of comedy and the eco-hero.

For us, *Local Hero* begins with a typical "big guys versus little guys" premise: The "big guy" Knox Oil and Gas CEO Happer sends his surrogate Mac to attempt to buy this village near Aberdeen, Scotland and acquire the land for an oil refinery from the "little guys," the town's "accountant" and representative Gordan Urquhart (Denis Lawson) and its local hermit and beach scavenger, Ben. In most eco-comedies, this set-up would promote community opposition, with help from what could be described as a comic eco-hero. As an early proponent of comic ecological narratives and heroes, Joseph Meeker defines the eco-hero, claiming that comedy reflects mature nature and its actors and "depicts the loss of equilibrium and its recovery," demonstrating that humans "muddle through" without concern for "progress or perfection."[11] According to Meeker, once ecosystems mature, tragic heroes like those found in recent cli-fi films like *Snowpiercer* and *Noah* become not only unnecessary but also subordinate to the group.[12] Meeker argues, in a mature or climax ecosystem, "it is the community itself that really matters, and it is likely to be an extremely durable community so long as balance is maintained among its many elements."[13] *Local Hero* complicates this vision of the comic narrative and eco-hero by disrupting the binary opposition Meeker establishes between tragic "pioneer" and comic "communal" narratives and heroes.

Mac offers the most obvious example of such a disruption. As an outsider seeking to exploit villagers and their land for Knox Oil and Gas profits, Mac seems more tragic than comic. Yet he also serves as the object of multiple laughter-inducing devices. He especially infuses the eco-plot of the film with ridiculous dramatic irony, providing half of a double perspective offset by the more knowledgeable villagers. In one scene, for example, the villagers hide from Mac and Oldsen (Peter Capaldi) in the village church to discuss their potential profits from the sale. When Mac arrives, they send Scottish African Reverend Murdo Macpherson (Gyearbuor Asante) out to distract him, using their conversation to conceal the villagers' quick escape from the sanctuary and add a bit of humor to the scene. Audience members are in on the joke and watch the human parade with amusement. As Eli Rozik explains, this double perspective adds comedy in the context of the film's humorous mood, "a precondition for presenting a character as ludicrous."[14] In *Local Hero*, the dramatic irony also amplifies the blurring of boundaries between exploited and exploiter. Mac may think he is there to acquire property. With Gordon's help, the villagers believe they're the ones with the better half of the deal, without revealing they have no ownership of the bay Mac is there to purchase.

Mac also offers multiple examples of verbal irony and contributes instances of compulsive repetition and sexual innuendo, and most of these instances enhance the film's eco-comic narrative. While talking with Reverend Macpherson, fighter planes shriek overhead, disappearing into an eruption of fire and smoke. The Reverend takes it in stride, explaining, "They practice here. As long as they're bombing the beach, they can't be bombing anywhere else. It's kind of comforting." But Mac offers an ironic response that connects explicitly with the film's eco-narrative: "I don't know about those jets. They really spoil a very nice area," he declares, refusing to acknowledge the damage his petro-project will cause. And, in a move that highlights the goal to "break" the beach with an oil project, Mac's relationship with ex-girlfriend Trudi is transferred to an injured rabbit in oddly suggestive ways when he names the bunny Trudi, since Mac's new object of desire, innkeeper chef Stella (Jennifer Black), cooked the casserole de lapin. Mac's ridiculous responses translate well to the film's carnivalesque atmosphere during the traditional Scottish cèilidh social gathering where Mac strips off his jacket to dance with Stella. As Bakhtin avers, "the suspension of all hierarchical precedence during carnival time was of particular significance . . . [since] all were considered equal during carnival."[15] By juxtaposing the dance with Mac's discovery of the Aurora Borealis, sexual innuendo again parallels attraction toward the natural world and, perhaps, obstructs possible ecofeminist readings by objectifying women and the local landscapes with which they connect.

Another laughter-inducing device, compulsive repetition showcases Mac's evolution from tragic outsider to comic wanna-be eco-Scot. Early in the film, Mac explains how his watch is timed to ring whenever it is best to call Houston. Each alarm ring grows more ridiculous, as villagers scurry to gather coins for the town's only phone booth, and, each time Mac makes the Houston call, an operator drones "Knox Oil and Gas" multiple times. The alarms begin to connect with environmental themes when Mac and his Knox Oil compatriot Oldsen walk along the beach for private conversations. At first, they walk in full business suits and shoes while carrying briefcases. With each walk (and timed alarm), clothes are discarded or changed until Mac even throws off the watch and leaves it for the rising tide to silence. After Mac has left the scene, we watch waves flap over the timepiece and listen to the water-logged alarm dim.

But the future of the beach seems less lucrative until other comic narratives and heroes emerge. Instead of moving linearly toward one comic or tragic resolution, for example, the narrative of Local Hero highlights two possible outcomes for the village and its presumed opponent Knox Oil and Gas. A model of the proposed refinery at the Knox Aberdeen Laboratory reveals these opposing possibilities. When Mac and Oldsen visit the lab, they are introduced to Marina, the oceanographer bent on preserving the Bay, and while she remains in the room, the first of these possibilities for Ferness Bay—a research center illustrated by a model and the sensors in "sector 421." When Marina leaves for lunch, however, the scientists reveal the second (destructive) possibility Happer and Mac propose, "the petro-chemical capital of the world." According to the scientists, the harbor "is a natural for blasting in the underground tanks. . . . Plus, the debris rock will be used to fill in the other beach for the refinery." They claim the site "will last 1000 years, forever! . . . It'll even survive the next ice age. We can divert the Gulf Stream and unfreeze the Arctic Circle." And instead of opposing this eco-disastrous proposal, villagers who find lobster they catch too expensive to eat see the proposal as a way out of their economic woes. These unexpected narrative possibilities highlight the complex approach *Local Hero* takes toward its environmental message and the concept of the ownership of nature.

Binaries are also blurred between tragic and comic eco-heroes. Instead of establishing Happer as a tragic pioneer working toward "survival through the destruction of all our competitors and . . . achieving effective dominance over other forms of life,"[16] *Local Hero* merges Happer's goals with those of Ben, the local hero of the film's title not to dominate and destroy but to preserve the natural world. We have written extensively about the conflict between pioneer and comic eco-heroes in films of multiple genres. For us, many comic eco-disaster films highlight comic eco-heroes that respond to the heroic motifs of tragedy by comically constructing the characters of drama to serve both a comic purpose and a satirical premise and plot. In such an eco-comedy, heroes with more than one tragic flaw are foregrounded. Our work here typically draws on Meeker's vision of a comic eco-hero who tends to bumble and requires a community of allies to succeed. As we noted in our readings of *Eight Legged Freaks* and *WALL-E*,[17] comic eco-films sometimes poke fun at extremists and provide a space where comic eco-heroes so flawed they nearly become ineffective can show us the positive consequences of placing the good of community—a climax ecosystem—above the individual.

Rather than drawing on bifurcations between tragic pioneer and comic eco-heroes, *Local Hero* defies expectations, resisting conventional approaches to eco-disaster situations and characters by viewing them through varied ironic lenses. The most obvious example of situational irony is found in the unlikely alliance between Happer and Ben, which merges pioneer and communal ideals in unexpected ways. Unlike the typical tragic pioneer hero of films like *Noah*, Happer embodies both a drive for resource consumption and a comic passion for community and the wonders of nature. And the film emphasizes these dual (and conflicting) roles from its opening forward. Although Happer first appears as an absurd comic bungler, snoring through a promotional video that announces, "Nature guards her secrets," and dozing through a whispered board meeting arguing for the "acquisition of part of Scotland for the refinery and storage base," he transforms into a pioneer when he awakens, declaring Knox needs to "buy Ferness Bay for $60 million" and suggesting they send a negotiator to the site because "we're not in a Third World situation." Happer's character highlights this conflict between comically ridiculous and tragically rapacious behaviors in nearly all of the scenes in which he appears. Happer chooses Macintyre to negotiate for Ferness Bay because he believes Mac is a Scot and will be "dealing with [his] own people," a claim debunked by Mac's own admission he is Hungarian. But Happer cuts this comic plea with a racist comment that aligns with tragic pioneer tendencies when he tells Mac, "You won't be dealing with a bunch of Indians."

Happer's eco-comic characteristics come to light because of his obsession with astronomy, especially because this passion is first revealed during an unorthodox session with abusive therapist Moritz (Norman Chancer). While Moritz declares Happer's life is "empty" and "hollow," Happer asserts, "Comets are important. They could be the key to the universe." In discussions with Mac, this astronomical eco-passion takes precedence over negotiations for Ferness Bay. Instead of providing advice about acquiring the Bay for the best possible price, Happer opens up his enormous office planetarium, revealing an artificial sky bright with constellations and asks Mac to keep him updated about the skies. He tells Mac, "The constellation of Virgo is very prominent in the sky now, in Scotland," and wants him to "keep an eye on Virgo" because he is "expecting something special from there." Happer does not want reports about the oil acquisition. He wants reports about "anything unusual in Virgo" like "a new star or even a shooting star" and tells him to call any time, even providing Mac with his private number. For Happer, "the northern sky is a beautiful thing," and Mac's job is to share it with him. In a phone call late in the film, for example, a drunk Mac admires a sky "doing some amazing things," exclaiming about the colors of the aurora borealis, a phenomenon Happer hasn't seen "since '53 in Alaska." Yet that eco-passion is diluted by Moritz's abusive messages on Happer's skyscraper windows and the real mission of Mac's trip, acquiring the bay and making it the refining petrocapital of the world. Happer moves beyond the tragic pioneer in these scenes, trying out eco-comic inclinations in sometimes productive ways.

Ben, too, shows a penchant for both tragic and comic eco-heroic characteristics. We are introduced to Ben gradually, first as a lone man in the distance blending into the beach he works, then as the eccentric inhabitant of a beach shack seemingly constructed of mismatched driftwood. But each of these off-center portraits serve as parallels to the action on display. The first distant shot of Ben on the beach highlights his interconnection with the natural world around him, but it also amplifies the clandestine meeting of townspeople in the village church. While Mac meanders toward the church, Gordon tells the group and its Minister Macpherson, "I've got the Knox man on the hook. Give me time to land him in style. He's got a bag full of money. So stay calm and let me handle him." Their bickering over price powerfully diverges from Ben's austere and sustainable life on the beach. The closer view of Ben in his Shack also contrasts with a scene of consumption, this time a literal consumption of a meal that includes Mac and Oldsen's rescued rabbit Trudi. Trudi serves as a potential symbol of the village and beach. With a leg broken by Oldsen and Mac's car, Trudi resembles a bay broken by economic desolation. And like Trudi, the bay may be consumed by the oil company vying for its resources. Ben highlights the potential eco-disaster Knox Oil and Gas will bring by illustrating what will be lost if the company succeeds. Everyone is lying to everyone else in these scenes. The town does not have anything to sell, and Ben will not reveal he is the owner. Mac and Oldsen, too, hide their predatory behavior.

Yet Ben's eco-role also blurs under scrutiny and showcases a productive nostalgia that draws on a past in which both the beach and its human inhabitants thrived. Instead of completely opposing Knox Oil and Gas and its mission to acquire the beach, Ben shows an affinity for the company's owner Happer's obsession with the stars, when Gordon and Mac drop in to discuss the sale. Ben laughs when Gordon suggests Mac "was asking . . . how much I thought the bay was worth," but he perks up when Mac asks him if he knows anything about the stars. Ben exclaims, "I know my way around this sky," proving it with his telescope. Ben explains, "if you want to find a comet, you just have to look long enough in the right place," and suggests, "I would look in Leo" to find one, before Mac grows overwrought by a meteor shower. When Mac calls Happer to share his discovery, the connection between Happer and Ben is accentuated, since Happer is listening to the radio program *Astronomy Tomorrow* while he marvels over Mac's report. And the link between Ben and Happer further strengthens when Gordon finally informs Mac that Ben owns the beach, and Happer tells Mac he is coming to meet the owner. During negotiations with Ben, Mac, Gordon, and Russian fisherman Victor (Christopher Rozycki), they discover Ben's surname, which just happens to be Knox, broaching one example of productive nostalgia. The beach has "been in the family for 400 years," and "the Lord of Isles gave it to" one of his ancestors. Ben tells them "he helped him out of with a spot of trouble. Killed his brother for him . . . something like that," and the deed is "in the museum in Edinburgh. It's a historical document."

Despite this bond between Ben Knox and Happer, Ben views his beach through a sustainable ecological lens that amplifies productive nostalgia, rather than the fair use economic ecology lens shared by Knox Oil and Gas. When Mac offers to buy Ben another beach, he tells Mac, "I have this one. I don't need another one. Besides, I'm not sure that there's a living in any of those beaches." By offering his family's historical memory, Ben also explains the negative externalities associated with colonialism, globalization, and over-consumption. Mac may claim that four hundred to five hundred people could make a living if Knox Oil and Gas transformed the bay into a petrochemical nightmare, but Ben explains, "That wouldn't be the first time. . . . Local history. . . . This beach used to be a good living for 300 people. They gathered seaweed and extracted the chemicals. Two hundred years ago, this beach was turning over 15,000 a year. Then the trade routes opened up again to the east, and so, 'farewell, Ferness.' The business went, but the beach is still here. If you got the place, it would be good-bye beach, forever, wouldn't it?" To prove his point, Ben offers Gordon and Mac oranges found in the rocks on Tuesday. As Ben declares, "I found a coconut once. Lord knows where that came from." For Ben, the outside world and Ferness can share an interconnected relationship that benefits both, providing seaweed and trade routes and sharing oranges and coconuts on its way. The project Knox Oil and Gas proposes would destroy the beach, focusing only on consuming its resources for economic gain.

The conflicting goals Ben and Happer seem to embody in binary opposition break down when Happer travels to Ferness Bay and meets with Ben to negotiate with him for the beach. Instead, Happer and Ben blend their visions, highlighting a merger of comic and tragic eco-narratives and heroic characteristics. Ben agrees to share his beach, not for an oil refinery but for a research institute. And Happer acquires the beach, as he planned, while preserving its natural beauty. As Happer tells Mac, "the refinery was a mistake." Happer "want[s] this place" but "see[s] a kind of institute here, a place for research and study, an observatory, so to speak, with radio and optical telescopes." With Oldsen's guidance, Happer includes the sea in his plans, since the bay is "a natural place for a marine laboratory." Happer and Ben seem to demonstrate the power of connection, finding a "middle way" over food, drink, and conversation. By the end of their talk, Ben even blames Mac for the original petro-nightmare plan, exclaiming, "I'm glad I managed to stop your refinery caper," and transmitting Mac's role to Oldsen to prepare for a night with Ben on the telescope. Although the eco-comic ending is diluted by Happer's instructions to maintain the project in a location closer to the models and move oil storage offshore, the Bay is "saved." In this eco-comic narrative, both the "little guys" and the "big guys" win, and so does the natural world. As if answering Gordon's claim, "you can't eat scenery," Happer's research institute will provide a meal.

But Ben and Happer's resolution is complicated by the conclusions of two more segments of the film's plot—those driven by Marina and Mac. Unlike the real hand-shaking moment that saved the beach, Marina and Mac highlight the continuing conflicts between fantastic hope for the environment and lonely and tragic perpetuation of its destruction. As Oldsen declares to Marina, the marine lab is going to happen as she had predicted, but instead of offering a rational scientist with five oceanography degrees, the film leaves us watching Marina's fantastical mermaid tail shooting through the waves. We have had suggestions for this conclusion when Oldsen admired her webbed feet, but this ending leaves the eco-message on more fragile magical realist ground. Much has been written about Mac's return to Houston and his unanswered call to the Ferness phone booth, but it too ultimately highlights a less positive outcome for the natural world, since Mac will presumably continue his work for Knox Oil and Gas, merely moving the refinery to a less astronomically stimulating spot. The village and bay, then, serve a nostalgic purpose, illustrating the "before" picture in an oil culture (see fig. 9.2).

The story most resembles a proposed North Sea gas reception terminal construction near Crimond, Aberdeenshire in the early 1970s. Graeme Baxter outlines how the North-East Environmental Liaison Group and the Buchan Action Group thwarted the Gas Council and the oil corporation Total and, like the Knox Oil and Gas of the film, "found an alternative terminal site, a few miles away at St. Fergus." Baxter compares this victory with reactions to Donald Trump's 2010 development of "the greatest golf course anywhere in the world," highlighting how the press adopted pro-Trump bias and dismissed, ridiculed, or ignored the development's opponents.[18] This continuing bias against the environment and toward economic gain resonates powerfully in more recent oil comedies. Forsyth's comments on the 2008 DVD release of *Local Hero* highlight at least one reason for the change. As Forsyth asserts, "I think an audience nowadays coming to the film would not be moved so much by any environmental message, because it is a very, very low-key message."[19] For the 2008 DVD release, however, Forsyth suggests, "maybe nowadays we need harder messages and louder messages."[20]

Fubar: Balls to the Wall and the Power of the Carnivalesque

Fubar: Balls to the Wall gives us this harder and louder message with gas flares illuminating frozen fields of pump jacks like paper under flame. It also showcases the choice missing from *Local Hero*, providing the "after" bookend to the nostalgic "before" oil image on the beaches of Ferness. As a mockumentary

Fig. 9.2. Although the eco-comic ending is diluted by Happer's instructions to maintain the project in a location closer to the models and move oil storage offshore, the Bay is "saved." In this eco-comic narrative, both the "little guys" and the "big guys" win, and so does the natural world. (*Local Hero*, written and directed by Bill Forsyth, [Enigma Productions, 1983], film)

loosely connected with *American Movie*,[21] *Fubar: Balls to the Wall* continues the story of the two misfit losers and what Rozik would define as "ludicrous characters"[22]—Terry and Dean—introduced in the original *Fubar*.[23] Set five years after *Fubar*, *Fubar: Balls to the Wall* shows these two headbangers celebrating Dean's fifth year of remission from the testicular cancer that was the plot driver of the first film. Tired of barely scraping by on menial jobs in Calgary, the pair seek their fortunes in Canada's oil sands. Although Terry quickly becomes a welcome member of Tron's pipeline crew, Dean flounders. An infertile but confident Terry even starts dating Trish (Terra Hazelton), a promiscuous waitress at the local strip bar.

Strategic and far-reaching pipeline crew layoffs complicate this comic rags to riches story, especially when coupled with Terry's new wife Trish's unlikely pregnancy and Dean's returning cancer. These issues highlight multiple negative externalities associated with Alberta's oil fields. Even though *Fubar: Balls to the Wall* maintains its comic tone (including the expected happy ending), it also serves as a visual warning and stark contrast to the idyllic village and bay preserved in *Local Hero*. By revealing the human costs of "tough" oil excavation in the tar sands of northern Alberta through multiple comic lenses,

Fubar: Balls to the Wall powerfully exposes the "devastating scale"[24] of tough oil's environmental externalities. Although, like *Local Hero*, *Fubar: Balls to the Wall* complicates expectations for comic eco-heroes, it also amplifies the potential revolutionary effects of the carnivalesque and, for its eco-comic message, draws on what David Farrier calls the toxic pastoral "in which pastoral certainties are degraded, permitting an engagement with and celebration of the ambivalence in human interactions with the more-than-human world."[25] The film reels in audience sympathy with this human focus, while comically and slyly unmasking the eco-disaster of oil culture and offering a communal eco-comic solution to exploitation of human and nonhuman nature.

As a metalhead gross-out mockumentary, *Fubar: Balls to the Walls* most obviously applies lenses drawing on repetition, a more traditional comic device. Arguably the most prevalent and blatant tool used to induce laughter and expose eco-disastrous consequences of the oil sands is the repetition of night shots of refinery stacks, seeming to breath fire and smoke as they establish the horrific location for most of the film, Fort MacMurray, Alberta. They also serve as a stark contrast to the idyllic Scottish village, beach, and bay of *Local Hero*, and a portent of what might have become of Ferness if Happer's research center were replaced by a sea of glowing refineries. The first shot of these fiery refineries comes early, introducing Terry and Dean to the oil sands. Seen from a distance, Terry and Dean call these erupting smokestacks the "Northern Lights," infusing the scene with comedy and an ironic eco-message. The refinery lights make an appearance in each scene highlighting a change for the comic pair. After Tron warns Terry and Dean about "the Mac," horrifying scenes show us refineries that look like burning monsters turning the night sky red. These nearly demonic flames welcome Terry and Dean to their first day working on Tron's pipeline crew and to their two-week anniversary when the two are hired more permanently for the pipeline construction. The refinery lights connect with the landscape in a montage of images signaling a transition to the Christmas season, as well, connecting the refineries with holiday lights, ice skating, elves, and (to emphasize the costs of oil extraction) the unemployed Dean in a homeless camp syphoning gasoline for the car that is now his winter shelter.

But the film also powerfully draws on carnival and the carnivalesque to reveal and amplify human relationships and their interaction with the natural world. According to Bakhtin, "Carnival is not a spectacle seen by the people; they live in it, and everyone participates because its very idea embraces all the people. While carnival lasts, there is no other life outside it."[26] For Bakhtin, carnival is not an extension of real life, it turns the problems and hierarchies of the world upside down. Because of this "upside down" worldview, "during carnival time life is subject only to its laws, that is, the laws of its own freedom."[27] Because Bakhtin's carnival includes this breakdown of hierarchies and binaries, "it has a universal spirit; it is a special condition of the entire world, of the world's revival and renewal, in which all take part."[28] For Bakhtin, carnivalesque imagery is always both dualistic and ambivalent, uniting conflicting poles such as change and crisis, birth and death, old and young, down and up, and wisdom and stupidity. To highlight this breakdown and merging of opposites, objects and devices in the carnival are reversed: clothes are worn upside down, household items serve as weapons, and the clown is king. According to Bakhtin, "Such free, familiar contacts were deeply felt and formed an essential element of the carnival spirit. People were, so to speak, reborn for new, purely human relations. . . . The utopian ideal and the realistic merged in this carnival experience, unique of its kind."[29]

In *Fubar: Balls to the Wall*, carnivalesque scenes subvert and liberate dominant cultural and ecological assumptions through humor and chaos, but they also highlight the reproductive potential of a unified interdependent worldview. The opening hyperbolic party preparation and event illustrates this focus on freedom and universal spirit of renewal. Sounds of a forklift and its unskilled operator Terry talking about a party that "won't run out of beer" open the film and its carnivalesque moments of escape. Terry's car trunk is not even big enough for the beer forklifted into it. This ridiculous party scene begins to highlight the subversion of hierarchies when Dean's Mom Rose (Rose Martin) yells, "Yay, my boy and his ball!" When occasional friend Tron arrives, both cultural and ecological assumptions are subverted. As he drives up in his oversized pickup truck, Tron deliberately knocks down an aspen sapling, seeming to resent the tree's taking any space in Terry and Dean's yard. And it is Tron who instigates an "eviction party" when he discovers Terry and Dean have been forced out of their home, encouraging party goers to smash walls, furniture, and appliances. Tron even grabs his chainsaw using it to cut a hole in a wall to extract a naked and high Dean after he accidently lights the house on fire. Ultimately, Tron throws the saw out a window through a sheet of smoke and drives off, leaving an environmental disaster in his wake. In later Fort MacMurray scenes, too, Dean, Terry, and Tron subvert hierarchies. Dean and Tron vandalize Terry's truck when Terry succumbs to traditional patriarchal norms with Trish. Dean and Terry break into a hardware store to steal hockey knee pads for Dean's daughter, Chastity (Hannah Lawrence). And a drunken, drugged out, and suicidal Tron wets himself on Christmas, denigrating the sacred holiday.

Other carnivalesque scenes explicitly highlight how both degradation and renewal unite all humanity and the more-than-human. As Bakhtin explains, "The people do not exclude themselves from the wholeness of the world. They, too, are incomplete, they also die and are revived and renewed."[30] Multiple drunken gatherings at the local Ft. McMurray strip club emphasize carnival's grotesque "concern . . . with the lower stratum of the body, the life of the belly and the reproductive organs."[31] The carnivalesque "relates to acts of defecation and copulation, conception, pregnancy, and birth."[32] Terry's attraction to Trish illustrates this focus on the lower stratum, but their courtship also reveals our interdependence with nonhuman nature, moving from heavy metal slow dancing to a deer hunting video game emphasizing the natural world. Trish excels at this game, and we watch her shoot down bucks and does running gracefully across a constructed meadow background. A trip to an Edmonton mall parallels this interconnection, when a weekend of consumerism moves into hunting bow purchases and a comical scene at an indoor shooting range.

All of these carnivalesque acts mask the environmental degradation on display throughout the film (see fig. 9.3). The multiple shots of refinery lights do more than highlight transitions. These demonic fires also reify the disastrous environmental consequences of dirty oil extraction and refining: toxic smoke and CO_2 emissions, tainted water runoff from tailing ponds, and forest wildlife habitat and water resource destruction. R. P. Siegel sums up the pros and cons of oil sands extraction, revealing how the development of oil sands "began in the 1960s" on a "small scale," but recently, "with declining supplies and increasing prices" for traditionally extracted oil, production ramped up "after PetroChina acquired a 60% interest in two major wells in Alberta in 2009." Siegel notes a few benefits of the oil sands, including the very large supply of oil and enormous growth potential. In fact, the negative externalities are overwhelming: greenhouse gas emissions so large they comprise "Canada's largest source of CO_2 emissions," "relatively low net energy return compared to other sources," water requirements that are three times the oil produced, "roughly three million gallons of toxic runoff per day" resulting in polluted pools that cover at least fifty square miles, boreal forest destruction, and "widespread habitat destruction," which especially affects First Nations. Siegel compares the negative externalities associated with oil sands to those connected to coal, suggesting "these tar sands might even be worse."[33]

Fubar: Balls to the Wall presents many of these negative externalities with a comic mood and a mixture of what Freud calls innocent and tendentious laughter.[34] The repeated images of refinery lights we noted highlight the CO_2 and toxic emissions associated with the oil sands, while its "fiery furnace" effect

Fig. 9.3. *Fubar: Balls to the Wall* gives us this harder and louder message with gas flares il-luminating frozen fields of pump jacks like paper under flame. It also showcases the choice missing from *Local Hero*. (*Fubar: Balls to the Wall*, directed by Michael Dowse, written by David Lawrence, Paul Spence, and Michael Dowse, [FU2 Productions, 2010], film)

also serves as a symbol of the industry's environmental destruction. Terry and Dean's encounter with a hitchhiker broaches multiple negative consequences of oil sands. He is headed to Fort MacMurray not for work but to join a First Nations protest against the oil sands, noting the impact extraction, refining, and transporting oil from the fields have on water resources, lakes, and wild-life. As he explains, it takes ten barrels of water for every one barrel of oil. And water sources become so polluted, "birds fly into lakes of oil and drown." Although Terry and Dean ask him, "Where would you be if there wasn't any oil?" and declare, "I don't need ducks. Fuck ducks," adding a comic tone to the scene, their arguments gain a sense of irony during later unsuccessful hunting scenes when Dean kills a housecat and refuses to shoot a turkey for Boxing Day.

Not only do extraction and refining contribute to environmental degra-dation, so do oil pipelines. Xuejuan Su highlights the negative economic ex-ternalities associated with extraction, refining, and pipeline transport of oil from Alberta's oil sands. According to Su, "the construction and operation of an oil pipeline may have environmental impact on air quality, water qual-ity, noise level, contamination in case of oil leak or spill, wildlife habitat loss, etc.," and Su notes how such externalities can be reliably calculated.[35] Su also notes that greenhouse gas emissions associated with oil sands development "is mainly a result of upstream extraction and downstream refining and consumption."[36] As an economist, Su suggests ameliorating these externalities with solutions such as a carbon tax levy, but he admits "it is indeed the case that WSC [Western Canadian Select] oil sands generate more GHG [greenhouse gas] emissions than some other sources of crude oils."[37] Both Siegel and Lu demonstrate that the environmental and human costs of oil sands exceed any economic benefits to the region. As a part of the pipe crew, Terry and Dean showcase some of the environmental destruction associated with building an oil pipeline. Most emphatically, scenes at the work site highlight destruction of boreal and deciduous forests. The crew has clear-cut a wide strip of the forest for the pipeline, leaving a barren clay highway behind. In the distance we see rows of trees lined by the broken stumps that remain. When Tron rams into the tree in Terry and Dean's front yard, he foreshadows this eco-disaster, but he also demonstrates the violence necessary to raze a forest. Such responses persuade feminist film critic Barbara Creed to ask regarding the cinema of eco-trauma, "are we either too aggressive or too fearful to share the planet and its resources?"[38]

Tron's crash into the aspen does more than illustrate forest destruction, then, it additionally highlights a way humanity copes with environmental degradation and the eco-trauma associated with it: human-upon-nature violence. For clinical psychologist Tina Amorok, eco-trauma is "a traumatic loss of intimacy with the Earth and the cosmos" and "creates a deficit in the realm of eco-Being and is a core cause of human-upon-nature and human-upon human violence."[39] Amorok and eco-psychologist Eduardo Duran assert eco-trauma "is in a state of constant retraumatization with the continual devastation of the land."[40] Amorok also asserts that eco-trauma originated in "harmful effects" of "aberrant human violence," a violence that continues in our methods of protecting ourselves from despair caused by our separation from the environment.[41] As ecocritic Anil Narine suggests, "a traumatized earth begets traumatized people,"[42] a point that becomes tangible in *Fubar: Balls to the Wall*. Terry, Dean, and Tron experience this trauma and reveal negative consequences connected explicitly to the oil sands. Dean faces the most disastrous repercussions, discovering his cancer has returned during a checkup for a failed workers' compensation attempt. When gas prices plunge, Tron and his boss lay off both Terry and Dean without compensation, forcing the overextended Terry into a job at a gas station and Dean into homelessness. Drugs and alcohol are the most prevalent method of coping with eco-trauma, beginning from early shots of Fort MacMurray's homeless drunks passed out along the roadway. Tron's drug addiction serves as a peak eco-trauma response. His despair grows so unbearable, he makes a suicide pact with Dean. And in a tragicomic scene on Boxing Day, Tron nearly smothers Dean and wets himself after passing out. Their experience with the oil sands has led to eco-traumatic results.

But *Fubar: Balls to the Wall* is a comedy and provides a sense of eco-recovery like that Amorok explains, arguing that "to begin healing what is broken in ourselves and in our relations to the natural world, we need to see and feel what is within us and all around us."[43] To promote such reconnections, the film showcases comic toxic pastoral scenes that recall a ridiculous camping trip in the original *Fubar*. For ecocritic David Farrier, linking classical pastoral and comedy provides a way to add "harder edge" to "pastoral's sentimental expressions." *Fubar: Balls to the Wall* has this harder edge and moves comic pastoral toward the "toxic pastoral" that "foregrounds the 'impure' and symbiotic rather than the 'pure,' separated (albeit mutually reinforcing) civic and rural spaces of conventional pastoral."[44] Tron's transformation into Santa after Dean dresses him in red pajamas and washes his urine-stained clothing broaches one of these impure pastoral scenes. After Dean's daughter Chastity mistakes him for St. Nick, Tron's despair lifts, and he hands her a battery as an odd gift. Later, Tron joins the family at an outdoor hockey rink and distributes eccentric gifts surrounded by a pastoral scene of white purifying snow and distant views of trees and "impure" smokestacks.

After leaving the oil sands behind them, Terry and Dean's relationship with the natural world draws on the dual and overlapping goals of a toxic pastoral that resists separation between humanity and nature. According to Farrier, "toxic pastoral insists upon the interdependence of ecocentric and anthropocentric values and expounds a more 'biotically imbricated' and 'elastic' version of pastoral."[45] The various hunting scenes illustrate Terry and Dean's evolving relationship with nature. The videogame hunting game connects Terry and Trish but offers only a constructed view of wild nature there only for gamers' pleasure and illusion of success. After Dean smashes his foot for workmen's compensation, Terry and Dean take off on a snowmobile with their crossbows to the field where Dean shoots the housecat. Here the natural world is a real and covered with purifying snow, but so is the housecat Dean nonchalantly takes as his token prey.

When Dean and Terry reunite after oil sands layoffs and a clash over Trish, however, their connection with the nonhuman nature seems to mature during another hunting trip. In an absurd turn, the two buy a wild turkey and set it free to hunt for Christmas dinner, even claiming, "we're going to murder you."

Instead, Dean demurs, attempting to hug the turkey in friendship. A sledding party mingles ecocentric visions of purifying snow and relationships with anthropocentric views of cancer and reproduction, as well. This beautiful pastoral setting is disrupted by Dean's conversation with his ex-wife Trixie (Tracey Lawrence). She knows about Dean's loss of a second testicle and fears he may commit suicide. But Dean explains suicide is out of the question because he has another baby on the way, the child Trish believes the infertile Terry fathered. Dean's bodily functions demonstrate his connection with the natural world. He gives Trish's child life, but after losing another testicle to cancer, Dean is reborn, collecting an absurd reward from his hormonal changes—a falsetto voice that allows him to hit the high notes of his favorite toxic pastoral song. As Dean croons, "Every rose has its thorns," he highlights Tron's original warning about the Mac as a cruel mistress while providing the backdrop for Terry and Trish's wedding and a family portrait that includes Dean and their communal son.

Conclusion

As in *Local Hero*, the toxic pastoral happy ending in *Fubar: Balls to the Wall* becomes possible only after Terry, Dean, and Tron leave the oil fields behind. In both the "before" picture of oil culture found in *Local Hero* and the "after" eco-horror exhibited in *Fubar: Balls to the Wall*, oil does not mix well with either human or more-than-human nature. As we noted in *Film and Everyday Eco-Disasters*, however, conflicts between oil and the natural world have been whitewashed by media representations of their relationship because, as Vermont Public Radio asserted regarding oil drilling in the Gulf of Mexico, "The local fishermen feared their way of life was in jeopardy when the first oilmen arrived in Cajun south Louisiana. But over the last half century, the two industries learned to live together. Oil and gas brought jobs and opportunity for many families."[46] For NPR Reporter Debbie Elliot and other representatives of the media, locals whose living depends on nature and oil companies learned to live together because oil brought money and jobs to the region. Even after the BP Horizon Oil Disaster, the final report of the National Commission on the BP Deepwater Horizon Oil Spill and Offshore Drilling claimed, "Drilling in deep water does not have to be abandoned. It can be done safely."[47] The last chapter of the report outlines how best to implement the safety precautions that will avoid such disasters and facilitate more offshore oil drilling. Neither *Local Hero* nor *Fubar: Balls to the Wall* make such a ludicrous claim. Instead, in the context of fantastic, ridiculous, and satirical comic situations, these two films provide the environmental message made possible when the "shit and sex" of oil extraction, refining, and transport come to the fore.

NOTES

1. *Local Hero*, written and directed by Bill Forsyth (Enigma Productions, 1983), film.
2. *Fubar: Balls to the Wall*, directed by Michael Dowse, written by David Lawrence, Paul Spence, and Michael Dowse (FU2 Productions, 2010), film.
3. *The Paleface*, written and directed by Eddie Kline and Buster Keaton (Buster Keaton Productions, 1922), film; *Boom Town*, directed by Jack Conway, written by John Lee Mahin (MGM, 1940), film; *All Dogs Go to Heaven*, directed by Don Bluth and Gary Goldman, written by Don Bluth et al. (MGM, 1989), film; *Son of Rambow*, written and directed by Garth Jennings (Hammer and Tongs, 2007), film.
4. *Oklahoma Crude*, directed by Stanley Kramer, written by Marc Norman (Stanley Kramer Productions, 1973), film.
5. Stephanie LeMenager, *Living Oil: Petroleum Culture in the American Century* (Oxford: Oxford University Press, 2014), 92.
6. Robin L. Murray and Joseph K. Heumann, *Film and Everyday Eco-Disasters* (Lincoln: University of Nebraska Press, 2014).
7. Bill Forsyth, "Comments," *Local Hero*, written and directed by Bill Forsyth (1983; Channel 4, 2008), DVD.
8. Christopher Meir, *Scottish Cinema: Texts and Contexts* (Manchester: Manchester University Press, 2015), 15–16.
9. Jonathan Murray, *Discomfort and Joy: The Cinema of Bill Forsyth* (New York: Peter Lang, 2011), 91.
10. Dorothy Howell, *Entertainment Stewardship: Images from Popular Culture* (Westport, CT: Greenwood Publishing, 1997), xi.
11. Joseph Meeker, *The Comedy of Survival: Literary Ecology and the Play Ethic* (Phoenix: University of Arizona Press, 1997), 159, 160.
12. *Snowpiercer*, directed by Joon-ho Bong, written by Joon-ho Bong et al. (Moho Film, 2013), film; *Noah*, directed by Darren Aronofsky, written by Darren Aronofsky and Ari Handel (Paramount Pictures, 2014), film.
13. Meeker, *Comedy of Survival*, 163.
14. Eli Rozik, *Comedy: A Critical Introduction* (Sussex: Sussex Academic Press, 2011), 48.
15. Mikhail Bakhtin, *Rabelais and His World*, trans. Helene Iswolsky (Bloomington: Indiana University Press, 1984), 10.
16. Meeker, *Comedy of Survival*, 162.
17. *Eight Legged Freaks*, directed by Ellory Elkayem, written by Ellory Elkayem, Randy Kornfield, and Jesse Alexander (Warner Bros. Pictures, 2002), film; *WALL-E*, directed by Andrew Stanton, written by Andrew Stanton, Pete Docter, and Jim Reardon (Pixar Animation, 2008), film.
18. Graeme Baxter, "Local Heroes or Village Idiots? Press Portrayal of Two Controversial Coastal Developments in North-East Scotland," *Aberdeen Business School Working Paper Series* 8, no. 2 (December 2015), https://openair.rgu.ac.uk/handle/10059/1366.
19. Quoted in Murray, *Discomfort and Joy*, 91.
20. Quoted in Murray, 91.
21. *American Movie*, directed by Chris Smith (Bluemark Productions, 1999), film.
22. Rozik, *Comedy*, 22.
23. *Fubar*, directed by Michael Dowse, written by Michael Dowse, David Lawrence, and Paul Spence (Busted Tranny, 2002), film.

24. LeMenager, *Living Oil*, 3.
25. David Farrier, "Toxic Pastoral: Comic Failure and Ironic Nostalgia in Contemporary British Environmental Theatre," *The Journal of Ecocriticism* 6, no. 2 (July 2014), https://ojs.unbc.ca/index.php/joe/article/view/559.
26. Bakhtin, *Rabelais*, 7.
27. Bakhtin, 7.
28. Bakhtin, 8.
29. Bakhtin, 10.
30. Bakhtin, 12.
31. Bakhtin, 21.
32. Bakhtin, 21.
33. R. P. Siegel, "Tar Sands Oil: Pros and Cons," Triple Pundit, April 16, 2012, https://www.triplepundit.com/special/energy-options/tar-sands-oil-pros-cons.
34. Sigmund Freud, *Jokes and Their Relation to the Unconscious*, trans. James Strachey (New York: W. W. Norton, 1963), 171.
35. Xuejuan Su, "Evaluating Environmental Concerns in Oil Pipeline Proposals: The Pricing of Externalities," (working paper, Department of Economics, University of Alberta, November 2014), 5, http://citeseerx.ist.psu.edu/viewdoc/download?doi=10.1.1.706.3155&rep=rep1&type=pdf.
36. Su, 11.
37. Su, 15.
38. Barbara Creed, "Exolution, Extinction and the Eco-Trauma Film: *Darwin's Nightmare* (2004) & *A Zed and Two Naughts* (1985)," in *Eco-Trauma Cinema*, ed. Anil Narine (New York: Routledge, 2014), 26, 25–45.
39. Tina Amorok, "The Eco-Trauma and Eco-Recovery of Being," *Shift: At the Frontiers of Consciousness* 15 (June–August, 2007), 29.
40. Amorok, 30.
41. Amorok, 30.
42. Narine, *Eco-Trauma*, 13.
43. Amorok, "Eco-Trauma," 31.
44. Farrier, "Toxic Pastoral."
45. Farrier.
46. Debbie Elliott, "A Love-Hate History: Oil and Fishing in the Gulf," July 22, 2010, in *Morning Edition*, produced by Evie Stone, National Public Radio, http://www.npr.org/templates/story/story.php?storyId=128463645.
47. National Commission on the BP Deepwater Horizon Oil Spill and Offshore Drilling, "Deepwater: The Gulf War Disaster and the Future of Offshore Drilling," January 2011, https://www.govinfo.gov/content/pkg/GPO-OILCOMMISSION/pdf/GPO-OIL COMMISSION.pdf.

CHAPTER 10

Boom/Bust: Tragic Logistics and Accelerationist Comedy in Petroleum Transport

C. Parker Krieg

Gather the wind, though the wind won't help you fly at all. Your back's to the wall.
Chain the sun, and it tears away to face you as you run, you run, you run!
    —Ronnie James Dio (Black Sabbath), "Die Young," *Heaven and Hell*, 1980

This chapter explores boom-and-bust narratives set in the peripheral industries that support fossil fuel extraction, in operations that are obscured by the more visible sites of the petrocultural economy. By turning to the infrastructures that support extraction, we might expand our understanding of how contemporary narratives articulate culture and economy in an accelerating, warming world. This chapter offers a comparative reading of the Smithsonian Channel reality series *Boomtowners* (2015) and the Canadian mockumentary *FUBAR II* (2010).[1] By juxtaposing the tragic frame of logistics with what I call accelerationist comedy, I argue that the emotional economies depicted in these texts illustrate contradictory social imaginaries and frustrated forms of agency embedded in the movement of petroleum.

Climate change encourages people to think in global terms yet often relies on abstract, aesthetic descriptions of flows and processes without subjects. It is easy to think of fossil fuel modernity as a constituted power or system, and much more difficult to think of it as *built*, and indeed, something still being made, assembled, moved around, and reproduced, by constituent subjects. To this end, Anna Tsing discusses the need to "reopen the question of contingent articulations" at the human scale that link particular forms of production and circulation to planetary networks.[2] Attending to the ways that people are unevenly implicated allows for different ways of knowing an "energy system" that often appears as a totality with its own epistemology and homogenizing world-historical trajectory.[3] Resisting leaps to new periodization, Sandro Mezzandra and Brett Neilson suggest an analytical turn to the "operations of capital"—extraction, logistics, and finance—to describe the various ways "contemporary capitalism is mutating in and beyond its returning crises."[4] Between finance and extraction, logistics offers the narrative potential to "make public" *things* that are ontologized into the background, a move that Ash Amin and Nigel Thrift, following Bruno Latour, call a *Dingpolitik*.[5] Such narratives illustrate that "politics is no longer limited to humans and incorporates many issues to which they are attached."[6] The recognition that human economies are inextricable from climate requires narratives that "ventilate" these attachments to quite literally create "new atmospheres of democracy."[7] Logistics and infrastructure may "make worlds"; yet, as these scholars argue, ontological approaches to technology and environment must be accompanied by an account of labor as a living (and critical) form of subjectivity that "escapes measure."[8]

Paralleling the emerging discourse on logistics is accelerationism, a theoretical and cultural tendency that affirms the intensifying modernization of late capitalism as a strategy for overcoming it. Accelerationism contains a desire to push contradictory capitalist tendencies to the extremes leading to simultaneous exhaustion and transcendence. Benjamin Noys is credited with both naming the tendency and for offering the most sustained critique of its limitations.[9] In *Malign Velocities*, Noys traces this strain of Nietzschean affirmation through the work of Gilles Deleuze and Felix Guattari, Jean-François Lyotard, and Jean Baudrillard, among others, identifying similar sensibilities in cyberpunk and technoculture. In response to the increasingly abstract and precarious labor under neoliberalism, accelerationism reaffirms it. The answer is "not to withdraw from the process, but to go further, to 'accelerate the process.'"[10] This "road of excess" sets about "integrating labor into the machine"; it offers "the fantasy of integration, the man-machine (note the gendering) that might save and transcend the laboring body."[11] In short, what begins as transgressive desire turns masochistic. "*Defeat* is registered in these forms of theoretical accelerationism," Noys argues, "in the form of ecstatic suffering, of *jouissance*, experienced in our deepening immersion."[12] Accelerationism might be understood as a disappointed idealism that is uncomfortable with immanence, or which tries to recover the experience of transcendence through figures of speed or intensity. It is no surprise then that Donna Haraway, whose ironic figure of the cyborg owes more to the Nietzsche of American pragmatism, is largely absent. Her playful and experimental figures of posthuman relations offer comic relief to the bipolar drama of acceleration.[13] While Noys sees this dark affirmation as a symptom of precarious intellectual workers, its high-tech *amor fati* may also obtain in precarious networks of logistical labor.

Instead of asking *can accelerationism take a joke?* I wonder whether it, in fact, *is the joke*. Or rather, I wonder if accelerationism is more useful as a form of comedic critique that acts out the contradictory expectations, feelings, and drives that underpin the energy economy. In her call for an "irreverent ecocriticism," Nicole Seymour confesses: "Surely, I'm not the only one who has taken sick satisfaction in the idea that going to hell in a handbasket means we get to say 'I told you so' to the global-warming deniers as we all drift on down."[14] What is often dismissed in ecological circles as misanthropy contains this accelerationist kernel of weaponized masochism animated by a sense of defeat. This feeling is never far from laughter. Comedy bursts boundaries and "takes the piss" out of pretensions, making us aware of our ambivalent attachments to the objects of humor. For Michael Branch, environmental humor is "the serious business of addressing the troubling gap between what our ideology promises and the often disappointing outcomes that our policies and practices actually produce."[15] Walter Benjamin argued that "there is no better trigger for thinking than laughter."[16] Laughter reveals situatedness even as it unsettles and dislodges. Benjamin's "demand *to think*" is at the same time a demand to "reflect on [one's] position in the process of production."[17] If the bodily affirmation of laughter allows one to recognize oneself as a producer rather than a spectator, perhaps comedy in the era of climate change can irreverently probe the tragic logistical attachments that constrain mobilities in our fossil-fueled late liberalism.

The 2008 financial crisis inaugurated a new cycle of intensified energy transport and extraction in North America. This was aided by the 2005 Energy Policy Act that exempts hydraulic fracturing companies from the Clean Water Act. "America is addicted to oil," George W. Bush announces the following year, "which is often imported from unstable parts of the world."[18] Yet the rhetoric of national energy independence, with its promise of stability and individual freedom, fails to describe the reality of many whose hope for a future entails a deepening attachment to new forms of dirty and tough oil. Just as "subprime" describes a set of bad assets with no financial future, people now live and work to reproduce an arrangement with no environmental future. "Living oil in the U.S.A. of the twenty-first century is living subprime," writes Stephanie LeMenager.[19] It means "persisting, holding on . . . in the infrastructure that oil made."[20] It is a form of self-destructive preservation, a kind of modernization that mobilizes the economizing neoliberal subject through levels of debt which can only be sustained so long as oil prices (and paychecks) remain high enough to cover the interest. Maintaining an infrastructure perpetually on the edge of a bust requires a fury of movement and conceals exhaustion beneath the appearance of vitality. "Ideology is not just the bad dream of the infrastructure," Terry Eagleton observes, "in *deformatively* 'producing' the real, it nevertheless carries elements of reality within itself."[21] Infrastructure with "no future" is assembled by and through subjects who inhabit a similar loss of futurity. In what follows, I examine how this boom/bust condition shapes cultural narratives of transport in the petroleum industry.

Logistics as Tragic Narrative

The docuseries *Boomtowners* is the Smithsonian Channel's 2015 foray into reality television. Set in the long wake of the 2008 financial crisis, the first line narration informs viewers that "the Bakken shale formation has been a beacon of recovery for the rest of the nation."[22] This beacon is not what it appears to be. The show follows individuals and families adapting to overburdened domestic infrastructure in cities like Williston, ND, and Sidney, MT, municipalities which face an influx of workers, rising drug use, and violent crime, as oil companies gain increasing hold over local government. According to the executive producer, the intent is to illustrate the "human side" of the Bakken oil boom.[23] He describes *Boomtowners* as a "character driven series" that captures contemporary expressions of that "truly American phenomenon" where people try to escape debt and poor job prospects by following a gold rush.[24] The theme song is a rendition Johnny Cash's cover of Soundgarden's "Rusty Cage," performed by Indigenous Canadian folk-rocker Tom Wilson. Wilson sings: "I'm gonna break my, gonna break my, gonna break my rusty cage and run."[25] The reference is to the rust belt. Cash's Grammy winning album *Unchained* (1996) has provided the cinematic and commercial soundtrack of twenty-first century "grit" and nostalgia for Fordist masculinity.[26] He has become the voice for a time when America "made things" and "built stuff," usually out of materials whose symbolic hardness stands in opposition to the immaterial, "feminized" sphere of "communicative capitalism."[27] When the country rediscovered the rust belt in 2008, it renewed its search for ways out of the cage.

The boomtowners are described as a collection of "locals under siege," "fortune seekers," "the hopeful," "the desperate," "the realists," and "the dreamers."[28] Their middle-class aspirations intimately connect their lives to the logistics of the boom and volatile price per barrel of oil. The show may be "character driven" but the characters are driven by a sense of uncertainty. Even successful people are struggling to create stable lives outside of industry rhythms. As evidenced by the show's social media tags, "America," "Engineering," and "Infrastructure," *Boomtowners* tells its human story through the chain of transportation logistics and national symbolism. Their profiles compose a list of fracking's peripheral industries. There are truckers, welders, well-testers and inspectors, and lease operators whose job is upkeep on wells once they are in place. There is the massive concrete industry, sand industry, housing construction, as well as religious and education organizations. Trucking transport offers a sense of the scale of these logistics. According to the show, an average of 645,000 barrels of oil are transported each day from remote well sites to shipping facilities. Making three separate trips over twelve to fourteen hours, one truck can haul 600 barrels per day. This makes for 1,100 trucks moving crude on local roads daily. Between 2005 and 2014, Bakken oil extraction expanded from under 3,000 barrels to one million barrels per day. One million barrels requires over 1,600 trucks. Additionally, each well site requires two million gallons of water, which also has to be trucked. Despite this incredible demand, trucking is one of the most unsteady occupations since competition for short-term contracts favors small, "lean" enterprises.

While the majority of the characters are in the transportation and infrastructural industries, *Boomtowners* profiles Liberty Oilfield Services, a fracking company described as "high tech fortune hunters."[29] Here, fracking is viewed as an expression of entrepreneurial dynamism in the national character where personal sacrifice and tenacity is celebrated as a natural part of the tragic cycle that produces ghost towns and sacrifice zones. The ambiguous thrill of sex and death is invoked as a foreman unironically describes the "triple love machine," a specially designed rig that penetrates and shatters the ground with exceptionally high-pressure (and dangerous) pipes. As the name implies, Liberty evokes the independence and personal freedom that accompanies petroleum-fueled "entrepreneurial life."[30] Yet here one encounters the ecological limits to Lockean liberty. If private property is understood as a hybrid produced by the mixing of labor with nature, industrial humans find themselves increasingly *entangled* with the nonhuman, whether natural or technological, rather than masters over it.

The show incorporates this entanglement into its episodic narratives, yet the logistics narrative brackets ecological and moral questions by shifting attention to either technical problems or market values. Just as environments are produced as accumulations of capital, and framed as an instrumental means to that end, logistics supports a subjective ethos of self-worth through the struggle to "get the job done." On the one hand, this limited horizon helps rationalize resource use within the industrial process as when, for instance, *Boomtowners* highlights efforts to reduce the amount of natural gas burn off at wells or a small business dedicated to recycling fracking water. However, the logistical sleight of hand is at work in the first episode, where the narrative conflict is *a missing part* in Liberty's operation.[31] In episode two, *rocks in the water supply* threaten to ruin pump valves.[32] In episode four, a project stalls while waiting for *load restrictions* to be lifted from connecting public roads.[33] The threat of lost revenue builds tension as drills remain idle and the land untapped. The viewer is oriented toward the operation with a narrative desire to see it go smoothly, to complete the supply chain and resolve the conflict, rather than question the context or purpose of the action. It illustrates Neilson and Rossiter's provocative suggestion that logistics "actively produces environments and subjectivities."[34] However, the show's effort to avoid politicizing the issue of fracking carries a politics of its own, as illustrated by the tragic drama of a naturalized economy.

A self-conscious discourse about inhabiting a boom and the inevitability of a bust pervades the show, from the series title to the interviewed subjects. In this naturalized economic backdrop, we encounter contemporary ideology. To paraphrase Slavoj Žižek, the tragedy is not that people are ignorant about inhabiting a boom-and-bust cycle, but that they *know* it, and do it anyway.[35] Here, one encounters the production of contemporary economic subjects. In *Undoing the Demos*, Wendy Brown argues that neoliberalism has become a "deeply disseminated governing rationality," akin to "a normative order of reason."[36] This change in the very conception of life in common transforms "every human domain and endeavor, along with humans themselves, according to a specific image of the economic."[37] Brown follows Michel Foucault's description of *homo oeconomicus* as one who "accepts reality" by conflating the market with nature. "The person who accepts reality or who responds systematically to modifications in the variables of the environment," Foucault observes, "appears precisely as someone manageable, someone who responds systematically to systematic modifications artificially introduced into the environment." In short, "*homo oeconomicus* is someone who is eminently governable."[38] Logistics plays on this reality principle as it builds, assembles, and constructs publics through its conflation of economic and natural necessity. So-called non-market values like ecological and social sustainability only become legible if they can be articulated to concerns over secure employment or managerial oversight. When the show registers opposition to the "controversial practice" of fracking, informing viewers that "their voices are outnumbered by those who stand to profit from the boom," one finds an example of the reduction of democracy to an extension of the market.[39] The series ambiguously reaffirms the reality principle of energy markets while using logistics-driven narratives to "make public" transport infrastructures whose activity often remains hidden.[40]

The logistics narrative naturalizes an economic landscape by presenting reasonable action within an irrational set of choices. Yet it also enables viewers to understand certain risk calculations integral to middle-class aspirations of many families. "The oil boom," says Ben Moorhead, "has given us an opportunity to be a better family unit."[41] In this father's imagination, the market discipline of the boomtown has transformed his family into an *entrepreneurial* unit. In between long bursts of driving as a well tester, he invents an antitheft device for trucks. With the high crime rates, he hopes his invention will be his family's ticket to "a private jet." Identifying this level of mobility with family happiness, Moorhead's intensive work schedule puts their well-being in question. He *enjoys* the existential risk of his job. Riding on steep narrow roads through the badlands, Moorhead relishes the feeling of becoming one with his truck: "Man and machine versus the earth," he says.[42] Others respond to risk with a religious *amor fati*. Sean Banks works as a Christian pastor who supports himself and his wife by monitoring wells for hydrogen sulfide, the volatile and deadly gas generated by the fracking process.[43] At least 10 percent of wells they encounter release enough concentrated hydrogen sulfide to cause instant death. These forms of faith and discipline illustrate a "conduct of conduct," a practice of organizing one's beliefs and habits into an enterprise.[44]

Another recurring storyline follows Haley and Larysa, a young lesbian couple who run a trucking operation transporting sand. Each well requires roughly five million pounds of sand. Each ton must be trucked out, on distressed public roads, over treacherous terrain, by networks of small companies on short term contracts. Haley and Larysa are recovering from a bust after a single contract fell through and almost ruined them. To increase their flexibility, they accrue more debt to take on an additional truck and driver. A sign in their kitchen reminds viewers that "love is why we're here."[45] Like the Moorheads, their love facilitates an enterprise. In Haley and Larysa's version of queer family futurity, one sees the possible fate of what Haraway calls "multispecies kinship."[46] The couple has their purebred golden retriever impregnated as an investment, and will sell the puppies to cover the costs of a destination wedding in Mexico. In the boomtown, even pets can be turned into biopolitical capital to form a "more effective family unit."[47]

The show's lone voice of environmental opposition, "landowner" Sandi opposes the destruction of the landscape and rise in violent crime. The first episode stages a conversation at the county fair between her and the Moorhead family. Sandi argues that the oil companies are "raping the land."[48] The Moorheads nod and in a post-conversation interview say they *agree* with her. However, they interpret Sandi's concerns through a logistical frame of "mis-management." They claim Sandi is worried that the oil companies will build things up and leave, and that she is worried about "everything that goes with the oil," meaning that a post-boom Bakken would be unable to support over-developed cities.[49] This is emphatically not Sandi's point, but it illustrates the way environmental voices (including indigenous voices, which do not appear in the series) are often elided as concerns that extractive industries and infra-structural development will simply be poorly managed.

Despite their portrayal as figures tragically defined by the boom's uneven development, the resilience of *Boomtowners'* characters may also be inter-preted as a desire to change their conditions. However, a Williston oil worker expresses the impasses of this outlook. In the final episode, Liberty Oilfield Services lays-off a large segment of their six hundred workers and closes drill sites after the price per barrel drops by half in 2015. The laid-off worker con-soles himself saying, "When you're in a boom you're one day closer to a bust and when you're in a bust you're one day closer to a boom."[50] In the interstices of the petrocultural economy, the states of boom and bust exist simultane-ously. This self-conscious discourse further impedes initiatives for long-term, sustainable infrastructural development. Likewise, it relies on short-term, carbon-intensive trucking which demands public roads service private opera-tions. The imminent horizon of the bust demands mobile and flexible subjects, and encourages a desire for complete expenditure to make the most from the boom. In a historical sense, the ideological awareness of the boom-and-bust cycle is part of the very infrastructure that drives "tough oil" development. By locating individual and family dynamics within petroleum's peripheral in-dustries, *Boomtowners* illustrates the vast social infrastructure that makes it possible. Nevertheless, the series also reproduces the contradictory national rhetoric of energy independence secured through self-conscious "boom" de-velopment, aimed at making sure nothing changes in the American ideal of high consumption.

Acceleration and Exhaustion

The cities of the Bakken shale formation share parallel boom/bust temporali-ties with the Athabasca oil sands in Alberta's Fort McMurray. The 2015 drop in oil prices eliminated over 35,000 jobs in the tar sands, while an unprec-edented wildfire the following year forced 88,000 residents to flee the city in the largest evacuation in the province's history.[51] The Canadian mockumentary *FUBAR II* (or *Fubar: Balls to the Wall*) is set in pre-bust Fort McMurray. The film builds on the cult success of *FUBAR* (2002), sympathetically following two long-haired Calgary metalheads, Terry and Dean, when their hard-partying lives are disrupted by Dean's discovery of testicular cancer. The cancer is a crisis of both masculinity and futurity that returns in the sequel with the removal of his remaining testicle. They leave their big box warehouse jobs and move to "the Mac" on the promise of high-paying work on a pipeline construction team. Terry and Dean do not just want good work; they want to *live* the dangerous intensity of "the Mac." Soon enough, they wind up exhausted, indebted, and suicidal. On one level, the film might be read as an allegory of decadence. As "bad" economic subjects, the characters serve as a warning against desiring extremes. However, on another level, the film enables viewers to inhabit the destructive contradictions of "the Mac" from within. By perversely affirming the economy of pollution, debt, drugs, promiscuity, and generally living beyond one's means, *FUBAR II* exposes the libidinal undercurrents of the boom fantasy. In contradistinction to the tragic narrative of logistics, the comedy of *FUBAR II* combines an accelerationist attitude with the mockumentary genre to critique the petro-fueled suburban lifestyle that *Boomtowners* holds as an ideal.

The mockumentary has its precursors with the advent of film but comes into its own in the 1980s with films like *The Gods Must Be Crazy* (1980) and *This Is Spinal Tap* (1984).[52] Ethnographic convention and the camera's authority are made the object of laughter, while their ironic subjects defamiliarize viewer expectations through parody. The modernity-busting humor comes from the errant circulation and recontextualization of objects, whether a Coca-Cola bottle thrown from a passing airplane into a hunter-gatherer society or a touring rock band past their peak whose pretenses to stardom are out-of-joint with the present. The coke bottle, for instance, spurs the hero's journey into the city, which is skewered through the norms of "the original affluent society," and restages the *spatial* encounter of earlier modernisms in an era of accelerating urbanization.[53] Yet perhaps no film captures the modern epic of logistics better than Werner Herzog's *Fitzcarraldo* (1982), and its accompanying documentary, *Burden of Dreams* (1982).[54] Herzog's crew reproduces the efforts of Peruvian rubber baron, Carlos Fitzcarrald, by transporting a 340-ton steamship over the steep terrain of the Amazon.[55] The project unwittingly recapitulates the exploitation of indigenous crew members, even as they laugh at the quarrelsome white filmmakers and politely offer to kill the lead actor. This *doubling*, a documentary about making a film whose production is as "crazy" as its original subject matter, dramatizes the vast endeavor of logistics. Indeed, it is logistics all the way down. The late nineteenth-century demand for railroad infrastructure to transport Brazilian rubber for European manufacturing predates the automobile industry's demand for tires. The latter of course prompted Henry Ford's comically doomed efforts to replicate a middle-American city in the Amazon. Herzog's sincerity to the point of self-parody skirts the line between reaffirming the heroic endeavor of cinema as the interrogation of dreams, and an ironic performance of the brutal irrationalities that animate the dream of modernization. As a technique of second-order observation, the documentary opens up a gap between the ideal and the conditions that make it possible.

The comedy in *FUBAR II* is derived from the self-destructive fantasies of making "sweet cash in the oil patch."[56] Much like its neighbor to the south, Fort McMurray represents the promise of stability and economic development that ensures Canada's global status in energy. Yet this official narrative is subtended by the unofficial mythology of "the Mac" as a place of seductive danger, a volatile mix of extremes in temperature and income, as well as pain and pleasure. This would seem to contradict the first narrative, but the Mac's unstable vitality instead functions as an unofficial draw. It is a place to test one's masculinity, and for Terry and Dean a chance to overcome their delayed entry into middle-class adulthood. Tron, the "housebroken" character from the first film reappears robust and bearded, crushing a birch tree in the front yard with his massive truck, ready to party. His ex-girlfriend remarks that he has become a self-destructive animal, yet Tron's intensity seduces the main characters to come work for him in the oil fields. "The Mac," he whispers, "she's a cruel mistress, and she will freeze you if you don't love her."[57] This ethos of survival through embracing danger, and taking pleasure in dissolution, illustrates a provocative accelerationist claim by Lyotard, who suggests that death was part of the industrializing peasant's enjoyment. As a class, he claims, they "enjoyed the hysterical, masochistic, whatever exhaustion it was of hanging on in the mines, in the foundries, in the factories, in hell."[58] The party ends with Tron walking through their burning house carrying a chainsaw, flames reflecting in his sunglasses. This demonic image of Tron as a promethean figure of creative destruction parallels the film's hellishly sublime shots of Fort McMurray's night-time plumes. Tron's mythological status embodies the Mac's transgressive appeal beneath the official cover of stability.

The opening sequence introduces an accelerationist logic in the plot's movement to Fort McMurray. Dean's cancer-free celebration quickly escalates when Tron discovers that they are getting evicted. "It's a fuckin' eviction party!" he screams as he kicks in the refrigerator door.[59] Tron returns from his truck with a chainsaw and sledgehammer, and party-goers commence destroying the house. The soundtrack is Black Sabbath's "Die Young" (1980) sung by Ronnie James Dio.[60] The lyrics evoke a constrained relation between nature and freedom: "Gather the wind / though the wind won't help you fly at all / your back's to the wall / Chain the sun / and it tears away to face you as you run / you run, you run!"[61] Dio's imagery of wind and sun are associated with renewable sources of energy, but the emphasis on the *wall*, the *chain*, and *gathering* as an act of accumulation suggests bodily limits. The lyrics express a desire not to escape the bounds of nature so much as to escape the logistical constraints that turn the environment against the subject. A hallucinating Dean begs a Dio poster not to sing the chorus, "die young," as if it were a prophecy or command. Their response mimics Benjamin's "destructive character" that arrives, as Noys reminds us, like an "eviction order executed by a slob."[62] Pursuing the logic of eviction to its end, they make sure there is no going back.

Environmental opposition to tar sands is voiced by a hitchhiker picked up en route to Fort McMurray. "There's actually like a problem with the economy and gas and stuff. That's what I'm going to protest up there," he tells them. "It takes like ten barrels of water for one barrel of oil." "Water's free, man," they respond, "that seems like a fuckin' bargain."[63] As they smoke the hippie's weed, Terry and Dean repeat cliché accusations of activist hypocrisy, such as riding in a car on the way to a protest. Their defensiveness about the effect of oil sand tailing ponds on migratory bird populations, for instance, turns into hostility: "I don't need ducks, fuck ducks!" "I'd like to see you push [the car] ten feet," Terry says, "after that you'd be like, 'kill ALL the ducks!' "[64] In a compact way, this scene introduces viewers to Fort McMurray's ecological "externalities." Their stoned, defensive stupidity is a response to a threatened fantasy, while the outrageous delivery parodies routine conservative postures. It is the first scene to explicitly foreground the automobile as a narrative trope of movement implicated in the environmental critique of Fort McMurray, notably through its relation to *bodily* energy.

The suggestion to push the car makes a *physical* point about the enormous amount of embodied energy throughout transportation system in comparison to the frail human body. It is estimated that the average "energy return on investment" ratio for tar sands oil is about 4.5-to-1, which only accounts for the "front end of the life-cycle."[65] As energy analysts argue, this number would be much smaller if the entire operation of transport and logistics were accounted for. Eco-socialists have attempted this, developing Marx's concept of a "metabolic rift" between the reproductive cycles of the ecosystem and the cycles of accumulation in society.[66] The growing rift between these two temporalities has resulted in a drawdown and disruption of the earth system itself, portending exhaustion on the horizon. In the Mac, gas-guzzling pickup trucks become a necessity to reach remote job sites and are material symbols of individual power and mobility. Likewise, automobiles become narratively significant as they differentiate the opposing paths of the two characters. Terry attempts to join the Mac lifestyle and takes out a large loan for a truck, while Dean ends up living out of his old car and siphoning gas to stay warm after he deliberately injures his leg in an unsuccessful attempt to receive workers' comp.[67] Terry's truck is a false image of successful domestic life, while Dean's old car becomes the private space of someone with nothing left to lose. A brilliant cut brings the conflict to a head. Terry is at the gas station filling up his truck and cheers as the attendant lowers the price of gas. In the next scene, he is laid off. It dramatically illustrates the volatility of a high energy economy as well as the cognitive dissonance of those who live it.

The film moves through three accelerationist moments. The first is desire as transgressive production through creative destruction (Deleuze); the second is painful enjoyment, or *jouissance*, at the extremes of the libidinal economy (Lyotard); the final moment of exhaustion arrives as the economy outpaces its subjects (Baudrillard).[68] The eviction party scenario and the move to Fort McMurray are expressions of the first moment. The narrative conflict arises in the second moment when the characters are caught in the Mac's extremes. As Terry and Dean are living high on good paychecks and partying hard on extended lines of credit, their lives parallel the pipeline workers who are depicted smoking crystal meth and crack cocaine to maintain energy levels during the physically demanding hours in the cold. The moment of exhaustion occurs with the drop in oil prices. Terry is unable to make payments on his debt, and depression sets in for Dean after his workers' comp is denied and he is informed that his cancer has returned. Dean makes a suicide pact with Tron, whose outrageous behavior masks deep despair. *FUBAR II*'s narrative illustrates Noys' claim that in accelerationism the triad of "desire, libido, death," corresponds to the cycle of "production, credit, inflation."[69] These affective states integrate workers into the precarious "supply chain" of mobile labor, whether long-distance trucking or spacing pipelines for the transport of crude.

Reading accelerationism as comedic critique allows one to link the affective and economic conditions of a renewed project of modernity that leaves too many ecological questions unasked. Alex Williams and Nick Srnicek's *#ACCELERATE* manifesto resuscitates the Marxian celebration of capitalist modernity as a dissolving force.[70] They call for a militant constructivism untainted by nostalgia for the limits of nature and culture. In this, their manifesto resembles what Clive Hamilton calls the "theodicy" of the neoliberal eco-modernists, who claim that because industrial humans have conditioned the climate, they have duty to geoengineer the planet to greater extremes.[71] The authors of left-wing acceleration call for increased automation to the point that human labor will no longer be necessary for production. Terry and Dean would be on board with the goal of a post-work society but their Dionysian exhaustion, not unlike the tragic outlook of *Boomtowners*, calls into question the sacrifices required to attain such utopian ends. Following the Club of Rome's 1972 *Limits to Growth* report, the "no future" of 1977 punk, and the high-octane "this goes to eleven" of eighties metal, Terry and Dean are post-Fordist figures that embody and amplify the precarious limits of neoliberal extractivism. They might be compared to Charlie Chaplin, whose slapstick comedy and machinic speed inspired the Soviet avant-garde in their fascination with Taylorism. Chaplin embodies the intensity of modernization and pushes all of its contradictory tendencies until it erupts into comedy.[72] Russian futurists declared "Victory Over the Sun," in which the sun was "torn down from the sky" as a "representative of the decadent past."[73] Perhaps Ronnie James Dio's sun, that "tears away to face you as you run," is more appropriate in the era of anthropogenic warming.[74] It is an era that mocks the promise of freedom through controlling nature, understanding that extraction, debt, and logistics, are the real forces that move and constrain people, binding them to a planet whose future is being foreclosed through the very infrastructures that promised to liberate them.

Conclusion

In her reflections on the pedagogical irony of the mockumentary, Miranda Campbell argues the genre often assumes that "a critique has already been made."[75] By operating against an assumed critical background, the humor invites "the closing-down of assumptions" and "interpretive capacities."[76] While both *FUBAR II* and *Boomtowners* operate within and against national discourses surrounding new "tough oil" development, this is not the case. For the latter, it is precisely by avoiding ecological criticism of fracking that it is able to trace its effects through the lives and communities caught in the peripheral transportation industries. This bracketing may narratively reinforce the trap of logistics, but it also enables the docuseries to question a disruptive form of economic recovery whose social sustainability is as doubtful as its environmental sustainability. In accelerationist fashion, *FUBAR II* comically plays contradictory national narratives of Fort McMurray against each other, exposing their mutual reliance. These self-conscious documentaries are less a reflection *on* but a demonstration *of* the fissures between the lived and the represented on screen. If, as Benjamin claims, "spasms of the diaphragm generally offer better chances for thought that spasms of the soul,"[77] comedy might allow us to breathe when the soul fails to do anything more than shake.

By situating human labor in the peripheral networks of petroleum transport, these boom-and-bust narratives expose the cultural logic of an economy set on "eliminating friction and resistance."[78] As Fred Moten and Stefano Harney argue, the logic of modern transport was "founded *against* the Atlantic slave" as the original "containerized" commodity labor.[79] It wants to "dispense with the subject altogether."[80] Eliminating reference to the human enables power relations to be concealed. By neither abolishing the human from the ontological picture, nor by abolishing technological objects from the human frame, these texts can be read as a frustrated desire for democratic agency over the infrastructures that shape our common life. So long as the boom-and-bust cycle is accepted as a natural condition, that is, as a tragic necessity for economic recovery, even the acidic laughter of critique risks becoming one more lubricant for accelerating seemingly inevitable scenarios. However, if taken to be performing out loud what remains an unspoken dynamic of contemporary petroleum development, narratives like these perform a valuable service. Further exploration of transport industries may reveal still more friction that materially moves and constrains environmental imaginaries.

NOTES

1. *Boomtowners,* executive producer Jeff Stecyk (Virginia Beach: Landmark Media Productions and Wavelength Entertainment, 2015), on Smithsonian Channel and Amazon Video, TV series; *FUBAR II,* directed by Michael Dowse (2010; Montreal, CA: Alliance Films, 2010), DVD.
2. Anna Tsing, "Supply Chains and the Human Condition," *Rethinking Marxism* 21, no. 2 (2009): 148–176, 155.
3. Imre Szeman, "How to Know about Oil? Energy Epistemologies and Political Futures," *Journal of Canadian Studies* 47, no. 3 (2013): 145–168, 146.
4. Sandro Mezzandra and Brett Neilson, "Operations of Capital," *South Atlantic Quarterly* 114, no. 1 (2015): 1–9, 2.
5. Ash Amin and Nigel Thrift, *Arts of the Political: New Openings for the Left* (Durham: Duke University Press, 2013), 105.
6. Amin and Thrift, 105.
7. Amin and Thrift, 106.
8. Sandro Mezzandra and Brett Neilson, eds., *Logistical Worlds: Infrastructure, Software, Labour* 1 (2014): 72, http://logisticalworlds.org.
9. Benjamin Noys, *Malign Velocities: Accelerationism and Capitalism* (Winchester, UK: Zero Books, 2014).
10. Gilles Deleuze and Felix Guattari, *Anti-Oedipus,* trans. Robert Hurley (Minneapolis: University of Minnesota, 1983), 239.

11. Noys, *Malign Velocities*, 11.
12. Noys, 7.
13. Donna Haraway, *Manifestly Haraway* (Minneapolis: University of Minnesota, 2016).
14. Nicole Seymour, "Toward an Irreverent Ecocriticism," *Journal of Ecocriticism* 4, no. 2 (2012): 56–71, 57.
15. Michael Branch, "Are You Serious? A Modest Proposal for Environmental Humor," in *The Oxford Handbook of Ecocriticism*, ed. Greg Garrard (New York: Oxford, 2014), 377–390, 387.
16. Walter Benjamin, "The Author as Producer," *Understanding Brecht*, trans. Anna Bostock (New York: Verso, 1998), 85–103, 101.
17. Benjamin, 85–103, 101.
18. George W. Bush, "Address Before a Joint Session of the Congress on the State of the Union, 2006," January 31, 2006, *American Presidency Project*, https://www.presidency.ucsb.edu/node/214381.
19. Stephanie LeMenager, "Infrastructure Again, and Always," *Reviews in Cultural Theory* 6, no. 3 (2016): 25–29, 25.
20. LeMenager, 26.
21. Terry Eagleton, *Criticism and Ideology* (New York: Verso, 2006), 69.
22. "Wake up the Devil," *Boomtowners*, season 1, episode 1.
23. Ernest Scheyder, " 'Boomtowners' Looks to the Human Side of North Dakota's Oil Fields," Reuters, May 6, 2015, https://www.reuters.com/article/us-television-boomtowners-idUSKBN0NR0S920150506.
24. Scheyder.
25. "Rusty Cage," performed by Tom Wilson, written by Chris Cornell.
26. Johnny Cash, "Rusty Cage," track 3 on *Unchained*, American/Warner Bros., compact disc.
27. Jodi Dean, *Democracy and Other Neoliberal Fantasies: Communicative Capitalism and Left Politics* (Durham: Duke University Press, 2009), 22.
28. "Wake up the Devil," *Boomtowners*.
29. "Wake up the Devil."
30. Matthew Huber, "Refined Politics: Petroleum Products, Neoliberalism, and the Ecology of Entrepreneurial Life," *Journal of American Studies* 46, no. 2 (2012): 295–312.
31. "Wake up the Devil," *Boomtowners*.
32. "Bakken Drag Race," *Boomtowners*, season 1, episode 2.
33. "Here Comes the Chaos," *Boomtowners*, season 1, episode 3.
34. Brett Neilson and Ned Rossiter, "Logistical Worlds," *Logistical Worlds: Infrastructure, Software, Labour* 1 (2014), http://logisticalworlds.org/.
35. Slavoj Žižek, *The Plague of Fantasies* (New York: Verso, 2008), 139.
36. Wendy Brown, *Undoing the Demos* (New York: Zone, 2015), 9.
37. Brown, 9.
38. Michel Foucault, *The Birth of Biopolitics, Lectures at the College de France 1978–1979*, trans. Graham Burchell (New York: Picador, 2008), 270.
39. "Wake up the Devil," *Boomtowners*.
40. Amin and Thrift, *Arts of the Political*, 105.
41. "Shootin' Blanks," Boomtowners, season 1, episode 5.
42. "Wake up the Devil," *Boomtowners*.
43. "Wake up the Devil."
44. Brown, *Undoing the Demos*, 21.
45. "Bakken Drag Race," *Boomtowners*.
46. Donna Haraway, *When Species Meet* (Minneapolis: University of Minnesota, 2008), 296.
47. "Boom or Bust," *Boomtowners*, season 1, episode 6.
48. "Boom or Bust."
49. "Boom or Bust."

50. "Boom or Bust."
51. Ian Austen, "Oil Sands Boom Dries Up in Alberta, Taking Thousands of Jobs with It," *New York Times*, October 12, 2015, https://www.nytimes.com/2015/10/13/business /international/oil-sands-boom-dries-up-in-alberta-taking-thousands-of-jobs-with-it .html.
52. *The Gods Must Be Crazy*, directed by Jamie Uys (1980; Johannesburg: Ster Kinekor/20th Century Fox, 2013), DVD. *This Is Spinal Tap*, directed by Rob Reiner (1984; Los Angeles: Embassy Pictures/Criterion, 1998), DVD.
53. Raymond Williams, "Metropolitan Perceptions and the Emergence of Modernism," *The Politics of Modernism* (New York: Verso, 1989), 37–48.
54. *Fitzcarraldo*, directed by Werner Herzog (1982; Berlin: Filmverlag der Autoren/ Criterion, 2015), DVD. *Burden of Dreams*, directed by Les Blank (1982; Los Angeles: Criterion, 2016), DVD.
55. Greg Grandin, *Fordlandia: The Rise and Fall of Henry Ford's Forgotten Jungle City* (New York: Metropolitan, 2009), 7.
56. "Fubar: Balls to the Wall," IMDB, March 14, 2011, https://www.imdb.com/title /tt1555747.
57. *FUBAR II*.
58. Jean-François Lyotard, *Libidinal Economy*, trans. Ian Hamilton Grant (Bloomington: University of Indiana, 1993), 111.
59. Lyotard, 111.
60. Black Sabbath, "Die Young," track 6 on *Heaven and Hell*, Warner Brothers, 1980, vinyl.
61. Black Sabbath.
62. Noys, *Malign Velocities*, 86.
63. *FUBAR II*.
64. *FUBAR II*.
65. Charles Hall, Jessica Lambert, and Steven Balogh, "EROI of Different Fuels and the Implications for Society," *Energy Policy* 64 (2014): 141–152, 146.
66. John Bellamy Foster, Brett Clark, and Richard York, *The Ecological Rift: Capitalism's War on the Earth* (New York: Monthly Review, 2010), 121.
67. *FUBAR II*.
68. Noys, *Malign Velocities*, 5.
69. Noys, *Malign Velocities*, 5.
70. Alex Williams and Nick Srnicek, "#ACCELERATE MANIFESTO for an Accelerationist Politics," *Critical Legal Thinking*, May 14, 2013, http://criticallegalthinking.com/2013/05 /14/accelerate-manifesto-for-an-accelerationist-politics.
71. Clive Hamilton, "The Theodicy of the 'Good Anthropocene,'" *Environmental Humanities* 7, (2015): 233–238, 235.
72. Pluto Press, "Owen Hatherley Introduces 'The Chaplin Machine,'" YouTube video, 19:38, April 25, 2016, https://youtu.be/d7JviiO7KdM.
73. Isobel Hunter, "*Zaum* and Sun: The 'First Futurist Opera' Revisited," *Central Europe Review* 1, no. 3 (1999), http://www.ce-review.org.
74. Black Sabbath, "Die Young."
75. Miranda Campbell, "The Mocking Mockumentary and the Ethics of Irony," *Taboo: The Journal of Culture and Education* 11, no. 1 (2007): 53–62, 61.
76. Campbell, 53–62, 61.
77. Benjamin, "The Author as Producer," 101.
78. Mezzandra and Neilson, "Operations of Capital," 7.
79. Stefano Harney and Fred Moten, *The Undercommons: Fugitive Planning & Black Study* (New York: Minor Compositions, 2013), 92, emphasis added.
80. Harney and Moten, 87.

CHAPTER 11

Trafficking in Petronormativities: At the Intersections of Petrofeminism, Petrocolonialism, and Petrocapitalism

Sheena Wilson

Trafficking is at the core of a global infrastructural network that has greatly contributed to the culture of climate change. Here, I evoke two meanings of trafficking: the straightforward definition as the transportation of commodities by land, air, or sea for the purposes of commercial trade, as well as in its more common usage regarding the trafficking of illicit goods, including but not limited to women. Beyond the more obvious connections between traffic and climate change, today's ecological situation might also be attributed to more nuanced forms of traffic and trafficking—that is, the ways in which bodies (human and otherwise) are managed, (im)mobilized, and (dis)connected in the name of those extractivist, patriarchal, and colonial worldviews that perpetuate the (North) American Dream(s) of nationhood, prosperity, and petrocolonial futurity. Today's culture of climate change (i.e., rising CO_2 levels and greenhouse gas emissions), at least in North America, traffics in hegemonic fantasies of mobility that both reflect culture and shape it, producing and reproducing the limits that define a successful life.[1] These fantasies of freedom that make up the American Dream, as the moniker suggests, are aspirational notions of what we should be striving for. These imaginaries are circulated through media infrastructures that traffic in particular narratives of freedom shaping our individual and collective future(s). These freedoms, in reality, however, are only available to an elite few, and rely on the enclosure and containment of the many via our own indenture to the capitalist debt system that ties us figuratively and literally to mortgages and loans, and the waged labor necessary to pay off these debts. Whether we abide by or resist these dominant imaginaries, they function to delimit what is deemed possible when it comes to imagining the future, or what I call our *energy futures*.

In the age of the Anthropocene, or better yet, the Plantationocene and Capitalocene, an "era marked by ongoing enclosures of the commons and heavy reliance on slave labor and other forms of exploited, alienated, and usually spatially transported labor,"[2] the issue of trafficking necessitates not only analyses of mobility and transportation but also the inverse: analyses of stasis, stuckness, settlement, and occupation. Put another way, today's culture of climate change is not only defined by ecological devastation and an increasingly uninhabitable planet but also represents a profoundly material crisis anchored in *infrastructure*. Reaching across time, existing infrastructures link us to our past, while new infrastructures provide an opportunity to redesign the future.[3] Whether we are referring to the material infrastructures of transportation, the media infrastructures that play a key role in shaping the narratives that underpin our everyday experiences, the informal and often immaterial infrastructures of resistance movements, or the energy systems that undergird them all, infrastructure projects have the potential to create new pathways for moving into the future.

Taking this dynamic understanding of both trafficking and infrastructure as a starting point, this chapter interrogates the (dis)connection between mobility and the culture of climate change, particularly as it is represented in contemporary media, in order to unsettle current conversations and launch new discussions around energy transition projects, especially those designing more livable futures for all. In this chapter, I analyze two Canadian cultural texts: a CBC documentary film titled *Colonization Road* (2016)[4] that exposes the enclosures affected by hegemonic petrocultural fantasies, and a Canadian Ethical Oil commercial (2011)[5] that markets the colonization of women's lifeworlds[6] via what I call *petrofeminism*.[7] I do so in an attempt to unfold the ways that (auto)mobility and infrastructure are represented in contemporary Canadian media ecologies, and, in turn, examine how these representations illuminate an extractivist dream sustained through particular "energy imaginaries" that leave us at an impasse—an intersection, if you will—in desperate need of reimaginings.[8] Put briefly, these media texts offer a starting point to investigate how the tightly intertwined politics of "mobility" and "freedom" rely on patriarchal and colonial infrastructures, which necessitate the ongoing *extraction* of surplus value, whether by the colonization of commonly held lands or via the expropriation of human and nonhuman labor power. By unravelling the complex relations between infrastructures of (auto)mobility and the current culture of climate change represented in these media artifacts, this analysis seeks to investigate how mobility for some, be they people or ideas, necessarily relies on the immobility and confinement of others, and further, how this uneven power geometry limits possibilities for addressing the current energy impasse and thus the potential for imagining alternative futures.[9]

Trafficking in Extractivist Dreams

The current culture of climate change, or what is understood in this analysis as a dominant "petroculture,"[10] has developed over the past century and a half based on both the availability of (relatively) cheap carbon-based fuels *and* dreams of ever-increasing mobility: the transportation of commodities in commercial trade; the high-speed mobility of ideas (communication being yet another kind of commodity); and the migration and mobility of people as they commute and move through the everyday as well as more distant work, leisure, and vacation destinations. These forms of petrocapital mobility are associated with increased social mobility for those with the greatest access to and control of energy supplies, or those who have been able to shape global capitalism by extracting surplus value and labor from those "resources" (natural, human, and more-than-human) seen to be at their disposal. For example, the creation of a large mobile middle class that consumes goods transported via worldwide networks of global trade continues to be integral to sustaining a capitalist financial system and its necessary infrastructures, which are fueled by fossil power and driven by extractivist worldviews. That is, the status quo understanding of a *successful* (middle-class) life has been produced and maintained by marketing the Dream narrative that operates on a narrow and homogenous definition of mobility, revolving around a concept of freedom that is most often materialized through a house, a car, and a nuclear family. Today's fossil-fueled narratives of mobility rely on the often-unquestioned entitlement to private property (via a home and car) and conservative forms of social reproduction (via a nuclear family)—a Dream of success that is only possible, as I discuss further below, through an *originary theft*. In this way, the Dream that has come to constitute the vision of success is not so much a once-viable ideal now corrupted by an extractivist worldview, but is instead a necessary apparatus, or infrastructure, for concealing the primacy of extraction and exploitation on which illusory representations of the "good life" are founded.[11] Extractivist occupation is the very basis of the Dream of freedom via mobility.

While the post–World War II fantasy of the American Dream was designed to produce a white heteronormative middle class in the United States, its material origin is based in a petroculture whose extractive character is global.[12] In western Canada, where I write from Treaty 6 Territory in the province of Alberta, for example, we have our own cultural, financial, and infrastructural equivalents of the Dream.[13] Here, the extractivist worldview that sustains our contributions to global capitalism is deeply ingrained in the Canadian psyche and tied explicitly to the project of settler colonialism. Attention to the extractive basis of capitalism in settler colonial countries reveals that, despite the particularities of national histories, Canada's situation is not so very different from what has taken place in the United States, Australia, and throughout the colonized world. Canada's national identity, for instance, rests on the facts that Canada is a staples economy—whether the staples are those of the fur trade or the oil industry—and that the nation's worth and its political-economic raison-d'être relies on extracting value from "resources,"[14] thus informing the relationship that many Canadians have to the land, to other species, and to one another. This extractivist worldview also defines relationships beyond our borders and over time, much as the infrastructural networks powered by fossil energy weave power relations across time and space. In short, where mobility, be it physical or social, is defined by uneven processes of circulation across stolen lands and by the unquestioned extraction of resources necessary for maintaining the reproduction of a gas-guzzling middle class, the Dream and the freedoms it promises are intimately entangled with the infrastructures that enable the ongoing project of settler colonialism and that are invested in its perpetuation.

The Dream, secured in part through private property (white picket fences included) and (auto)mobility, exemplifies some of the great contradictions inherent to contemporary understandings of freedom and the good life. For example, home ownership in and of itself anchors the individual to a specific space and time, thus limiting both social and physical mobility. That is, the acquisition of private property requires that the buyer leverage their anticipated lifetime of labor to secure home mortgages and car payments, all in an effort to reproduce social life and support a family. This indebtedness is, contrary to any lived reality, packaged and sold as freedom—specifically, the financial freedom and/or purchasing power to buy other freedoms. However, the steady repayment demanded by the debt cycle requires that people maintain regular waged labor, which in turn inhibits mobility, while also limiting capacities for socio-political organizing and actions of solidarity with others for better working conditions. In addition to home ownership, (auto)mobility—or the necessity of personal vehicles (sometimes two or three per home!)—further highlights the contradictions inherent to today's extractivist Dream.[15]

In the current paradigm, at least in North America, traffic is made possible via personal vehicles, which, regardless of mythic tropes of the *freedom of the road*, have become more practically an extension of the domestic space whose anchored nature is affectively made up for by perceived physical and social mobility. But any promise of emancipation—particularly women's emancipation—linked to the automobile cannot hold up to much scrutiny. The freedom of the road, popularized in the early twentieth century, originates in market strategies that target women as consumers. And, within this patriarchal system, women become both consumers of automobile culture as well as commodities within the same circular network: both are objectified and both fetishized.[16] As I shall expand upon below, following the work of Silvia Federici,[17] the witch hunts of sixteenth- and seventeenth-century Europe were prototypes for both the colonization of populations around the world, as well as for the ongoing enclosure of women's lives under capitalism: a system that markets their un/underpaid labor back to them as emancipation under the banner of what I call *petrofeminism*, a term that I coin to indicate the co-optation of feminism by petrocultural capacities and logics. Rather than moving freely through space and time, women in North America often find themselves boomeranging back and forth along a largely predetermined course: moving from home, to work, to community destinations, to stores. On a weekly (if not daily) basis, women where I live now spend a significant number of hours driving to a variety of gigantic, widely dispersed commercial centers—accessible only by car—and shopping for food, clothing, and newly designed consumer goods marketed as necessities. The mobile woman is at the center of a consumer-oriented society. This is particularly true of mothers. The reality of automobility being quite different from the fantasy, the personal vehicle has been imbricated as a normal and necessary tool for personal independence and the successful management of a nuclear family, which has significant ramifications for women and everyone else.

The nuclear family is intrinsic to the neoliberal social and cultural construction of personal success, as well as to the perpetuation of cisheteronormative-patriarchal-petrocapitalism and to the ongoing project of settler colonialism. As Deborah Cowen argues, "In colonial and settler colonial contexts, infrastructure is often the means of dispossession, and the material force that implants colonial economies and socialities."[18] All of this is to say that the nuclear-family home at the base of the imagined fantasy of the nuclear family is, like the big box shopping outlets, in and of itself an infrastructure. It likewise shapes the infrastructural design of urban and suburban living in our modern petrocultures, just as the necessity to provide each family home with all of the goods and services to run a single residence has grown and maintained enormous consumer market.

Moreover, the Dream of freedom afforded by both private property and the personal vehicle are tethered to infrastructures—shipping networks, roads, telecommunications, energy grids, structures of financialization and debt, and so on—that rely on an originary theft of Indigenous lands. Sold as mobility, the Dream is simultaneously about occupation and settlement. It is about the soft and hard infrastructures of extraction and colonialism that promise the chimera of freedom to some (ironically all the while binding them to the systems of their own oppression), while ensuring the containment of Other bodies, restricting Indigenous Peoples through the infrastructures of cultural genocide, including residential schools and the many iterations of the child welfare system and the criminal justice system.[19] The Dream is about the domestication and "development" of nature that has destroyed local ecosystems and perpetuated ecocide on a global scale. Any transition away from extractivist practices of the environmental variety must be accompanied with a shift in worldview, raison-d'être, and relationality that includes human and more-than-human relationships. Decarbonization of the environment alone is inadequate to address the challenge of climate change. Rather, we must address the root cause: the worldview that relates to bodies and their potential labor, as well as other species and nature, for the profit that can be extracted from them.

(De)*Colonization Road:* Towards Deep Energy Literacy

Colonization Road

Examined through a critical lens focused on the extractivism that is central to the project of settler colonialism, and on the subtending constructs of mobility upheld through private property and personal vehicles, the Canadian Dream is quite literally founded on land that has been stolen from its rightful owners. That is, the land that we now call Canada legally belongs to the Indigenous Peoples whose territories have been colonized. This is the history and current lived reality that Anishinaabe comedian Ryan McMahon navigates in Michelle St. John's 2016 documentary film *Colonization Road.* The film's title comes from the many roads named "Colonization Road" throughout Canada (see fig. 11.1), and this documentary examines the idea of the road

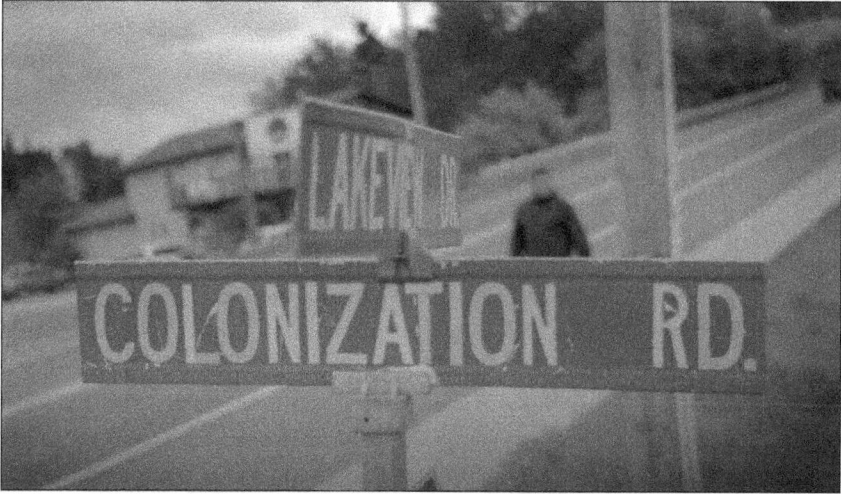

Fig. 11.1. Two green street signs crossed at an intersection with the street sign "COLONIZATION RD." in full focus. (Michelle St. John, *Colonization Road* [Toronto: Decolonization Road Productions Inc., 2016], aired on CBC, *Firsthand*, http://www.cbc.ca /firsthand/episodes/colonization-road, 7:22. Image from film.)

itself as both a literal and figurative or metaphorical manifestation of colonization in Canada. Released on the heels of Canada's Truth and Reconciliation Commission's reports, the film mobilizes political humor as one strategy to push Indigenous and non-Indigenous viewers alike to think through what reconciliation and decolonization mean for our future.[20]

The film opens with a clip of McMahon performing his stand-up comedy routine on the topic of colonization. He starts out with the following bit: "You ever notice that when you ask the government for *your* land back, they're all like, 'Ok, one sec—Ok, let me see, one second, ok, alright here, let me just, one—, ok, one, uh, uh [*Pause for dramatic effect*] NO!' "[21] The scene then cuts directly to McMahon doing a street interview with a Canadian passerby asking, "Have you ever heard of colonization roads?" The young woman replies "No." This scene is followed up by a media clip of former Prime Minister Stephen Harper (2006–2015) publicly declaring: "We [Canada] also have no history of colonialisms."[22] Following discussions with two Indigenous experts, who put Harper's comments into context, McMahon then asks more Canadians on the street if they know which leader made this claim. Two take a guess. Two definitely answer that they do not. When he asks yet another pair of young women, "Do we think this country has a history of colonialism?" one responds with a tentative "to a certain extent," while the other asserts "oh, most definitely. . . . That's kind of how we were founded."[23] Juxtaposing such responses with his own voiceover reflections, which are more serious in tone, and interviews with historical and legal experts, in addition to more clips of his stand-up, McMahon illustrates that while there is some awareness of colonization and its histories, many Canadians are not attuned in the same ways as Indigenous people in Canada are to the ongoing violences enacted through the performative slights of hand demonstrated by Harper—which become not only part of the mainstream (toxic) media ecology of the nation but also make their way from political rhetoric into law and policy. McMahon shows that it is precisely this chasm in understanding and attunement to the ongoing nature of colonization that needs to be bridged to even begin to address the impacts of historical and ongoing colonization in Canada. Media, political rhetoric, law, and policy are all soft infrastructures of the nation-state. One of the experts who speaks about Prime Minister Harper's understanding of colonization in this introductory segment is Hayden King. Since the release of this film in 2016, King has spoken out extensively about the ways in which Harper's successor, Prime Minister Trudeau and his government, understand the nation-to-nation relationships between Canada and Indigenous nations that further threaten to entrench colonial relations, this time mobilizing the infrastructure of the language of reconciliation.[24]

Where McMahon uses humor to point out discrepancies between public perceptions of historical and ongoing colonization, I look to decolonial and feminist frameworks to make evident the complex relations connecting land, extractivism, and fantasies of freedom, so as to offer more adequate approaches to addressing climate change by organizing around energy transition. Within our present petroculture, energy systems require the extraction of fossil fuels from "resource-rich" lands that ultimately belong to the Indigenous Peoples of these territories.[25] A move away from oil and fossil fuel energy systems, and by extension from the social-economic-political power relations and infrastructures they require, therefore necessitates the development of alternative relationships, both with the land and with the stewards of those lands. With this in mind, energy transition is not merely a technical issue (i.e., what new technologies will replace the old?) but also requires a deep and concerted effort to examine and dismantle power relations in order to develop energy imaginaries that allow us to design more livable futures for all.

Deep Energy Literacy

In other words, what is truly required of us at this time is a full-scale energy transition, informed by what I call *deep energy literacy*. This approach to literacy draws from theories of deep ecology that originated in the 1970s and argued that technocratic solutions were (and remain) inadequate to the challenges of ecological devastation. I make the allied claim that deep energy literacy is the understanding that all of our relationships are grounded in the energy systems that have fueled our networks of power and oppression—and thus deep energy literacy must be intersectionally feminist and decolonial in its mobilization. To be clear, both deep energy literacy and a more technology-based understanding of energy transition are needed. One is not more important than the other; rather, they round out one another. Installing a smart thermostat or taking public transportation might be part of engaging in energy transition depending on where you live in the world (because so many solutions will be oriented to local conditions), but so too is an understanding of how energy is social and how energy transition is—or could be—a galvanizing political force. In Canada, for example, full-scale energy transition and any new uses of the land must occur by first reconciling our relationships to the land and our concomitant relations with one another—Indigenous and non-Indigenous and also all manner of gendered, racialized, classist, ableist, relations in and between us—as well as our relations with the other species of flora and fauna, earth, air, water, and fire, with whom we coexist on this planet we call home. To dismantle and challenge the extractivist Dream that has come to undergird the way in which mainstream Canadians understand themselves in relation to land, to one another, and to energy, we need to practice alternative forms of literacy and understanding—again, deep energy literacy—to renegotiate power relations and reimagine more livable futures for all.

In *Colonization Road*, McMahon's inherently transgressive political humor provokes these same foundational issues about land, albeit in a different manner. As an Indigenous person, he is resisting the oppression and the genocidal dispossession of his people, for instance, by calling into question who owns so-called private property within ongoing regimes of colonial control and expansionism. In a particularly cutting segment, McMahon speaks to the then-recent report of the Truth and Reconciliation Commission (2008–2015), dedicated to documenting the history and legacy of Canada's residential school system, and its final report and ninety-four calls to action:

Oh, we are in a time that we have never seen before and we are not
ready, folks. We are not ready, 'cause I'm talking about nation-to-nation
shit, right? Like I'm talking about getting land back. Which, I don't even
know if that means you have to go back to where you came from. I'm
not sure yet. Maybe it does, I don't know. Oooh . . . feel that? That's the
assholes of . . .[26]

At this moment, McMahon gestures and laughs about the sphincters of his
white audience members tightening up, as he riffs on the very serious issues
of reconciliation and land rights and what they mean for the future of non-
Indigenous and Indigenous relations.

To further stress these points, *Colonization Road* moves viewers through
the history of Canadian colonization and Indigenous dispossession, including a short history of the Doctrine of Discovery, its inceptions, and its ongoing impacts into the present. As a recap, the Doctrine of Discovery "emanates
from a series of Papal Bulls (formal statements from the Pope) and extensions,
originating in the 1400s. Discovery was used as legal and moral justification
for colonial dispossession of sovereign Indigenous Nations."[27] It declared that
the first European nations to discover lands inhabited by "non-civilized"—in
other words, non-white and non-Christian—peoples would be given sovereign
ownership over those lands. While subsequent legal documents, such as the
Royal Proclamation of 1763 and numerous treaties would, in fact, recognize
that Indigenous Peoples have rights to their land, the long-held belief that
Christians were entitled to the land led to the Free Land Grants of the nineteenth century that parceled out Indigenous territory to settlers. As Indigenous
legal scholar and activist Pam Palmater explains in the film, Indigenous rights
are inherent and existed before settlement.[28] As Palmater asserts, "If you read
the Royal Proclamation, they say why they had to recognize those rights, and
it was because the only way that their 'colony' could be secure or have any justice is if they recognized and protected those rights, because we weren't giving
them up."[29] Treaties, she explains, do not undermine Canadian law, but are
instead foundational to it, and thus Canada must "recognize our [Indigenous]
sovereignty and nationhood in order to even exist as a state."[30] *Colonization
Road* weaves these historical and political facts shared by a range of Elders
and academic experts to illustrate that the dispossession of land central to the
colonial project is ongoing: *it is not an event but a structure.*[31] Put otherwise,
colonization is defined not only by historical events but also by the current
infra*structures* that enable its affirmation and continuation, in this case laws
that validate discovery and erode Indigenous Treaty Rights.

Accordingly, today's pressing political and economic hot topics—be they pipeline infrastructures, carbon pricing (an infrastructure of economy), or energy transition (another material infrastructure)—must be contextualized within the fraught history *and* present context of colonization; this is a process that necessitates deep energy literacy. That is, rather than trafficking in discussions about how to power the country through new technological innovations or ad hoc solutions, which often fail to address the ongoing exploitation of Indigenous Lands, we might instead redirect current conversations around climate change and energy transition towards more fulsome popular *energy imaginaries* that hold the capacity to speculate not only on a range of decarbonized possible futures but also futures in which the worldview that drives decision making shifts from extracting value to valuing all lives—human and more-than-human. As highlighted above, and as seen through the lens of deep energy literacy, McMahon's critiques of the land are part of a larger critique related to the current energy system. Implicitly, his demand for reorienting our nation-to-nation relationships and our relationships to the land is also a call to explicitly recognize who owns and controls "resources," how that land is "managed," and for whose benefit. In other words, he asks us to consider who profits from the way things are?

At this historical moment, when energy transition is needed as a first critical response to decarbonizing the environment, energy transition can also become a material reality and a politics around which we can begin to imagine and organize for new futures. As new "resources" and energy sources and systems are proposed for use (for example, rock bed formations with geothermal potential, or wide-open spaces ripe for wind-power capture or solar-power generation), we must rethink anew our relationships to the lands on which these projects are situated. As we embark on this renegotiation of land use for new low-carbon energy transition projects, it is also possible and necessary to renegotiate the deeper relationships we have to these spaces and places and to the people who live on them and have rights to them, especially Indigenous Peoples, given that Crown lands and Indigenous lands in remote areas of the country are often the sites and sources of new energy projects. In this way, decarbonized futures *could* help bring about more socially just futures for everyone in these territories, as well as those we are impacting around the world, through our ongoing petrocapitalist practices. Because if Indigenous Peoples are constrained by existing infrastructures, so too—to differing degrees at the intersections of power—are the majority of the population whose own mirage of freedom is, when exposed, another form of enclosure. While a solar farm in and of itself holds no promise of providing more equitable futures, the negotiations around these new infrastructures—from where they are built, on whose lands, to who controls those lands and who controls the means of power generation, and for whose benefit—could seriously reorient existing relations of power for Indigenous and non-Indigenous peoples and communities alike.

Paving the Road for Colonization: Infrastructures of (Im)Mobility

In addition to challenging the representations that have concealed the originary theft on which the Canadian Dream is founded, St. John's film explores infrastructural issues by identifying and debunking the metaphor of the road as benign, and of mobility as freedom. To begin, McMahon's voiceover narrative introduces the literal and metaphoric meaning of the road (see fig. 11.2):

> Colonization. We need to talk. I know you well. I wish I didn't, but I do. How crazy is this? There is a road named after you in my hometown. The road starts at the base of our traditional ceremonial grounds on my reserve: Koocheching First Nation in Northwestern Ontario. I played on this road. I swam off of it. I drove and walked this road. But I never knew what this road had done to my people. And, it turns out, there are colonization roads scattered across Manitoba and Ontario. Crazy.[32]

The same privilege that made it historically possible for European explorers to declare *terra nullius*[33] and claim dominion/*dominus*[34] over the discovery of the New World as their God-given right also works to mobilize settler colonial freedom fantasies that pave the way—quite literally by mapping, surveying, and building infrastructure such as colonization roads—for the cultural genocide and dispossession of Indigenous Peoples, their land, languages, and cultures. Further highlighting the power of roads as infrastructures of colonization, Palmater adds, "To me, roads, railways, they're like an infection, not just metaphorically but actually. It was a way of invading our territories without legal authority, without consent. And what are roads used for now? They literally bleed our territories dry of people, of resources, everything that matters to us. And, they pose a hazard."[35]

Both McMahon's and Palmater's comments invoke the invasive, predatory nature of roads at multiple levels, symbolic and infrastructural. For many Indigenous communities, roads not only allow for unofficial logging and mining operations that move resources unidirectionally out of Indigenous territories into the coffers of multinational corporations, but roads also play a role in other modes of illicit trafficking. For example, the Highway of Tears

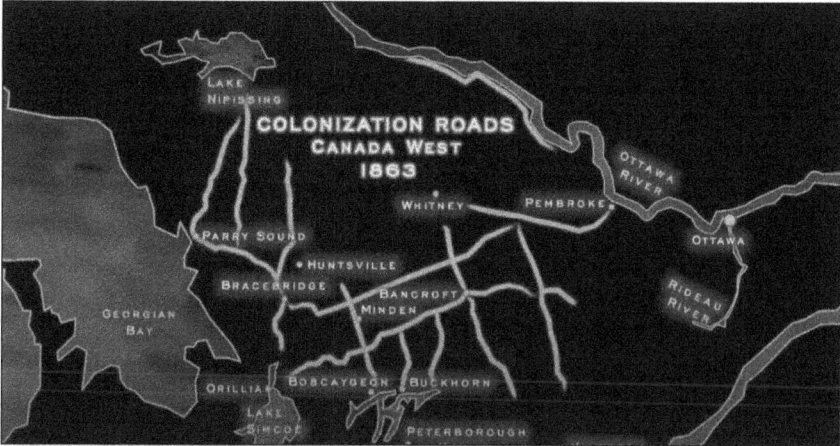

Fig. 11.2. Simplified map of colonization roads in 1863 running through what is now Ontario. (Michelle St. John, *Colonization Road* [Toronto: Decolonization Road Productions Inc., 2016], aired on CBC, *Firsthand*, http://www.cbc.ca/firsthand/episodes/colonization-road, 3:37. Image from film.)

(Highway 16 in British Columbia, Canada), where hundreds, by some accounts, and thousands by others, of Indigenous women have gone missing or been murdered since the 1960s, sparking a national inquiry, is also invoked by Palmater when she talks about invasion without consent. In a world of settler colonialism, women of color are more at risk than men of color or white women, and Indigenous women are often most at risk. Audra Simpson argues eloquently that this is because, according to Indigenous structures of governance, women are the original keepers of the land, and petrocolonialism therefore requires their ongoing dispossession and disappearance.[36] In the settler colonial reality of Canada's modernity, the Highway of Tears is a synecdoche for the many roads that have led to the dispossession and erasure of Indigenous women's power through the sociological phenomenon of missing and murdered Indigenous women and girls in Canada.[37]

Colonization Road, and the voices it gives space to throughout, speaks back to the Dream founded on a particular vision of success as "freedom" to own private property and freedom to access the open road and move through the world, as well as the freedom of class mobility narrated as the rightful reward of hard work (never of structural violence and privilege—which are unavoidably a foil for one another). In a world designed by white men for white men, the Dream built on freedom and mobility—both literal and metaphoric, both physical and social—that might be attained by the most privileged is experienced differently by those bodies situated differentially at the intersections of power. Furthermore, this same system and network of exploitation and extraction that has fueled colonial dispossession and reinforced an extractivist worldview is also responsible for the global warming that now presents a threat to us all. If we are going to address climate change, it will take more than technological shifts to slow and reverse the rampant rise of CO_2 issuing from these histories of extracting and moving value globally for the profit of a few. What is needed, instead, is deep energy literacy that interrogates and challenges power dynamics so as to develop full-scale transitions toward more just futures by dealing not simply with CO_2 emissions but with the deep causes of these emissions. The current media ecology traffics in the stolen Dreams necessary to sustain bankrupt capitalist financial worlds that continue to rely on colonialism. Our attachment to these fantasies contributes to our actions and inaction in response to the grand challenges of the twenty-first century, most pressingly, global warming.

Colonizing Women's Lives, Past, Present, and Future

Histories of Oppression: From Witch Hunts to the Nuclear Family

Having outlined how the infrastructures of the Dream narratives are inseparable from colonialism, in this section I aim to illustrate how the Dream is also cisheteronormative and patriarchal, illustrating by way of Silvia Federici's examination of historical witch hunts where and why feminist visions of the future that aim to subvert and overturn the infrastructures of modern social reproduction are, to my mind, inextricably linked to and have common cause with decolonization efforts.[38] Under capitalism, the lifeworlds of the majority are colonized, albeit in uneven and intersectionally different ways. The lives of oppressed people, Indigenous people, and women are colonized in different ways based on where our gendered, raced, classed, and abled bodies intersect with existing power structures. In addition to the house and car—private property and (auto)mobility—another central component of the Dream fueled by existing *energy imaginaries* is the nuclear-family unit. Indeed, the conversation often halts when we ask how transformations to energy infrastructure might impact the daily (and family-focused) privileges to which we have become accustomed. Further, and in addition to legitimizing the need for private property and personal vehicles, this heteronormative-familial mode of relationality also relies on (mostly) women's social reproductive labor, largely unpaid. For example, women are most often responsible for domestic work that is integral to the production of value, but is unrecognized as formal "labor" within capitalist logics of production and accumulation. Furthermore, when this labor is waged, it is often relegated to marginalized women such as women of color and poor women, those least able to benefit from the already scanty protections afforded to labor by the state. To ensure buy-in and thus the perpetuation of the status quo, colonial capitalism in Canada not only normalizes the exploitation of land and resources, and in so doing subsumes and represses the treaties and relationships on which this nation's own legitimacy rests, but it also continues to colonize the present and the future by normalizing the exploitation of the bodies and labor of women and women of color.

Looking to the histories that have led to the current moment, Federici has argued that European women's lives were colonized through the witch hunts of the sixteenth and seventeenth centuries in Europe, which involved the torture and killing of hundreds of thousands of women.[39] The historically overlooked "witch-hunt was a major *political* initiative" and "one of the most important events in the development of capitalist society," an "essential aspect of primitive accumulation and the 'transition' to capitalism."[40] During this period, women who engaged in traditional women's work—midwifery, medicine, the foraging and cultivation of food on commonly owned lands— were dispossessed of their access to these communal holdings and to their own expertise (i.e., the commons). These female bodies and knowledges were then integrated into a rationalized patriarchal capitalist market, a market in which women would henceforth participate only as poorly waged laborers, who earned half of what a man earned in the fourteenth century and one-third of what men earned by the mid-sixteenth century.[41] This history of oppression, which was multifaceted and included the aforementioned erasure of particular knowledge systems and subsistence practices, as well as tools of power such as the decriminalization of rape (which resulted in state-sanctioned rape and erased women's rights to their own bodies) and the mass killing of women, is intrinsically intertwined with the subjugation of the poor, people of color, and Indigenous populations. The witch hunts occurred "simultaneously with the colonization and extermination of the populations of the New World, the English enclosures, the beginning of the slave trade, the enactment of 'bloody laws' against vagabonds and beggars, and it [the persecution of witches] climaxed in that interregnum between the end of feudalism and the capitalist 'take off.'"[42]

Not unlike the history lessons provided by *Colonization Road* in relation to the Doctrine of Discovery outlined above, this historical account of women's history and specifically of the witch hunts also demonstrates how the control of land, bodies, and ideas (i.e., knowledge systems) is made possible by soft and hard infrastructures of the Dream of mobility and freedom, which enclose all but a very few. As Federici notes, "The colonized native Americans and the enslaved Africans . . . shared a destiny similar to that of women in Europe, providing for capital the seemingly limitless supply of labor necessary for accumulation."[43] Under capitalism, the colonized masses are positioned as resources from which value can be extracted. And, under modern petrocapitalism, women's labor and lives continue to be colonized through the division of private from public life that relegates *free* reproductive labor to the non-monetized domestic realm that sustains the *free* market.

Petrofeminism, (Auto)Mobility, and Ethical Oil

In my research around motivations for and resistances to energy transition, I have had to ask, what version of feminism is being trafficked to sustain petronormativity? An initial response might be articulated in relation to the second media text featured in this investigation—namely, the television commercial produced by Ethical Oil, a pro-Alberta oil sands organization with close connections to conservative politics in Canada. In 2011, the EthicalOil. org billboard campaign and associated television commercial in Canada mobilized both foreign and domestic women's images in numerous ways, not the least polemical of which invoked "foreign" women's deaths by stoning in Middle Eastern oil-producing nations.[44] In Ethical Oil's television commercial, the Canadian (or Western) woman is defined against the Saudi woman, as someone whose liberty is linked directly to her mobility, specifically her (auto)mobility, which enables her to move from home to work to shopping.[45] The commercial promotes a brand of feminism—what I call petrofeminism—that has been normalized as part of Western neoliberal petroculture. Petrofeminism reveals the ways in which oil, as an energy source, has shaped the lives of Western women not only through infrastructure, but also through explicit advertising strategies with well-defined consumer aims, as well as through political discourse that mobilizes the concept of "woman" as a means to justify resource extraction and international political relations of power.

In the West, shopping and consumer activity are largely defined as "feminine" and associated with the female-gendered or female-identified subject. As an example, the Ethical Oil commercial elaborates, in a voiceover, that through its purchase of Saudi oil, Canada "bankroll[s] a state that doesn't allow women to drive," a claim that is substantiated through subtitles that read, " 'Five Saudi women drivers arrested.' *Associated Press*, June 29, 2011," followed by " 'Saudi women . . . can't even leave the house to shop, let alone get a job, without a male family member's permission.' *Time*, October 19, 2009."[46] These "facts" about women's abilities to drive a car, shop, and work are placed on equal footing with Saudi women's lack of legal rights, as the commercial testifies to the fact that " 'Women also faced discrimination in courts, where the testimony of one man equals that of two women.' U.S. State Department."[47] While Ethical Oil strategists might have used Saudi women's continuously postponed access to the vote as an argument to illustrate their oppression, the automobile and consumerism were chosen instead. In this way, the extractivist Dream perpetuated in the Ethical Oil campaign, as well as in the current media ecology, reveals the powerful role of the automobile in the Western social imaginary as a symbol for autonomy and freedom, particularly as it has been constructed in relationship to women as petrofeminism: that is to say, a vision of women's lives that serves white supremacist cisheteropatriarchal colonial petrocapitalism. Petrofeminism is an easily exportable ideal of womanhood used to justify the continuation of business as usual, and to not only slow any transition away from fossil fuels to other energy sources but to potentially open up new female consumer markets in the East. Petrofeminism casts a broad petronormative net. The infrastructures of language mobilized by petrofeminist messaging recuperate the lives and limits of the imaginary for women in Canada and around the world about what futures are available to us.

This discourse builds on long-standing cultural narratives that tie women's freedom—or emancipation—to mobility, and specifically to automobility. The ideal of petrofeminism, like the "beauty myth" or the "mommy myth," mobilizes women's images, and largely white women's images, against all women, white or not, enclosing what is acceptable or possible for any of us.[48] For example, the petroleum-powered automobile has a symbolic resonance with firstwave feminism and the suffragette movements of the early twentieth century. The acquisition of the vote is a landmark moment in Britain, the United States, and Canada, and the Western suffragette campaigns that gained increasing visibility during the late nineteenth and early twentieth centuries popularly aligned women's emancipation directly with the automobile through media campaigns that photographed suffragettes campaigning for the vote in gaspowered cars, particularly US suffragettes before 1920 (see fig. 11.3).[49]

With this historical mobilization of petrofeminism in mind, the Ethical Oil commercial not only represents a denial of the deep and complex social transitions that are required as part and parcel of any just energy transition—that

Fig. 11.3. Image of Nell Richardson and Alice Burke photographed in their yellow Saxon automobile in 1916, while on the first cross-country suffrage trip by automobile, which was sponsored by the National American Woman Suffrage Association. (Library of Congress, Prints & Photographs Division, LC-DIG-ggbain-21391. Digital file from original negative.)

is, of any "ethics" of oil or energy—but it also defers entirely the issue of global warming in a desperate bid to maintain the power that fossil capital endows on the most privileged within the system. It is able to do this as part of a larger media ecology that has historically and ongoingly mythologized the role of the automobile, conflating it with individual autonomy and the Dream of freedom and success. The Dream and reality do not align for anyone, but least of all for women. Quite in contrast to the fiction, women's (auto)mobility drives an ever-expanding consumer market, rather than fulfilling any visions of feminist emancipation in the present or the future. As Andrew S. Gross argues, "the most common trope of driving—'the freedom of the road' "—popularized in the early twentieth century is linked to marketing strategies that were targeting women as consumers.[50] He goes on to argue, "the woman driver quickly became the central figure of consumerism. Gender, in fact, turns out to be an important strategy for mediating some of the conflicts and anxieties attending the transition to a consumer-oriented economy."[51] And, within this system, women also become commodities. Women and cars, in many instances, are made synonymous with one another, the automobile being perceived as an object of desire and either equated to or accessorized by the voluptuous and semi-naked woman draped on the hood (or over a motorcycle). The woman and the vehicle are culturally linked: both objectified and both fetishized.[52] It is a patriarchal double bind: Women = Car = Sex object. Women + Car = Independence. Either way, petrofeminism is part and parcel of the patriarchal petrocapitalist imaginary: and it is these imaginaries that must also be reclaimed and decolonized as part of future energy imaginaries.

Overworked and Perpetually Exhausted: Petronormative Social Reproduction

As highlighted above, the automobile is a symbol of a freedom, but the cultural myth has not been actualized for Western women.[53] Instead, as (middle-class) women fill their homes with consumer goods, so too do they fill their itineraries and their children's lives with an ever-increasing list of extracurricular activities. As a further example, throughout the twentieth century, as doctors' home visits became increasingly rare and health and hygiene standards rose, women were increasingly expected to travel to doctors' offices, dentist appointments, and hospitals, not only for emergency medical care but for regular check-ups and routine appointments.[54] By the mid-twentieth century, large segments of the female population had been relegated to the suburbs as part of the cisheteronormative petrocultural Dream, where they now labored alone in their own homes, reproducing on an individual level all of the tasks that were socially identified as within the purview of mothers and wives. Fast-forward to today, where women now spend a significant number of hours driving—commuting, running errands, and chauffeuring family members—and we can see how women's lives are not merely enhanced but also limited by their petrocultural inheritances. The Age of Oil gave rise to the Dream, designed and marketed to promote (auto)mobility in specifically gendered and racialized ways.

The automobile has been imbricated as a tool for personal independence and the successful management of a nuclear family, which in and of itself is intrinsic to the extractivist Dream that underlines the perpetuation of capitalism and, by extension, the ongoing project of settler colonialism. The promotion of the nuclear family as social norm has had significant ramifications for women, who must now independently reproduce in each household tasks that, had they been socioculturally constructed otherwise, could have easily been industrialized.[55] The infrastructural design of urban and suburban living in our modern petrocultures must be entirely remade at the relational level, whether the relations are to the ecosystems of which we are a part, to the territories we live on, to other species, or to our most intimate lived realities within our families and communities. A fulsome energy transition adequate to the challenge of climate change demands of us not only that we decarbonize the environment but also that we remake the relations of power that have led to this moment.

There are, of course, societies with radically different relational infrastructures. The late nineteenth and early twentieth centuries were rich with social experiments that sought greater gender equality.[56] Indigenous kin networks, in North America and elsewhere in the world, also provide alternatives in the ways they invite expanded definitions of family that include extended and community relations.[57] However, these alternative modes of relationality have been largely eradicated through the creation of normative standards that declared them un-Christian, uncivilized, communist, or some combination thereof. And so, cisheteropatriarchal colonial capitalism has become the norm. With this history of disappeared alternatives in mind, I'd argue that the Ethical Oil television commercial attempts to further erase any alternative to petrocapitalism by invoking a mythic understanding of the automobile and the open road as symbols of freedom that are necessary for the emancipation of, for instance, Saudi women. In short, according to Ethical Oil, *true* freedom involves the development of capitalist petronormativity, at the cost of any and all alternative energy imaginaries.

There is also the obvious fact, hidden in plain view, that personal vehicles are designed for optimum use on low-friction surfaces (roads), which are made possible through a series of public infrastructures, not the least of which are publicly maintained networks of streets, freeways, and highways, as well as local, national, and global financial marketplaces. In turn, these infrastructures create an interlocking set of path dependencies, not only in the way we construct and move through the material world but also in terms of what we deem possible when thinking through future energy transition scenarios. But what connects also divides, contains, and encloses. These roadways, as prerequisites for (auto)mobility, constitute, as McMahon and Palmater have illustrated above, an infrastructure of invasion and dispossession. Mobility through this space follows roads and networks used to conquer the Indigenous Peoples of these territories and to extract resources, including the fossil fuels that power this individual mobility. Having mapped the territory, these roads then work to colonize the lifeworld of the capitalist subject, who is endlessly relegated to the social reproduction of the nuclear-family home. The Dream of mobility and emancipation through that nuclear-family home, extended by personal vehicles, is held out as a lure for all, when in reality the Dream is designed to serve those who control/master it (*dominus*). If we want other more equitable futures for all, the fantasies that sustain the Dream and the Dream itself need to be reimagined by all for all.

While there are real and pressing issues related to the social, economic, and political status of women in Saudi Arabia, the rhetorical strategy of petrofeminism deployed by Ethical Oil neither proposes nor promises any solution or aid to the women of Saudi Arabia. Instead, the narrative relies on naturalized elements of women's lifestyles in Western petrocultures—driving, shopping, and employment—as though these activities equate directly with autonomy and feminism. The standard against which Saudi Arabia is being judged is not a feminist standard, nor even a standard of liberal human rights. It is a capitalist standard. The Ethical Oil campaign is invested in a certain brand of feminism—petrofeminism—that can serve as the handmaiden to reinforce and sustain global fossil-fueled capitalism. This system is bankrupt. Quite literally, capitalism went bankrupt in 2008 as part of the global financial crisis. It is furthermore socially bankrupt in that it more recently persists only through its subsidization with public tax dollars that further impoverish those most devastated by the cisheteronormative patriarchal colonial power relations of petrocapitalism. Further still, it is bankrupt in terms of providing alternative energy imaginaries—and this is where our investments for the future, I argue, should be going. We must replace the existing petrocultural Dreams that have always required and continue to demand the ongoing colonization of the stolen territories that make up Canada through the extraction of resources (the tar/oil sands, to name the most obvious), and the continued exploitation of under- and unpaid domestic labor, as well as the opening up of new consumer markets, all in the name of emancipation and freedom.

Energy Transition: Toward More Livable Futures for All

Disrupting the "Freedom Dream": Land, Bodies, and Collective Action

We must build new Dreams that redefine success, not as (auto)mobility and speed and unlimited access, but in ways that reorganize our imaginaries around new energy futures. If we cannot imagine just energy transition or just futures for all, then we cannot build the necessary soft and hard infrastructure projects to get us there. Invoking humor and fun is one viable strategy for imagining, and *Colonization Road* is one such example, giving voice to Indigenous attitudes toward the land and reconciliation. As a serious comedy, dark even in its inflection and yet still laughter inducing, it offers a sharp contrast to ongoing discourses of liberalism and right-wing politics in Canada that claim Canada's moral superiority to other nations, justifying the historical exploitation of land and resources so clearly illustrated in the 2011 Ethical Oil advertising campaign. *Colonization Road* disrupts the hegemonic narratives promoted by texts like the Ethical Oil commercial, which suggest that the infrastructures of the Dream—whether the hard infrastructures of freedom and (auto)mobility such as the road, or its soft infrastructures such as petrofeminism—need to be reworked. If we are to exceed the limits of the hegemonic Dream narratives and the associated (infra)structural violences that have defined modern petrocultural subjects, then we need to start trafficking in new future energy imaginaries. To this end, we need to hack existing media ecologies—the infrastructures that move and/or enclose existing stories—and we must, with care, form new feminist and decolonial Dreams that can be organized around material energy infrastructures that newly account (literally account in the sense of valuing) for our relations to one another, other species, and the land. These are the infrastructures needed for our reworlding. Or, as Leanne Betasamosake Simpson puts it in *Colonization Road*, "So I don't think we're having the right conversations in this country. We're talking about reconciliation, but we're not talking about land. We are talking about Missing and Murdered Indigenous Women and Girls, but we are not talking about the land. Where the root causes of every issue that Indigenous people are facing right now in Canada comes from dispossession, and it comes from erasure, and it comes from this system of settler colonialism that keeps us in an occupied state."[58]

Genuinely reconciling Indigenous and non-Indigenous relations requires that we deal with issues of land ownership, dispossession, and use—past, present, and future.[59] It requires us to not only reconceptualize our relations but also create new language for them: language and communication, while one of the most important infrastructures, is also an infrastructure that is susceptible to redesign when glitches present themselves. While the negotiation of Indigenous and non-Indigenous relations has been drawn out for centuries by the powers that be, climate change and the rising CO_2 levels that are an outcome of extractivist dispossession now force the issue. Or at least they should. At this historical juncture, on the lands known as Canada, the calls to action by the Truth and Reconciliation Commission are being put to us at the very moment that Indigenous and non-Indigenous peoples in Canada must urgently address global warming. The threat of a warming planet has the potential to force a reckoning with the impacts of cisheteronormative patriarchal colonial capitalism that have produced climate change and ongoing social injustice at the intersections of power and oppression—whether we are able to effectively mitigate rising CO_2 levels or not. These problems all originate in the land and in bodies, which are so intricately connected. We cannot deal with one without the other. Nor can we address either without first addressing our human and more-than-human (multispecies) relationships to the ecosystems in which we live.[60] If we understand the exploitation of social reproduction and unpaid labor—even when it is sold back to us as a freedom—as part of and not separate from the colonization of land and resources and the dispossession and erasure of Indigenous people and other people of color, then it becomes possible to organize against the common denominator of capitalism and neoliberal life, which rely on the individuation and atomization of the modern subject to foreclose collective action.

Energy Transition as a Feminist, Decolonial Collective Practice

With the above analyses in mind, I propose that energy transition, driven by deep energy literacy, provides one of the most important material realities around which to organize climate justice action on the ground. The current energy transition underway is being embarked upon as a largely technical problem that presents financial opportunity for those able to seize the market potential of new multisourced energy systems organized around the local geological and cultural conditions best suited to solar, wind, geothermal, hydro, and nuclear forms of power. However, by engaging in varied and ongoing processes of deep energy literacy, for instance by analyzing the current trafficking of the extractivist Dream within Canadian media ecologies, we might be able to not only recognize but also dismantle those modes of relation that have come to limit future energy imaginaries. To merely add to or tweak the system that has gotten us to where we are is insufficient; instead, we need to hack existing media ecologies. Lauren Berlant talks about the glitches that appear during times of crisis: "an interruption within a transition, a troubled transmission . . . the revelation of an infrastructural failure." She is interested in how the repair or replacement can generate "a form from within brokenness beyond the exigencies of the current crisis, and alternatively to it too."[61] We need to create these types of productive "glitchfrastructures" wherever possible: these alternative solutions that allow us to remake the infrastructures of the present in ways that mobilize for Other futures.

We can do this in the language we use, in the medias we mobilize, in the relations we reorient.[62] We need wholly different systems—new infrastructures based in decolonial and feminist approaches—that expand our capacity to imagine more livable futures for human and more-than-human life. This means collectively creating the conditions to live less energy-intensive and more socially, economically, and politically empowered lives in search of decolonized feminist futures.

Just as the histories of these oppressions are linked, so too are any possibilities for our liberated futures. In Canada, Indigenous communities often have the strongest legal standing from which to resist industrial expansionism into their territories, because of their inherent rights as First Peoples and because of the treaties that are recognized by international law, despite the ways in which they are disregarded by the Canadian governments and run roughshod over consistently as part of ongoing colonization. However, these communities should not be required to sustain, alone, the emotional and financial strains of long-term litigation when the population at large benefits from these legal maneuvers; all of us benefit from choosing life-affirming relations with the land that protect air, water, and multispecies health. We must all take responsibility and avoid succumbing to the capitalist drive, articulated as "development," "expansion," "growth," and a series of other capitalist nomenclature that linguistically reclaim extractivist practices as implicitly positive. We must *all* interrogate our relationships to our ecologies, as central to energy transition discussions and actions, where the struggle for women's rights, Indigenous rights, land rights, and so on can find common cause and paths for solidarity.

Feminist praxis is about these solidarities. As Angela Davis puts it, "When we identify into feminism, we mean new epistemologies, new ways of producing knowledge and transforming social relations."[63] What I'm asking for, in particular, is for us to organize these solidarities around energy transition projects, as a material reality on the ground that will implicitly bring with it certain social transformation. I'm also asking that where we recognize common cause, we must likewise recognize that common cause does not equate with one-size-fits-all solutions to energy transition. Here, for example, I think of the ways that many "environmental solutions" are urban-centric, classist, and racist and will not apply across cultures and cannot be scaled across both urban and rural spaces and logics. Berlant reminds us that the commons, for instance, has too often been invoked as "an uncontestably positive aim, [that] cover[s] over the very complexity of social jockeying and interdependence it responds to . . . the commons concept is a powerful vehicle for troubling troubled times" but one that also means living "with some loss of assurance as to one's or one's community's place in the world, at least while better forms of life are invented and tried out."[64] That is, we cannot continue to separate out issues of energy transition from other deeply interrelated rights issues. In Canada, in particular, post–Truth and Reconciliation Commission (2015), with its ninety-four recommendations, and post–United Nations Declaration on the Rights of Indigenous Peoples (2008), we need to think deeply about what it means to decolonize and indigenize our ways of thinking, doing, and being. This must happen simultaneously with the decisions we have to make about how we either "use" our resources to make a transition or transition to other ways of living in relation to our local and global ecosystems.

A feminist and decolonial approach is central to how we must think about energy transition and our energy futures. We need to organize our solidarities around energy transition projects because energy transition is a first critical step in decarbonizing the environment. It needs to be done. We absolutely need to make decisions about energy transition if we are to even continue to pretend that we are aiming for internationally agreed-upon targets limiting global warming to 1.5 degrees above preindustrial levels.[65] Plus, energy transition is a material problem that we can address and imagine incrementally, unlike, for example, the more amorphous problem of climate change—a hyperobject[66]—which is even more multifaceted and difficult to organize around politically. And a transition in power—*a powershift*—both literally and figuratively provides a fulcrum around which to mobilize feminist and decolonial politics in the interest of just futures. For instance, we can organize around community-networked energy systems, taking control of the materiality of energy production and distribution, as well as the politics and economics of these systems. Those who control energy and who benefit from it socially and financially have power, and so I am simply advocating that we take control of the means of production. We can get involved in making sure that the transition—energetic and social—is orchestrated for the maximum potential benefit of all. Taking into account the "all" also forces us to account for the fact that it is not just humans but also countless other species that will be the benefactors of humans thinking our relationships anew in these ways on this planet we share. Any energy transition that imagines a perpetuation of the status quo—or worse, an ever-growing demand for energy—demonstrates a vested interest in maintaining a system that promotes the privilege of some by externalizing the human, nonhuman, and more-than-human casualties of state-sponsored cisheteronormative patriarchal colonial capitalist violences. Whatever the bodies we are identified with, we must, as Angela Davis counsels us, take our identity/ies from our politics and not our politics from our identity/ies.[67] Any energy transition that does not reconsider human-to-human relations, and any energy transition that does not conceptualize of us all as part of our ecologies, not superior to them, is a failed transition. Any energy transition that does not fundamentally reorient the conceptualization of the Canadian economy as a staples economy—and problematize the fact that our current lives and economies are built on stolen lands, labor, and extractivist Dreams—is, from my perspective, inherently incapable of the re-imagining necessary to save not only the planet but our humanity.

The energy imaginary of our culture of climate change often promotes purely scientific approaches to energy transition that seek to optimize and maintain our current ways of living. These techno-scientific solutions fail to recognize that energy is social. Energy shapes the societies we build, create, and live in. Thus, any sort of energy transition also holds the potential for social and cultural transformation. Understanding energy transition as synonymous with social change reveals that our current crises cannot be reduced simply to replacing oil with solar, wind, or geothermal energy. Instead, it demands the complete reinvention of daily lived reality. It requires that we rethink every-thing from the clothes we wear, to where those clothes are manufactured, to what we eat and where it is grown, to how we wash those clothes and dishes. It requires that we rethink how we collect and use "natural resources," including water, solar, and wind, and ultimately how, and how fast (or slowly), we move about in the world and how we live together in community, sharing our food, energy, shelter, labor, and lives. It also demands that we question not only gender roles and the gendered division of labor but the nuclear family that is currently at the core of social organization. A full-scale energy transition also requires a rethinking of our gendered, classed, and racialized relationships: it requires the erasure of gender binaries that limit our potential to fully realize our humanity.

Conclusion

In sum, we must thoughtfully organize to work through a range of energy scenarios and fully investigate the paths forward. We need to recognize what we stand to gain or lose, not just financially, but in terms of (if not survival, then at least) more equitable, livable lives. This can only happen, however, if our energy transition plans are informed by deep energy literacy in order to recalibrate social inequities, whether our goal is to reverse climate change, mitigate it, be more resilient to it, or merely die better on an ailing planet.[68] Far better than trafficking in false petronormative Dreams of freedom and mobility that rely on our own enclosure, indebted to a system that is always already exploitative and exploiting, we must seize the current moment to interrogate and disrupt existing energy imaginaries and the infrastructures that enable or limit our ability to do so.

A shift away from our global petroculture requires that ongoing energy transition conversations move into a dialogue with feminist and decolonial knowledge in order to imagine other more ecological ways of being into being less autonomous, more collaborative, more community-oriented lives. Instead of mobilizing for the purpose of accumulating capital, which defines the culture of transportation and trafficking during the age of oil, I advocate mobilizing for justice. "Justice is love in the public sphere."[69] We must find the joy and the pleasure in resisting, where possible, the extinction of so many species of flora and fauna, including but not limited to our own. To my mind, this is a radically necessary response if any of the solutions imagined by us as local or global decision makers are to undo the infrastructures of extractivist injustice, past and present. We are at an impasse in desperate need of reimaginings and new action. This is an impasse that requires deep energy literacy: a way of being that resists petronormativity in all of its guises—petrofeminism, petrocolonialism, petrocapitalism—and that instead gives its all towards decolonized feminist energy futures—in other words, *just* futures for all.

NOTES

1. In this chapter, I explore the relationship between mobility and North American petro-imaginaries of freedom as mobility, with specific attention to what types of occupation and stasis are required to colonize these ideals of mobility. What I do not have space to explore in this chapter are other types of mobilities and immobilities of the petrocultural socio-scape, including the forced diasporas and mobilities required for many people to secure paid labor, who must either relocate or work at long distances from their families and lives. For more information on that, from a feminist perspective, please look to the work coming out of On the Move: Employment-Related Geographical Mobility in the Canadian Context (2012–2019) (www.onthemovepartnership.ca), a seven-year Social Sciences and Humanities Research Council of Canada Partnership project based at Memorial University and led by Barb Neis; Sara Dorow, a member of the Just Powers (www.justpowers.ca) team, is the Alberta team lead for On the Move, and explores these issues in specific relationship to the oil and oil sands industry of Northern Alberta. Another important aspect of mobility studies is done under the umbrella of critical mobility studies. For more information on this approach, see the work of Danielle Peers, among others, and the work coming out of their Media in Motion Lab (www.media inmotion.ca).
2. See Donna Haraway, Noboru Ishikawa, Scott F. Gilbert, Kenneth Olwig, Anna L. Tsing, and Nils Bubandt, "Anthropologists Are Talking—About the Anthropocene," *Ethnos* 81, no. 3 (2015): 335–64. Riffing off the term *Anthropocene*, a term used to signal an era where, through its activities and its growing population, the human species has emerged as a geological force now altering the planet's climate and environment, the *Plantationocene*

was introduced by Donna Haraway et al. (2015) to acknowledge how the current geological era is also marked by ongoing enclosures and a heavy reliance on indebted and exploited laborers. While the Anthropocene and the Plantationocene are not direct synonyms, these terms both refer to the human impacts of modernity on the geological and ecological form of the planet; however, they differ on how far back we can or should trace the roots of the heteronormative, patriarchal, and colonial forms of capitalism that define modernity, and thus where critical energy might be directed in addressing these geological transformations. See also Jason Moore, *Anthropocene or Capitalocene?: Nature, History, and the Crisis of Capitalism* (Oakland, CA: PM Press, 2016).

3.   Deborah Cowen, "Infrastructures of Empire and Resistance," *Verso Blog*, January 25, 2017, https://www.versobooks.com/blogs/3067-infrastructures-of-empire-and-resistance.

4.   Michelle St. John, *Colonization Road* (Toronto: Decolonization Road Productions Inc., 2016), aired on CBC, *Firsthand*, http://www.cbc.ca/firsthand/episodes/colonization-road.

5.   Ethical Oil, "Saudi Arabia (The Ad Saudi Arabia Doesn't Want You to See)," YouTube video, 00:45, posted August 26, 2011, https://www.youtube.com/watch?v=1SjZlqbDudI.

6.   By "women" I mean all those interpolated into the gender category, structurally, as a function of a patriarchal social order.

7.   For more information about the theoretical underpinnings of petrofeminism, see Sheena Wilson, "Gendering Oil: Tracing Western Petro-Sexual Relations," in *Oil Culture*, ed. Ross Barrett and Daniel Worden (Minneapolis: University of Minnesota, 2014), 244–66; Sheena Wilson, "Gender," in *Fueling Culture: 101 Words for Energy and Environment*, ed. Imre Szeman, Jennifer Wenzel, and Patricia Yaeger (New York: Fordham University Press, 2017), 174–77; and Sheena Wilson, "Petrofeminism and Petrointersectionality," *Deep Energy Literacy*, November 7, 2017, http://deepenergyliteracy.csj.ualberta.ca/2017/11/07/petrofeminism-and-petrointersectionality.

8.   See Sheena Wilson, "Energy Imaginaries: Feminist and Decolonial Futures," in *Materialism and the Critique of Energy*, ed. Brent Ryan Bellamy and Jeff Diamanti (Chicago: MCM Prime Press, 2018), 377–412.

9.   See Doreen Massey, especially "Power Geometry and a Progressive Sense of Place," in *Mapping the Futures*, ed. John Bird, Barry Curtis, Tim Putnam, George Robertson, and Lisa Tickner (London: Routledge, 1993), 59–69.

10. Petroculture, as a concept, refers to the ways twentieth- and twenty-first-century global systems and the associated networks of economic and political power have been shaped by energy-intensive carbon-based fuels, but more specifically it names the fact that these systems have shaped modern life and us, as moderns, into petrocultural subjects through and through. Our values, our habits, and our ways of being in and with the world, with others, and other species, have all been shaped by the availability of energy-intensive fossil-fueled mobility, telecommunications, and the plethora of products made available to us by these fossil-fueled networks—everything from the food we eat, to those things we never even knew we needed until the desire was manufactured, to the garbage we dispose of in such great abundance. For more information on the concept of petroculture, see Sheena Wilson, Imre Szeman, and Adam Carlson, "On Petrocultures: Or, Why We Need to Understand Oil to Understand Everything Else," in *Petrocultures: Oil, Politics, Culture*, ed. Sheena Wilson, Adam Carlson, and Imre Szeman (Montreal: McGill-Queen's University Press, 2017), 3–20.

11. See Lauren Berlant, "Cruel Optimism," *differences: A Journal of Feminist Cultural Studies* 17, no. 3 (2006): 20–36, especially 24–27.

12. For more on the exclusionary history of the New Deal, see Matthew Huber's *Lifeblood: Oil, Freedom, and the Forces of Capital* (Minneapolis: University of Minnesota Press, 2013), particularly chapter 2, "Refueling Capitalism: Depression, Oil, and the Making of 'the American Way of Life.'"

13. Treaty 6 covers a vast territory in the center of the provinces of Alberta and

Saskatchewan. It was signed in 1876. (See Michelle Filice, "Treaty 6," in *The Canadian Encyclopedia*, last edited October 11, 2016, https://www.thecanadianencyclopedia.ca/en /article/treaty-6). The British Crown signed eleven numbered treaties with Indigenous Peoples on the lands now called Canada between 1871 and 1921. (See Michelle Filice, "Numbered Treaties," in *The Canadian Encyclopedia*, last edited August 2, 2016, https:// www.thecanadianencyclopedia.ca/en/article/numbered-treaties.) However, there is ongoing debate about what that relationship entails, and there has been a long history of the conflict between the way Indigenous communities understand these treaties and their relationships to the Canadian governments (largely provincial, territorial, and federal, but also at other levels), and the way the Canadian government(s) understand their relationships and obligations to Indigenous Peoples. See note 24 for more details. The Idle No More Manifesto, for example, explains the relationship as follows: "The Treaties are nation to nation agreements between First Nations and the British Crown who are sovereign nations. The Treaties are agreements that cannot be altered or broken by one side of the two Nations. The spirit and intent of the Treaty agreements meant that First Nations peoples would share the land, but retain their inherent rights to lands and resources. Instead, First Nations have experienced a history of colonization which has resulted in outstanding land claims, lack of resources and unequal funding for services such as education and housing" (IdleNoMore.ca, http://www.idlenomore.ca /manifesto).

14. I use the term *resources* with the awareness that this term objectifies nature as something from which profit can be extracted.

15. As David Harvey argues, borrowing for homeownership is the control mechanism that stabilizes restive lower-income populations. He explains that "there was a wonderful phrase the business-class used to use, 'Incumbent homeowners don't go on strike!' " Vincent Emanuele, "Rebel Cities, Urban Resistance and Capitalism: A Conversation with David Harvey," *Counterpunch*, February 1, 2017, https://www.counterpunch.org/2017 /02/01/rebel-cities-urban-resistance-and-capitalism-a-conversation-with-david-harvey.

16. I address the discourses of (auto)mobility, women, and the family in a *Deep Energy Literacy* blog post. See Sheena Wilson, "Women and the Car," *Deep Energy Literacy*, November 13, 2017, http://deepenergyliteracy.csj.ualberta.ca/2017/11/13/women-and -the-car.

17. Silvia Federici, *Caliban and the Witch: Women, the Body and Primitive Accumulation* (New York: Autonomedia, 2004).

18. Cowen, "Infrastructures of Empire and Resistance."

19. The child welfare system and criminal justice system are populated by disproportionately high numbers of Indigenous people in Canada. For more on the implications and intersections of Indigenous Peoples in Canada and the criminal industrial complex, see Lisa Monchalin, *The Colonial Problem: An Indigenous Perspective on Crime and Injustice in Canada* (Toronto: University of Toronto Press, 2016).

20. The Truth and Reconciliation Commission of Canada (2008–2015) had the mandate to document the impacts of residential schools in Canada. In 2015, it released an executive summary that included ninety-four calls to action. See *Truth and Reconciliation Commission of Canada: Calls to Action*, https://nctr.ca/assets/reports/Calls_to_Action _English2.pdf.

21. St. John, *Colonization Road*, 0:09–0:20.

22. St. John, *Colonization Road*, 2:00.

23. St. John, *Colonization Road*, 2:00.

24. In February 2018, the federal government, under Prime Minister Justin Trudeau, introduced the *Indigenous Rights, Recognition and Implementation Framework*, which claims to be aligned with reconciliation efforts. However, this framework, which has led to the rapid deployment of a string of legislations, is the subject of much critique by Indigenous

and non-Indigenous scholars who see it as part of the ongoing colonization of Indigenous Peoples. In brief, the new framework raises questions about how Section 91(24) of the British North America Act of 1867 is understood in relationship to Section 35 of the Constitution Act of 1982, on Treaty and Aboriginal Rights. Section 91(24) undermines nation-to-nation rights, seeing Indigenous Peoples and lands as under federal jurisdiction, while Section 35 of the Constitution recognizes Indigenous rights to self-government. In their June 2018 report, King and Pasternak express their concern that "the federal government will now make a distinction between its constitutional obligations, organizing First Nations into Section 91(24) or Section 35 categories" (11). See the King-Pasternak report online: Hayden King and Shiri Pasternak, *Special Report: Canada's Emerging Indigenous Rights Framework: A Critical Analysis* (Toronto: Yellowhead Institute, 2018), https://yellowheadinstitute.org/rightsframework. And for another perspective, see the two-minute video-short featuring Indigenous legal scholar and Idle No More organizer Janice Makokis explaining the situation in lay terms: Just Powers, "Janice Makokis on Trudeau's Indigenous Framework," Vimeo video, 2:18, posted March 4, 2019, https://vimeo.com/321275450.

25. I use *belong* here with the understanding that many lands in Canada are unceded, which means that Indigenous Peoples never gave up their original rights to the land. In other contexts, there are signed treaties, which recognize Indigenous rights to the land.

26. St. John, *Colonization Road*, 14:00.

27. Assembly of First Nations, *Dismantling the Doctrine of Discovery* (Ottawa: Assembly of First Nations, 2018), http://www.afn.ca/wp-content/uploads/2018/02/18-01-22 -Dismantling-the-Doctrine-of-Discovery-EN.pdf.

28. Dr. Pamela D. Palmater is a Mi'kmaw citizen and member of the Eel River Bar First Nation in northern New Brunswick. She has been a practicing lawyer since 2001 and is currently an associate professor and the Chair in Indigenous Governance at Ryerson University.

29. St. John, *Colonization Road*, 17:00.

30. St. John, *Colonization Road*, 19:00.

31. In the film, interview subject Jeff Denis, associate professor of sociology, paraphrases theorist of settler colonialism Patrick Wolfe to remind viewers that "colonization is not just something that happened in the past . . . It is a structure, not an event. It is an ongoing process, something that we reproduce everyday through our actions" (4:00).

32. St. John, *Colonization Road*, 4:00.

33. *Terra nullius* is Latin for "nobody's land," because "nobody" signaled non-civilized peoples or rather non-Christians.

34. The term *dominion/dominus* means master or owner, in this case land controlled by the subject of a king or divine ruler.

35. St. John, *Colonization Road*, 36:00.

36. Audra Simpson, "The Chiefs Two Bodies: Theresa Spence and the Gender of Settler Sovereignty," lecture, Unsettling Conversations, Unmaking Racisms and Colonialisms, R.A.C.E. Network's 14th Annual Critical Race and Anticolonial Studies Conference, University of Alberta, October 2014, https://vimeo.com/110948627.

37. Simpson, "The Chiefs Two Bodies," 34:00.

38. Federici, *Caliban and the Witch*.

39. Federici, *Caliban and the Witch*.

40. Federici, *Caliban and the Witch*, 168, 165.

41. Federici, *Caliban and the Witch*, 77.

42. Federici, *Caliban and the Witch*, 164–65.

43. Federici, *Caliban and the Witch*, 198.

44. In one billboard, a red banner message reads "Conflict Oil Countries: Women Stoned to Death," superimposed over the black-and-white image of a burqa-clad woman being buried alive in preparation for stoning. This woman is not identified and simply stands in

as a synecdoche for the perceived oppression of women in Muslim areas of the world. The use of this image is part of a larger rhetorical practice that fails to read and understand exceptional moments of gender violence in other contexts. Instead, these images of violence against women are invoked because they appeal to the Western narratives of the foreign woman as victim, while denying violence against women in Western cultures. See the *Globe and Mail*, "Ethical Oil Ad Campaign," In Pictures, July 28, 2011, https://www .theglobeandmail.com/news/politics/ethical-oil-ad-campaign/article637242/.

45. The female voiceover narrator of the Ethical Oil television commercial explains the situation in Saudi Arabia to viewers as follows: "Fact. Last year we bought over 400 million barrels of oil from Saudi Arabia. We bankrolled a state that doesn't allow women to drive, doesn't allow them to leave their homes or work without their male guardian's permission, and a state where a woman's testimony only counts for half of a man's. Why are we paying their bills and funding their oppression? Today there is a better way. Ethical Oil from Canada's oil sands. Ethical Oil, a choice we have to make." There are also text and subscript citations, indicating their sources, which appear throughout the commercial, provided to support further the information in the voiceover. They are as follows: "North Americans bought over 400 million barrels of oil from Saudi Arabia. U.S. Energy Information Administration. ["Five Saudi women drivers arrested." *Associated Press*, June 29, 2011.]" "Saudi women . . . can't even leave the house to shop, let alone get a job, without a male family member's permission. [*Time*, October 19, 2009.]" "Women also faced discrimination in courts, where the testimony of one man equals that of two women. [U.S. State Department.]" (Ethical Oil, "Saudi Arabia").

46. Ethical Oil, "Saudi Arabia."

47. Ethical Oil, "Saudi Arabia."

48. See Naomi Wolf, *The Beauty Myth* (Toronto: Vintage Books, 1991) and Susan J. Douglas and Meredith W. Michaels, *The Mommy Myth: The Idealization of Motherhood and How It Has Undermined Women* (New York: Free Press, 2005).

49. Julie Wosk, *Woman and the Machine: Representations from the Spinning Wheel to the Electronic Age* (Baltimore: Johns Hopkins University Press, 2001), 125.

50. Andrew S. Gross, "Cars, Postcards, and Patriotism: Tourism and National Politics in the United States, 1893–1929," *Pacific Coast Philology* 40, no. 1 (2005): 85.

51. Gross, "Cars, Postcards, and Patriotism," 85.

52. See Sheena Wilson, "Gendering Oil: Tracing Western Petro-Sexual Relations," in *Oil Culture*, ed. Ross Barrett and Daniel Worden (Minneapolis: University of Minnesota, 2014), 244–66; and Cecily Devereux, " 'Made for Mankind': Cars, Cosmetics, and the Petrocultural Feminine," in *Petrocultures: Oil, Politics, Culture*, ed. Sheena Wilson, Adam Carlson, and Imre Szeman (Montreal: McGill-Queen's University Press, 2017), 162–86.

53. For more details on the transformations to women's domestic work and roles, see Ruth Schwartz Cowan's award-winning 1983 monograph *More Work for Mother: The Ironies of Household Technology from the Pen Hearth to the Microwave* (New York: Basic Books), which documents and analyzes how "industrialization transformed every American household sometime between 1860 and 1960" (3).

54. Cowan, *More Work for Mother*, 84–85.

55. Cowan details social moments or specific social experiments in industrializing aspects of women's domestic work, such as laundry and cooking, which ultimately failed in the face of sociocultural pressures and advertising campaigns. For example, a market for the washing machine was created by undermining industrial laundries through discourses of suspect hygiene linked to racism. Cooking as the responsibility of each mother-wife was reinforced through concerns about how communal kitchens and other social-housing experiments that eliminated this task from daily life posed a threat to Western family values and insinuated parallels with communism.

56. For an extensive history of the "lost feminist tradition" of American material feminists

who worked between the Civil War and the start of the Great Depression to challenge industrial capitalism by creating "feminist homes with socialized housework and child care," often through communal living, as a means to achieve equity, see Dolores Hayden, *The Grand Domestic Revolution: A History of Feminist Designs for American Homes, Neighborhoods, and Cities* (Cambridge, MA: MIT Press, 1981), 3.

57. These include polyamorous, polygamous, polyandrous, multigenerational, and communal ways of living, and the creative remakings of these relationalities for the twenty-first century. See Kim Tallbear, *The Critical Polyamorist* (blog), http://www.criticalpolyamorist .com, and Kim Tallbear, "Disrupting Settlement, Sex, and Nature," lecture, Future Imaginaries Lecture Series from Concordia University, Montreal, Quebec, October 14, 2016, http://abtec.org/iif/output/lecture-series-kim-tallbear.

58. St. John, *Colonization Road*, 25:00.

59. Lauren Berlant writes at length about language as an infrastructure that can be mobilized when the glitches, those aspects of the infrastructure that aren't working, appear. See Lauren Berlant, "The Commons: Infrastructures for Troubling Times," *Environment and Planning D: Society and Space* 34, no. 3 (June 2016): 395, https://doi.org/10.1177 /0263775816645989. Ryan McMahon, in his own way, also addresses this issue in his stand-up routine in *Colonization Road*, when he jokes about the pronouns and the way Indigenous and non-Indigenous people are put at odds with the "us"/"we" he uses for "Native people" and by association the "them" and "you" he associates with non-Indigenous folks. Language too needs reimagining if we are to think through our solidarities across political divides and even species divides. We must remake our language so that it is not so binary, so anthropogenic, so isolating and alienating in its orientation. And, in this, we can learn from the queering of language that is necessary for the queering and expansion of relationality and Other futures.

60. See Kirsty Robertson, "Oil Futures/Petrotextiles," and Janine MacLeod, "Holding Water in Times of Hydrophobia," in *Petrocultures: Oil, Politics, Culture*, ed. Sheena Wilson, Adam Carlson, and Imre Szeman, (Montreal: McGill-Queen's University Press, 2017), 242–63, 264–86; Maya Weeks, "Closed Loop Dead Matter," *Guts Magazine*, November 5, 2015, http://gutsmagazine.ca/dead-matter, and "Myth of the Garbage Patch," *New Inquiry*, May 2015, http://thenewinquiry.com/essays/myth-of-the-garbage-patch.

61. Berlant, "The Commons," 393.

62. Berlant, "The Commons," 396.

63. Angela Davis, *The Meaning of Freedom: And Other Difficult Dialogues* (San Francisco: City Light Books), 197.

64. Berlant, "The Commons," 395.

65. Intergovernmental Panel on Climate Change, "Summary for Policymakers," in *Global Warming of 1.5°C. An IPCC Special Report on the impacts of global warming of 1.5°C above pre-industrial levels and related global greenhouse gas emission pathways, in the context of strengthening the global response to the threat of climate change, sustainable development, and efforts to eradicate poverty*, ed. V. Masson-Delmotte et al. (Geneva: World Meteorological Organization, 2018).

66. See Timothy Morton, *Philosophy and Ecology after the End of the World* (Minneapolis: University of Minnesota Press, 2013).

67. Davis quoted in Natalie Loveless, "Review of *Desire Change: Contemporary Feminist Art in Canada*," *RACAR: Revue d'art canadienne/Canadian Art Review* 44, no. 1 (2019), https:// www.jstor.org/stable/26654447.

68. See Roy Scranton, *Learning to Die in the Anthropocene: Reflections on the End of a Civilization* (San Francisco: City Lights Open Media, 2015).

69. See Cornel West, "Justice Is What Love Looks Like in Public," sermon, Howard University, Washington, DC, April 2011, https://www.youtube.com/watch?v=nGqP7S_WO6o &feature=youtu.be&t=21s.

Contributors

Brent Ryan Bellamy studies and teaches in the areas of energy humanities, science fiction studies, and American literature and culture. Bellamy coedited the climate crises issue of *Science Fiction Studies* and a book-length speculative dictionary titled *An Ecotopian Lexicon*. His book-length study on the post-apocalyptic mode and US hegemony is forthcoming from Wesleyan University Press. He has published articles in *The Cormac McCarthy Journal*, *Mediations*, *Open Library of the Humanities*, *Paradoxa*, *Postmodern Culture*, *Science Fiction Studies*, and *Western American Literature*.

Brian C. Black is Distinguished Professor of Environmental Studies and History at Penn State Altoona, where he also currently serves as head of the Division of Arts and Humanities. He is the author or editor of several books, including *Petrolia: The Landscape of America's First Oil Boom*, *Crude Reality: Petroleum in World History* and *Gettysburg Contested: 150 Years of Preserving America's Most Cherished Landscape*.

Jeff Diamanti teaches literary and cultural analysis at the University of Amsterdam. With Imre Szeman, he is the editor of *Energy Cultures: Art and Theory on Oil and Beyond* (WVU Press), and with Amanda Boetzkes, he co-organizes "At the Moraine," an ongoing research project on the political ecology of glacial retreat in Greenland. In addition to coediting the Climate Realism book and journal collection with Lynn Badia and Marija Cetinic, he also has two forthcoming book chapters in the Duke University Press Elements Series.

Megan Hayes is a researcher and visual artist from Australia, currently based in Amsterdam. A graduate of cultural analysis from the University of Amsterdam, her research interests lie at the interstices of the environmental humanities, marine science, and cultural anthropology. Her current project considers ocean acidification in the coral sea region, and emergent concepts of immersion in feminist science studies.

Joseph K. Heumann is professor emeritus of communication studies at Eastern Illinois University, where he continues to teach various film courses. He and Robin L. Murray have coauthored six books exploring ecocinema: *Ecology and Popular Film: Cinema on the Edge, That's All Folks?: Ecocritical Readings of American Animated Features, Gunfight at the Eco-Corral: Western Cinema and the Environment, Film and Everyday Ecodisasters, Monstrous Nature: Environment and Horror on the Big Screen*, and *Ecocinema and the City*.

C. Parker Krieg is a postdoctoral researcher in environmental humanities at the University of Helsinki, affiliated with the Faculty of Arts and the Helsinki Institute of Sustainability Science. His research and teaching focuses on American literature, environmental justice, and cultural memory, particularly on issues related to energy and the cultural economy of post-Fordism. His articles appear or are forthcoming in *Studies in American Fiction, A/B: Auto/ Biography Studies*, and *Ecozon@: European Journal of Literature, Culture, and Environment*.

David LaRocca is the author, editor, or coeditor of ten books, including *The Thought of Stanley Cavell and Cinema: Turning Anew to the Ontology of Film a Half-Century after* The World Viewed, *The Philosophy of War Films*, and *The Philosophy of Documentary Film: Image, Sound, Fiction, Truth*. He has held visiting research and teaching positions in cinema, English, and philosophy at Binghamton, Cornell, Cortland, Harvard, Ithaca College, and Vanderbilt. He has participated in a National Endowment for the Humanities Institute, a workshop with Abbas Kiarostami, Werner Herzog's Rogue Film School, and the School of Criticism and Theory at Cornell University. Find out more at www.DavidLaRocca.org.

James Longhurst is a historian of urban and environmental policy and the author of *Bike Battles: A History of Sharing the American Road*. He is a professor at the University of Wisconsin–La Crosse, with a PhD in history and policy from Carnegie Mellon University. His first book, *Citizen Environmentalists*, described the rise of local environmental organizing in Pittsburgh and the United States in the 1960s and 1970s. Recent publications include articles in the *Journal of Policy History* and the *Transportation Research Record*, the journal of the Transportation Research Board, as well as op-eds in the *Pittsburgh Post-Gazette* and the *New York Daily News*. More at http://bikebattles.net and https://www.uwlax.edu/profile/jlonghurst.

Patrick D. Murphy is professor emeritus and former chair of the department of English at the University of Central Florida. Prior to that he taught at Indiana University of Pennsylvania. Founding editor of *ISLE: Interdisciplinary Studies in Literature and Environment,* he is the author of *Transversal Ecocritical Praxis, Persuasive Aesthetic Ecocritical Praxis, Literature, Nature and Other,* and other books. He has also edited or coedited a dozen books, including *Ecofeminist Literary Criticism* and *The Literature of Nature: An International Sourcebook.* Murphy began his ecocritical studies in 1983 with a master's thesis on spirituality and place in the poetry of Gary Snyder and Wendell Berry. He now lives in Galveston near the rising water's edge.

Robin L. Murray is professor of English at Eastern Illinois University, where she teaches film and literature courses and coordinates the film studies minor. She and Joseph K. Heumann have coauthored six books exploring ecocinema: *Ecology and Popular Film: Cinema on the Edge, That's All Folks?: Ecocritical Readings of American Animated Features, Gunfight at the Eco-Corral: Western Cinema and the Environment, Film and Everyday Ecodisasters, Monstrous Nature: Environment and Horror on the Big Screen,* and *Ecocinema and the City.*

Tatiana Prorokova-Konrad is a postdoctoral researcher in the department of English and American studies at the University of Vienna, Austria. She holds a PhD in American studies from the University of Marburg, Germany. She was a visiting researcher at the Forest History Society (2019), an Ebeling Fellow at the American Antiquarian Society (2018), and a visiting scholar at the University of South Alabama, USA (2016). She is the author of *Docu-Fictions of War: U.S. Interventionism in Film and Literature* and a coeditor of *Cultures of War in Graphic Novels: Violence, Trauma, and Memory.*

Gordon M. Sayre is a scholar of colonial American history and literature and professor of English and folklore at the University of Oregon. He is participating faculty in environmental studies and teaches an undergraduate course entitled Car Cultures that examines the history of the car industry and the environmental issues caused by automobility. He is also the author of "The Humanity of the Car: Automobility, Agency, and Autonomy," published in the journal *Cultural Critique.*

Barry L. Stiefel, is an associate professor in the historic preservation and community planning program at the College of Charleston. He is interested in how the sum of local preservation efforts affect regional, national, and multinational policies on cultural and natural heritage. Recently he has taken an interest in automobiles as a metaphor for rethinking the way we approach the conservation of the built environment. Dr. Stiefel has published numerous books and articles, including *The Routledge Companion to Automobile Heritage, Culture, and Preservation* (coedited with Jennifer Clark). Originally from southeastern Michigan, where the automobile industry was key to the region's heritage identity, Dr. Stiefel now resides in South Carolina with his family and where his primary mode of transportation is a bicycle.

Matthew C. Swanson is a PhD student in the department of English at the University of California, Los Angeles, where he studies twentieth- and twenty-first-century American fiction, environmental humanities, and the Anthropocene. In addition to his interest in transportation and sustainability, his research is concerned with narrative representations of environmental degradation resulting from the extraction and consumption of natural resources as well as the development of the logic of plenitude and material excess in American culture.

Sheena Wilson is professor of English and cultural studies at the University of Alberta, cofounder and director of the international Petrocultures Research Group, and research lead on *Just Powers*. Her research interests involve an interdisciplinary and intersectional approach to studying how the extractivist worldview that has contributed to climate change through the exploitation of land and resources, likewise allows for the exploitation of gendered, classed and racialized bodies, and the erasure of knowledge held by those bodies. Given that mobilizing against climate change can be overwhelming, she argues for a focus on *power shift*—literally in terms of energy transition, and figuratively in terms of social justice—as a means to anchor feminist and decolonial political movements striving for climate justice. Wilson's publication highlights include *Petrocultures: Oil, Politics, Cultures* with Adam Carlson and Imre Szeman; "Gendering Oil: Tracing Western Petrosexual Relations"; and *Sighting Oil* with Andrew Pendakis. Her monograph in process is called *Deep Energy Literacy: Toward Feminist Energy Futures*.

Index

accelerationism, 211, 212–13, 219, 220, 222, 223
acidification, 174
Acura, 91
Adventures of Ozzie and Harriet, The (1952–66), 111
aesthetics, 15, 84, 173–74, 176, 178, 179, 180, 187, 188, 211
Alas, Babylon (1959), 152–53, 156, 158, 165
All Dogs Go to Heaven (1989), 192
American Flyers (1985), 53, 56–59
American Graffiti (1973), 111, 124, 127
American Movie (1999), 201
"Andy's English Valet" (1963), 60
Anthropocene, 2, 127, 228, 253–54n2
apocalypse, 14, 146, 152, 154, 155, 159, 160, 162–65, 166n1; post-apocalypse, 3, 14–15, 151–66, 166n1, 166–67n3, 167n16, 168n35, 169n43
Atrocity Exhibition, The (1970), 148n1
Audi, 92
Ausgebrannt (2007), 169n43
automobile, 3–4, 7–8, 12–14, 21–38, 38n13, 42, 44, 45, 46, 47, 48, 49, 60, 63–64, 66–68, 71–73, 76, 78, 85, 88–89, 91–96, 101n28, 103–6, 110, 112, 115–16, 123, 126, 134, 135, 137, 139, 140, 142, 143, 150n66, 154, 157, 168n33, 220–22, 231, 243–46
See also autonomous vehicle; car; personal vehicle
autonomous vehicle, 27, 85, 98, 116, 118, 147
See also automobile; car; personal vehicle
autonomy, 23, 133, 243–44, 247

Baby Driver (2017), 110
Badlands (1973), 124, 127
Baker Motor Vehicle Company, 34

Bel Geddes, Norman, 83, 85–87, 95, 98
bicycle (bike), 1, 10, 12, 13, 41–60, 61n30, 68–69, 71–73, 75, 77, 78, 89, 90, 91, 92, 93–94, 97–98, 100, 108, 115, 168n35
See also CicLAvia; Flying Pigeon; Plan de la Bicicleta de Sevilla; Victory Bike
Bicycle Clown (1958), 47
Bicycle Flirt, The (1928), 50
Bicycle Today, Automobile Tomorrow (1969), 48
Bicycling with Complete Safety (1939), 45
Bike Behavior (1948), 46, 61n30
Bike Safety (1950), 47
biofuel, 27, 34, 35
biomimicry, 28
bioplastics, 33, 34
See also plastics
Bird (company), 64, 68, 75
Blinded by the Light (2019), 145
Blob, The (1958), 112
Bloodshed Motors, 31
BMW, 91, 92, 113
Boom Town (1940), 192
Boomtowners (2015), 16, 211, 214–18, 219, 223
Born to Run (2016), 125
Breaking Away (1979), 53–56, 58, 59
Bullitt (1968), 124
bunker fuel, 173
Burden of Dreams (1982), 219
Bush Mechanics, 32–33

Cadillac, 104, 126, 128, 129, 132, 133, 148n4
Can't Buy Me Love (1987), 52
capital, 2, 15, 67, 151, 159, 161, 164, 174, 176, 179, 181, 187, 188, 212, 215, 217, 242, 244, 253
capitalism, 3, 4, 6, 7, 13, 16, 89, 92, 123, 132, 141, 142, 145, 159, 164, 174, 177, 178,

capitalism (*continued*)
179, 185, 187, 212, 214, 222, 227, 229, 230, 231, 240, 241, 242, 245, 246, 247, 249, 250, 251, 254n2, 258n56; petrocapitalism, 16, 153, 197, 227, 229, 231, 237, 242, 243, 245, 246, 247, 253

Capitalocene, 228

car, 1, 3, 4, 5, 7, 8, 10, 11, 12, 13, 14, 21, 25, 27, 28, 29, 30, 31, 32, 34, 35, 41, 43, 46, 47, 48, 49, 50, 51, 52, 55, 59, 60, 63, 64–67, 68, 70, 71, 72, 73, 74, 76, 77, 78, 83–86, 87–93, 95–100, 100n12, 103–18, 123–40, 142–47, 154, 157, 159, 161, 165, 198, 202, 203, 221, 222, 229, 230, 231, 240, 243, 245

See also automobile; autonomous vehicle; personal vehicle

Car, The (1994), 4

carbolization, 14, 83, 84, 88–89, 90, 92, 93, 94, 97, 98, 99

carbon dioxide (CO$_2$) emissions, 14, 26, 28, 76, 83, 84, 89, 96, 97, 101n34, 106, 108, 109, 240, 248, 249

See also carbon footprint; pollution

carbon footprint, 25, 63, 64, 66, 67, 76, 77, 78, 104, 113

See also carbon dioxide (CO$_2$) emissions; pollution

carbonization, 1, 6, 12; decarbonization, 14, 64, 69, 70, 75–78, 232, 237, 246, 251

Carhullan Army, The (2007), 169n43

Chery, 91

Chevrolet, 46, 51, 105, 125

Chrysler, 84, 95, 107

CicLAvia, 67–68

See also bicycle (bike); Flying Pigeon; Plan de la Bicicleta de Sevilla; Victory Bike

climate change, 2, 3, 4, 5, 6, 10, 11, 12, 13, 14, 15, 16, 22, 36, 42, 60, 84, 96, 108, 109, 114, 115, 116, 117, 118, 127, 165, 173, 174, 175, 184, 186, 188, 211, 213, 227, 228, 229, 232, 234, 237, 240, 246, 248, 249, 251, 252, 258n65

See also global warming

coal, 2, 5, 6, 76, 77, 94, 104, 116, 117, 155, 204

See also fossil fuels

Colonization Road (2016), 16, 228, 232–40, 241, 248, 258n59

comedy, 3, 15, 41, 44, 50, 52, 53, 59, 60, 91,

128, 191–209, 211–24, 232, 233, 248; eco-comedy, 192, 196

See also humor; laughter

commodity, 3, 6, 86, 153, 157, 159, 165, 166n2, 177, 181, 182, 224, 227, 229, 231, 245

consumerism, 6, 12, 13, 14, 15, 145, 204, 243, 244

containerization, 177, 188

See also intermodal shipping container

Corporate Average Fuel Economy (CAFE), 96–97, 105, 119n13

Crash! (1970), 148n1

Crash (1973), 14, 123, 124, 128, 131, 132–35, 140, 143, 148n1, 149n41

Crash (1996), 14, 123, 128, 135–41, 142, 149n41, 150n55

Crash (2004), 148n1

Death Proof (2007), 139

Dick Van Dyke Show, The (1961–66), 111

Dirty Girl (2010), 112

Dodge, 127, 128

Dog Stars, The (2012), 14, 155, 159–62, 165

Dr. Strangelove (1964), 133

Drive Your Bike (1955), 47, 48

Dylan, Bob, 144

e-scooter, 13–14, 63–64, 67–78, 98

E.T. the Extraterrestrial (1982), 52

Earth Day, 124

eco-hero, 192, 193, 194, 196, 197, 202

eco-horror, 208

eco-trauma, 206–7

Ecotopia (1975), 114, 115, 116

Ecotopia Emerging (1981), 114, 115, 116

electricity, 24, 25, 26, 59, 76, 77, 104, 116, 117, 152, 153

See also energy; fossil fuels

Empire of the Sun (1984), 132–33

energy, 1, 2, 5, 6, 9, 10, 11, 12, 13, 14, 15, 16, 21, 25, 26, 27, 28, 29, 31, 32, 33, 35, 36, 42, 49, 67, 68, 76, 77, 88, 90, 96, 108, 109, 115, 116, 117, 144, 151–56, 158–66, 166n2, 167n5, 167n15, 168n33, 173, 176, 191, 204, 211, 213, 217, 218, 220, 221, 222, 228, 229, 230, 232, 234, 235, 237, 240, 242, 243, 244, 245, 246, 247–53, 254n2, 254n10, 257n45

See also electricity; fossil fuels

engine, 1, 10, 21, 24, 27, 30, 31, 34, 35, 76, 90, 93, 95, 96, 115, 125, 130, 133, 136, 137, 140, 146, 150n66, 154, 162, 168n35, 173
    See also motor
environmental documentary, 3, 180
environmental humanities, 16, 188
Ethical Oil, 16, 228, 242–48, 256–57n44, 257n45
    See also fossil fuels; oil; oil sands (tar sands); petroleum
exhaustion, 24, 34, 95, 96, 182, 212, 214, 218, 219, 220, 222, 223, 245
Exposed (2016), 112
extinction, 123, 133, 253

Fast and Furious (2001), 110
feminism, 16, 176, 183, 206, 231, 234, 235, 240, 242, 243, 244, 247, 248, 249, 250, 251, 253, 253n1, 257–58n56; antifeminism, 192; ecofeminism, 195; petrofeminism, 16, 227, 228, 231, 242, 243, 245, 247, 248, 253, 254n7
Fish Story (1989–95), 177
Fitzcarraldo (1982), 219
Flying Pigeon, 90, 91
    See also bicycle (bike); CicLAvia; Plan de la Bicicleta de Sevilla; Victory Bike
Ford, Henry, 28, 85, 93, 104, 118n8, 220
Ford Motor Company, 30, 31, 33, 34, 36, 84, 85, 95, 96, 104, 106, 138, 214, 223
Foreign Affair, A (1948), 52
Forgotten Space, The (2012), 15, 175–79
fossil fuels, 1–6, 9–12, 24–27, 36, 67, 77, 78, 96, 151–54, 157, 160, 161, 162, 164, 166, 166n2, 168n33, 173, 181, 211, 213, 229, 234, 243, 246, 247, 254n10
    See also coal; electricity; energy; Ethical Oil; natural gas; oil; petroleum
freedom, 7, 8, 14, 91, 103, 104, 106, 111, 113, 114, 116, 126, 127, 129, 203, 213, 215, 221, 223, 227–32, 234, 237, 238, 239, 242, 243–49, 252, 253n1
French Connection, The (1971), 124
Fubar (2002), 201, 207
Fubar: Balls to the Wall (2010)/*FUBAR II* (2010), 15, 16, 191–92, 200–8, 211, 219–23
FuelRod, 35
Futurama, 83–85, 88, 89–90, 93, 95, 97, 98, 99

Gattaca (1997), 112
Geely, 116
gender, 123, 212, 235, 240, 242, 244, 245, 246, 252, 254n6, 257n44
General Motors, 22, 28, 35, 49, 51, 83, 84, 85, 95, 99, 106, 116
gentrification, 74, 75
global warming, 3, 4, 6, 9, 10, 11, 13, 16, 96, 104, 108, 109, 115, 116, 118, 175, 213, 240, 244, 249, 251, 258n65
    See also climate change
globalization, 6, 84, 173–80, 187–88, 199
Gods Must Be Crazy, The (1980), 219
Gone in 60 Seconds (2000), 110
Grapes of Wrath, The (1939), 4
Grease (1978), 110
green revolution, 152, 167n7
Guthrie, Woody, 131, 144

Handlebars (1933), 50
Hansen, James, 5
Happy Days (1974–84), 111
hazardous materials, 25–27, 33, 36–37
health, 24, 30, 38n13, 42, 44, 45, 46, 54, 55, 70, 71, 96, 98, 108, 118, 186, 245, 250
Heat (1977), 114, 115
highway, 7, 11, 42, 66, 73, 84, 86, 89, 90, 92, 98, 126, 129, 130, 131, 144, 145, 146, 147, 162, 168n33, 206, 239, 246; Highway of Tears, 238, 239; superhighway, 83, 85, 86, 88, 89, 93, 95
    See also road
His First Ride (1907), 50
Honda, 91
Honeymooners, The (1951–57), 110
humor, 41, 116, 192, 194, 203, 213, 219, 223, 233, 234, 235, 247
    See also comedy; laughter
Hyundai, 91

I Am Legend (2007), 146
I Like Bikes . . . But (1978), 49–51
I Love Lucy (1951–57), 60, 111
Ill Wind (1995), 163, 168n37
I'm No Fool with a Bicycle (1956), 47
impasse, 218, 228, 229, 253
Indiana Jones and the Last Crusade (1989), 52
Industrial Revolution, 5
industrialization, 4, 6, 83, 100n12, 220, 246, 257n53, 257n55
Infiniti, 91

infrastructure, 11, 12, 15, 22, 35, 63, 64, 66, 67, 68, 70, 71, 72, 73, 78, 84, 88, 90, 97, 105, 152, 153, 155, 156, 159, 167n5, 168n33, 177, 178, 179, 211, 212, 213, 214, 215, 217, 218, 220, 223, 224, 227–32, 234, 236, 237, 238, 240, 242, 243, 246, 247, 248, 249, 250, 253, 258n59
Intergovernmental Panel on Climate Change (IPCC), 6, 89, 116, 173, 174
intermodal shipping container, 173, 174, 177, 178, 179, 188
International Convention for the Prevention of Pollution from Ships (MARPOL), 173
International Harvester, 105
International Maritime Organization (IMO), 173, 175
Isuzu, 110
Italian Job, The (2003), 110
It's a Mad Mad Mad World (1963), 52
It's a Wonderful Life (1946), 110

Jaguar Land Rover Automotive, 29
Jetsons, The (1962–63), 111
Jinping, Xi, 92

Kia, 91
Kyoto Protocol, 6

Lady in Question, The (1940), 50, 52
laughter, 194, 195, 202, 204, 213, 219, 224, 248
See also comedy; humor
Leave It to Beaver (1957–63), 111
Leviathan (1651), 184
Leviathan (2012), 15, 175, 180–84
Leviathan Cycle (2017–), 15, 176, 184–88
Lexus, 91, 104
liberalism, 92, 176, 179, 183, 184, 213, 247, 248; neoliberalism, 89, 92, 151, 212, 213, 216, 223, 231, 242, 249
Lime (company), 68
See also Bird (company)
Lincoln, 30, 104
Local Hero (1983), 15, 191–200, 201, 202, 205, 208
logistics, 15, 153, 154, 174, 178, 180, 211, 212, 214–17, 219–21, 223
Lolita (1955), 139
Long Pants (1927), 50, 51

Machine Stops, The (1909), 133
Mad Max (1979), 4, 146, 162, 167n4
Magic Motorways (1940), 83, 85, 95
Magnificent Ambersons, The (1942), 147, 150n66
masculinity, 42, 44, 54, 214, 219, 220
materialism, 15, 176
Matrix, The (1999), 133
Mercedes, 34, 91, 104, 146
mobility, 1–3, 6–13, 16, 22, 23, 32, 33, 37, 43, 66, 67, 68, 71, 72, 74, 75, 91, 93, 103, 113, 147, 151, 179, 217, 222, 227–32, 238–40, 242–48, 253, 253n1, 254n10, 255n16; automobility, 12–14, 21, 22–24, 26, 27, 29, 31, 32, 33, 37, 38, 42, 43, 50, 60, 83–86, 88–90, 92–95, 99, 100n7, 124, 140, 151, 152, 154, 155, 157, 158, 161, 162, 165, 167n16, 230, 231, 240, 242–48, 255n16; cyclomobility, 43; immobility, 238; micromobility, 13, 14, 63, 64, 67–69, 71–74, 77, 78
mockumentary, 16, 200, 202, 211, 219, 223
Model A, 85
Model T, 1, 28, 34, 36, 85, 96, 104, 106
modernity, 44, 94, 97, 152, 156, 158, 159, 166n3, 187, 211, 219, 222, 239, 254n2; petromodernity, 151
Monster Trucks (2016), 4
motor, 21, 23, 47, 49, 68, 75, 94, 96, 104, 108, 111, 113, 132, 162
See also engine
motorcycle, 21, 44, 46, 245

National Historic Vehicle Register, 36
National Oceanic and Atmospheric Administration (NOAA), 174
natural gas, 6, 76, 104, 216
See also fossil fuels
nature, 1, 3, 4, 6, 8, 11, 12, 14, 15, 16, 28, 54, 64, 66, 67, 68, 75, 78, 93, 132, 139, 150n51, 167n15, 191, 192, 193, 194, 196, 202, 204, 206, 207, 208, 215, 216, 221, 222, 223, 231, 232, 234, 238, 255n14
Naughty Grandpa and the Field Glass (1902), 50
Never Let Me Go (2005), 169n43
New York 2140 (2017), 114
Night the Lights Went out in Georgia, The (1981), 124
Nissan, 91
Nixon, Richard, 96
Noah (2014), 194, 196

nomadism, 4
nostalgia, 15, 85, 147, 152, 158, 161, 192, 198, 200, 214, 222

Obama, Barack, 97
ocean, 15, 143, 174, 175, 176, 179, 180, 182, 184, 185, 192, 195, 200
oil, 3, 5, 6, 9, 11, 12, 13, 15, 32, 34, 84, 85, 87, 115, 124, 131, 132, 133, 136, 146, 152, 153, 154, 157, 159, 162–65, 166n2, 168n26, 168n33, 168n37, 169n40, 173, 191–95, 197–202, 204–9, 213–15, 217, 218, 220–23, 230, 234, 242, 244, 245, 252, 253, 253n1, 254n7, 254n10, 254n12, 256n44, 257n45, 257n52, 258n60
 See also Ethical Oil; fossil fuels; oil sands (tar sands); petroleum
oil sands (tar sands), 191, 201–2, 204–7, 218, 221, 242, 247, 253n1, 257n45
 See also Ethical Oil; oil; petroleum
Oklahoma Crude (1973), 192
Olmsted-Bartholomew Report, 64–67, 78
Omega Man, The (1971), 146
One Got Fat (1963), 48

Pacific Edge (1990), 168n35
Paleface, The (1922), 192
Paper Hangers, The (1921), 50
Parable of the Sower (1993), 154, 165, 168n35, 169n43
Paris Climate Agreement, 188n2
patriarchy, 16, 203, 227, 228, 231, 240, 241, 243, 245, 246, 247, 249, 251, 254n2, 254n6
Peddlin' Safety (1974), 49
Pee Wee's Big Adventure (1985), 53
personal vehicle, 72, 73, 103, 116, 118, 231, 232, 240, 246, 247
 See also automobile; autonomous vehicle; car
petroculture, 2, 3, 9, 15, 16, 151, 158, 159, 166n2, 176, 211, 218, 228, 229, 230, 231, 232, 234, 242, 245, 246, 247, 248, 253, 253n1, 254n10, 257n52, 258n60
petroleum, 2, 3, 11, 15, 16n1, 23, 24–25, 26, 30, 34, 36, 37, 43, 63, 152, 163, 166n2, 168n37, 211, 214, 215, 218, 224, 243
 See also Ethical Oil; fossil fuels; oil; oil sands (tar sands)

Plan de la Bicicleta de Sevilla, 73
 See also bicycle (bike); CicLAvia; Flying Pigeon; Victory Bike
Plantationocene, 228, 253–54n2
plastics, 6, 24, 25, 27, 32, 33, 34, 136, 184
Points for Pedalers (1943), 45
pollution, 2, 4, 6, 9, 12, 14, 26, 31, 36, 76, 85, 88, 89, 93–100, 116, 123, 147, 173, 174, 204, 205, 219
 See also carbon dioxide emissions (CO_2 emissions); carbon footprint
posthumanism, 176, 178, 183, 212
Premium Rush (2012), 53

Quicksilver (1986), 53

Rad (1986), 53
Rambo: First Blood Part II (1985), 57
Reagan, Ronald, 116
Remember Me (2010), 112
resiliency, 21, 24, 25, 29, 32, 35, 37
road, 1, 3, 8, 11, 16, 21, 22, 23, 28, 33, 41, 43, 48, 52, 54, 56, 58, 64, 67, 71, 72, 77, 84, 85, 88, 89, 90, 91, 92, 93, 94, 96, 97, 101n34, 103, 104, 108, 110, 111, 112, 113, 116, 117, 118, 124, 125–31, 134, 135, 138, 139, 140, 144, 145, 146, 147, 149n49, 162, 169n43, 177, 207, 212, 215, 216, 217, 218, 220, 228, 231, 232, 233, 235, 236, 238–39, 241, 244, 246, 248, 258n59
 See also highway
Road, The (2006), 169n43
Rocky IV (1985), 57
Runaway Match (1903), 109
rural, 22, 34, 90, 104, 108, 109, 111, 115, 207, 250

safety, 14, 21, 36, 42, 44–50, 68–72, 85, 95, 112, 124, 146, 192, 208
science fiction, 114, 162, 166n2, 167n3, 168n35, 168n37
sexuality, 8, 123, 133, 134, 139, 142, 167n3
She's Having a Baby (1988), 52–53
ship, 15, 85, 109, 173, 174, 175–77, 179–82, 185–88, 215, 219, 232
Six Day Bike Racer (1934), 50
Sloan, Alfred P., 28, 85

Slow Apocalypse (2012), 14, 155, 162–66, 168nn36–37
smog, 95, 96, 116
Smokey and the Bandit (1977), 110
Snowpiercer (2013), 194
solar panel, 25, 26, 27, 35, 160
Son of Rambow (2007), 192
speed, 2, 3, 6, 8, 13, 23, 31, 35, 49, 52, 54, 56, 60, 68, 72, 85, 112, 114, 124, 135, 139, 147, 150n66, 151, 212, 223, 229, 247
Springsteen, Bruce, 14, 57, 123–32, 134, 138, 141–46, 148n3
Station Eleven (2014), 14, 155–59, 160, 165, 167n24
Subaru, 105, 106, 118–19n11
Sugarland Express, The (1974), 124, 127
survival, 7, 11, 111, 115, 116, 146, 147, 151, 152, 157, 158, 159, 160, 162, 167n3, 168n37, 196, 220, 252
sustainability, 1, 10, 21–26, 28, 29, 31, 32, 36, 37–38, 38n8, 88, 103, 109, 115, 118, 160, 193, 198, 216, 218, 223, 258n65

tailpipe, 4, 21, 25–26, 30, 94, 103
Tesla, 107, 116
That '70s Show (1998–2006), 111
thirtysomething (1987–91), 60
This Is Spinal Tap (1984), 219
Thunder Road (1958), 110, 111
Titanic (1997), 112
To New Horizons (1940), 88
Tomorrow's Drivers (1954), 46
Top Gun (1986), 57
toxicity, 14, 15, 25, 26, 27, 28, 36, 96, 176, 178, 179, 202, 204, 207, 208, 234
Toyota, 91, 103, 118n4
traffic(ing), 14, 16, 45, 47, 52, 58, 63, 65, 66, 67, 72, 73, 85, 88, 92, 93, 94, 98, 109, 111, 112, 114, 118, 124, 132, 147, 162, 227–29, 231, 237, 238, 240, 242, 248, 249, 252, 253
trans-corporeality, 176, 186

Transporter, The (2002), 110
Tricopian, 35
Trump, Donald, 97, 118, 200
Twenty Thirty (2011), 163, 168n37
2 or 3 Things I Know About Her (*2 ou 3 choses que je sais d'elle*, 1967), 141
2001: A Space Odyssey (1968), 133

Uniform Vehicle Code, 42, 45
United Nations Conference on Trade and Development (UNCTAD), 173, 175
Unsafe at Any Speed (1965), 124
urban, 13–14, 22, 24, 37, 38n8, 38n13, 41, 42, 52, 53, 58, 64–72, 74–75, 78, 85, 88, 89, 95, 98, 100, 100n14, 104, 105, 106, 108, 109, 110, 111, 112, 115, 117, 152, 163, 179, 219, 232, 246, 250, 255n15

Victory Bike, 45
    See also bicycle (bike); CicLAvia; Flying Pigeon; Plan de la Bicicleta de Sevilla
Volkswagen, 95, 116
Volvo, 104, 146

waste, 24, 27, 29, 33, 38–39n13, 77, 85, 88, 93, 152
Western Stars (2019), 128
White Heat (1949), 110
windmill, 35
World Made by Hand (2008), 163, 168n37, 169n43
World's Fair (1985), 83, 98
Wrong Mr. Fox, The (1917), 50

Xenogenesis Trilogy (1987–89), 169n43
Xiaoping, Deng, 90

Yank at Oxford, A (1938), 51
You and Your Bicycle (1948, 1959), 47, 49

Zedong, Mao, 89

www.ingramcontent.com/pod-product-compliance
Lightning Source LLC
Chambersburg PA
CBHW050343270326
41926CB00016B/3589